Plant Production and Protection

D1101807

TRANSHUMANT GRAZING SYSTEMS IN TEMPERATE ASIA

Edited by
J.M. Suttie and **S.G. Reynolds**

FOOD AND AGRICULTURE ORGANIZATION OF THE UNITED NATIONS
Rome, 2003

ISBN 92-5-104977-7

FOREWORD

The Food and Agriculture Organization of the United Nations (FAO) has long been concerned with pastoral development issues, both through various field-based activities and through its Regular Programme work.

The primary focus of FAO's activities is to improve food security; one way to achieve this is through the development of sustainable agricultural and pastoral systems. Pastoral development and the study of transhumant systems have been focus areas of the Grassland and Pasture Crops Group within FAO's Crop and Grassland Service.

The Grassland and Pasture Crops Group has for a number of years implemented some of its field activities through various Working Groups, formed on the basis of similarity of ecological and production systems. In temperate Asia, it was agreed that there was a general lack of knowledge about transhumant production systems. Therefore, since the mid-1990s, the Grassland and Pasture Crops Group has supported the production of a number of case studies, mostly of transhumant systems, through the Temperate Asia Pasture and Fodder Working Group or Network. This work has been complemented by additional studies, including on transhumant systems and haymaking in Mongolia; grassland studies and work on the development of cold-tolerant lucerne in China; and a number of studies of country pasture resources.

Following the International Year of Mountains, for which FAO was the lead agency, it is hoped that this publication will contribute to our understanding and better use of the vast grasslands in mountain and plateau areas of temperate Asia, and support the conservation and sustainable development of mountain regions.

The contributions of authors and the considerable input made by the editors are much appreciated by FAO in its efforts to disseminate information on pastoral systems and transhumance. Thanks are particularly due to retired staff member James Suttie and to Stephen Reynolds of the Grassland and Pasture Crops Group of the Crop and Grassland Service for ensuring that the book was brought to publication.

Mahmoud Solh
Director
Plant Production and Protection Division
FAO Agriculture Department

CONTENTS

ACRONYMS

GDP	Gross domestic product
ICIMOD	International Centre for Integrated Mountain Development
NWFP	North West Frontier Province [Pakistan]
OM	Organic matter
VDC	Village Development Committee
WFP	World Food Programme of the United Nations

Contributors

Adhikary, J.R. Pasture and Fodder Research Division, Nepal Agricultural Research Council, Khumaltar, Lalitpur, Nepal.

Bhattarai, B.N. Extension Programme Officer, RNRRC, Yusipang, Bhutan.

Erdenebaatar, Batjargal. Head, Large Animal Department, Research Institute of Animal Husbandry, the State University of Agriculture, Ulan Bator, Mongolia.

Hu, Zizhi. Grassland Science College of Gansu Agricultural University, Lanzhou, P.R. China.

Lkhagvajaw, V.I. Geobotanist, High Altitude Research Station, Ikh Tamir, Arkhangai, Mongolia.

Min, Jichun. Faculty of Agronomy, Xinjiang Agricultural University, No. 42, Nanchang Road, Urumqi, 830052, P.R. China.

Misri, Bimal K. Principal Researcher, Indian Grassland and Fodder Research Institute, Regional Research Centre, Palampur HP, India.

Mukhtar, Ahmed. Natural Resources Management Officer, Environmental Rehabilitation Project, Swat, Pakistan.

Nyima, Tashi. Mountain Farming Systems, International Centre for Integrated Mountain Development (ICIMOD), Kathmandu, Nepal.

Pariyar, Dinesh. Pasture and Fodder Research Division, Nepal Agricultural Research Council, Khumaltar, Lalitpur, Nepal.

Pradhan, S.M. Pasture and Fodder Research Division, Nepal Agricultural Research Council, Khumaltar, Lalitpur, Nepal.

Reynolds, Stephen G. Senior Officer, Grassland and Pasture Crops Group, Crop and Grassland Service (AGPC), FAO.

Sanaullah, Khan. Senior Technical Adviser, Environmental Rehabilitation Project, Swat, Pakistan.

Sardar, Muhammad Rafique. Range Management Officer, Pakistan Forest Institute, Peshawar, Pakistan.

Shrestha, K.K. Pasture and Fodder Research Division, Nepal Agricultural Research Council, Khumaltar, Lalitpur, Nepal.

Suttie, James M. FAO Grassland and Pasture Crops Group Staff Member (Retired).

Tsering, Gyaltsen. Sector Head, Feed and Fodder Sector, RNRRC, Yusipang, Bhutan.

Wang, Wan Lin. Foreign Funds Project Executive Office, Xinjiang Animal Husbandry Bureau, Urumqi, Xinjiang, P.R. China.

Zhang, Degang. Grassland Science College of Gansu Agricultural University, Lanzhou, P.R. China.

ACKNOWLEDGEMENTS

This publication is based on a series of case studies carried out by a number of authors, who are acknowledged in the text. The editors are also very indebted to many of these authors for assistance, advice and companionship given during field trips, often in remote areas and under difficult conditions. The participation of many of them in a number of meetings of the Temperate Asia Pasture and Fodder Working Group, with enlightening discussion both of the transhumant study methodologies and the case study results, is also appreciated. The country coordinators of the Working Group were deeply involved in the design of the Himalayan case studies and formulated the questionnaire that was the basis for much of the field work. Particular thanks are due to Dr Panjab Singh, who did so much to found the Group and initiate the Himalayan studies. Thanks are also due to John Morrison for his contribution in setting up and advising the Group, from the earlier UNDP-funded regional project, through to the fourth meeting, held in Peshawar in June 2000.

Thanks are due to Anthony Fitzherbert for information on Kyrgyzstan; to Olaf Thieme for assistance with Afghanistan; and to the authors (A. Karagoz, B. Misri, D. Pariyar, E. Kosayev, Hu Zizhi, Zhang Degang, Kinzang Wangdi, M. Al Jaloudy, M. Makhmudovich, and R. Tumanian) of a number of Country Pasture/Forage Resource Profiles on the FAO Grassland Group Website, from which information has been drawn (see www.fao.org/ag/AGP/AGPC/doc/pasture/forage.htm).

Photographs, unless otherwise acknowledged, are by the editors. Maps were prepared by Christopher Aurich, and many of the sketch maps were re-drawn by Lucie Herzigova. The cover was designed by Pietro Bartoleschi and Etra Studio Associato.

Final editing for consistency of language and style and preparation for publication was by Thorgeir Lawrence.

EXECUTIVE SUMMARY

Extensive grazing lands cover vast areas of temperate Asia, and are important both environmentally and as a source of livelihood for herders. Both transhumant (nomadic) and agropastoral systems are involved. The area can be divided into two zones: temperate areas, above 1 000–1 500 m in the Himalaya – Hindu Kush area (referred to as Himalaya); and the cold semi-arid to arid zone north of the Himalaya, through the Tibet-Qinghai Plateau and northern China to the Asian steppe.

FAO has supported a series of case studies, mostly on transhumant systems, since the mid-1990s, which were carried out by national staff using local means and methods. The studies generated a series of reports, and the quality and interest of those reports is such that they merit a wider readership; they are now brought together in book form.

Studies are reported from Bhutan, China, India, Mongolia, Nepal and Pakistan, on transhumant systems and allied subjects, including haymaking and the development of cold-tolerant lucerne. The pastoral situation in the major areas of extensive grazing is described briefly, by zone, to put the studies in context.

The book is in 17 chapters, with summaries for each. After an introduction, Chapter II introduces Cold Temperate Asia, and discusses the effects of decollectivization on herding. Chapters III and IV present two case studies from Mongolia: the first describes systems in two provinces of the great lakes basins (the steppe and mountain-steppe systems are already well known), where a clear set of climatic and social indicators govern movements. Timing of movement is restricted since routes use passes that are only negotiable for very limited seasons. Mixed flocks are kept by all herders: horses, cattle and small stock are important, and camels are kept for baggage transport. A second Mongolia study describes haymaking in the mountain and steppe zone. Now that centrally provided hay is unavailable, techniques using animal drawn or manual equipment were demonstrated on herder's land with their full participation.

Chapter V describes the grazing and fodder situation in China. Chapters VI and VII are two case studies from Xinjiang: one on a herding system allied to irrigated haymaking, and the second on breeding lucerne for irrigated hay. Irrigated lucerne for winter feed has been introduced to a transhumant system in Altai, Xinjiang. Transhumance continues, but only the herders migrate. The scheme began in the late 1980s – it will take time to convert traditional herders, with no cropping experience, into good irrigated cultivators. Only one local landrace of lucerne was in use, so it was deemed desirable to widen the genetic base. Introduced "cold-tolerant" cultivars failed to overwinter. Local selection has produced an improved cultivar, which is well adapted to the area and more productive than the one in use. A system of seed multiplication and maintenance of mother seed has been installed. Chapter VIII describes the pastoral situation in Tibet, and some ambitious plans for its development.

Chapter IX describes the systems of the western Himalaya, followed in Chapter X by a case study from India of a classical vertical transhumance system of the Gaddis, a pastoral tribe in Himachal Pradesh, where their route goes from the plains to the snow-line on ranges that have peaks as high as 5 500 m, although the average altitude is about 2 500 m.

Chapters XI and XII are two studies from Pakistan. One involves two groups of herder who use the same summer pastures: local farmers who take their herds to the high pastures in summer, and herding nomads who move between the high pastures and the plains. A second study describes how, in Swat, which was a traditional winter grazing area for transhumant herds, change in political structures and land-use patterns over the past thirty years has led to a great reduction in the grazing area available to nomads in winter, as well as blocking many of their transhumance routes.

Chapter XIII deals with the eastern Himalaya, and is followed by two studies on transhumance with large ruminants from Bhutan (Chapters XIV and XV) and a study on high-altitude raising of cattle-yak hybrids in Nepal (Chapter XVI). The first Bhutan study involves a community based between 2 600 and 3 000 m, with some crops. Cattle and cattle x mithun (*Bos gaurus*) crosses are the main stock. A system of entrusting stock to the care of other groups for part of the year is described – in this case, for the winter. The second system is wholly dependent on yaks. In Nepal, two grazing systems based on raising bought-in chauris for milk were studied: one is highly commercialized and based around a milk-purchasing organization; the other has no outlet for fresh milk, so sells only ghee and local dried cheese. Grazing areas are between 2 500 and 3 100 m; up to 2 800 m they are in the vicinity of forest, while higher pastures are open and treeless. There are problems of overgrazing, compounded by the summer grazing areas being also the winter grazing of yaks belonging to other communities, and the winter areas are used, in summer, by buffaloes from the lower areas.

Findings and conclusions are summarized in Chapter XVII. Two kinds of transhumant herding systems have been identified, which developed under different geographical conditions. Those in the Himalayan region overwinter in lower, warm areas, but in cold semi-arid Asia they have no access to warm pastures. Grassland is by far the most important vegetation type, although browse is locally important in the subtropical end of Himalayan systems. Cyperaceae form a major part of the grazing in the highest areas, especially for yak grazing.

Land tenure problems, or lack of clarity in grazing rights, were identified as a serious problem in most of the zone. This has been exacerbated in those countries that had collectivized extensive stock rearing, since livestock were distributed long before any attempt was made to define grazing rights. The methods of decollectivization varied, as has their impact on the herding industry. Throughout the Himalayan zone, conflict of interests between settled farmers and herders is increasing with rising population pressure and intensification of agriculture.

Poor pasture condition figures highly among technical constraints. Since there is no baseline data, the evolution of degradation can only be guessed; there is a serious need for more monitoring of pasture condition and trends as a management tool, and to measure environmental impact. Winter and spring feed are major problems throughout the area, and, in cold semi-arid areas, winter shelter is highly desirable. Water supply is a local problem, especially in the steppe, where artificial water points have often been neglected in recent times. Fire is rarely mentioned; it is little used, neither as a pasture management tool nor in agriculture in the zone, and does not seem to be a serious problem.

Technical problems are not usually the main ones facing transhumant herding: the major problems are socio-economic. There is an urgent need to clarify problems of grazing rights. The "technical" approach advocated for improving extensive pastures and livestock production in the past has not been successful, and, in most cases, an integrated methodology would be needed. Educational levels among herding communities in the study areas vary greatly, but it is not obvious that the level of literacy affects the main traditional herding skills. In the Himalaya, herders were generally perceived as being poor, but in cold semi-arid Asia they are in the mainstream population and are not a poor group. The studies overall have shown that most of the usual technical "grassland" suggestions for improving pasture management and herding productivity (such as better grazing management, reseeding with high-yielding species, and herder training) are impracticable, not least until the various land tenure and grazing rights issues are addressed.

The main methods of improving pasture condition involve manipulation of grazing pressure and grazing management. It is necessary, therefore, that the grazing rights to the land involved be clear, that the necessary laws and regulations be in force, and that the mechanisms exist to see that they are respected. Application of regulations for improvement, such as only grazing land at the correct season and regulating the overall stocking rate, require the agreement and compliance of all who have right to graze a particular piece of land – participatory methods are indicated, but the whole issue can be very complicated. Where the human population is dense, and the pasture – even when correctly managed – cannot provide a reasonable livelihood, it is very difficult to get agreement on destocking. However, better grazing management is essential, not only for improving pasture conditions and for improved pastoral livelihoods, but also for improving the overall grassland cover on areas that constitute some of the most important and fragile watershed areas of the region.

In the Himalaya zone, many of the settled stock owners who use the same pastures as transhumants have considerable opportunity for improving feed supply through growing hay crops.

Throughout most of the area there is lack of information on pasture condition and trends, although China has just completed a national grassland survey. Even grazing areas are often only approximately known. If management of grazing land is to be improved, more information is required for both planning of work and monitoring vegetation trends. Transhumant systems are potentially less damaging than sedentary ones because they exploit the herbage at fixed seasons, and leave it to recover for the remainder of the growing season. While many herders would prefer a more settled life, and many governments would like to settle nomads, alternative employment would have to be found. In the Himalayan context, this would mean finding livelihoods in an already oversupplied labour market. In the cold semi-arid zone, extensive herding seems to be the only practical way of earning a living from the land. It is likely that transhumant herding will continue for many years yet.

Chapter I
Introduction

Temperate Asia has vast areas of grazing lands, which, as well as being important environmentally, provide livelihoods for herders. Both transhumant and agropastoral systems are common and involve both full-time nomads and settled farmers who take their stock to summer pastures. While some of these systems have been studied previously in detail, there is a general lack of knowledge, particularly of many of the transhumant systems. Since the mid-1990s, FAO has been supporting the production of a series of case studies, mostly on transhumant systems, which have generated a series of reports. The quality and interest of these reports are such that they merit a wider readership, so they have been brought together in book form.

Some definitions are in order:

- **Extensive grazing land.** There is no clear definition of extensive grazing land, except that it is grazed and unenclosed. Definitions for national statistics vary, and much that is "waste" land will probably be grazed at some time of the year. Where forests occur, these are usually also subject to grazing, with or without control.

- **Pastoralism or herding.** This is a form of occupancy. It is the commonest form of land use in arid grazing lands. Pastoralists' strategies of resource use focus on risk management and food security. In the harsher, drier climates it is mainly a subsistence activity, with commercial aspects and supply for urban consumers a secondary consideration.

Mobility is the principal strategy for making the best use of resources on offer and for dealing with fluctuation and spatial variation in precipitation and feed supply. Large seasonal shifts are supplemented by local movements. Seasonal shifts in temperate Asia are mainly imposed by climatic factors, but can also be caused by other factors, such as snow cover, lack of water or plagues of biting insects.

- **Temperate Asia.** No precise definition of "temperate" has been used, and any area is included that is not subtropical and is snow-free for part of the year.

Two main zones and a subzone can be distinguished in the study area:

- the Cold Semi-arid Zone in high latitude areas, with no warm lowlands for overwintering;

- and a second zone, with a large altitude range and where stock overwinter in warmer plains and lowland in more southerly areas, mainly Himalayan; and

- at high altitudes throughout most of the region there is a subzone where the yak forms a major part of the livestock.

Thus there are two main parts. The most northerly is the cold, semi-arid zone embracing part of the Eurasian steppe, that great arc of grazing land which runs from Manchuria to the eastern boundaries of Hungary. It is bounded on its north by the taiga (the swampy coniferous forest of high northern latitudes) and the cold mountain masses of the Qinghai-Tibet Plateau, Pamir, Tien Shan and Kunlun. There are, of course, transhumant grazing systems north of the taiga, based mainly on reindeer, and indeed their southern tip is in Mongolia, but these are not dealt with here.

The other great area of transhumant herding is in the mountain masses of the Himalaya–Hindu Kush region (referred to hereafter as Himalaya for brevity), where the temperate zone is defined by altitude and the winter end of many transhumance systems is in the subtropical foothills or plains. The area is bounded to the south by the limit of subtropical vegetation; the altitude of this decreases progressively from our most southerly country, Bhutan, along the northwesterly progression of the Himalaya. In Nepal, the limit of temperate vegetation – the "mountain region" in contrast to the tropical and subtropical "hills" – is about 2 000 m; by the time the Indus is reached, the oak and olive forests are down below 1 000 m. The latitude range is from a little over 50°N in northern Mongolia to about 27°N in Nepal and Bhutan.

The cold semi-arid zone includes Mongolia, north China, the Tibet-Qinghai Plateau, Buryatia, Kyrgyzstan and Kazakhstan. There winter shelter is a necessary grazing resource and a major survival strategy is to have the herd fat enough in autumn to survive through winter and spring. In much of this area, grazing lands are either steppe or at least much less precipitous than those of the Himalayan zone, and horses are used for herding as well as being kept for meat and milk. Mixed herds are the rule, involving large and small ruminants, horses and often camels. Herders have little interaction with crop producers since there is little farming and crops are limited to favoured, often irrigated, sites. Winter camps are in relatively cold areas and do not usually have

access to alternative sources of employment or sources of bought fodder. Herders' diets are very much based on animal products, meat as well as dairy produce, and cereals are a very minor food in most of the herding area.

In the Himalayan zone, transhumance patterns are vertical, going up to mountain pastures in summer and descending to relatively warm areas in the foothills, plains or desert fringe in winter. This travel pattern, as well as following feed availability, avoids both the great summer heat of the lowlands and the winter cold. The transition routes and summer pastures are often very steep, if not precipitous. Winter grazing is often close to arable and urban areas that provide sources of seasonal employment, the possibility to buy fodder and access to markets.

Throughout the Himalayan area there is considerable interaction between herders and settled farmers. Herds have to traverse settled areas during their migrations, and meet local stock on the summer pastures. Crop residues and stubble grazing are part of the winter feed and are paid for in cash or kind; cereals and sometimes fodder are purchased in winter. Horses are relatively unimportant, although ponies may be used for transport. Herds are usually much less mixed than in northern areas, and groups usually specialize in types of stock. The western Himalaya and the Hindu Kush are generally areas of low precipitation, and small stock form the major part of transhumant flocks, although Gujars take cattle and buffalo to mountain pastures in Pakistan and western India. In the much wetter eastern Himalaya, large ruminants predominate. Herders' diets are generally based on cereals, purchased with the proceeds of livestock sales, and on dairy products.

The yak-rearing subzone is not treated in detail in the text, apart from the very interesting Soe Yaksa study from Bhutan. The subzone covers a large area, but yak numbers are not well defined, partly because they interbreed with cattle, with which they are often included in livestock counts. Yaks form a major part of the livestock in both the northern and southern parts in cooler areas at higher altitude. They are present in most of the countries of temperate Asia, from Afghanistan eastwards, but in the western Himalaya yaks are very few and only found in some extremely mountainous places. They become much more important in the eastern Himalaya, and the greatest number of yaks in the world are on the Qinghai-Tibet Plateau. Mongolia also has quite a large yak population. Air temperature is a major factor determining yak distribution. According to Cai Li and Weiner (1995), yaks thrive provided that the mean annual temperature is under 5°C and the mean temperature of the warmest month does not exceed 13°C. Temperature is strongly influenced by altitude. In Tibet, yaks live normally up to about 5 500 m, but can be used as pack animals up to 7 200 m; further north, in Mongolia, they come down to 2 000–2 500 m.

Extensive pastures, be they exploited by transhumant or sedentary herds, have many uses other than as a source of feed for livestock, and are of great environmental importance. They are usually important hydrologic catchment areas, and are important as wildlife habitat, for the *in situ* conservation of plant and other genetic resources, and are frequently used for sport and tourism. This makes the apparent neglect of their management all the more surprising. While poor grazing management is probably by far the most serious cause of damage to the natural vegetation, collection of medicinal plants, uprooting shrubs for fuelwood, and uncontrolled felling all play a part.

The great mass of mountains formed by the Tibet-Qinghai Plateau and the adjacent Himalaya, Karakoram, Pamir, Hindu Kush and Tian Shan ranges is the source of most of the rivers of China, as well as the Irrawaddy, the Mekong, the Brahmaputra, and the Indus and Ganges systems. Afghanistan's agriculture is mainly dependent on irrigation from its rivers, and the Amu and Syr flow north into the Aral Sea. From the case studies and general observation, it is clear that the vegetation of the upper catchments of these rivers is under severe pressure and is often seriously degraded. This decreases infiltration and speeds up runoff, thereby increasing flooding. It will also increase the silt load, with consequent damage and cost to agriculture and structures far downstream. The primary means of reducing such damage is the rational management of grazing and forest resources.

The problems of mountains and mountain communities have been a subject of concern for some time. The International Centre for Integrated Mountain Development (ICIMOD) is based in Kathmandu, Nepal, and deals with both the temperate and subtropical zones. Such is the importance given internationally to mountains that the United Nations declared 2002 to be the International Year of Mountains (IYM). Mountains, in this context, include uplands, be they steep or not, and most of temperate Asia's grazing, plateaus and steppes, as well as true mountains, are at relatively high altitude, so the studies described in the following

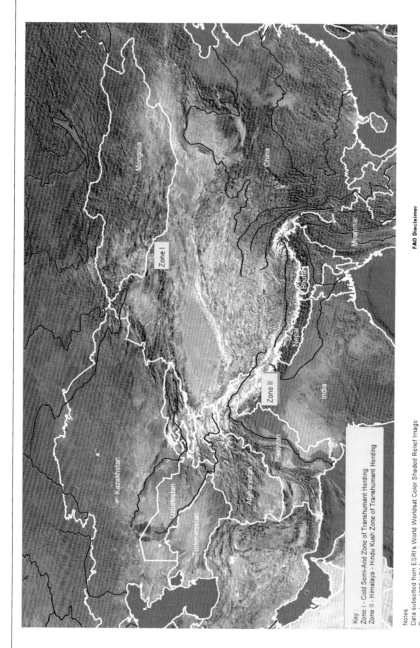

Key:
Zone I - Cold Semi-Arid Zone of Transhumant Herding
Zone II - Himalaya - Hindu Kush Zone of Transhumant Herding

Notes
Data subsetted from ESRI's World Worldsat Color Shaded Relief Image
Based on 1996 NOAA weather satellite images, with enhanced shaded
relief imagery and ocean floor relief data (bathymetry) to provide a land
and undersea topographic view. ESRI Data and Maps 1999 Volume 1.
Projection = Geographic (Lat/Long)

FAO Disclaimer
The designations employed and the presentation of the material in the maps
do not imply the expression of any opinion whatsoever on the part of FAO
concerning the legal or constitutional status of any country, territory or sea
area, or concerning the delimitation of frontiers

FIGURE 1.1

Map showing the study areas in temperate Asia and the two main zones of transhumant herding.

chapters are highly relevant to "Mountain Development".

The production systems studied vary from the purely livestock systems of the steppe to those where farmers in mountain valleys take or send their stock to alpine pastures in summer, and from situations where herders are the majority of the population to others where they are minority groups that have to move through the lands of others or through state-controlled forests during part of their migration.

The common features throughout are that transhumant systems are used and that their major part is in areas of temperate vegetation. **Transhumance** is also loosely defined: often it is defined as a system of pastoralism wherein livestock are moved between mountain pastures in summer and lower areas for the rest of the year. That is the common pattern in most of the region, but in the steppe and mountain-and-steppe the choice of winter camps is based on shelter from wind and relative freedom from snow, and some summer movements may be dictated by the need to avoid biting insects.

Some authorities use the term transhumance when herders have a permanent home: only the herds and the people necessary to tend them travel, as opposed to nomadism, when the whole family lives in tents all the year round, moving with the herds. For our purpose, any system where livestock move over considerable distances to seek grazing, in set seasonal patterns, is considered to be transhumance – whether by full-time nomads or by stock owners with settled homes. A novel system is described from western Bhutan, where in the *nothoue* system there is a partnership agreement in rearing migratory cattle, whereby the herds are looked after by different groups at different seasons, i.e. the herds migrate between two sets of herders – the people stay put.

In parts of the area, especially in the eastern Himalaya, two or more transhumance systems may overlap on the same land but at different seasons. Cases are reported from Bhutan and Nepal where three lots are involved: yak graze in winter on the summer pastures of cattle and hybrids, while the winter grazing areas of the cattle and hybrids is the summer pasture of buffaloes that overwinter yet lower down.

Transhumant herding is not the only system of grazing management throughout the region. In some parts, especially in the Himalayan zone, there are many settled communities with mixed farming systems involving livestock. These frequently interact with, and may be in conflict with, transhumant graziers. Settled systems are mentioned where they affect the transhumance under discussion, but no attempt is made to describe or discuss in detail the many and varied settled production systems.

Sedentary livestock production systems, usually combined with cropping, have received a good deal of attention in the Himalayan zone. An International Symposium on Livestock in Mountain Livelihoods, jointly funded by ICIMOD, FAO, the International Potato Centre (CIP) and the System-wide Livestock Programme (SLIP), was held in Pokhara, Nepal, in December 1999 as part of the preparations for the International Year of Mountains. The proceedings of the Symposium (Tulachan *et al.,* 2000) mainly deal with the more densely populated agricultural and agropastoral tracts, especially insofar as the Himalaya is concerned. The emphasis is on livestock and economics, with only passing reference to the pasture component. A joint ICIMOD-FAO study prepared for the Symposium – *Livestock in farming systems of the Hindu Kush–Himalaya* (Tulachan and Neupane, 1999) – gives details on livestock systems and trends. In settled systems there is a move towards intensification and an increase in the proportion of buffaloes and goats, while sheep are decreasing.

Many types of livestock are involved: sheep and goats are almost universal, and cattle occur in most systems; yak and their hybrids graze areas too cold for cattle; and in Bhutan, mithun (*Bos gaurus*) are part of the stock. Horses and mounted herding are the rule in the steppe and adjacent areas. Camels are important throughout the drier areas as transport and are the major livestock in the driest areas. In China, central and northern Asia the Bactrian camel (*Camelus bactrianus*) is kept; from Afghanistan through the western Himalaya the Arabian camel (*Camelus dromedarius*) is used. Water buffalo are common in the lower parts of the Himalayan transhumance areas, and some are managed in transhumant systems.

Since the aim of grazing systems is livestock production, the animal aspects of the systems are dealt with in enough detail to make the study clear. Some of these stock may be unfamiliar to readers from other zones: the yak, and its hybrids, is important in all the subzones (although in the western Himalaya it is limited to a few very high peripheral areas); yaks and yak husbandry and that of hybrids are described in detail in another FAO publication (Cai Li and Weiner, 1995).

Over the past decade the FAO Grassland Group has encouraged studies on the grazing lands of the region. Some of the studies were through a subregional working group, which coordinates collaboration between national pasture specialists. The Pasture and Fodder Working Group for Temperate Asia [members to date: Bhutan, India, Nepal, Pakistan] was established in 1995 and covers a wide ecological zone where animal husbandry is important. In the Himalayan region, livestock production systems in the semi-arid and alpine areas are not independent of the lower moister areas. Other studies in China and Mongolia have been supported by the Grassland Group. The studies generated a series of reports and their quality and interest is such that they merit a wider readership, so they have now been brought together in book form.

Morrison (2000a), in discussing the Himalayan studies at the meeting of the Temperate Asia Pasture and Fodder Working Group, stated:

> *In the Himalaya the high altitude systems – at elevations above 2 500 m to 5 000 m – embrace the entirely migratory sheep/goat systems found in Pakistan and India which graze alpine pasture in summer, the yak and yak hybrid systems which use alpine and subalpine range in the northern Areas of Pakistan, Ladakh in India, the northern parts of Nepal and Bhutan. Transhumance, the annual migration from lower to summer grazing in alpine areas, is the common feature of these systems. These entirely pastoral systems overlap with high altitude agropastoral systems that graze mainly subalpine pastures.... Pastoralists are skilled at exploiting these grazing resources and appreciate rangeland plants – those of value and undesirable ones. But these systems are essentially exploitive. The migratory systems*

have fascinated people and there are many general descriptions of migratory routes, but there have been few systematic studies of the dynamics and present status of such systems. Although 'improvement' and 'improved range management' are suggested, there is no clear definition of appropriate improvement practices or opportunities for their effective application. The systems studies conducted within the Working Group addressed some of these issues.

The studies, from their origin, emphasize the technical, "grassland", aspects of transhumant systems, but recognize that socio-economic, ethnological and land tenure factors are fundamental to the organization and improvement of grazing management and the livelihoods of herding families. The studies have proved very useful to the institutions involved since they provided an opportunity to become familiar with the system-wide problem of extensive grazing, whereas previously they had often concentrated on "technical" problems.

While the studies reported were partly funded by FAO, the subsidies were very modest indeed and the work has been carried out mostly by the efforts of the national institutions and staff concerned – often under isolated and difficult conditions and with a minimum of equipment and no accommodation. Taking even basic equipment to high, steep pastures, far from motorable tracks, requires a lot of effort and organizing – transporting fencing and exclosure cages by pack animals and porterage, sometimes up to nearly 5 000 m, is very difficult. On at least one site, researchers suffered from altitude sickness.

Recently a series of "Country pasture/ forage resources profiles" was initiated and is available on the FAO Web site. To date

(autumn 2002), profiles are available, in the region, for Afghanistan (Thieme, 2000), Armenia (Tumanian, 2001), Azerbaijan (Kosayev, 2002), Bhutan (Kinzang Wangdi, 2002), China (Hu Zizhi and Zhang Degang, 2001 – summarized here in Chapter V), India (Misri, 1999), Kyrgyzstan (Fitzherbert, 2000), Mongolia (Suttie, 2000b), Nepal (Pariyar, 1999), Pakistan (Dost, 1999), Turkey (Karagoz, 2001) and Uzbekistan (Makhmudovic, 2002).

Over the past decade FAO has paid particular attention to the socio-economic problems of herding in temperate Asia, especially Central Asia, where extraordinary social changes in herding communities have been brought about by the abandonment of collective production for private ownership of livestock, and social patterns based on centrally planned systems had to give way, almost instantly, to a free-market driven existence. An FAO-sponsored International Conference on herding was held in Mongolia in 1990, which identified many of the problems as well as fields for study. A summary document was produced – *Trends in Pastoral Development in Central Asia* (FAO, 1996) – which gives a good picture of the situation immediately post-decollectivization, but many changes have taken place since, and few to the herders' advantage. Another study on Mongolian herders' income and employment (FAO, 1992b) gives a more detailed study at national level of the very early post-decollectivization years.

A round-table discussion was held in 1992 at Shah e Kurd, Islamic Republic of Iran, in conjunction with the International Conference on Nomadism and Development, which was organized by the Government of the Islamic Republic of Iran (FAO, 1992a). At the opening of the meeting, problems mentioned by the Minister included drift of herders to the towns; dependence of herding communities on urban markets; nationalization of grazing lands leading to unclear access rights; poor access of herders to services; and the need to re-establish the ecological balance between the grazing land and the livestock.

The local definition of nomadic people is those:

- whose main source of subsistence is domestic livestock grazed on natural pasture;
- who live, for at least some of the year, in mobile shelters within a common and recognized set of boundaries; and
- who have a perception of belonging to a tribal social structure, i.e. one where pressing loyalties of the individual are to a tribe, not to the state.

Most of that definition was thought applicable throughout the region, although the "tribal" proviso was problematical. There were two other points of general application:

- Lack of clear tenure arrangements for grazing land lies at the root of much existing overuse. Without tenure reform there is little chance of halting pasture deterioration nor of improving pasture productivity. Wherever possible, the starting point for reform should be the customary tenure system.
- There is a clear need for basic studies on pasture ecology, which should contain ecological analytical work, including ecosystem studies and monitoring of ecological changes.

This present publication aims to consolidate the results of FAO pasture work from the past decade in temperate Asia, and to make it available to a wider readership by bringing together the results

of a series of studies on transhumant grazing systems. It attempts to put the studies in a framework of the overall pastoral situation, using information from country profiles and the editors' experience in the field. Studies on transhumant production systems are reported from Bhutan, China, India, Mongolia, Nepal and Pakistan. Two articles on subjects closely related to transhumance are included: one on haymaking by pastoralists in Mongolia and the other on breeding cold-tolerant lucerne for a scheme that integrates irrigated hay with transhumant stock rearing in Xinjiang, China.

The studies are grouped into four zones: Central Asia, which includes parts of northern Asia; China; the western Himalaya; and the eastern Himalaya. To put the studies in context, there are also chapters giving a brief introduction to each subregion and brief notes on the main countries where there is transhumant stock rearing. A whole section is devoted to a concise description of China's pastoral and forage sector, one of the greatest and most varied in the world. A final chapter discusses the findings of the studies, the problems they raise and areas for action or further study.

Other recent Grassland Group Publications on related topics include those on *Hay and Straw Conservation* (Suttie, 2000a), *Grassland Resource Assessment* (Harris, 2001), *Silage in the Tropics* (t'Mannetje, 2000), *Managing Mobility in African Grasslands* (in conjunction with Beijer International Institute of Ecological Economics and IT publications) (Niamir-Fuller, 1999), and a comic book for children on *Discovering the natural resources of the Hindu Kush – Himalayan region* (FAO, 2002).

Chapter II

Cold, semi-arid Asia

SUMMARY

Cold semi-arid Asia is a great belt to the south of the taiga. Much of it, apart from some mountains and deserts, is steppe. It includes parts of Russia, Buryatia, Mongolia, much of Central Asia including Kazakhstan, Kyrgyzstan and Tajikistan, as well as vast areas of China, including Inner Mongolia, northern Gansu, Xinjiang and the Tibet-Qinghai Plateau. China is dealt with in detail in later chapters. Climate is arid to semi-arid and winters are arctic. The area is unsuitable for large-scale fodder conservation, so stock have to be fattened adequately during the short growing season and autumn to survive until next spring. Winter shelter and feed are major problems. Over most of the area there is little interaction between herding and cropping. There are no warmer areas for overwintering (unlike the Himalayan systems, described in later chapters), and winter and early spring is a prolonged period of food scarcity. A major herding skill is getting stock fat enough in summer and autumn to survive the winter.

Many of the herding peoples are of similar ethnic origins and lifestyles. Those to the west of the Altai mountains are Muslims. All were originally full-time nomads, living in circular felt tents, or in Tibet in black woven tents. Herders' diets are based on dairy products and meat. Two case studies are presented from Mongolia (Chapters III and IV): one describing two transhumance systems in mountainous areas, and another on haymaking by herders using animal-drawn equipment, with some trials on ice-irrigation. Detailed studies on China are given in later chapters.

In the twentieth century the livestock industry of most countries in the region was collectivized for a period. Decollectivization has taken place in all the countries during the past ten to fifteen years, with varying results. These are described briefly for Buryatia, China, Kyrgyzstan and Mongolia. From the outcome of collectivization and the various degrees of "modernization" that have been applied to the extensive stock rearing systems of the various countries of cold semi-arid Asia, it appears that deviating too far from mobile systems using hardy stock is fraught with risks. Use of exotic breeds brings dependence on shelter and on imported feed, which may not be economic. Sedentarization seems to bring localized overgrazing, as well as undue exposure to weather risks. The use of imported feed for winter feed may lead to overstocking and damage to pastoral vegetation. Most of the countries of the region report serious to very serious degradation of their grazing lands. By far the least affected is Mongolia, which has maintained herding mobility, with hardy local breeds throughout.

INTRODUCTION

The case studies, although in contiguous countries, Mongolia and China, involve both northern and central Asia. The herding systems of the region have much in common: mixed herds of several species are general, since they make better use of the natural vegetation, provide a range of products for communities that live entirely by herding, and spread risk in an area of climatic extremes. Horses are very important for meat and milk (Plate 1),

Plate 1.
Horse herd, Ikh Tamir, Mongolia.

Plate 2.
Yaks take over from cattle at high altitudes. Yaks at 4300 m in Linzhou County, about 70 km from Lhasa, Tibet.

and essential for herding – all herders are mounted. Sheep, goats and cattle are all important, while yaks and their hybrids are kept in higher areas (Plate 2). Bactrian camels are common for transport (Plate 3). Since time immemorial, transhumant stock rearing has been the main land use in this vast region (Plate 4), as the semi-arid climate, with long, cold winters, is unsuited to crops. The region – mostly steppe except for some mountains and deserts – lies south of the taiga and includes Buryatia, Tuva, Mongolia, Kyrgyzstan and Kazakhstan. Parts of China, including Inner Mongolia, northern Gansu and Xinjiang, would fit in here, but are dealt with in a separate chapter because of their size and the vastness of the grazing lands.

The climate is generally semi-arid to arid, and winters are arctic. Winter feed and shelter are major problems. There is little interaction with crop production in most of the area as the climate is unsuitable for cropping, although the lowlands of Xinjiang and a few parts of western and southern Mongolia have a short, hot summer where crops can be grown if irrigation is available. Unlike the Himalayan systems described later, where herds move more or less avoiding extremes of heat and cold by spending the summer on alpine pastures and winter on or near the subtropical plains, herders in northern Asia cannot avoid the winter cold. Winter is also a long period of feed scarcity, so a major skill in herding is to get the stock fat enough in summer and autumn to be able to survive until spring.

Many of the peoples of the area are of similar ethnic origins and lifestyles: those to the west of the Altai mountains are generally Muslims. All were originally full-time nomads, living in the characteristic circular felt tent or *ger* (*yurt* in Russian) on a folding frame (Plate 5), which can be rapidly struck or erected, or, in the case of Tibetans, in black, woven tents. Herders' diet is largely based on meat and dairy products. In the recent past the herding industry of many countries of the region was collectivized. Decollectivization has taken different forms and had varying results.

BURYATIA

Buryatia – a republic of the Russian Federation – is at the junction of the steppe and taiga zones, on Mongolia's northern border, with Tuva – another republic of Russia – to its west. The main river of Buryatia is the Selenge, which rises in Mongolia and drains to Lake Baikal. About 70 percent of the land is taiga, so its dependence on livestock is much less than that of Mongolia. Forest-based industry, trapping and minerals are all important. In 1992, 22 percent of national income and 12 percent of employment were in the agricultural sector. Precipitation is generally less than 500 mm/yr. Forest dominates the natural vegetation and grazing lands are mainly in valleys – with large tracts of meadow.

In 1993, the natural pasture was estimated at 21 200 km², of which 3 400 km² were used for hay and 17 800 km² for grazing. Total grazing land comprises 12 220 km² of improved meadows, 6 541km² of natural meadow and 6 560 km² of bush and rocky land. About 1 840 km² of the meadow is marshy, frozen in winter and early spring and therefore of limited access for grazing. The following pasture zones are distinguished:

- dry valley meadow steppe, hayfields and pastures on high plateaus and mountain

Plate 3.
Camels are common pack animals in much of the steppe. Near Ikh Tamir, Mongolia.

Plate 4.
A Mongolian herders' camp in autumn.

Plate 5.
Mounting a ger, the common tentage of the steppe. Roof poles rest on a concertina frame, and all is covered with felt and cloth. There are no ropes or tent pegs, yet gers withstand very high winds.

slopes, with chestnut, free draining soils and low to medium herbage yields;

- lowland-meadow hayfields and pasture on chestnut-meadow soils, with high yields;
- well or excessively watered areas, riparian or marshy meadow hayfields and pasture covered by small bushes and low trees mixed with tall grasses;
- marshy hayfields and pastures in peaty meadows and permafrost-peaty soil, lowland river basins and lakes – areas that produce low quality herbage; and
- high mountain pastures and hayfields above 1 200 m, with reasonable productivity.

The dominant species in pasture communities are: *Festuca lenensis, Stipa baicalensis, Leymus chinensis, Agropyron cristatum, Potentilla acaulis, Veronica incana, Artemisia frigida, Sanguisorba officinalis, Hemerocallis minor* and some species of *Carex, Filifolium, Oxytropis, Polygonum* and *Pulsatilla*. On average, the estimated annual forage production of natural pastures is 2 500–3 000 kg/ha of green matter. Pasture degradation is estimated at 60 percent and uncontrolled grazing has led to drainage problems. Available grazing and hay is sufficient only for 50–60 percent of the feed requirements of the national herd.

Nomadic herding was the production system until the 1930s, when collectivization, in the form of collectivization and sedentarization of the population, was introduced as a matter of policy. This brought joint cultivation and haymaking. Livestock production became dependent on external inputs, including feed and fodder.

TABLE 2.1
Evolution of livestock numbers in Buryatia (head).

	1990	1991	1992	1993	1994
			Total livestock		
Cattle	560 600	559 100	549 600	502 700	455 300
Sheep and goats	1 493 600	1 384 000	1 262 700	1 091 500	822 200
Horses	73 500	76 500	73 700	73 700	73 000
			Livestock on peasant farms		
Cattle	0	100	4 400	11 800	18 400
Sheep and goats	0	1 500	32 900	35 000	34 800
Horses	0	0	600	1 500	2 200

SOURCE: Adapted from FAO, 1996.

Restructuring of the agricultural sector began in 1992, with a redistribution of land of collectives; land under private gardens and grazing land were unaffected. In the initial phase, many former agricultural enterprises collapsed because of migration of workers to private holdings; now many villages have organized new public enterprises as partnerships or companies. State enterprises maintained a strong presence in the livestock sector, and in 1994 only 25 percent of the livestock was privately owned.

Recently, difficult living and market conditions have encouraged migration to urban areas of the rural population, which was 36 percent of the total. In 1990, rural employees numbered 150 000, of which 60 percent were in animal husbandry, 25 percent in cropping and the remainder in related activities. Livestock was distributed about 33 percent in the dry steppe, 23 percent in the steppe, 27 percent in the forest steppe and 17 percent in the mountain taiga zone.

Since decollectivization there has been a sharp decline in livestock numbers (see Table 2.1), especially sheep. Part of the reduction is due to the collapse of the public sector and may be compensated by the rise in private herds, but much is due to lack of feed. Increased slaughter for home consumption has been an important factor in the decrease, accelerated by low market prices for livestock products.

PEOPLE'S REPUBLIC OF CHINA

Chapter V is devoted to a description of China's pastoral sector, and Chapters VI to VIII to three Chinese case studies.

Hu, Hannaway and Youngberg (1992) give a comprehensive description of China's grassland vegetation. Here some aspects are discussed to compare the various approaches to decollectivization that countries have taken.

Herding communities in China are generally "minority nationalities", including Mongolians, Kazakh, Kyrgyz and Tibetans. In the past decade the Government of China put the "Long-term contract grassland use system" into force, with great effort. Under this system, grassland productivity is improved by subdividing pastures and allocating long-term grazing rights to individual families, based on the number of family members. This has been basically completed nationwide, but it has not been put into practice totally on summer pastures because of their long distance from settlements, complex topography and difficulty of management. This is discussed in more detail in Chapters VI to VIII. The China study, however, indicates that, during the same decade, the degree of pasture degradation rose alarmingly.

Intensification, with enclosure of family grazing land, some upgrading of stock, pasture improvement and integration of crop production and herding, has been adopted with apparent success under the somewhat more clement conditions of the Autonomous Region of Inner Mongolia. Supplementary feeding is an integral part of the system, but herders have access to forage and concentrate feeds from agricultural areas, as well as a vast internal market for their products. The Altai case study describes a system where there has been a considerable upgrading of cattle, less so with sheep, but transhumance has been maintained, partly because of the Prefecture's mountainous nature and its excellent alpine pastures for summer grazing. The introduction of a new winter feed supply, through irrigated hay production, has improved overwintering condition and survival, but has increased pressure on the transition pastures. There are probably few sites where land and water for haymaking are available in herding areas. Again, the area has access to China's large market for its products.

The Autonomous Region of Inner Mongolia has developed much more towards individual holdings rather than continuing with the traditional, transhumant system. It has a slightly less harsh climate than Mongolia and Xinjiang, which allows some cultivation of crops, sown pasture and hay, as well as access to feed from neighbouring agricultural

areas. It also has good access to a vast national market for livestock products. Pasture degradation has become a major problem in the Region: between 1957 and 1980, the number of livestock rose by 57 percent. Major policy changes have taken place in the past half-century (Ma Rong and Li Qu, 1993): first the livestock of rich landowners and herd-masters were distributed to poor herders. Collective production units were established and step by step developed into collective, brigade and commune. Recently, land and livestock have again been redistributed among the residents. Grazing land is now leased to residents on a contract for a fixed term, and they are responsible for all production, planning and management. Because of the national market, the prices of livestock products rose sharply and this led to increases in stock numbers and overexploitation of the pasture. This short-sighted strategy caused serious ecological problems and the concept that natural pasture could be used without limit was proved fallacious.

After 1980, some 70 percent of the grazing land was leased to individual households. Policies are based on the carrying capacity of the land and appropriate stocking rates and management practices. Contracting farmers are encouraged to create and improve the pasture, and quality has obviously improved with their greatly increased enthusiasm to improve grazing areas. All collective stock was sold to pastoralists at a discount on market prices, to be paid for in instalments over 10–15 years, with the monies to be taken for public accumulation and used for development of grassland as a communal facility. Collective farms have completely disappeared. State farms are divided between production farms and stud farms, and state production farms contract their livestock to herders. After nearly three decades of collective ownership, agricultural capital now has been transferred to producers through the contractual system of "family responsibility".

Ho (1996) gives a depressing description of the situation in Ningxia, where mismanagement and overgrazing has led to ever-worsening erosion, pasture degradation and associated difficulties, even with the "responsibility system" to persuade herders to manage their grazing lands correctly.

KYRGYZSTAN

The Kyrgyz pastoral scene is described by Fitzherbert (2000). Kyrgyzstan is mountainous and mainly pastoral, with most of it above 1 500 m. Traditionally,

horses were the main livestock, being best suited to long transhumance and foraging in deep snow. Kinship-based groups had rights over recognized areas of pasture along their transhumance between the lowlands and the mountains. Winter feed supply limited stock numbers. By the late nineteenth century, winter camps had permanent buildings and simple stock shelters had come into use. Collective production was developed from 1930, and by 1940 collectivization was complete. Sheep became much more important and profitable; less hardy, fine-wool breeds were developed and raised. The rural population remained in villages; livestock were taken to the high summer pastures (Plate 6) by a small number of salaried herdsmen. Transhumance was maintained for the livestock while settlement gave families permanent housing and access to services.

A. FITZHERBERT

Plate 6.
A camp on the high pasture in Kyrgyzstan.

Privatization of state and collective enterprises took place in 1992. Livestock were shared out among individuals working in the enterprises, and private herding then developed. Currently, three-pasture transhumance continues, but multispecies herds are now normal. While crop land has been let on 49-year leases, natural pasture is almost all common grazing.

Livestock numbers rose steeply between 1960 and 1989. The number of small stock rose by 66 percent, cattle by 50 percent, but horses by only 25 percent, with a maximum herd size of 18 million sheep equivalents in 1989. This was made possible by an increased reliance on imported grain. In the three years following privatization, sheep numbers fell by 30 percent and cattle by 12.5 percent, while horses increased by 23 percent. With the change of system, many stock were slaughtered to pay for services and fodder. This was exacerbated by low prices for livestock products. The local transhumance system – *otgonne* – aims at maximum use of grazing, with build-up

of bodily reserves for winter, and minimal use of conserved fodder.

Sheep numbers in particular have declined most dramatically since the early 1990s, for a number of reasons (van Veen, 1995). After collectivization in the 1930s and 1940s, Russia harnessed the herding skills and transhumance traditions of the Kyrgyz and the rich seasonal grasslands of the Tien Shan mountains into a wool farm for the USSR. They developed new (to the area) breeds of sheep based on the merino, the Rambouillet and other classic western fine-wool breeds, to produce the "Kyrgyz fine-wool" and others. Wool rather than mutton was the government's priority, so large flocks of wethers were maintained as well as ewe flocks, and flock numbers increased, often regardless of good pastoral management, to meet Central planning quotas.

After independence, in 1991–1992, one of the first things that happened, even before land reform had started, was splitting up the flocks and herds among the members of the sovkhozes

TABLE 2.2
Stock numbers in Kyrgyzstan, 1990 to 1999 ('000 head).

Year	Sheep	Goats	Cattle	Yaks	Horses	Sheep equivalents	Change from previous year
1990	9 544.40	428.10	506.10	57.20	312.60	14 536.17	
1991	9 106 60	418.30	518.60	55.30	320.50	14.188.90	-347.27
1992	8 361.70	379.80	514.70	53.60	313.00	13 034.06	-1 154.90
1993	6 972.60	349.70	511.20	50.20	322.00	11 990.89	-1 043.17
1994	4 783.00	293.40	480.90	40.70	299.00	9 390.38	-2 600.51
1995	3 899.30	375.50	470.90	33.10	308.10	8 506.68	-883.70
1996	3 322.20	393.90	459.90	22.60	314.10	8 476.15	-30.53
1997	3 333.50	471.40	473.50	17.90	325.40	7 895.03	-581.12
1998	3 308.50	502.10	492.20	16.70	335.20	7 906.33	+ 11.30
1999	3 263.80	542.70	511.50	16.90	349.80	8 215.67	+ 309.34

Note: Official stock counts are in January, before the main spring births. Previously, official stock numbers reflected the 'state-owned' herds and flocks, without the individually owned animals, so that the figures for the years 1990/92 may have been higher than recorded here, especially for sheep.
Source: Kyrgyzstan GoskomStat, cited in Fitzherbert, 2000.

A. FITZHERBERT

Plate 7.
Kyrgyzstan pastures at 2500 m in June.

and kolkhozes [types of collective]. There was also a collapse of the logistic support they had previously received from the Soviet State to maintain large numbers of animals and people up in the high valleys in the summer.

Cheap concentrate feed ceased to be available. Intensive livestock units – beef, dairy, poultry – collapsed. Very few remain. It became much more difficult to maintain large numbers of sheep over winter. The acreage of lucerne shrunk dramatically, ploughed up to grow wheat to feed a population that had previously been fed by Ukraine, the Volga Region and Kazakhstan. The Russian market for wool collapsed. The fall in sheep numbers has been the most dramatic: from over 9 million in 1990 to under 3 million now. Breeding programmes and controls collapsed, except on a few farms that managed to hold on to their flocks. Here opinion is divided between some manag-

ers who hang on to previous policies and try to maintain their fine-wool flocks, and others, who are now deliberately breeding back to fat tailed–fat rumped breeds, as clearly the market is now for meat rather than wool. Yak numbers have also declined sharply, since nobody wants to undertake the hard transhumance to the high pastures. Some outlying areas have been almost abandoned for grazing, and wildlife there is said to be on the increase.

After an extensive trip through Kyrgyz mountain pastures in 2001, Fitzherbert (personal communication) found that pasture condition had greatly improved (Plate 7) and that traditional grazing practices were once more being used.

> *Generally we have found them in marvellous condition – with exceptions of course – but to our surprise many of what they call the prisebni pastures, i.e. those closest to the settlements, appear to be in a very recovered, even in excellent state. The mountain Kyrgyz are increasingly returning*

Plate 8.
Milking at a transit camp, moving to summer pastures, with much of the gear on lorries.
The animals group by species at a few words from the herders. Tarialan, Mongolia.

to a more traditional and rational use of pastures. Fewer animals are being kept round the villages all the year round, and more are being sent up to the jailoo in the summer. That does not mean that all owners are going, but that traditional systems of bada (hiring a group herdsman), and kesu of shared rotational herding responsibility among a group of families, as well as larger flock masters herding their own individual flocks and herds of horses and cattle, mean that most animals are now away from the villages by the end of May or early June, and off to the more distant pastures. We also know much more about the use of south facing slopes for wintering (the sunny side or kungoi) and the shady side (snowy side or teskey) slopes of valleys for spring and early summer pasturage.

Pastures at all levels, and seasonal locations, which every herdsman agrees were grazed down to dust in the 1980s as the result of increasing quota demands from Moscow and seriously heavy stocking, have recovered amazingly well, dem-onstrating the innate resilience of these pastures and their species, both perennials and ephemerals. There was no evidence of pasture degradation or deterioration to no, or very light, stocking, as predicted or stated by a number of armchair pastoralists; rather the reverse.

MONGOLIA

In Mongolia stock rearing is, and always has been, almost the only industry in the country. Traditionally the land was managed, under feudal tenure, by transhumant systems – the only way of using such inhospitable land. While stock movements (Plate 8) are generally, as elsewhere, dictated by the availability of feed, water and shelter, in some regions during summer movement is also made necessary by the presence of biting insects. The case studies show how, in mountainous country, topography and the seasonal closure of passes by snow also has a marked influence. Uvs *aimag* [province], one of those studied, has a particularly extreme continental climate – it has the hottest summers and coldest winters of anywhere on its latitude and is the northernmost limit of desert.

The cold, arid climate is well suited to extensive grazing and transhumance, which makes best use of pastures where forage availability in any one place can vary greatly from season to season and year to year. The ancient, original systems were transhumant with a wide range of possible travel. In the late thirteenth century, Marco Polo described Mongol transhumance and their *gers*. The country's pastures have probably always been heavily stocked, and hard grazing is a historical phenomenon, not something of recent development. Kharin, Takahashi and Harahshesh (1999) quote Przhevalsky (1883), who said that "all suitable agricultural lands were reclaimed and all grazing lands were overloaded by livestock." Feudal land ownership was done away with on the founding of the Mongolian Communist State in 1921; transhumance continued, with government supervision.

A fundamental change took place in 1950, with the collectivization of the livestock industry. While this facilitated the provision of government services and marketing (and probably control of a nomadic population), it decreased the range over which herds could travel and thus reduced opportunities for risk avoidance in times of feed scarcity. The unit of management was the *negdel*, covering the same area as a single district (*sum*); it was primarily an economic unit responsible for marketing livestock products, supplying inputs and consumer goods, as well as fodder and transport services to members,

and it provided health, education and veterinary services. Although livestock was collectivized, each family could keep two livestock units (*bod* – a large-animal unit, where 1 camel = 1.5 bod; cattle and horses = 1; and 7 sheep or 10 goats = 1 bod) per person, so about a quarter of the herd was under private control.

During the collective period, the government intervened heavily in livestock production through the provision of breeding stock, fodder, marketing, transport and services. It was a heavily subsidized production system, which did not allocate resources efficiently. The loss of mobility through collectivization was compensated by the production of supplementary forage, and a State Emergency Fodder Fund (SEFF) was established to provide feed during weather events that would threaten survival, but, with heavily subsidized transport and undervalued prices, herders soon became dependent on it as a regular source of feed. By 1991, SEFF, handling 157 600 tonne, had become a major component of the state budget. A network of stock routes allowed slaughter stock to be trekked to market, fattening en route. There were marketing and primary processing facilities for hides, skins, wool and cashmere.

Eighteen *aimags* were subdivided into 225 *sum*, in turn divided into brigades. *Negdel* headquarters had administration, schools (boarding), medical facilities, a veterinary unit, communications, recreational facilities and shops. *Negdels* were set production quotas and paid accordingly with bonuses – the system was production driven. A vast number of salaried administrators and specialist staff was built up at all levels, especially in the capital.

Political change was rapid in the early 1990s. Policy was to privatize half of the livestock and turn the rest of the negdel's assets into companies, with the former negdel members as shareholders. Some companies were never formed, others collapsed quickly. All stock was soon distributed amongst negdel members. This created a large class of "new herders" from the ex-salaried workers – some with little or no relevant experience or training. No legislation was drawn up to define rights to pasture so private stock graze on uncontrolled public land. There is a ministerial dichotomy: livestock is under agriculture, but pasture under natural resources! Because of lack of title, no maintenance occurs on pasture infrastructure, so at least 85 percent of mechanized wells are not functioning.

An overall description of herding in Mongolia, as well as a summary of changes in its structure, is given in the FAO Pastoral Resource Profile for Mongolia (Suttie, 2000b). The basic system is four-season grazing, with specific winter, spring, summer (Plate 9) and autumn pastures, using mixed herds (Plate 10), usually of five species of hardy local breeds.

Otor – travel to distant pastures – is also an important part of the system. There are three major periods of otor: (i) spring otor for grazing young grass; (ii) summer otor for development of enough muscle and internal fat; and (iii) autumn otor for consolidation of fatness. There can also be emergency movement of large stock to grazing reserves in a hard winter. Some social reorganization has begun to appear, usually at the level of a few families collaborating for herding tasks, but no larger association, capable of participating in overall land management, has yet appeared.

Plate 9
Mongolian summer camp in the Great Lakes basin.

With decollectivization, most of the technical services previously available to herders – including veterinary care, improved quality breeding stock, organized marketing of livestock and products, emergency fodder, and shops in outlying centres – have been suspended.

Privatization of livestock has created many problems for grazing management. With private livestock on public land there is no control over how herders use pasture. Market and social forces have brought about changes in pasture use. The collapse of markets and social services have encouraged herders to move close to cities and service centres. New herders, mostly ex-employees of negdel and state farms, have difficulties in gaining access to grazing (especially winter grazing), and this leads to conflicts. The influx of new herders is leading to frequent disputes over territory. Grazing rights are not clear at local level, which makes dispute settlement difficult for administrators. Controls on land use cannot be enforced effectively by sum officials; the areas are too great and the government resources too small to do such work, even if it were practicable. A self-regulating and community-based system of management is needed. Several suggestions have been made, varying from grazing associations to a return to traditional units.

The vast grasslands of Mongolia are part of the steppe, a prominent transition belt in inner and central Asia between the forest and desert belts. Steppe vegetation is characterized by a predominance of grasses, especially *Stipa* spp., *Cleistogenes soongorica* and *Festuca* spp. Legumes are scarce, and the commonest are *Medicago falcata* and *Astragalus* spp. *Artemisia*

Plate 10.
Cattle being milked beside calf pens. Cattle, yaks and their hybrids are kept. Ikh Tamir, Mongolia.

frigida is frequent and is the main steppe-forming plant of the desert steppe. The montane forest steppe has *Festuca* spp. and *Artemisia* spp. as dominants.

Opinions on the present state of Mongolia's pastures vary widely, especially those of external missions. There is general agreement that overstocking now occurs close to agglomerations, especially the capital, and along roads. Damage through random track-making by vehicles in valley bottoms is also widespread. Thereafter opinions have varied from declaring that the nation's pastures are seriously degraded, risking an ecological disaster, to the view that overstocking is a localized phenomenon and labour availability, not pasture production, is the main constraint to herding.

While stock numbers are at an all-time high since recording began in 1918, the 1996 levels were only marginally higher than those of 1950. The consensus is that problems vary from place to place, and that outlying (summer and autumn) pastures are underutilized while winter-spring pastures are often being abused. Natural control of stock numbers is the traditional way to correct overstocking. Periodic *zud* – a term applied to various types of winter weather event in the cold season, mostly deep or frozen snow making feed inaccessible, but also lack of snow preventing access to grazing where there is no water in winter, blizzards, very low temperatures, etc. – or prolonged drought kills large numbers and puts the grazing stock back in equilibrium with the forage supply. Nevertheless, however effective natural disasters are in protecting the grazing vegetation, they inevitably lead to poverty and suffering among the herders. The

spring of 2000 saw a particularly severe *zud* over a large area.

Previously, mechanized wells and bores had supplied water to large areas in the steppe; most of these are now out of use since their ownership is unclear and they have not been maintained, so these areas are now unavailable to domestic stock, but are being recolonized by gazelles.

Eighty percent of Mongolia is extensive grazing, and a further 10 percent is forest or forest scrub, which is also grazed. Its climate is arid to semi-arid and the frost-free period of most of the steppe is 100 days; transhumant herding on natural pasture is the only sustainable way of using such land. There is hardly any crop production. Natural pasture is the only animal feed, and since it is impossible during so short a growing season to conserve feed for the unproductive nine months, survival of herds depends on having the stock fat enough in autumn to survive winter and spring. Animals not essential for breeding are sold, or slaughtered and frozen for domestic use, at the onset of winter.

The livestock population rose very rapidly from 1918 until 1940 (Table 2.3), but was severely affected by bad weather in the 1940s, and remained almost stable throughout the collective period. There has been a very steep increase since decollectivization, to over 28 000 000 in 1996, and even the zuds of 1999 to 2001 have not brought numbers down to 1996 levels. The evolution of stock numbers, as stock units (using the traditional *bod* units), is shown graphically in Figure 2.1.

In the absence of other employment opportunities, families must keep livestock (Plate 11). The evolution of stock numbers, therefore, is probably associated

TABLE 2.3
Stock numbers in Mongolia, 1918–2000 ('000 head).

Year	Camels	Horses	Cattle	Sheep	Goats	Total
1918	228.7	1 150.5	1 078.7	5 700.0	1 487.9	9 645.8
1924	275.0	1 389.8	1 512.1	8 444.8	2 204.4	13 826.1
1930	480.9	1 566.9	1 887.3	15 660.3	4 080.8	23 675.7
1940	643.4	2 538.1	2 722.8	15 384.2	5 096.3	25 384.8
1950	844.2	2 317.0	1 987.8	12 574.6	4 978.6	22 702.2
1961	751.7	2 289.3	1 637.4	10 981.9	4 732.6	20 392.9
1970	633.5	2 317.9	2 107.8	13 311.7	4 204.0	22 574.9
1980	591.5	1 985.4	2 397.1	14 230.7	4 566.7	23 771.2
1985	559.0	1 971.0	2 408.1	13 248.8	4 298.6	22 485.5
1992	415.2	2 200.2	2 840.0	14 657.0	5 602.5	25 714.9
1996	357.9	2 270.5	3 476.3	13 560.6	9 134.8	28 800.1
2000	322.9	2 660.7	3 976.0	13 876.4	10 269.8	31 105.8

Source: ADB, 1998.

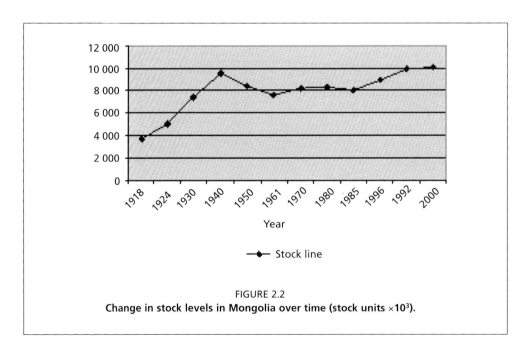

FIGURE 2.2
Change in stock levels in Mongolia over time (stock units ×10³).

with the rise in the human population. The total population has risen sharply, more rapidly than livestock numbers, tripling in half a century, from 772 400 in 1950 to 2 422 800 in 1998, and the degree of urbanization rose very steeply on collectivization. Whereas previously the urban dwellers were only 15 percent, after a decade of collectivization they had risen to 40 percent, and were 57 percent by 1989, the end of the collective period. These figures include those in the sum centres. The 1997 figures show a slight decrease in the proportion (but not number) of town dwellers, perhaps reflecting some families returning to herding. While the rise since 1950 has been large and rapid, the projections for the next twenty years show no slowing down, but instead predict a near doubling!

The degree of urbanization may seem surprising, given the lack of towns of any size, but many of these people are living around the small townships at sum and aimag centres, originally as employees of negdels and many now semi-unemployed, not having succeeded in herding after decollectivization.

Two consecutive years, 1999/2000 and 2000/2001 have had the harsh combination of drought followed by *zud*: stock suffered on thin pastures in the growing season and were unable to feed because of hardened snow in winter. This is, of course, a regular risk in herding under such climatic conditions (Plate 12). The greatest disaster was 1944/45, when 8 million adult stock were lost. Eight zud winters have been recorded since then, the worst pre-2000 being in 1967. The figures used to define zud are stock losses, not meteorological data; for much of the time when zud has been recorded there was a well organized system of grazing management. Shelters were maintained and winter feed conserved, emergency systems were probably better equipped as well. It is not clear, therefore, to what extent the recent losses are a reflection of severe weather events, and how much is due to lack of preparedness by herders and authorities. Stock numbers had risen very steeply since 1990, and this may have been a contributing factor to the severe losses. The government is now very aware that good stock and pasture management, coupled with preparation at local level, is necessary if further such dis-

Plate 11.
Cashmere goats are an important source of revenue in cold climates. Early October, Mongolia.

Plate 12.
Winter can come early. Mongolia, mid-October.

asters are to be mitigated or avoided. It is recognized that "relief" is generally ineffective and expensive; similarly, restocking herders is to little avail if the underlying faults that put stock at risk are not attended to.

In response to the damage caused by *zud*, the government drew up a Programme for Combating Zud and Drought (Resolution of the Government of Mongolia, 13 March 2001, No. 47, Ulan Bator). This sets out the responsibilities of central and local government at various levels, as well as those of the herders themselves. Herder responsibility mainly concerns adequacy of winter preparedness. The programme has a set of integrated goals:

• to devise and put into operation all available mechanisms to protect livestock from drought and zud,

• to improve the system for disaster reduction and relief,

• to establish relief aid networks and to identify responsibilities and roles of livestock owners, herders and various government agencies in emergencies, and

• to provide strong policy, monitoring and guidance to national natural risk management.

An FAO TCP project studying Herding Risk Strategy concluded:

The main key to winter survival of livestock is having them in as good a condition as possible, adequately fat, by the onset of winter. Herd survival and herders' risk avoidance is not a seasonal activity: it depends on proper grazing management throughout the year. Grazing management principles are well known in Mongolia but, since the early 1990s, have been largely ignored. Preparation of stock for winter is not only an autumnal activity; it depends on proper herd and grazing management throughout the year. Proper seasonal use (and protection) of pastures is the key to good grazing management. Otor is an essential strategy both for autumn fattening and winter emergencies. Suitable areas for otor reserves at both inter-aimag and inter-sum level have been identified, but require infrastructure as well as regulation of use. Many otor areas are already well known, but all should be prospected and their use planned. Otor areas at all levels should be delimited and agreements made on their use – depending on their situation, collaboration between sums or aimags will be required. Herders should be encouraged to go on autumn otor for fattening. Winter emergency otor reserves should be equipped with necessary infrastructure.

The potential area of hay land was mapped some time ago; it does not always take into account suitability for the various methods of haymaking (manual, mechanized, horse-drawn), potential hay quality nor accessibility to users. More information is needed both to estimate potential hay production and to assess likely needs in machinery and spares.

Local rules for pasture use, with emphasis on control of seasonal movement, are necessary so that herders know where they should (and should not) be at a given season. These have existed but require revision and updating; their drafting should be a consultative process. Once the rules are drawn up, herders have to be made aware of them. Their observance should be assured by involvement of herders and local administration. Grazing management plans indicating seasonal grazing areas and times for moving from zone to zone should be revised and updated, sum by sum, in consultation with herders. Out-of-season grazing should be avoided, and this includes exclusion of trespassers from other sums. The bag khural

[local-level parliament] should assist in the implementation of the plans.

Winter preparedness involves much more than good grazing management. Other activities include animal health, household preparedness in food, fuel and housing, timely construction or cleaning and repair of shelters and pens, and assurance of water supply.

Correct grazing management and respecting of seasonal use can probably be organized at sum and bag level if herders' participation is obtained. If, however, herds from outside the sum use its pastures in an uncontrolled fashion, the sum's work will have been in vain.

RISK IN HERDING

Risk is inherent in extensive stock rearing, partly because it is carried out in areas that are marginal for other forms of agriculture. This is discussed in detail, with reference to cold, semi-arid areas, by Swift (1999), and Baas, Erdenbaatar and Swift (2001). Three main categories of risk affect the pastoral economy:

- Environmental – adverse weather events; drought; fire; and predation.
- Economic – derived from stock theft; market failure (abrupt shock followed change in terms of trade subsequent to disappearance of the subsidized sum shop and collapse of markets); education costs; illness; and sudden health costs.
- Political – resulting from a reduction in the ability of the state to be effective in remote areas; declining government resources and services; declining legitimacy and authority of the state, with no alternative source of legitimate authority; and conflict.

The different types of risk are interrelated: for example, bad weather may weaken surviving animals. Market failure exacerbates other risks. The word 'risk'

Plate 13.
Horses in the eastern steppe, Hentii, Mongolia. These are kept for milk and meat, as well as work. Large stock are usually left to graze free without herders.

itself carries many different meanings. It is often used in a very general, but negative, way: 'risk refers to uncertain events that can damage well-being'. Risk is also used in English in positive ways, as when we talk about risk-taking by entrepreneurs.

While herders can lose drastically in bad years, they can build up capital in a series of good seasons. In the Himalayan zone, many herding groups are also stock traders. This may be more lucrative than the actual stock rearing. The studies here deal with transhumant people who are mainly engaged in looking after stock; this does not mean that their whole ethnic group are poor herders. Those who build up stock and capital can move to a more settled existence, buy land and property and live by trading. The subsistence crop-grower has far less chance of escaping from a cycle of poverty. Gujars in India and Pakistan (see Chapters X to XII) are

renowned stock traders, as well as being milk dealers in peri-urban areas; it is the poorer ones who go on transhumance. The Kuchis of Afghanistan are also great traders. In the ex-communist countries, any tradition of trading would have died out under many years of centralized marketing, and clear trading patterns have yet to appear.

STRATEGIES FOR COLD SEMI-ARID GRAZING LAND

Several strategies for exploiting extensive grazing land are used in the Region, or have been used in the recent past, with very varying degrees of success and sustainability.

Intensification through the use of exotic or upgraded stock, with higher production potential, has been widely advocated, sometimes with fencing of pastures. Use of exotic stock immediately leads to loss of mobility and hardiness, so shelter, even housing, will be necessary for overwintering. Such livestock are unable to subsist and produce entirely by foraging, so external inputs of feed are needed. Such production systems are usually sedentarized. "Improved" stock rarely stand up to long transhumance, so mobility cannot be used for risk avoidance, precluding making full use of far-off, high-altitude or arid grazing. Intensive production in areas of low pasture yield, with a very short growing season, are dependent on external inputs and thus can only survive when they have access to a good market for their products. This was the policy of the intensive livestock sector in Mongolia, which supplied urban demand for dairy, pork and poultry products; it made little use of the natural grassland and collapsed because of changes in the economic situation.

Sedentarization of the herding population and "improvement" of livestock by cross-breeding has been widely used in the pastoral regions of the former USSR since the 1930s. In some instances, upgrading to fine-wool sheep produced herds that required shelter in winter as well as supplementary feed; such herds have difficulty in surviving without external inputs and, with current low wool prices, upgraded sheep are being sold or slaughtered in Kyrgyzstan, and a slow start made to redeveloping local, adapted meat breeds.

Mongolia has maintained mobility (Plate 13) for its vast extensive livestock sector throughout the changes of system. Transhumance, with few if any external inputs, has clearly demonstrated its resilience and sustainability. The negdel, although restricting transhumance dis-

tances compared to the original traditions, still covered sufficiently large areas to cope with many weather events. Selected stock of local breeds were used, and some crossing of cattle took place in favoured areas, but the overall livestock population has remained hardy, productive, good foragers and suitable for mobile herding. Under the negdels there was an excessive use of subsidized fodder, which may have contributed to their eventual economic collapse, but they left behind both herders and stock adapted to the conditions and economic realities of the country's grazing lands. The lack of orderly transfer of grazing rights, however, has led to some transitional problems. It is clear that improvement of grazing management in Mongolia must be within traditional transhumance and based on the proper use of grazing land, with the minimum use of external inputs. In addition to making best use of the available grazing in an organized manner, the redevelopment of family haymaking, from natural herbage, in those regions where hayfields can be developed, is a primary area for encouragement.

In China (see Chapter V) grazing land has been allocated on Long-term Grassland Use Contracts; this usually involves sedentarization of the families and often of the livestock. It is still too early to judge the effect of this on pasture condition, nor whether reseeding is sustainable.

It appears, from the outcome of collectivization and the various degrees of "modernization" that have been applied to the extensive stock rearing systems of the various countries of cold semi-arid Asia, that deviating too far from mobile systems using hardy stock is fraught with risks. Use of exotic breeds brings a dependence on shelter and imported feed, which may not be economic. Sedentarization seems to bring localized overgrazing as well as undue exposure to weather risks. The use of imported feed for winter feed may lead to overstocking and damage to pastoral vegetation. Most of the countries of the region report serious to very serious degradation of their grazing lands. By far the least affected is Mongolia, which has maintained herding mobility, with hardy local breeds throughout.

Chapter III
Mongolia case study 1: Studies on long-distance transhumant grazing systems in Uvs and Khuvsgul aimags of Mongolia, 1999–2000

B. Erdenebaatar

SUMMARY

The entire study area is extensive grazing land, used by highly mobile production systems. The study looks at transhumance patterns that have re-appeared since privatization of the livestock industry in 1990, after forty years of collectivization. The study sites are in two western, mountainous provinces, both in great depressions surrounded by high mountains, where mountains and other physical features impose restrictions on the migration routes available. Both sites have a wide range of ecological conditions. Topographic features as well as weather and feed availability influence the itineraries chosen for migration, and in some cases the summer move is prompted by the arrival of biting insects. In both areas, all movements are longitudinal (west-east) to make better use of pasture resources and climatic differences. In Turgen, the movements cross five ecological belts, travelling twice yearly over two sets of passes: one for the spring journey and another for the return. The distance travelled annually is between 90 and 140 km. Rinchinlkumbe herders traverse only two ecological belts, making two long movements: from winter to summer pastures, and back. The distance travelled is between 90 and 180 km. There is a clear set of climatic and social indicators governing seasonal movements. The period of the study, 1999 and 2000, was a time of disastrous weather events. A severe drought, lasting several years, was followed by the severe winter of 2000, which caused much misery and economic loss. Herders were obliged to modify their travel patterns to save their stock as best they could.

Multispecies herding using hardy local landraces is the basis of the system. Horses, cattle, yaks, sheep and goats are the main stock, with some camels for transport. Success in herding lies in having stock fat enough in autumn to survive the winter-to-spring near-starvation period. Turgen herders move twice a year over the same passes between their summer and winter camps; those of Rinchinlkumbe make one movement to and from winter pastures. No herders stay at higher altitudes in winter. Seasonal, especially winter, camps are on one side of a mountain range that routes must cross. Herders of both sexes are highly literate, most to secondary level.

Since decollectivization, public services, including technical support to herders, have deteriorated, leading to problems of marketing and procurement of necessities. The major problem, however, is the lack of clear title to grazing and haymaking rights, which has led to trespass and squatting, and obliges many herders to restrict transhumance movements so that they can protect their winter camps. This exacerbates the deterioration of standards of pasture management, and some outlying areas are neglected while others are overgrazed and used at the wrong season.

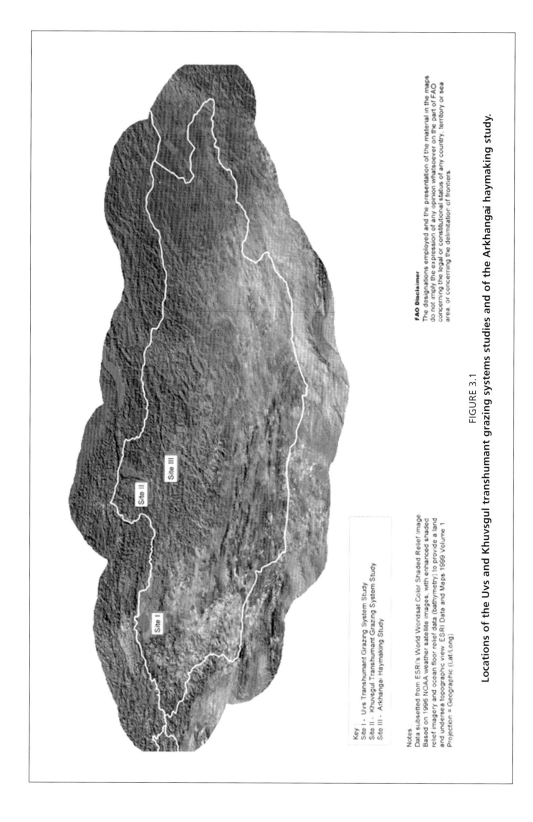

FIGURE 3.1

Locations of the Uvs and Khuvsgul transhumant grazing systems studies and of the Arkhangai haymaking study.

FAO Disclaimer

The designations employed and the presentation of the material in the maps do not imply the expression of any opinion whatsoever on the part of FAO concerning the legal or constitutional status of any country, territory or sea area, or concerning the delimitation of frontiers.

Key :
Site I - Uvs Transhumant Grazing System Study
Site II - Khuvsgul Transhumant Grazing System Study
Site III - Arkhangai Haymaking Study

Notes :
Data subsetted from ESRI's World Worldsat Color Shaded Relief image
Based on 1996 NOAA weather satellite images, with enhanced shaded relief imagery and ocean floor relief data (bathymetry) to provide a land and undersea topographic view ESRI Data and Maps 1999 Volume 1
Projection = Geographic (Lat/Long)

SELECTION CRITERIA

The Mongolian livestock industry has undergone a great transformation since privatization in 1990. This study was designed to determine how herders now manage their livestock and to identify problems associated with their new situation. A major concern was to identify and select viable households representative of the community in terms of regularity of transhumant grazing movements and availability of necessary information. Criteria for household selection included:

- permanent membership of a society where long distance transhumance is traditional or newly formed. Newly formed means that, in some areas, herders had to change movement patterns to strengthen their rights over grazing land;
- distance of transhumance to be over 100 km, one way; special attention was paid to determine whether a household had taken the same itinerary in the past five years. The movement pattern in the collective period was also studied as an additional source of information;
- herd composition to include four or more species; herders owning many species need more diverse and productive grazing resources to maintain herd productivity;
- adequate labour and availability of the additional workforce needed for long-distance migrations; shortage of labour is a potential limiting factor to herd mobility. Additional labour is needed at peak times, like lambing, moving animals and repairing shelters and camps; and
- representative of a range of social and economic status of herding lifestyles. It is commonly believed that female-headed households are less able to be

efficient transhumant grazers and that most poor herding families in rural Mongolia are female-headed.

STUDY SITES AND SAMPLE HOUSEHOLDS

Thirteen herding households were chosen in Turgen sum, Uvs aimag, and fourteen (with six more selected in 2000) in Rinchinlkumbe sum, Khuvsgul aimag (Figure 3.1). Of those in Turgen, ten household heads were male and three were female; herding experience varied from 8 to 42 years. In Rinchinlkumbe, 12 heads were male and 2 were female; herding experience was from 5 to 38 years.

In addition to the selected households, studies in 2000 covered other families to cross-check data on livestock production and consumption at household level, and to gain more information on marketing and sale opportunities. Special attention was given to identifying alternative routes for long-distance movement; this necessitated interviewing more herding households and also local government officials.

Data were collected using participatory techniques, with group and individual interviews, semi-structured discussion, matrix ranking, etc. Special attention was paid to female informants. Secondary data covering the last three to five years were collected from the annual census and other valid statistical documents. The territory of the sums, the areas of the movement routes and camping sites of sample households were mapped, marking the seasonal movement routes of a group of households. Valuable forage plants in main seasonal pastures were identified and data on their natural productivity obtained by field observation and talks to herders. Data on herd performance of sums and sample households were gathered to estimate annual output of livestock products. Socio-economic and customary points directly and indirectly related to the transhumant movements, and factors determining the patterns of such movements, have been carefully considered and some indicators identified for cross-checking and verification.

ECOLOGICAL AND NATURAL CONDITIONS OF THE STUDY SITES

Turgen is in the Great Lake Depressions along the Uvs and Khyargas lakes (Buyanorshikh, 1994). Most of Turgen is to the north of Uvs lake, stretching over the Kharkhiraa-Turgen mountains to the top edges of the Bairam-Yamaat ranges to the west. There are dry desert belts where, on the west side of swampy willow lowlands and dry desert, Uvs lake meets the forest belt of Kharkhiraa mountain and

the basin of Uureg lake. Various authors (Buyanorshikh, 1994; Badarch, 1971) note that Turgen has an exceptionally harsh and extreme continental climate. Sum headquarters (Plate 14) is at roughly 49°15′ N, 92°04′ E, at the break of slope between the plains at around 1 100 m and the mountains, which rise to over 3 000 m. The highest areas have permanent snowfields and glaciers; the lowest areas are below 800 m.

Turgen is divided by a range of high, steep mountains running roughly north-south. Spring pastures are on the plains to the east of the mountains, and winter grazing is on the other, western, side. At the lowest, easterly, extremity there are large areas of marshland, suitable for autumn and spring grazing and hay-making (Plates 15 and 16). It is arid to semi-arid, according to altitude (average annual rainfall at Ulaangom is 154 mm).

Plate 14.
Turgen sum headquarters. Herders and their herds cross these mountains four times each year.

Lowland vegetation is desert steppe, except in marshes. Part of western Turgen is a nature reserve. The climate is extreme, with very cold winters in the lowlands. Winter camps are in the hills.

The total area is 225.3 km². Usable land covers 210.5 km², of which pasture is 98.5 percent (Table 3.1). Turgen has vast winter-spring pastures, which provide plenty of room for seasonal camping and grazing for both transhumant and short-distance migration. The sum is famous for its natural diversity, which has attracted herders and people from other sums to settle, making some seasonal pastures more crowded, leading to overconcentration of livestock and people in some parts of the territory. Geographically, the winter-spring pastures are unsuitable for grazing at other seasons; they are in a defined part of the

TABLE 3.1
Land resources in Turgen sum, Mongolia.

Land category		Turgen		Aimag total	
		km²	percent	km²	percent
Land utilized		210.5	93.4	6 229.0	89.2
of which pasture land		207.5	98.5	6 064.0	97.3
comprising	– summer-spring pasture	37.9	18.0	2 109.5	33.8
	– summer-autumn pasture	53.0	25.2	2 661.1	42.7
	– winter-spring pasture	116.6	55.4	1 195.6	19.2
Land not available		14.8	6.6	756.6	10.4
Total territory		225.3		6 985.6	

Plate 15.
Manual haymaking in the Uvs Lake basin.

sum and have strict boundaries and conditions for grazing.

Rinchinlkumbe sum headquarters is at 51°01′ N, 99°40′ E, at 1 583 m. It is also in a very mountainous area, but with much higher rainfall, 284 mm annually. It has an area of 1 400 km², with some 18 percent covered by water and the rest is a state reserve. Pasture areas are as shown in Table 3.2. It has a large area of seasonal pastures on both sides of Bayanuul (Rich Mountain). In comparison with Turgen, it has a great network of surface water, including Khuvsgul Lake – the largest in Mongolia. Over 800 ha of land are reserved for haymaking.

Rinchinlkumbe is less varied in terms of landscape and altitude range. It has

TABLE 3.2
Major land categories in Rinchinlkumbe sum, Mongolia.

Land category		Area	
		km²	percent
Land utilized		1 288.1	92.0
of which pasture land[1]		1 092.0	85.2
comprising	– spring-summer pasture	253.3	23.2
	– summer-autumn pasture	233.6	21.4
	– winter-spring pasture	542.7	49.7
Total territory		1 400.0	

NOTE: (1) Includes sparsely distributed and lowland forest.

Plate 16.
Measuring primary production in the marsh haylands, Uvs Lake basin.

five major landscapes, all belonging to the Sayan-Khuvsgul region, namely:
- alpine and taiga high mountain to the west;
- taiga, meadow and forest steppe in the Darkhad Depression;
- Ulaan taiga and mountain top edge formations;
- steppe at the foot of the high mountain areas; and
- lowland areas lying along the basin of Khuvsgul lake.

LAND-FORMS AND ALTITUDE RANGE

Turgen contains all the ecological zones of Mongolia: from desert steppe to high alpine, including steppe, forest steppe and Gobi-type landscapes. Based on literature sources (Erdenebaatar, 1996; Buyanorshikh, 1994) and information from herders, the topographical elements in Turgen and their use patterns are:
- high mountains (over 3 000 m) with alpine climate and vegetation provide room for some wildlife at all seasons; large livestock put for short fattening, lost or unattended can survive there during the warm period (summer, autumn and late spring);
- medium mountains (2 000–3 000 m) are summer grazing for all kinds of livestock in some competition with wildlife; low mountains are where herders camp in summer, late autumn and early spring;
- high hills (1 000–1 500 m), where herders stay in late spring for lambing or in late autumn before moving to winter camp; and
- lowlands between the west bank of Uvs lake, medium mountains and high hills, which are used as grazing in late summer and post-lambing in late spring.

Rinchinlkumbe has interesting land forms, with elements of alpine, taiga, lowlands and high mountains. Lowlands (1 200–1 500 m) for late spring-summer and summer-autumn grazing are between mountain ranges over 2 500–3 000 m, whereas winter areas are in medium-altitude forest steppe and steppe between 1 000–1 400 m. Some transhumant herders stay at 1 900–2 300 m over winter and early spring. No single area is used all the year round; there is a strict seasonal division according to ecological type and topographical conditions. Land such as high hills, low mountains and lowlands will be used several times in a year because of the linear location of resources and west-east direction of grazing movements: all upward movements are westwards and the return to lowlands eastwards.

SOILS

Dominant soils are light brown in the steppe and desert light brown in desert-steppe. Brown and light brown soils are found along mountain sides and the slopes of low hills and hillocks. Small areas of mountain meadow, with alpine dark soils, are present in high mountains like Kharkhiraa, Turgen and Bairam. Saline soils are widespread in the proximity of Uvs Lake and the dry margins of swampy lowlands. There are no sands or sand dunes in Turgen, except small stony plain lands and alluvial fans at the base of mountains. Some mountain areas are not used for grazing due to excessive bare rocks, steep clefts between mountains and permafrost.

Soils in Rinchinlkumbe are fertile compared to Turgen, but a variety of permafrost, high mountain and lowland soils can be found. Most soils of the mountain edges are tundra, mountain meadow and permafrost meadow dark brown. Lowland areas form permafrost meadow, meadow-swamp dark and meadow-swampy brown soils. Soils around Khuvsgul are lake meadow dark brown and mountain dark, as well as chestnut. Carbonate soils are present in lowland areas and riparian land of the lake.

CLIMATE

Buyanorshikh (1994) reports annual temperature fluctuations of 80–90°C in the Uvs Lake Depression, which contains a third of the sum grazing land. This occurs as a result of specific geo-ecological patterns of the area: land-locked and heavily dissected by sequenced mountains and lowlands which hinder the exit of free flows of arctic winter and north summer Siberian cyclones/anticyclones. The Kharkhiraa-Turgen mountain ranges, which are less cold and snowy, are the winter camps of most of the herders. Badarch (1971) suggests that winter camping areas in Turgen have a cold Altai winter, a medium-continental climate.

These topographic peculiarities determine the annual temperature regime: mean annual temperature is +1.8 to 3.6°C. The annual range is some 70°C – from a maximum (in July) of +30°C to a minimum (in January) of -40°C. Annual precipitation in the Uvs Lake depression is 123–218 mm; 200–250 mm in the Kharkhiraa-Turgen mountains; and around 180–200 mm in other parts of Turgen. Rainfall is very unimodal: 85–90 percent falls in April–October, with over 30 percent in July alone. Snowfall is 4–30 mm, but heavy snow occurs around Uvs Lake. The prevailing wind is from the west, with an annual average speed of 1.3–3.0 m/second.

Records from Rinchinlkumbe indicate an annual average temperature of -2.1°C, with average isothermic values of -25°C in January and +23°C in July. The minimum temperature recorded was -43°C and the maximum +32°C. The climate of the sum is largely determined by east Siberian cyclones and microclimatic flows off Khuvsgul lake. Annual precipitation in the lowlands of Rinchinlkumbe is under 250 mm, about 300 mm in mountainous areas and over 400 mm in alpine and tundra. Rainfall is unimodal: much falls in June to August (over 60 percent of the total). Snow arrives from mid-November to January, with 12–20 cm (maximum 32 cm in a normal year). Summer areas of the sum are classified as dry cool, while most of winter camps of the sample herders are cold. Tundra and alpine zones are the coldest. The growing period is 75 to 115 days.

VEGETATION FORMS AND SPECIES COMPOSITION
Turgen

Turgen is in the Kharkhiraa-Turgen vegetation subregion of the Mongol Altai mountain steppe province, and in the Sagil-Davst and Ulaangom areas of Uvs lake semi-desert subregion of the North Gobi desert-steppe province of Eurasian Steppe region. Major ecological zones and belts were identified with the help of the overview of Buyanorshikh (1994). Samples were collected from permanent sites and randomly selected areas to determine major plant species composition and approximate condition and productivity of pasture types. Plants were grouped into forage, toxic and unpalatable. The following range types and major plant species were identified in Turgen.

Semi-shrub – tussock grass desert steppe
Caragana pygmae, C. bungei, Stipa glareosa,

Artemisia frigida, A. xerophytica, Kochia prostrata, Agropyron cristatum, A. nevskii, Stipa krylovii, S. gobica, Allium mongolicum, Oxytropis aciphylla, Anabasis brevifolia, Cleistogenes soongorica and *C. squarrosa.*

Grass – semi-scrub desert steppe *Allium polyrrhizum, A. mongolicum, Reaumuria soongarica, Anabasis brevifolia, Ajania achilleoides, Caragana pygmae, C. bungei, Oxytropis aciphylla, Stipa glareosa, Hedysarum fruticosum, Artemisia frigida, Cleistogenes squarrosa* and *C. soongorica.*

Riparian meadow – swampy lakeside Salix-grass meadow *Salix ledbouriana, Betula microphylla, Caragana spinosa, C. bungei, Leymus angustus, Phragmites communis, Achnatherum splendens, Iris lactea, Agropyron cristatum, Oxytropis salina, Halerpestes ruthenica, Saussurea salsa, Kalidium gracile, Nitraria sibirica, Stipa glareosa, Oxytropis aciphylla, Plantago salsa, Poa pratensis, Carex lithophila, Juncus salsuginosus, Sium suave, Inula linariaefolia* and *Hordeum brevisubutum.*

Tussock grass dry steppe *Caragana pygmae, C. bungei, Agropyron cristatum, Stipa krylovii, S. orientalis, Poa attenuata, Koeleria macrantha, Veronica pinnata, Cleistogenes squarrosa, Festuca lenensis, F. valesiaca, Arenaria meyerii, Leymus chinensis, Bupleurum bicaule, Youngia tenuifolia, Aster alpinus, Astragalus mongholicus, A. brevifolius, Ephedra sinica, Artemisia monostachya, A. frigida, A. rutifolia, A. santolinifolia, Allium prostata, A. mongolicum, A. eduardii, Thalictrum foetidum, Elymus sibiricus* and *Orostachys spinosa.*

High mountain meadow *Festuca lenensis, Poa attenuata, Koeleria altaica, Koeleria*

sp., Potentilla sericea, Aster alpinus, Festuca krylovii, Leymus chinensis, Stellaria pulvinata, Arenaria formosa, Potentilla nivea, Carex rupestris, C. amgunensis, Silene repens, Kobresia smirnovii, Saxifraga ceruna, Rosa acicularis, Geranium pseudosibiricum, Galium boreale, Vicia cracca and *Bromus korotkiji.*

Tundra alpine meadow *Kobresia* sp., *Carex rupestris, C. pediformis, Poa siberiana, Festuca altaica, Polygonum viviparum, Hedysarum alpinum, Astragalus frigidus, Vaccinium vitis-idaea, Launaea* sp. and *Pyrola incarnatus.*

Coniferous (**Larix sibirica**) ***forest*** *Larix sibirica, Pinus sibirica, Lonicera altaica, Vaccinium vitis-idaea, Calamagrostis obtusata, Cicerbita azurea, Geranium albiflorum, Trollius asiaticus, Festuca altaica, Polygonum viviparum, Hyloconium splendens, Aulaconnium palustre, Climatium dendroides* and *Rhytidium rugosum.*

High mountain herbs – tussock grass meadow steppe *Helictotrichon desertorum, Elymus aegilopoides, Polygonum alpinum, Potentilla evestita, P. biflora, Artemisia monostachya, A. laciniata, Helictotrichon schellianum, Carex pediformis, Dasiphora fruticosa, Leontopodium ochroleucum* and *Vicia multicaulis.*

Rinchinlkumbe

The sum territory contains the following vegetation types.

Polytridrum rocky mountain tundra and high alpine *Polytridrum* sp., *Carex bigelowii, Waldheimia tridatylites, Sourea coracephola, Logatis altaica, Lloydia serrotina* and *Saxifraga sibirica.*

Polytridrum, Carex–Polytridrum *and* **Polytridrum–***semi-bush treeless high alpine* Carex sp., *Betula rotundifolia, B. humilis* and *Cladonia cetraria.*

High mountain sparse rocky and grass *Caragana jubata, Carex* sp., *Carex microglochin, C. capitata, Eriophorum brachyantherium, Lloydia serrotina* and *Logotis altaica.*

Abundant **Carex–Koeleria–Festuca** *grass* **Larix** *forest* *Larix sibirica, Polytrichum cladonia, Kobresia bellardii, Festuca lenensis, Polygonum viviparum, Ptilagrostis mongolica, Salix berberifolia, Cetraria sausurea, Claytonia joanneana, Ledum palustre, Potentilla nivea* and *P. gelida.*

Koeleria–Festuca *mountain steppe* *Kobresia bellardii, Festuca lenensis, Polygonum viviparum, P. angustifolia, Ptilagrostis mongolica, Potentilla nivea, P. gelida, Koeleria macrantha, Poa attenuata, Aster alpinus, Artemisia comutata, Bupleurum bicaule, Potentilla sericea* and *Pulsatilla turzcaninovii.*

Picea–Betula–Caragana jubata–Carex *meadow* *Picea obovata, Betula rotundifolia, Caragana jubata, C. tenuifolia, C. capitata, C. microphylla, Carex melanantha, Salix reticulata, S. saxatilis* and many other herbs.

PASTURE CONDITION

In order to assess the condition of major types of natural pasture in Turgen sum, Uvs, and Rinchinlkumbe sum, Khuvsgul, seasonal sampling was done in May, August and November 1999 and 2000.

An overview by Buyanorshikh (1994) was used as reference to cross-check findings.

Data from field surveys (1999-2000) require several observations on the natural productivity of pasture: precipitation was extremely poor, with little snow in winter, and few, late, short-lived heavy showers in summer; so that precipitation was 70-80 percent lower than normal. The spring, especially, was very hot and dry, which greatly delayed regrowth. Surveys in Turgen in 2000 showed a very different situation; with the exception of the early spring months until the thaw, it was pleasant due to abundant snow in winter and more rain in summer. Pasture growth, which had been considerably affected by drought, recovered to a reasonable extent and forage was readily available (some 30–40 percent more compared to 1999 in all areas in all seasons).

In 1999–2000, the weather in Rinchinlkumbe was relatively pleasant in terms of temperature fluctuations, precipitation and pasture grass growth. The data in Tables 3.3 and 3.4 show natural forage available to livestock by season, and earlier data from the literature. The 1999 data were collected from areas where few animals and people concentrated. No fencing was used but some attempts were made to prevent continued and heavy grazing, so that the real availability of natural forage could be approximated. Herders were interviewed to find out the initial productivity of each pasture type; their simple calculations indicated that yields were 10–30 percent below what non-grazed pasture can produce.

The comparable usable pasture in summer and autumn of 2000 (real winter begins from late November), is seen by experienced herders of Turgen to be the result of two major factors:

• heavy, deep (20–40 cm in winter grazing areas) and long-lasting snow (first heavy snow in late December 1999 and the heaviest in early February 2000; lasted to mid-April 2000) and snow cover in winter 2000 provided reserve moisture for the early spring herbage growth; and

- continued and adequate rainfall in summer 2000 provided a vital support to the vegetation to recover so quickly and made the warm season most pleasant.

Meteorologists suggest that the normal range of snow depth in Turgen is between 7 and 15 cm and snowfall is mostly in November-December. This is completely different from that reported for winter 1999-2000 and spring 2000, which caused a number of unusual changes in the transhumant movements of local herders.

Areas with some soil moisture reserves (rich underground water, permanent swamps and other non-rainfed sources)

grew some young grass, but were grazed immediately by all graziers in a very competitive manner. This led to localized overconcentration of livestock, making forage availability even lower at all seasons. Neither herders nor meteorologists expected so severe a drought in 1999. In the project studies, for example, a 75-year-old, who has been herding all his life, could not remember a drought like the summer of 1999, nor a severe winter like 2000. According to his assessment, the 1999 drought and 2000 snowfall covered a large area and affected all neighbouring sums (Sagil, Tarialan, Chandmana and Davst); and covered all ecological areas, leaving herders with no chance to use grazing elsewhere.

The weather of 1999 and part of 2000 is stressed because of its effect on studies of pasture productivity and range condition.

TABLE 3.3
Forage productivity of types of natural pasture in Turgen sum, Mongolia (kg/ha).

Range types	Field survey (1999)			Buyanorshikh (1994)
	May	August	Nov.	
Semi-scrub – tussock grass desert steppe	470	1 050	630	1 600–3 500
Grass – semi-scrub desert steppe	230	450	210	1 500
Riparian and swampy *Salix* – grass meadow	2 460	4 530	2 180	10 000
High mountain meadow	1 020	2 100	870	4 800
Tundra alpine meadow	430	1 000	860	800–1 000
Coniferous (*Larix sibirica*) forest	970	2 800	1 000	3 500
High mountain herb – tussock grass meadow steppe	1 200	2 700	780	4 700–6 300

TABLE 3.4
Approximate forage production of natural pastures in Rinchinlkumbe sum (kg/ha).

Pasture type	Season			
	spring	summer	autumn	winter
Lowland *Salix* meadow	1 000–1 200	3 300–4 300*	2 000	1 200–1 300*
Woodland and mountain foot	800–1 000	3 900–4 700*	3 100–3 600	700–2 100
Mountain valley and woodlands	500–600	5 500–8 800*	5 200–7 800*	3 300–3 500
Low-hill pasture	1 500–1 700*	1 700–1 900	2 100–3 400	1 300–2 100*

NOTES: * data presenting production of forage in grazing-free seasons

Due to the atypical weather, past experience had to be relied on to provide details of movements, seasonal grazing patterns, pasture condition and other important details.

Conversations and interviews with herders suggest that they sense a deterioration in the condition of the sum's natural grazing, because of ecological and social factors:

- global warming (herders refer to it as warming) shows clearly in terms of milder winter; longer spring; shorter and cooler summer; and longer and warmer autumn; and
- herders define rainfall distribution over the year as irregular and late. For instance, the first snow, expected in late October, was delayed till mid-November; the first heavy rain, expected in late May, sometimes falls in mid-June. Useful rain (two or more days) in mid-September is now rare, but Turgen had heavy snow in early September, mostly in mountains, which quickly melted away.

These changes in the rainfall distribution have a strong influence on grass growth, and on grazing patterns as well, as some areas of Turgen have suffered large-scale trespass by herders and stock from other sums. This was partially described by Erdenebaatar (1996). Serious cases of trespass and unauthorized (informal) residence have two consequences:

- first, overconcentration of people and livestock in areas where more forage is available; and
- second, local herders have to give up parts of their traditional grazing areas to the newcomers to avoid conflicts.

No reasonable solution has been found for this situation. Although summer and winter in 2000 were good, local herders still worry seriously about trespass. Since the first arrival of trespassers in Turgen, herders have had, each year, to cede parts of the area where they have been grazing since time immemorial; they are worried that this will continue unless there are emergency measures to stop trespass (some herders argue that they would be pushed out of the sum territory). A conclusion from the above is that herders who are displaced from their home areas are forced to change their seasonal camping patterns, and a knock-on effect causes others to do the same. Herders who formerly made long movements had either to shorten the distance or move even farther. Some herders have changed seasonal movement routes completely and stay two seasons in the same area, thus violating the informal land tenure system and legal land rights.

A visual assessment and a partial transect over crowded grazing areas suggest that crucial changes in the vegetation cover, species composition and overall productivity have taken place due to several factors, including:

- severe overgrazing leading to soil damage and pasture degradation. From a brief estimate, almost 34 percent of spring and autumn pasture, 12 percent of summer pasture and over 5 percent of winter pasture had undergone some degradation. This assessment was based on simple evidence and was supported by herders;
- an increase of non- or less-palatable indicator plants, namely *Chenopodium album, Artemisia sieversiana, Caragana bungei* and aromatic species of *Artemisia*;
- increased bare ground near the sum centre, and in areas that have been grazed

in all or more than two seasons the plant cover has declined significantly, with bare ground reaching 70–80 percent. These areas are usually infested by most of the negative indicator plants;

- bush encroachment, with herders noting that *Caragana pygmae* has been spreading in lowland areas of Turgen, notably in traditional haymaking and spring and autumn camp areas. *Caragana* is good browse for camels; cattle and goats may eat it if there is deep snow. In Rinchinlkumbe, increased herbs in summer and autumn pastures and the appearance of moving dunes indicate serious damage to soils and grazing areas;

- shorter grass as heavy grazing damages the long vegetative shoots of valuable species, causing a decrease in overall height. In Khangai, Lkhagvajaw (1998) observed that heavy grazing transformed the major communities into short, creeping (horizontally-spreading) ones. The decline in the overall height of major plants leads to a decline in pasture productivity and forage availability. Herders in Turgen report that *Thalictrum* communities were so tall in autumn and spring camp areas that sometimes they lost horses and cattle; children who attended small stock would get lost if timely shouts were not given. Elderly herders of Rinchinlkumbe remember grass being twice as high in the 1960s and early 1970s along the rivers Sharga and Shishkhit, where herders now spend the entire warm season; and

- non-systematic grazing patterns, as it is widely believed that the condition of natural pasture is reasonably good. This view is common among young herders who do not know the history of

land use patterns, and some old herders who still think that pasture growth is entirely governed by "weather", i.e. total rainfall. The latter group believes that sufficient rain accelerates grass growth while dryness causes a temporary decline in productivity, which is easily recompensed by heavy precipitation in following years.

Despite obvious pasture degradation in parts of the sum, herders share a common perception that the pasture is in good condition. This is indefensible for two clear reasons:

- lack of evident information regarding the changes in the productivity and species composition. Herders measure pasture condition by year-to-year comparison; they find poor grass in a dry year, but it may be different next year if rainfall is enough. Such simplistic comparisons do not take the real situation into account and only vegetation and other measurements can record what is really happening; and

- a belief in the self-recovering capacity of natural pastures. Herders perceive it as something which is not related to physical disturbances, and they ignore the negative effects of excessive grazing pressure and non-seasonal grazing. Some herders argue that animals never damage the roots of grasses and so long as the roots are intact, grasses will always grow again.

Data on pasture degradation in Turgen are consistent with the latest information on the pasture condition in many parts of the country. Tserendash (1999) identified the condition of seasonal pastures in Uvs as shown in Table 3.5.

High mountains (the highest in Uvs) and some swampy willow forest areas

TABLE 3.5
Proportion of degraded pasture, Turgen sum, Uvs aimag.

Area	Degree of degradation (percent)				
	intact	slight	moderate	heavy	severe
Uvs aimag[1]	5	25	35	35	0
Turgen sum[2]	~20	~30	~30	~10–15	~3–5

SOURCES: (1) Tserendash, 1999.   (2) Approximate estimates, 1999.

of Turgen remain intact because they are inaccessible to stock. Some areas at the outlets of mountain passes are heavily degraded. In late May, there were signs in Rinchinlkumbe of the result of regular movement of large herds at least twice yearly: in early November to winter camps and in March–April on the way back to warm areas.

Conversation with herders showed that they do not really believe that these areas are degraded. They think that they are in a biological rest, beyond the grazing frontier. This is hard to believe if the movement patterns followed by herders in Turgen are studied. The above-outlined pasture degradation has taken place in all grazing areas used by transhumance systems.

Long distance movement in the study site involves several clear patterns:
- it is really long distance because of the remoteness from each other of the seasonal camping areas. To reach seasonal pasture, herders need to travel by short-stay camping. In the study area, stock and gers have to cross mountain ranges, so animals are first

Plate 17.
Temporary camps on the autumn migration. The ranges have to be crossed yet again. Tarialan, Uvs, Mongolia.

walked up and down the mountains and continue to the destination areas, passing over medium elevations and hills. In this sense, transhumant long-distance movements in Mongolia differ from those of the Central Asian highlands and Tibet, which follow routes up and down mountains;

- opportunity for change of itinerary is very limited, as routes are through passes (Plate 17), some of which are closed by snow in late autumn, winter and early spring. Land on both sides of the passes is heavily degraded as a result of periodic, but very high, overconcentration of a large number of herds;
- herds comprise four to six species herded and move almost together, so the areas used must suit them all;
- there is little opportunity for separating herds into small groups by species, age or sex, for travel over different routes or at different times. All stock must move together, to save time (movements are made in response to any sign of sudden and irreversible changes in the weather and grass availability) to reach destination camps and to avoid horses and people being overloaded with additional tasks.
- In the best cases, herders with enough labour and transport split their herds into two: one group with small animals

with milking females or females with newborn young, and a second group with large, unproductive animals; and
- herders need to transport all living facilities, especially for winter migration; they have to stay at permanent residences for a long time without back-up visits to other seasonal areas, so movement requires sufficient transport capacity.

Any seasonal or long-distance migration has, therefore, to be organized on the basis of routes defined by passes (there are no routes they can use all the time); the need for suitable pasture; and available transport. The lack of permanent facilities where they can store items not required on migration increases the cost and labour requirements for moving. Long movement in the study area has strong traditional roots, as well as practices inherited from the collective period. To determine how households secured, or are securing, grazing rights and camp sites, all family heads were interviewed. The results are summarized in Table 3.6.

Herders secured their grazing rights in several ways: some trespassed on a neighbouring sum; others moved to areas where they had had access in the collective period. A case of trespass in Turgen began as a result of a dispute in early 1992: some moved into Turgen from neighbouring sums and pushed out some local herders from their lowland and winter areas.

TABLE 3.6
Criteria for security of grazing rights.

	Respondents	
	Turgen sum (n=14)	Rinchinlkumbe (n=8)
Grazing rights secured because:		
– grazed since collective period	9	5
– selected voluntarily (mostly by joining others)	2	3
– trespassed (i.e. without official permit)	3 (winter camps in Sagil sum)	0

In search of new space, these displaced herders entered Sagil and were accepted by the local community, but the "new" residence area straddles the border of two sums, which is why the local community had to allow their settlement. According to the environment protection officer of Turgen, trespassers are "plotting" to occupy more land by clandestine means, building camps in the heart of winter and summer areas, as they start their first settlements in distant lowlands.

In 1999, many herders (four from sample households) from Turgen had no choice but to enter part of the winter pasture of Sagil sum to share existing resources, due to hard drought and short grass in summer 1999 and deep snow in winter 2000. Neither local nor visiting herders consider this trespassing, saying it is a part of reciprocal access to key or available resources; it is an important assistance that herders always expect at a time of disaster in their own area. They strongly believe that the only way to cope with similar shocks is to seek reciprocal permission from neighbours.

In February–March 2000, many herds were crossing the border of Turgen and Sagil sums. Many of the large animals, however, were left behind in the mountains, unattended, because, first there was not enough grazing on the way to support big herds, and, second, large animals are usually not friendly to small ones in sharing grass. Large animals push ahead of small ruminants and graze throughout the night, while small animals suffer heavy predation by wolves and snow leopards, but herders were not greatly concerned, saying that it is cleaner and more acceptable than having their animals dead at the edge of the khot – the herders' camp area.

HUMAN POPULATION

Turgen has three bags: two rural and one at the sum centre. In 1998, it had a population of 2 483, of which 1 839 belonged to 365 households that were purely herding. The sum had 62 104 head of livestock in 1998: 765 camels, 4 579 horses, 7 435 cattle, 32 726 sheep and 16 599 goats. In the survey, family size varied from household to household. Average family size was 4.7 (range 2 9), of which 2.92 were male and 1.78 female. According to national age classification, the number of working age per family would be 2.6 (1.7 males and 0.9 females). Each family had 1.14 children under 16, a source of labour in the peak period outside the school term.

In late 1998, sample households in Rinchinlkumbe had a family size of 5.2: 23.8 percent under 16 years old; 59.5 percent of active working age; and 16.7 percent pensioners and members of early pension age. The sample households in both sums owned five species of animals, following the common patterns of multi-species herding. The species composition and age and sex groups of livestock of the sample households are shown in Tables 3.7 and 3.8.

The number of livestock per household in Turgen varied widely: from none to 800 or more. Average herd size was 267 head in 1993, and increased to 358.2 in 1998. Livestock per family member was 76.2, and 135.7 per member of working age. There was no increase in the number of people engaged in herding, so the herd-upgrading strategy common in the Mongolian pastoral economy has been taking place here too.

Adult females in herds were 22.3 percent for mares, 32.1 percent for cattle, 39.0 percent for ewes and 38.3 percent for does. There was enough young stock for herd replacement:

TABLE 3.7
Sample herd composition statistics, Turgen sum, 1998.

| Species | Total | | of which | | | | | | | |
| | No. | % | males[1] | | females | | others[2] | | offspring[3] | |
			No.	%	No.	%	No.	%	No.	%
Camel	70	1.4	51	72.8	16	22.8	1	1.42	2	2.85
Horse	246	4.9	115	46.7	55	22.3	45	18.3	31	12.6
Cattle	401	8.0	52	13.0	129	32.1	124	31.0	96	23.9
Sheep	2 953	58.9	332	11.2	1 150	39.0	398	13.5	1 073	36.3
Goat	1 345	26.8	237	17.6	515	38.3	158	11.7	435	32.3
Total	5 015	100	787	15.6	1 865	37.1	726	14.4	1 637	32.6

NOTES: (1) Including stud males. (2) Male and female are aggregated. (3) As of December 1998.
SOURCE: 1998 Livestock Census Report, Governor's Office, Turgen sum.

TABLE 3.8
Sample household herd composition, Rinchinlkumbe sum, 1999.

| Species | Total | | of which | | | | | | | |
| | No | % | males[1] | | females | | others[2] | | offspring[3] | |
			No	%	No	%	No	%	No	%
Camel	21	0.44	16	76.2	4	19.0	–	–	1	4.7
Horse	637	13.4	356	55.9	175	27.6	60	9.3	46	7.2
Cattle	1 118	23.6	167	14.9	362	32.5	284	25.4	305	27.2
Sheep	1 858	39.4	193	10.4	823	44.3	200	10.7	642	34.6
Goat	1 092	23.1	105	9.6	417	38.2	244	22.3	326	29.8
Total	4 726	100.0	837	17.7	1 781	37.6	788	16.9	1 320	27.9

NOTES: (1) Including reproductive males. (2) Male and female aggregated. (3) As of December 1998.
SOURCE: 1999 Livestock Census Report, Office of the Sum Governor.

11.7–31.0 percent. The species and age composition of herds depends on personal preference and the herding goals of individual families. It is not possible to give standard figures to describe herd growth strategies among sample households. Rinchinlkumbe herders own more yaks than those in Turgen, perhaps because they need male pack yaks for transport and have a lower herd offtake. Horses are important for riding and herding.

In early 2000, livestock per household in Rinchinlkumbe were 315: 63.8 per family member or 98.4 per member of working age. No remarkable increase in the number of people of sample households engaged in herding was identified, explained on the basis that the wealth of the herders of Turgen selected for the study was relatively high, since long distance movement is mostly made by rich herders; and, in Rinchinlkumbe, all herders must move long distances because of specific climatic and geographical conditions; sample herders were selected randomly, including ones with fewer or more animals.

The low proportion of adult female and young camels is due to the high number of castrated males. Turgen and Rinchinlkumbe are not traditional camel-breeding areas. Some camels are used as transport during migrations and for short-distance transport of living needs. Turgen herders use male camels for riding

TABLE 3.9
Stud males, breeding females and male:female ratio, Turgen sum, 1998.

Species	Stud males	Breeding females	Ratio [1]
Camels	1	16	1:16
Horses	10	55	1:5.5
Cattle	8	129	1:16
Sheep	36	1 150	1:32
Goats	19	515	1:27

NOTE: (1) Number of female stock per stud male.

more in winter months than herders from Rinchinlkumbe. This can be easily explained as camels are exceptionally hardy and endure chronic feed shortage; and the geographical and topographical characteristics of winter ranges in Turgen are flatter than in Rinchinlkumbe, and camels are more popular for riding, whereas Rinchinlkumbe winter areas are heavily dissected and dangerous for humans and animals to walk over.

Herders believe that overall herd growth depends on the number of stud males and the number of females per male. The male:female ratio of small ruminants of the Turgen sample households (Table 3.9) does not match national averages; there is very high mating pressure on rams and bucks. The pattern appeared similar in Rinchinlkumbe. Nevertheless breeding pressure on rams and bulls seems to be less than in Turgen as a whole. From individual household statistics, many households have no male camels, bulls or stallions, so there is a risk of low conception, or they borrow males. Some herders have to delay mating until others loan males, or are told to keep their females away until the end of the season, especially camels and mares.

The low numbers of breeding male stock reflects the small herd size of most households, which does not support a large number of mating males nor provide broader opportunities to select good sires. As some herders have to keep the breeding males with their herds all year around, this makes keeping many male stock difficult because of a high probability of out-of-season mating.

CURRENT MANAGEMENT

Mongolian pastoralism is based on nomadic grazing of seasonally available pasture and other grazing resources, such as naturally-available minerals, water and other deposits, to cope with a harsh environment and frequent natural disasters.

Some official sources suggest that natural disasters (known as zud, an aggregation of hardships) have become more frequent. Previously, the expected zud occurrence interval was 7–10 years, but recently it has been 3–8 years. At the same, the size of the area affected has been expanding. The 1999–2000 zud covered 13 aimags out of 21, and 157 sums out of 300. So serious a disaster has been recorded only once since 1944–1945. In 2000–2001, zud conditions were also widespread and devastating.

In such circumstances, better herd survival and improved returns from stock raising depend on open grazing of natural forage. So pastoral livestock management, in terms of long-distance transhumance, focuses purely on careful and effective use of available sources of natural pasture. Grazing efficiency under transhumance is determined by many internal and external factors, affecting the timing, distance and other arrangements.

TIMING AND PATTERN OF HERD MOVEMENT AND HOUSEHOLD

It is known (Erdenebaatar, 1996) that the fundamental principles of traditional grazing management are based on cyclic grazing in the four seasons of the year. The long movements in the study area are strongly seasonal, so some criteria have been identified for the timing of migrations between grazing areas, including macro-level indicators and natural processes.

Change in pasture quality or productivity of grazing areas determines the timing of seasonal movements, and this productivity is determined by two primary factors:

- seasonal changes in the growth processes, in the sense of spring regrowth (May-June) and drying to standing dead forage and litter (early September); and
- decrease in forage, depending on the grazing offtake within a season and between seasons.

The comments of herders (see Box 3.1) show that herding movements are not spontaneous, but a clearly determined process. Seasonal movements allow herds to graze fresh forage and protect them from exposure to extreme climatic shocks.

Differences in relief and topographic conditions in different areas are important if long-distance movements have to be made. This is largely a case of the selection of seasonal camping areas and pastures. This shows how herders recognize macro- and microclimatic differences that are significant for them. Selection of seasonal pastures is based on several factors that assist herders in deciding on herd and family movements. In Box 3.2, a herder from IV bag in Rinchinlkumbe comments about local knowledge when selecting seasonal pastures.

The herder's comments show that each seasonal pasture in Rinchinlkumbe has unique conditions that the herders can exploit. Very similar information can be found for Turgen, but herders do not stay in lowlands in summer and woodlands in winter.

Changes in pasture quality are due to weather and seasonal forage consumption

---

BOX 3.1
Seasonal movement timing and changes in pasture productivity

Mr A., a herder in Bayankhairkhan bag, commented on how changes in pasture productivity determine the timing of long-distance movements. From experience over many years, he says that in late August, when all stock must move to lowland autumn pasture, the average yield of pasture is 500–800 kg/ha, falling to 100–200 kg/ha by mid-September. This serious drop in available herbage spurs herders to move to areas between autumn and winter camps because, if they linger, their stock will not be sufficiently fattened and their ability to survive the winter will be reduced. When the end of a season has less forage than usual then immediate moves are necessary. When there are sharp changes of weather herders cannot stay and must move. There is, therefore, a set of weather factors and norms which tell herders when the time to move to another seasonal area is approaching.

BOX 3.2
Herder's perception of selection criteria for seasonal camping area and pastures

Seasonal movements aim to make the best use of positive differences in the overall climatic conditions between grazing sites.

– Spring camping (*khavarjaa*) areas and pastures are in areas where grass regrowth and production starts early, so that animals can get fresh grass to recover their body condition. It is also important for young animals to get more milk. These pastures have to be capable of supporting herds for a month or more until early summer pastures are well grown. Spring pastures must be sheltered from cross winds and not exposed to winds coming over high mountains (locally known as "mountain cold daily winds"). For Rinchinlkhumbe herders, spring camps are in the bottom of stream canyons and valleys.

– Summer (*zuslan* – from mid-April to late August) areas have to be purely in lowlands in the Darkhadyn Khotgor (a 200 km-long lowland along the west slopes of the Khordil Sardig Range), where more open, mosquito-free pastures are available. These areas are not suitable for use in cold months due to continued low temperatures and deep permanent snow. High and open hill tops and open hollows are most suitable for summer residences. Abundant natural soda, open water and high grass are also important conditions for summer pastures and camp sites.

– Autumn pastures (*namarjaa*) are chosen in low mountain-foot woodlands and mid-valley slopes facing the sun. Autumn pastures are a staging area between summer and winter pastures, where animals find fresh and slowly drying grasses to put more weight on to obtain better consolidated body condition.

– Winter camping sites (*uvuljuu*) and pastures are on the eastern side of the Khordil Sardig Range, mostly in open areas in narrow valleys and woodlands. The most important conditions for selecting winter areas are high standing forage and less cold. The informant confirmed that their winter area has temperatures higher by 5-10°C than other parts of the sum, and hopefully protected from cold and snow winds.

---

by livestock. This means that if weather is far worse than normal, some areas have to support more animals for longer in a grazing season, and important grasses are quickly and heavily grazed, leaving less palatable species. Thus pasture quality changes, necessitating movement to other areas. In such cases, herders, including some who usually move short distances, have to go in search of land with available forage. When weather conditions are inclement in one place, an overconcentra- tion of households and herds in a com- paratively small area may occur, which in turn leads to quicker depletion of existing resources, and all herders have to move – both resident herders and newcomers.

SEASONAL AVAILABILITY OF OTHER RESOURCES (WATER, NATURAL SALT LICKS, ETC.)

Herders of the study sites argue that water availability at cold times of the year and naturally-available mineral sources make

TABLE 3.10
Weather- and resource-based indicators for seasonal migration timing in Turgen sum.

Seasonal movement	Typical timing	Criteria and indicators
Leave winter camp for spring area	20 March – 10 April	Melting of snow cover; cross-winds; poor forage availability.
Move to summer pasture	10–20 June – early July	Hot; arrival of mosquitoes; rare rainfall.
Return movement to autumn pasture	10–20 August	Cool; early frost; heavy wind and rain (more frequent and heavy hail); poor pasture.
Move to winter camp	Early November	Cold cross-winds and heavy breezes; early snow in lowlands; poor forage availability.

them move long distances. Herders say that "natural minerals stop worsening animal body condition and help consolidate animal fatness, and a mouthful of stream water in winter is equal to a *khormoi* [a traditional measurement unit equal to 3–5 kg of dry and frozen materials] of snow". In winter, spring and late autumn – the hard times of the year – animals suffer if they have to walk unnecessarily to find water and minerals.

Other important conditions looked at and carefully evaluated when planning immediate and future movements are natural indicators, including:

- arrival of biting insects and hot weather, which limit grazing and cause discomfort to humans and livestock;
- daily temperature changes, and frequency and type of natural precipitation;
- changes in livestock behaviour; and
- changes in the daily temperature and wind speed in parts of seasonal areas cause changes in the other areas, which determines the timing and direction of transhumant movements.

Centuries-old herding practices and modern scientific information are the basis of how herders select the timing and organization of migrations. These are widely referred to as movements between seasonal camps; some criteria for deciding on the timing of movements

are summarized in Table 3.10. There are, however, some camp-changing moves in particular seasons which are do not have strictly fixed timing.

The number of intermediate camps depends on the distance between the area of departure, the destination area and the season. Sample herders in Turgen make 5–6 temporary camps of 1–3 days to reach winter camp, covering a distance of 20–25 km daily. Herders of Rinchinlkumbe say that the distance between two consequent temporary camps for small ruminants is 12–18 km per day, sometimes less. The duration of long migrations is limited by how far small stock can walk daily. Topography also determines daily movement. Herders in the study area have to cross huge mountain ranges, so intermediate moves are short. Rinchinlkumbe herders need to make 6–8 intermediate camps to get to winter areas and move back to spring areas. The daily distance is shorter than in Turgen because of difficult topography: high passes, narrow and steep ravines, and single-track trails along which to walk herds and pack animals.

Animals are moved almost together. Small stock walk with the caravan or are trekked as a single flock; large animals may be moved separately. Herder interviews were indecisive as to whether there was any noticeable difference if personal belongings, including ger and furniture, are moved by motor transport or by pack animals.

In areas with very difficult relief, people prefer pack animals; more open, less broken, areas allow use of motor vehicles. Use of motor transport is common for spring moves, when many young stock have to be moved. Moving the dwelling and other facilities by motor transport does not change any of the important components of migrations since transhumance itself is the action of moving herds from one area to another. Around 90 percent of sample households in Rinchinlkumbe use male yaks, cattle and a few camels for transporting gers and furniture; over 60 percent of herders in Turgen move using camels.

In winter-spring 1999–2000, sample herders in Turgen organized wintering of their animals in a specific way: large animals, like horses, bulls and dry cows and some camels, were sent for free range, unattended grazing on distant pastures in high mountains and flat valleys, while small stock remained at the herders' camps.

COMMUNITY DECISION-MAKING

Formal decisions about long seasonal migrations are not made communally, but herders who are to move to the same area (within certain locations) consult each other. Moving as a single family is not desirable, but neither is many households moving together encouraged. Two to three families prefer to start together. Sometimes herders may agree to hire motor transport and make a common accord on timing and payment. They did not comment on whether they need community decision making procedures to make migration more organized and effectively arranged.

An important issue in decision-making could be delegating somebody to visit the destination area to see if all previous camps are ready to receive traditional residents and any more households. If they found insufficient resources to accommodate all herds and households, then a limited range of consultation might decide who moves and who does not, or how to arrange sites for the extra animals.

MOVEMENT PATTERNS

Turgen belongs to a society where herding mobility is the only way to cope with the harsh climatic and ecological conditions. This mobility helps make better use of natural resources, and the success of herding depends on flexible, mobile herding.

Discussions with sample herders identified two main types of grazing movement: short-distance and transhumant. The study thereafter focused on the transhumant systems (known as *kholyn nuudel* [where nuudel is a general term for any kind of moving of things, including livestock], sometimes *alsyn nuudel*). According to local herders, *alsyn nuudel* is migration between autumn pasture and winter camping. The local definition of transhumant movements can be summarized as: moving livestock to distant seasonal pastures or camps to ensure better productivity and survival through mobilizing all material means and social linkages.

In an attempt to determine the reality of long transhumance, households without close kinship relations were selected. This aimed to clarify whether distant movements by individual households are made purposely and to check how mutual help mechanisms work in areas where a typical *khot-ail* [a group of a few families that work and camp together – with or without family links] structure does not exist (Erdenebaatar, 1996). Small-scale interviews to check if this definition was acceptable to our respondents also involved six non-sample families. An impressive set of information was provided (summarized in Table 3.11) confirming that herders in the study area have ideas on seasonal long migrations that differ from those elsewhere (such as Arkhangai and central areas (Erdenebaatar, 1995)).

Sample respondents put better productivity and survival of herds in first place because they are totally dependent on animal production in an extremely harsh and risky natural and social environment. Social linkages are not thought important, while access to markets and services worry them less. Herders do not expect services for marketing and other needs to improve in the near future. They believe that they can no longer expect such services because the government does not do what it ought on behalf of the public.

While distance was a basis for determining whether a movement is called *alsyn nuudel*, some herders specified another type of transhumance, namely summer movement. Most (over 90 percent) of herding families and the majority of livestock keepers migrate to escape the mosquitoes that are abundant in lowland areas from late June to mid-August in Turgen (Plate 18).

To get away from early summer areas, herders start moving livestock and *gers* to the highlands at the start of the mosquito season, ca. 15–25 June. This is an upward movement. When mosquitoes have disappeared, herders migrate downwards, ca. 15–20 August. Many herders also make long moves between autumn-winter and winter-spring camping areas.

Movements by Rinchinlkumbe people differ in that herders move to autumn pastures, in the woodland at the foot of the mountains in late August–early September, and stay there until late October, whereas Turgen herders migrate from their winter pasture to spring pastures around mid-March or early April, stay six weeks, then move again over the mountains to reach summer areas at higher altitudes, where they remain until mid-August. Their next movements are towards winter camps or areas, in late October or early November, where herders select to stay over winter in bad years.

The specific patterns of seasonal migrations and long-distance movements are strict and depend on the location of seasonal pastures. There are very few opportunities for herders to act in any other way, and this holds generally for both Turgen and Rinchinlkumbe.

TABLE 3.11
Cross-checking of local definitions of transhumant migration between the sample and voluntary respondents, Rinchinlkumbe, August 1999.

Interview points	Male respondents (n=11)	Female respondents (n=8)	Average scores
Social linkages	3	3	3
Better productivity	5	5	5
Better survival	4	5	4.5
Residence area	5	3	4
Access to market	4	3	3.5
Access to services	3	3	3

NOTES: 2 = lowest score; 5 = highest score.

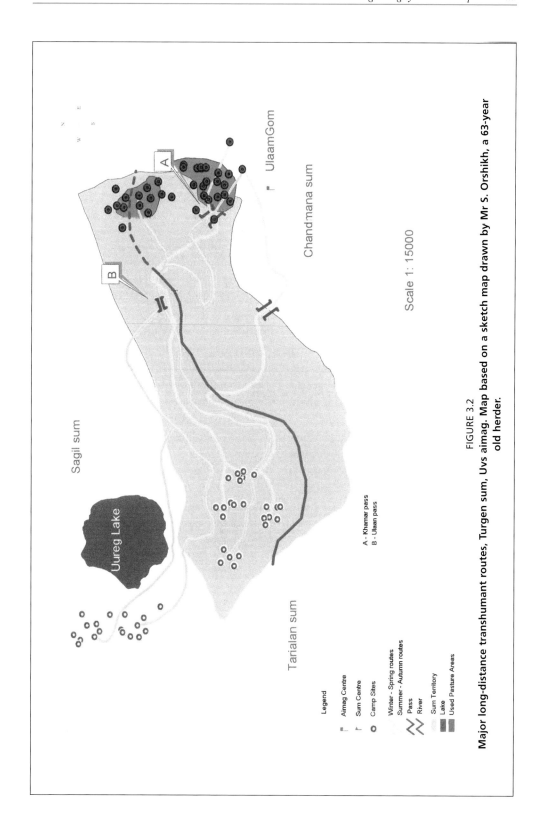

FIGURE 3.2

Major long-distance transhumant routes, Turgen sum, Uvs aimag. Map based on a sketch map drawn by Mr S. Orshikh, a 63-year old herder.

Plate 18.
Turgen summer pastures. These are at higher altitude to avoid the insects of the lake basin. Winter camps are also in the hills, to avoid the cold air that collects in the lake basin.

In Rinchinlkumbe, movements are strongly seasonal. A long migration is made between summer grazing and winter camping areas. Herders leave summer areas in late August towards winter camps, and en route they stay for some months elsewhere in the mountains (western side of Rinchinlkumbe and eastern end of Khoridol Sardig range) till it gets colder and snows. Then they move closer to their winter camps, which are the final destination of one of two major long-distance migrations.

The sample households were followed on their pastoral movements, and sites of intermediate and final camps were identified and total duration and distance noted in both areas. Respondents in both sums were questioned about routes taken in the last five years. In 1999, the routes

over which Turgen herders moved were carefully tracked as a case study, and mapped. Overall, the Turgen make a circular transhumance (Figure 3.2):

- from winter camp to lowland spring areas;
- from lowland spring-early summer areas to summer areas;
- from summer areas to lowland autumn areas; and
- from autumn areas to winter camp.

The topographic location of Turgen seasonal pastures and the seasonal division of grazing areas is shown in Figure 3.4.

Due to common spring and summer areas, where herders stay from mid-March to early to mid-September for summer grazing and late October to early November for autumn grazing,

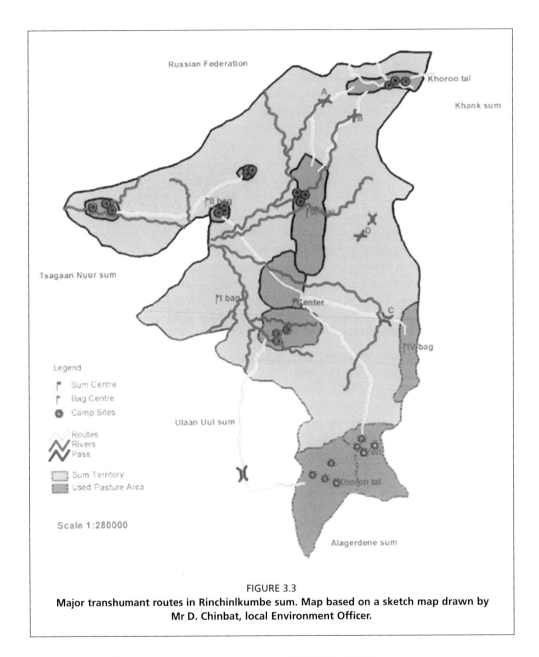

FIGURE 3.3
**Major transhumant routes in Rinchinlkumbe sum. Map based on a sketch map drawn by
Mr D. Chinbat, local Environment Officer.**

herders in Rinchinlkumbe have two long
movements (see Figure 3.3):

- from winter camp to spring and summer
  areas; and
- from autumn areas to winter camps.

The Rinchinlkumbe pastures and their
seasonal division are shown in Figure 3.5.

TURGEN SUM

Interviews with herders and the survey
identified two major long-distance
movements made by the sample
households: via *Khamar davaa* (Khamar
pass), and via *Ulaan davaa* (Red pass).

The first route is for moving from

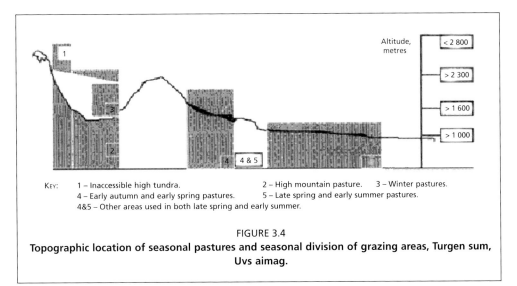

KEY: 1 – Inaccessible high tundra.   2 – High mountain pasture.   3 – Winter pastures.
        4 – Early autumn and early spring pastures.   5 – Late spring and early summer pastures.
        4&5 – Other areas used in both late spring and early summer.

FIGURE 3.4
**Topographic location of seasonal pastures and seasonal division of grazing areas, Turgen sum,
Uvs aimag.**

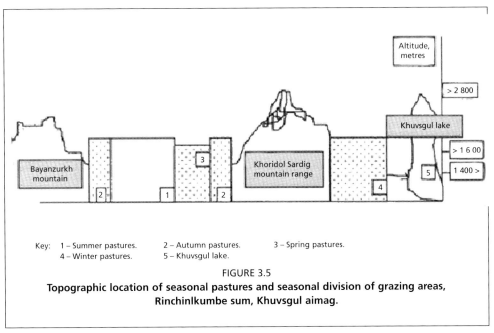

Key: 1 – Summer pastures.   2 – Autumn pastures.   3 – Spring pastures.
        4 – Winter pastures.   5 – Khuvsgul lake.

FIGURE 3.5
**Topographic location of seasonal pastures and seasonal division of grazing areas,
Rinchinlkumbe sum, Khuvsgul aimag.**

spring–early-spring areas to summer areas, and back to autumn areas, but a second route is followed to reach specific areas. The sample households formed two migration groups based on their transhumance routes. They follow similar routes to reach and return from the final areas and camps.

The first group use the *Khamar davaa* to summer and spring areas, but take different routes to return from winter camps to spring areas and return to winter camp from autumn areas.

Differences in duration and number of intermediate stops between migration

TABLE 3.12
Distance, duration and number of intermediate camps of long transhumance, Turgen sum.

Migration route	Total distance (km)		Duration (days)[1]		No. of intermediate stops[2]	
	group I	group II	group I	group II	group I	group II
Route A	118–137	138–153	9	7	7	5
Route B	102–121	89–104	3	3	2	2
Route C	102–116	93–113	3	3	2	2
Route D	118–137	108–113	6	6	4	5

NOTES: (1) Includes first day of migration. (2) Excluding initial and final camps.

routes (cf. Table 3.12) depend on two factors: season and distance per day. In warm weather, animals walk over 40–50 km daily; in cold months, when animals are exhausted and some lambs and kids have been born, migratory groups walk only 25–30 km daily. The range was 15 to 35 km. In warm seasons, herds move rather quicker than in winter and spring. Herders attributed this to:

- in late spring or early summer, herds are urged to walk faster to escape mosquitoes;
- animals are in better body condition and young stock have grown enough to cover long and continuous moves; and
- grass is abundantly available so that animals can graze as they walk, and some grazing is possible while camped overnight.

RINCHINLKUMBE SUM

To reach winter camps Rinchinlkumbe herders migrate over four major mountain passes of the *Khordil Sardig* range to enter areas west of *Khuvsgul* lake: (i) moving up *Sharga gol* [river] to winter grazing, and (ii) moving over *Uliin davaa*, (iii) moving up *Arsain gol*, and (iv) moving over *Khoroin gol*. Distances and duration are shown in Table 3.13.

The routes herders follow are largely dictated by the timing of long movements: routes W and X lead herders and livestock from the winter camps to spring

areas, whereas routes Y and Z direct the migration from summer areas to winter camps. There is a difference in duration and number of intermediate stays between Turgen and Rinchinlkumbe because:

- the starting points (camping or camp site) for movements differ. For example, in late August or early September, herders move up to woodland pasture (Rinchinlkumbe) or low hill areas (Turgen) before they head off to winter camping pastures. In spring, herders tend to select low-altitude areas protected from cross winds, where an early growth of pasture is likely and more water available, so they start from different points to arrive at different seasonal pastures; and
- body condition and herd structure are decisive factors determining the overall duration and number of intermediate camps. In autumn, body condition and fatness of all categories of animals is at its peak and they can tolerate long daily travel. In spring, herds are very vulnerable and have many heavily pregnant stock, and sometimes newborn offspring, so have to move much more slowly.

Herds need some rest on the way to their final destination because prolonged walking of well-fattened animals without rest leads to unproductive loss of body

TABLE 3.13
Distance, duration and number of intermediate camps of long transhumance movements, Rinchinlkumbe sum.

Migration route	Total distance (km)	Duration (days[1])	No. of intermediate stays[2]
Route W	160–180	9–11	6–8
Route X	96–108	7–9	5–8
Route Y	90–120	5–7	5–6
Route Z	105–110	6–7	5–6

NOTES: (1) Includes first day of migration. (2) Excluding initial and final camps.

condition, which inevitably accelerates further decline in body condition. Spring is also when animals tire easily, so a stop to allow grazing and rest is essential when about to walk over long distances in the next days. Herders argue that one, two or even more days are needed between stages in the spring movements, so that herds graze more and newborn offspring get more milk. Such stays take place in the middle of the journey, unless there are other reasons for stopping or good areas are found in other parts of the route. A decision on which routes to take depends on the location of summer areas and winter camps. Those with summer areas in the southwest corners of the sum and winter camps in the south end near Khuvsgul lowlands take route Y both ways. Some exceptional cases were observed: in 1998: five herders who moved along route W to winter camps took route W to return to summer areas because of exceptionally late melt of snow drifts in Sharga river valley, which forced them to leave already exhausted winter pastures before the main lambing.

EXCEPTIONAL 1999 SUMMER AND 2000 WINTER-SPRING MOVEMENTS IN TURGEN

It became obvious that both general and special cases had to be studied, instead of focusing all activities on a single year, so some details regarding the overall patterns of long-distance migrations in both sums are described. In 1999–2000, there were strong variations in the seasonal transhumant movements of herders of Turgen due to severe summer drought. This demonstrates that seasonal movements in Mongolia are complex and multipatterned. There was insufficient forage in all seasonal pastures in 1999–2000, and lack of haymaking accompanied by weather disasters and continued cold. The local meteorological stations recorded 28 days with temperatures of -35°C and colder at night, and -25°C during the day. Very deep snow, 20–30 cm on the plain and over 35–50 cm in the mountains, altered the movement patterns for a large number of herders. Many had to take a variety of manoeuvres to seek space for temporary accommodation, and to share available grazing resources. In the course of these movements, all habitual practices of long transhumance were modified to some extent, as the numbers of intermediate stays were increased and distances between two consequent camps also varied significantly.

There are very specific forms of transhumance in Mongolia and the variations mentioned above are not usual. Herders believe that transhumance, as an important component of pastoralism, is subject to natural spirits, as in other pastoral societies.

On a trip to Uvs *aimag* in early November 2000, the author met a widow and discussed how she survived the 1999–2000 winter and 2000 spring. The substance of that interview is summarized in Box 3.3. The decision-making process,

errors and realities show that 1999–2000 movement patterns were completely abnormal for some sample herders.

In eleven months, Ms S. and her family had moved over about 180 km, with 18 intermediate (overnight and camp changing) stays. There were some changes in terms of date of major herd movements:

- she moved all small stock in late

BOX 3.3
An interview with a Turgen family head

Ms S. made exceptional movements in the first three quarters of 1999. On the basis of instinct and personal observations she (a family head) recognized that the winter camp area could not support her animals any longer, so decided to move to spring lowlands 20 days earlier than normal, which is mid-March. Before deciding, she consulted other herders but found no support. However, having confidence in her decision, she moved her herds and reached a spring shelter after five intermediate camps. She expected the spring area to provide forage for her animals. She was partially correct and animals grazed some standing dead grass. Some experienced herders play on the specific behaviour of animals, whereby changing the grazing area motivates animals to forage more actively than before. Taking advantage of this natural instinct, they use prolonged moves, spending two, three or more days at an intermediate site. When the rest of the herders reached the spring shelters, Ms S. had already grazed what her areas had to offer, so she looked for a place to keep animals until the appearance of young grass. There was some forage for other herders who arrived later than hers but she chose not to trespass and instead moved to an unknown area lying across the borders of Turgen and Tarialan sum, where she had never stayed before. Young grass did not appear, although long expected, but instead came a drought. Herders competed for access to better areas before others and Ms S. found no room. She did some short moves within the area where she was. When the time came to move up to summer areas she could select one of two routes: route B or take a new one. She chose the latter option, and moved her herds and *ger* over totally unfamiliar land, spending eight days before reaching the traditional summer area. Dry and stunted pasture met her, promising inadequate support for her animals. Following other herders, she moved back to the spring area. As of early October 1999, she had made over 23 moves, including short-term camp changing. She estimated that for the rest of the year she might need to make at least 10 more moves. Based on heavy summer drought, which led herders to adopt non-standard decisions, her strategy for the 1999–2000 winter-spring season looked to be:

- separate the herd into two parts: small animals (sheep and goats) and large animals (horses, cattle and yaks);
- send large animals to her winter camp in Baruun salaa valley; and
- set up a temporary camp in Abilga valley for a month while the other herders find room for them, and move to areas near the Russian border.

February down Turgen river to an area lying across Abliga and Khuk Tokhoi, where her son's family stayed with some animals to reserve some pastures and she stayed there for a month;

- she made a risky decision, namely to move early to spring pasture in the hope of finding some better grazing before other herders; and
- she followed strictly the strategy she had planned. By making a risky decision on dates of movements, she benefited and was able to find more forage. Luckily, warm weather arrived earlier than normal and grass grew well enough so that animals achieved much improved body condition. Summer months in her resident area were exceptionally fine and her animals had good grazing. Her talks with the author confirmed that she would be following the movement rules set up for normal years, and she believed that there was no evidence to force her to make an alternative decision.

Ms S. said that the survival rate of her herd was much higher than that of other herders due to circumstances and correct decision-making. Her strategy worked very well for:

- efficient use of labour and division of herding tasks. Leaving large stock on their own, grazing with minimal supervision, allowed her to concentrate more on small animals, which showed a comparatively high survival rate;
- efficient utilization of pasture and reserved grazing areas. Removing large stock left more forage for stock kept near the camp; and
- an early move to spring pastures ensured better lambing and recovery of herd condition.

In conclusion, overall success of pastoral mobility, including long-distance transhumance, largely depends on the strategy herders choose and implement. Some herders prefer to move a long distance, while others prefer better herd and grazing management.

TREES

Trees are not considered fodder, either in Turgen or in Rinchinlkumbe. *Larix* forest is an area where cattle and horses can be herded in warm months, with regular supervision. Herders identified *Salix* trees and *Caragana* bushes as useful browse for camels and goats in hard times. Trees provide protection from periodic high wind, rain and snow storms. They provide fuelwood at all seasons and shade on hot, sunny days. No trees have been cultivated for fodder, and nor did herders entertain such a proposal. A family uses about 6–8 m^3 of fuelwood annually in Turgen and 12 m^3/yr in Rinchinlkumbe, at a cost of tugrik 800–1000 (US\$ 0.7–0.95)/m^3.

COMMUNITY AND HOUSEHOLDS

All herders and their family members were literate and had completed primary (fourth class) and secondary school (8 to 10th classes). Some children study at Universities and Colleges in Ulan Bator and Darkhan. Young people have a higher education level than the older generations thanks to Government policy on secondary education. No herders had training in matters related to livestock production and herd management. A young nursing graduate had returned to herding to help her mother; she provided health assistance to herders voluntarily. Four young men in both sums were trained professional drivers but were not

TABLE 3.14
Annual labour profile (percentage basis).

Task	Turgen	Rinchinlkumbe	Average
Cultivation	0	0	0
Sowing[1]	1-2	0	1–2
Weeding	0	0	0
Harvesting[1]	0	0	0
Collecting of fodder	8–10	10–15	9–12.5
Livestock herding	80	80	80
Fuelwood collecting	5	5	5
Work outside household	3	3	3

NOTE: (1) Two herders contributed some money and labour to a grain grower and helped with harvesting.

driving. Twelve herders' children of Turgen and eight of Rinchinlkumbe went to secondary school. Four (Turgen) and five (Rinchinlkumbe) children had left school for various reasons, mostly a parent's decision to have more labour for herding.

All households are wholly engaged in herding and all work patterns are determined by it and related activities, see Table 3.14. On average, over 80 percent of annual labour is devoted to herding; there are almost no crops. Three Turgen herders sowed vegetables in 1999, but did not tend them so the harvest was small. Two herders assisted in grain growing in 2000, and shared a small harvest – three sacks (120 kg) of unprocessed wheat.

WORK OUTSIDE THE HOUSEHOLD

Labour division between men and women is very similar to other herding societies in Mongolia. The respondents shared a common perception that herding needs good cooperation between households. Major forms of cooperation in the study areas are similar to those elsewhere in the country: labour pooling and resource sharing. Men and boys are responsible for outdoor work, whereas women perform household activities. Herding in summer is done by children of pre-school and school age, while men and grown boys have to herd animals in winter and spring, because of extreme cold and snow.

A similar profile of outside household work was described by respondents

TABLE 3.15
Profile of work outside the household (percentage – the total comprises 3 percent of annual labour).

Major activities	Turgen	Rinchinlkumbe
Haymaking	15–20	15–20
Wool shearing	15–20	15–20
Goat cashmere combing	20–30	20–25
Felt making	7–10	5
Help in migration	3–5	15–20
Cutting and collection of fuelwood	10	15
Collecting mineral additives and salt	2–3	3–5
Other	10	5–10

TABLE 3.16
Typical average animal production values.

	Rinchinlkumbe	Turgen
Liveweight (autumn weight; kg)		
Cattle adult bulls	245	260
Cattle adult cow	210	220
Sheep – ram	60	60
Sheep – ewe	48	45
Goat – billygoat	40	40
Goat – nannygoat	35	35
Milk production (litre)		
Cow (per 160-day lactation)	340	370
Mare (annual estimate)	15	15
Ewe (annual estimate)	6	6
Goat (annual estimate)	12	11
Fibre		
Cashmere fibre (gram)	320	290
Sheep wool (kg)	1.43	1.36

(Table 3.15), as all herding households are entirely pastoralists. Herders provide labour (people come to help) and some items (tools, pack animals, pack harness). No monetary assistance is given as loans or charity. During the 1999–2000 natural disaster, herders of Turgen received some assistance from donors and NGOs, and from the state.

PRODUCTION ESTIMATES

Production estimates of sample households' herds are all low, and little information on herd productivity was available (see Table 3.16). Herders never measure individual productivity of animals; sometimes information provided by local livestock inspectors was used to estimate production. Some indexes were measured by the survey team. The yield of mares may seem very low, but this is because, in the area studied, they are not milked much. Sheep in the study area produced 0.1–0.3 kg more wool and weighed 2.8–3.5 percent more than the Khalkh breed, due to a greater proportion

of the Bayad and Darkhad mutton strains.

Sale of livestock and livestock products are the main source of household income (Table 3.17). The amount sold varies depending on herd size and household needs. Most income comes from sale of meat, animals (live and bartered for food and goods), skin, hides and cashmere. Income per family member was US$ 173.9. The figures in Table 3.17 do not include items given as gifts or assistance.

FODDER BALANCE

Natural forage comprises over 90 percent of total animal feed. This was the case in the study area. Interviews revealed that they cut a little hay in 1998, but only 0.2 kg per animal fed. No crop residues or trees were used. Only a very little (240–400 kg) manufactured fodder was bought for exhausted animals and riding horses. Visits in 2000 showed that the impact of lessons herders had learned from the 1999–2000 natural disaster was uneven amongst sample households. Herders showed high interest

TABLE 3.17
Annual sales of livestock produce (total annual income per household).

Product		Average amount sold		Income (US$)	
		average	range[1]	average	range[1]
Milk (frozen)	kg	40	16–200	3.1	1.23–7.69
Wool	kg	189	148–470	50.7	39.7–126.0
Cashmere	kg	12	8–57	253.7	92.3–657.3
Hair	kg	1.2	0–1.5	0.32	0–0.40
Meat (all categories)	kg	175	90–600	50.4	26.0–173.0
Dairy products	kg	18	12–70	51.9	3.46–20.2
Animals	head	17	11–28	302.4	304.2–1 209.6
Sheep skin	piece	12	6–21	69.2	69.2–121.1
Goat skin	piece	4	2–13	15.4	7.7–40.0
Cattle hide	piece	1.2	1–3	13.8	12.5–37.7
Horse hide	piece	0.4	0–2	1.15	0–3.3
Sheep intestines	metres	56	8–120	5.38	0.76–11.5
Total				817.45	
Income per family member				173.9	

NOTE: (1) Maximum and minimum amounts

in making more hay in early summer, but a visit to Turgen in mid-September showed some drop in enthusiasm. Nevertheless, the amount of hay prepared had increased. A household cut hay in the range of 350 to 900 kg, which was said to be 10–35 percent higher than that made in 1998 (almost no hay was mown in 1999). Much more natural mineral lick was collected, as herders thought it was abundant because of the dry summer. Wild hay comprised 90 percent and more of the feed balance, and provided opportunities for supplementary feeding to some livestock. No other materials were available to improve structure and nutrient value of animal feed.

The only supplementation was to some (on average 3–5 percent of total herd) animals in winter and spring; supplementary feeding is short, depending on needs. There are no planned feeding schemes. Year-round grazing was the only way of feeding animals. As a rule, small stock and cattle grazed during the day and returned to camp overnight, whereas

horses and camels are left at pasture far from main camps and seasonal pastures for small livestock. Checking on animals at pasture varied by season. In summer they are checked weekly, and every 2–3 days in winter to offer minerals and see if all animals are well.

There are different ways of providing minerals (mostly natural soda licks). In spring and autumn, Turgen herds have free access to bulk licks. In late autumn, herders go to natural deposits near Uvs lake to collect soda and store it for winter and summer. In Rinchinlkumbe, herders from the southern part of the sum walk their animals to a source in Khurgany khooloi – small ponds full of salty water. Herders in the northern pastures have open access to swampy areas with minerals.

Rinchinlkumbe herders make more hay than Turgen people. In September 2000, five households were interviewed on this topic to find out what they do to make feed. Usually herders travel to their winter camping areas where there are

---

BOX 3.4
Private haymaking and supplementary feeding strategy, Rinchinlkumbe sum
From an interview with Mr B., fourth bag, Rinchinlkumbe.

Three households agreed to stay together over winter. Three men and a boy went to make hay and stayed 26 days, including four travelling by horse. Total hay prepared was 4.5 tonne. These households own 350 livestock and expect to give supplementary feed to about 8–10 percent of them (30–35 head) if winter and spring are normal. Duration of winter-spring supplementation is about 50–60 days. Gross daily consumption of these animals is 50–65 kg of hay, and the hay made is enough for another 10–20 animals. He is happy and sure that his hay will cover all his needs. As a reserve for newborn stock, he cut another tonne of hay at his late spring camp in the lowlands where herders arrive in early April direct from winter camps.

---

fields for cutting wild hay. All respondents said that they went to make hay in mid-August, when the hayfield grass growth was at its peak, and stayed for 25–30 days. Their description shows that the haymaking areas are productive enough: yielding 1 240–2 000 kg/ha. Herders measure the amount of hay by the numbers of stacks they make: each weighs 50–100 kg. Total haymaking by sample herders ranged from 56 to 100 stacks.

Turgen sum has some good areas for hay which could provide enough for local herders, but, because they are close to the *aimag* centre, there is a high level of competition from trespassers (Plate 19). Hay is divided into two parts: that for winter feeding, and hay reserved for young stock. Herders of study sites have two distinct plots for haymaking: one in the lowlands and one in the mountains. Hay for newborn animals is made near spring camps, cutting small areas in the lowlands. Hay prepared from the mountain fields at the winter area is used in winter.

COMMUNITY PARTICIPATION

To enhance community participation in the studies, a range of activities were undertaken:

- In the early days of the first visit to each site, the *sum* administration and the people concerned were informed of the tasks and expected outputs of the case studies. This enabled the team to establish goodwill and obtain assistance from the local government and officials.
- To ensure a broad and active participation of communities, an informal group was set up in each *sum* after discussions and consultations. Groups included the *sum* livestock inspector, bag governors, key herders and hired local representatives.
- A meeting involving key herders and *bag* governors identified sample households and discussed the organization and implementation of studies. Methods and techniques for data gathering and information sources were agreed.
- Two days of training were provided for the sample households and sum officials to introduce methodological approaches and the participatory role of herders for the provision of valid and correct data, and systematic record keeping. The training organized in Turgen involved eight men and six women (three of them family heads), while in Rinchinlkumbe the training was attended by seven men and one woman (family head).

Plate 19.
Hayfields must be protected and respected. Camels from migrating camps destroying lucerne hay fields, Turgen, Mongolia.

In each case, study sites were visited, a brief introduction about the studies was made, and major issues concerning the achievements and constraints discussed and agreement reached.

- One man at each site was hired and trained to collect primary and secondary data, and to measure pasture productivity and yields of animal products. Record keeping techniques were also introduced.
- No cooperation with the extension service was feasible because of the lack of any local infrastructure.
- A strong need and demand for improved sires for herd improvement was identified. Some herders in Turgen expressed an interest in obtaining seed to grow cereals.
- An interesting community activity among herders of Rinchinlkumbe was

identified: they agree on timing of movements because the tracks along which herds must move are very narrow, with steep, sharp side slopes. There are not many sites available for intermediate stays if all herders move at the same time. As far as Turgen is concerned, the mountain passes are high, but not so long as to take longer than half a day, which make them easy to cross, so no exact timing or movement sequencing is needed.

CONCLUSIONS

- Two major types of long-distance transhumance movements have been identified:
  - seasonal movement across five different ecological belts (in Turgen *sum*); and
  - seasonal movement across two ecological zones (in Rinchinlkumbe *sum*).

- All movements are longitudinal (west–east) to make better use of the variety of forage resources and climatic differences. There are a clear set of climatic and social indicators governing seasonal transhumance movements.

- The study shows that transhumance movements are not of the same direction and frequency: Turgen herders move twice a year over the same passes between their summer and winter camps; those of Rinchinlkumbe make one movement to and from winter pastures. No herders stay at the higher altitudes in winter. Seasonal, especially winter, camps are on one side of a mountain range that routes must cross.

- Various routes were identified by tracking the migration of households and groups of households. Due to the limited options for seasonal pastures and camping areas, mostly involving traversing mountain passes, herders in both sums must follow the same routes to reach particular areas and to return. This is an extremely important pattern that distinguishes the complexity of the system and its integrity.

- The major herding strategy is a multispecies herd with upgrading for subsistence, with marketing of surplus produce. The average family size is 4.7, comprising people of all ages.

- Pasture condition varies in different areas of the *sums*, from seriously degraded to underused. Increase in the proportion of negative indicator plants indicates the degree of damage to natural pastures.

- Long-distance transhumance movements consist of a number of intermediate camps and the final destinations. Geotopographic conditions of localities along the routes determine how many intermediate camps are required. The number of intermediate camps also depends on herd ability to walk long distances each day: shorter and slower in spring and longer and faster in summer and late autumn.

- Moving from autumn camps to winter areas is one or two days shorter than the return to spring areas because newborn stock walk slowly and all animals are exhausted, having lost 10–15 percent or more of their autumn weight.

- Herders sell animal products, using various marketing options, to earn income for buying food and goods. In 1999, average sale income per household was US$ 817.5. Household consumption was 60–70 percent of the annual sale income.

- Natural grazing is the main source of animal feed for both areas. Haymaking is a common form of fodder supply. Sown forage and cropping are practically absent.

DISCUSSION

There are a range of factors contributing to the adoption of long-distance transhumance as a single strategy, but the primary need is for all involved to agree.

Local conditions in both *sums* differ markedly from other areas of Mongolia, where short distances and fewer seasonal and grazing movements are made. For instance:

- pastures appropriate for winter–early spring are concentrated in special parts of the territory;

- snowfall in non-winter-spring areas is abundant and intense, forming a deep cover, which protects grazing to a greater extent;

- extreme cold in the lowlands due to accumulation of cold air in depressions (both *sums* are located in well-known lowland depressions: Turgen in the Great Lake Depression and Rinchinlkumbe in Darkhad Depression); and

- spring-summer and autumn pastures are only suitable for grazing at these seasons, and winter areas are suitable because of mild climate and good forage resources to support all kinds of animals for a short time.

Marked and strong seasonal changes in the weather dictate when to move, because early and hard frost transforms green forage grass into standing litter; herders always worry that early snow in the mountains may make movement over the passes difficult or even impossible: at a sign of early heavy snow they move 15–20 days earlier than normal.

Herders in some areas move in a very short time to another area. This is a need-based strategy that ensures the temporal and spatial dimensions of pastoral grazing. Herders call it "moving as frightened birds take off", leaving behind them all the pastures totally free of grazing.

Herders do not believe that catastrophic damages to traditional movement systems was wrought by pastoral collectives (*negdel*) under the planned economy. They provide a lot of their own arguments to show that collectives did much to strengthen pastoral production in all aspects of its functioning. They noted some development statistics for the livestock sector: in 30 years of existence, collectives provided water to over 75 percent of natural pastures at national level; after 10 years of post-liberalization, the water supply to pastures had fallen by 40 percent.

Chapter IV
Mongolia case study 2: Haymaking from natural pasture in Arkhangai, Mongolia

V.I. Lkhagvajaw and B. Erdenebaatar

SUMMARY

Stock raising in Mongolia relies on natural pasture. The thermal growing season is around one hundred days. Conservation of natural herbage for winter and spring supplementation is highly desirable. Since the privatization of the livestock sector in the early 1990s, collective systems of haymaking have collapsed and small-scale haymaking has yet to replace them. Herders have little experience of haymaking. Trials and demonstrations carried out from 1996 to 1998 at Ikh Tamir in Arkhangai Aimag are described.

Spreading of animal manure and irrigating by forming ice-sheets with spring water over potential hay land were used as possible ways of increasing yields. Drought prevailed throughout the period, limiting the availability of water to form ice, as well as restricting growth of rainfed herbage. Nevertheless, all treatments had a positive effect on hay production. Mineral fertilizer had the greatest effect, but is unlikely to be economically interesting. Simple haymaking techniques, using animal-drawn equipment, were satisfactory, and the demonstration effect of the work has encouraged herders to increase haymaking on their own initiative.

INTRODUCTION

The pastoral situation and the effect of decollectivization on Mongolian herding have been described in Chapter II. Centralized hay production was discontinued soon after the change of system, and nothing came in its place. This chapter describes studies carried out in Arkhangai on methods of haymaking suitable for herding families, the possibility of increasing hay yield by water (ice) spreading, and the use of dung.

Traditional livestock are all, of necessity, well adapted to the harsh climate; they can regain condition and build up fat reserves rapidly during the short growing season. The hump of the camel and the fat rump of local sheep breeds provide energy reserves to help tide them over winter and spring. Yaks, camels and cashmere goats develop winter down in their coats,

which helps reduce heat loss. All can survive outdoors throughout the long, cold winter with little or no shelter nor supplementary feed. The young are generally born in spring and their dams benefit from the fresh grass. The livestock are generally small. The herders' strategy is therefore to get the stock into as good condition as possible in autumn so that they survive on dried-off or frozen pasture until the grass regrows in late spring; non-breeding stock are sold or slaughtered in late autumn and frozen naturally.

While it is not possible in a growing season of a little over three months to conserve feed for the rest of the year, it is highly desirable that some reserves of conserved fodder be available to assist the survival of young, breeding and weak stock. Hay from natural pasture is probably the only source of conserved feed available to herders, and then only in areas where sufficient moisture is available. Historically, each herder was entitled to possess defined areas of common land for many years, where hay was cut. Following the nationwide privatization of the early 1990s, however, every hayfield became the focus of local disputes between individual herders and within herding groups, as well as with herders from neighbouring communities. Apart from this, the repeated cutting which had become common in the later decades of the planned economy led to a serious decline in the natural productivity of haymaking areas, and there is no sign as yet that herders have invested in improvements, or will do so. There are several reasons for this:

- the poor economic capacity of herders and herding groups for investment;
- lack of experience and readiness to take care of natural hay land;
- lack of equipment and financial resources for simple haymaking – the mechanized equipment of the *negdel* was dispersed and there is a scarcity of animal-drawn mowers and rakes;
- a series of relatively mild winters for five years in the late 1990s led to complacency (the very severe spring of 2000 caused enormous losses); and
- the low yield of most hay fields means that production is very labour consuming and there is a lack of machinery and other inputs.

In 1997, at national level, only 667 000 tonne of hay was made, or about 4.8 kg/animal – one fifteenth of the official supplementary feed norm.

The High Altitude Research Station of the Mongolian Research Institute for Animal Husbandry has its headquarters at Ikh Tamir *sum* in Arkhangai *aimag*.

It was the base for this work because it is in a suitable agro-ecological zone and has high calibre pasture specialists. According to geographic zoning, Ikh Tamir belongs to the high mountain area, where the size of natural hay fields is limited by relief and geomorphological conditions.

Because of its altitude, Ikh Tamir has a harsh, continental climate. The warmest months are June–August, with mean temperatures between 13.8°C and 16.6°C; the coldest season is December–February, with average temperatures between -12.9°C and -16.0°C. The absolute maximum is 34.5°C, recorded in August, and the lowest is -36.5°C, recorded in January. The average mean temperature measured at the soil surface is 4.1°C, with a maximum of 65.6°C in June and a minimum of -41.0° to -42.5°C in December–January. The annual precipitation at Ikh Tamir *sum* is 363 mm, with about 80 percent falling in May–August. The thaw takes place about 20 May, and the first frosts come in early September. There are an average of 100 frost-free days, but with a wide range of 70–131 days.

Trials extended over three growing seasons, studying the conversion of natural pasture into hay land to assess the impact of simple techniques, mainly based on local materials; on the productivity of previously constantly grazed areas; and to study the feasibility of making hay from natural herbage. Specific activities were:

- assessing methods of delivering nutrients and moisture and their effects on the productivity of natural pastures and hay fields;
- testing the effect of manures and fertilizers on the immediate and short-term performance of natural plant communities, in terms of positive species

and botanical changes, and variations in the yield of natural hay;

- designing and testing an animal-drawn cart suitable for the transport and spreading of dung; and

- drawing up recommendations on the improvement of pasture and hay land in high mountain areas.

EXPERIMENTAL TREATMENTS AND TECHNIQUES

The treatments were:

(i) Provision of moisture to the soil in late spring through forming an ice sheet (ice cover) over the fields during winter.

(ii) Spreading animal dung at 50 tonne/ha.

(iii) Ice irrigation + dung.

(iv) Mineral (N+P) fertilizer at 60 kg/ha N and 90 kg/ha P.

(v) Ice irrigation + mineral fertilizer.

Ice irrigation has been known in the area for a long time, and was used in the pre-collective period; it involves spreading water from streams or springs over hay land so that a sheet of ice is formed. When this thaws in spring it supplies moisture at a time when the vegetation has great need of it. The water from the thawing ice is distributed over the pasture by digging ditches. This can, of course, only be done where water supply and topography permit. The technique is seemingly also used in Russia and FAO (1959) quotes Larin (1953) as reporting on the "Liman" irrigation of fodder crops with ice.

The dung used was the dry excreta of cattle, horses and small ruminants, taken from night shelters; no bedding is used but there may be some soil admixture. This dung (which is also used as fuel) is hard and compacted by trampling and drying, and has to be broken up before

spreading. The herders grow no crops so there is no competition with other agricultural enterprises for the dung, which was hand-spread over the plots. Spreading is done in spring and has to be carried out relatively quickly, before plant growth is well started.

With such treatments, especially ice irrigation, and broken terrain, formal experimentation was not possible. In any case, large differences are being sought at this exploratory stage. Large observation plots were therefore used. The areas of the various treatments were: dung – 2.76 ha; mineral fertilizer – 0.9 ha; and fertilizer + dung – 2.67 ha. In addition, investigations were continued on the plots treated in 1996: 1.5 ha of ice irrigation plus dung; 0.25 ha dung plus mineral fertilizer; and 0.38 ha mineral fertilizer. In addition, areas of pasture were fenced as exclosures to serve as controls.

Geobotanical description was used to determine botanical composition; bare ground was estimated visually as a percentage. Height of the dominant species was measured on thirty plants selected at random. The above-ground phytomass was measured by clipping 5 plots of 0.5 m^2 at a height of 0.5–1.0 cm. To determine botanical composition and changes in the proportion of the different botanical groups, 0.25 m^2 plots were cut and separated into grasses, legumes, sedges and other forbs.

THE EXPERIMENTAL SITES

Eight plots at five sites in different areas of Ikh Tamir (Plates 20 and 21) were selected, taking into account botanical composition and distance to winter camps. All sites belonged to private herders and had been used for both grazing and haymaking. Some sites were where an ice cover could

Plate 20.
Haymaking study. Protected plots at Ikh Tamir, Arkhangai, Mongolia.

Plate 21.
Haymaking study. Plots about to be sampled, Ikh Tamir, Arkhangai, Mongolia.

be formed in winter through spreading spring water. Three sites were on south-facing slopes, two in open valleys, two in the lower parts of forested valleys and one on an open plain (see Table 4.1). In general, the sites represented most of the grazing and haymaking areas of the high mountain zone, and reflected their previous use. Some areas of the *sum* have been damaged by poor management (uncontrolled cutting and grazing, water and wind erosion, and damage by vehicle tracks).

Site 1 is mountain steppe with sandy brown soil on a 3–5° slope. In years of adequate rainfall, an ice sheet forms from a spring at the top of the slope. It is a degraded *Festuca lenensis–Stipa krylovii–*forbs pasture, which has been grazed at all

seasons. Ice irrigation began here in 1996.

Site 2 is riparian land in a north-facing narrow valley; its slope is 3–5° and the surface is even. Ice sheets may form if summer rainfall is adequate to feed the river. The soil is dark brown alluvium. The vegetation is a *Carex–Leymus chinensis–*forbs community. This site had been mown until 1993 and thereafter used as summer grazing. Considerable surface damage has been caused by burrowing rodents. A partial trial with ice irrigation began in 1996.

Site 3 is in a short, narrow mountain valley facing northwest; the slope is 10–15°. The ground water is near the surface. The plant communities and use are similar to those of Site 1.

TABLE 4.1
Summary description of project sites.

Site	Altitude (m)	Topography	Plant communities	Major species
Site 1 Bulagt	1740–1800	Riparian meadow area in open valley on southern slope of mountains	Herbaceous–*Carex duriuscula–Leymus chinensis* mountain steppe	*Leymus chinensis, Stipa kyrlovii, Festuca lenensis, Koeleria cristata, Carex duriuscula, Artemisia laciniata, A. glauca, A. comutata, Plantago adpressa*
Site 2 Burgast	~ 1700	River side in narrow, north-facing valley	Herbaceous–*Leymus chinensis–Carex pediformis* steppe-like meadow hayfield	*Leymus chinensis, Koeleria cristata, Agropyron cristatum, Carex pediformis, Artemisia laciniata, A. mongholica, Potentilla tanacetifolia, P. anserina, Galium verum, Bromus inermis, Vicia amoena, Silene repens, Sanguisorba officinalis*
Site 3 Khusluurt	~ 1740	Basin of northwest high valley	Herbaceous–*Leymus chinensis–Carex pediformis* meadow-steppe type pasture	*Geranium simplex* plus species as at Burgast
Site 4 Chono	1840	Closed depression in southeast-facing valley	Meadow-type steppe Herbaceous–*Carex pediformis–*Poaceae grazing area	*Agropyron cristatum, Poa subfastigata, Festuca sp., Carex pediformis, Artemisia laciniata, A. dracunculus, A. glauca, Thalictrum simplex, Galium verum, Potentilla tanacetifolia*
Site 5 Mukhar	~ 1760	10–15° slope on northern face of mountain	Hay and grazing area in Herbaceous–Poaceae–*Carex pediformis* steppe meadow	*Bromus inermis, Calamagrostis epiodis, Elymus turczaninovii, Festuca sp., Stipa baicalensis, Carex pediformis, Artemisia laciniata, Geranium pratensis, Galium boreale, Vicia amoena, Hedysarum alpinus, Thalictrum simplex, Silene repens, Anemone crinata, Scabiosa comosa*

Site 4 is a rainfed mountain meadow on dark brown clay on an east-facing slope at the foot of a mountain forest. The plant community is forbs–*Carex pediformis*–Poaceae. In years of adequate growth it had been used for hay; otherwise it was grazed. Work began in 1997.

Site 5 is on the north-facing slope of a valley with mountain meadows on dark brown clay. The slope is 10–15°. The plant community is forbs–*Carex pediformis*–Poaceae. The site had been used for haymaking and for winter-spring grazing. Work began in 1997.

RESULTS

During the period of the work, the weather was far from ideal for haymaking; no rain fell from April to late July. Heavy dust storms in spring and hot, sunny days in summer led to serious damage to the vegetation. Runoff from heavy downpours in late July did not provide enough moisture for the plants to recover, and drought continued into August. At a meteorological station 27 km from the sites, total rainfall in 1996 was 94.7 mm and the annual average temperature was 1°C above average. Snow cover during the 1996–1998 winters was also low and the lowlands were "brown" – snow free. The first rain in the springs of 1997 and 1998 fell in mid-May.

Effect of ice irrigation

Two sites at head-points of small springs had winter ice cover, beginning around 20 November and thawing by 10–20 April. The average ice depth varied from over 18 cm in the centre to 3–7 cm at the periphery. Two key moments are noted when more moisture is absorbed by the soil: in the initial days as the soil profile becomes filled before all is frozen over; and at the thaw. Soil covered by ice throughout winter contains more moisture than bare ground. This is probably important for early growth so ice-irrigated plots showed better performance. Although ice cover was insufficient to provide a reserve of moisture for after the thaw, it assured a better intensity of grass growth for the rest of the growing period. Ice irrigation, there-

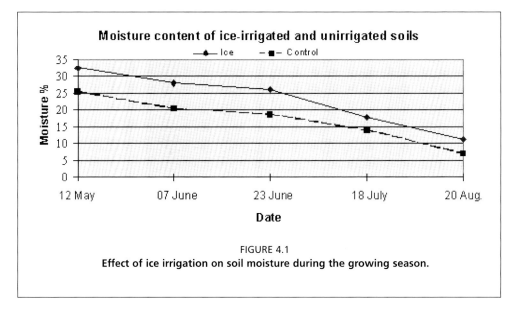

FIGURE 4.1
Effect of ice irrigation on soil moisture during the growing season.

fore, gives far better early growth than that which occurs in open areas. The moisture percentage of soils under the different irrigation regimes during the growing season are shown in Figure 4.1. In early spring, the ice-irrigated land contained over a third more moisture than the control, and the difference persisted through the season.

Effects on total phytomass

Since the nutrient treatments were applied to different plant communities at different sites, the aggregated results are shown (Table 4.2) by site. Annual variations, largely influenced by precipitation, are illustrated in Figure 4.2.

Application of dung and ice irrigation (although irrigation was inadequate due to drought) had a positive effect on yield; mineral fertilizer, as expected, gave a large, positive, response, but is unlikely to be economically attractive to herders.

Despite severe drought in the three consecutive years of the trial, a number of changes in the growth of the major plants and their abundance and role in the formation of plant communities were observed. These changes were attributed to the influence of the type of manure, as well as the basic characteristics of the plant communities involved, the microclimate and other ecoclimatic conditions of the mountain zone and the sites.

Dung gave a reasonable acceleration of plant growth, despite the drought, and brought about some changes in the development and appearance of young plants through the better distribution of stolons and rhizomes of valuable short and creeping tussock grasses (*Leymus chinensis, Bromus inermis, Festuca rubra, Hordeum brevisububatum* and *Poa subfastigata*) and some forbs. No loss of species in the plant communities was noted. An annual species, *Chenopodium album*, increased greatly in the first two years but was greatly reduced thereafter as it could not compete with well-established perennials. *C. album* was easily suppressed by more valuable species on the plots where mineral fertilizer was used.

With mineral fertilizer and the combination of fertilizer and dung, short tussock and creeping plants (*Festuca lenensis, Koeleria cristata, Agropyron cristatum, Plantago* sp., *P. adspera, Leontopodium*

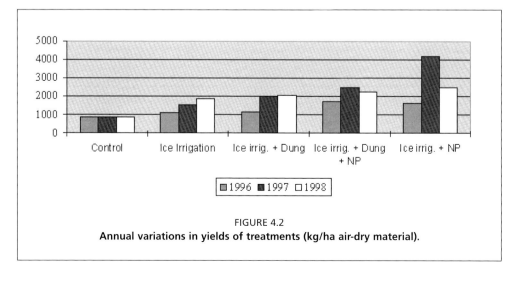

FIGURE 4.2
Annual variations in yields of treatments (kg/ha air-dry material).

ochroleucum, Heteropappus hispidus and *Potentilla anserina*) decreased, as they were dominated by taller species. In ice-irrigated plots, creeping herbs increased; this was especially obvious in 1996 and 1997. Grasses that increased under mineral and mixed fertilization were *Leymus chinensis, Bromus inermis* and *Poa subfastigata*. Forbs that increased were *Artemisia mongholica, A. vulgaris, A. laciniata* and *Silene repens*.

During 1996, shoot length of *Leymus chinensis* increased greatly in comparison to the control: by 37.4 percent under ice irrigation, 64.8 percent under ice irrigation + dung; and 141.8 percent with ice irrigation + dung + fertilizer. The same was noted in 1997/98 but real values were lower because of drought and insufficient ice cover. The results are shown in Tables 4.2 and 4.3.

In order to clarify the real effects of treatments on the vegetation, detailed observations were made at two sites, Burgast and Khusluurt.

Burgast (Site 2)

This was a forbs–*Leymus chinensis–Carex* hayfield. Major changes in the proportion of different plant groups in relation to treatments are shown in Table 4.4.

- Ice irrigation in 1996 and 1997 (there was no ice in 1998) increased the proportion of forbs and legumes, while sedges decreased. No obvious increase of any grass was noted. If the grasses are classified, however, creeping species increased and short tussock grasses decreased.
- Dung gave an increase of creeping grasses while sedges decreased. Interestingly, forbs showed no change.
- Mineral fertilizers, alone and in combination with dung, decreased the proportion of tussock grasses and forbs while increasing the percentage of creeping grasses (compared to control, dung and ice irrigation plots).

TABLE 4.2
Yields of hay trials by site (kg/ha air-dry herbage).

Site and Type	Control	Ice irrigation	Ice irrig. + Dung	Ice irrig. + Dung + NP	Ice irrig. + NP
Tsagaankhad, mountain steppe	280	340	420	1 170	720
Mukhar, mountain steppe meadow	1 450	2 060	2 060	3 570	4 340
Bulagt, mountain steppe	880	1 000	–	2 160	–
Khusluurt, mountain meadow	2 010	2 500	2 680	4 560	2 710
Burgast, steppe meadow	1 360	1 070	2 530	3 340	2 150
Mean	1 196	1 394	1 923	2 960	2 480

TABLE 4.3
Assessment of the effect of treatments on the bioproductivity of *Carex–Leymus chinensis*–forbs pasture community at Site 2.

	Absolute height of leaves (cm)	Plants per m²	Average fresh weight of single plant (gram)
Control	23.0	175	0.68
Ice Irrigation	23.7	582	0.62
Ice irrig. + dung	27.9	659	0.69
Ice irrig. + dung + NP	33.3	743	0.89
Ice irrig. + NP	43.6	877	1.02

TABLE 4.4
Change of plant groups in *Carex–Leymus*–forbs mountain-steppe hayfield (Burgast – Site 2) (average for 1996–1998; percentage).

Treatment	Grasses			Legumes	Carex	Forbs		
	Total	of which				Total	of which	
		Creeping	Tussock				*Artemisia mongholica*	Other
Control	32.1	8.2	23.9	3.7	16.4	47.8	3.5	44.3
Ice irrigation	30.9	27.6	3.3	8.6	3.9	56.6	13.3	43.3
Ice irrig. + Dung	44.4	36.6	7.8	4.8	2.8	48.3	3.3	45.0
Ice irrig. + Dung + NP	50.0	47.2	2.8	3.6	10.3	36.1	5.6	30.5
Ice irrig. + NP	53.6	51.5	2.1	3.1	2.8	40.5	8.7	31.8

TABLE 4.5
Change in plant groups in a *Carex–Leymus*–forbs mountain-steppe hayfield, average for 1996–1998 at Site 3 (Khusluurt) (proportion of plant groups in whole community; percent).

Treatment	Grasses			Legumes	Carex	Forbs		
	Total	of which				Total	of which	
		Creeping	Tussock				*Artemisia mongholica*	Other
Control	44.1	39.8	4.3	0.9	9.5	45.5	12.3	33.2
Dung	38.1	32.8	5.3	2.3	17.2	42.4	6.1	36.3
Dung + NP	44.2	41.4	2.8	1.2	4.0	50.6	7.3	43.3
NP	31.1	25.6	5.5	0.9	0.9	61.7	4.9	56.8

Khusluurt (Site 3)

This was a *Leymus chinensis–Artemisia–Carex* steppe meadow pasture. Here the proportions of different plant groups changed in a way different from Site 2, sometimes in an undesirable manner. The proportion of creeping grasses and forbs remained the same as the control under dung and dung + mineral fertilizer, while pure mineral fertilizer gave an enormous increase in forbs, including *Artemisia mongholica*. This increase in forbs caused a proportional decrease in grasses in the total yield (see Table 4.5). In contrast to the decrease of *Carex* in plots receiving mineral fertilizer, dung fields had a great increase of sedges. Shoot length of *Leymus chinensis* and *Bromus inermis* increased greatly in comparison with the control (see Table 4.6).

The strong increase in forbs, especially *Artemisia mongholica*, reflects their great ability to react to additional, easily available nutrients, and clearly limits growth of other plant forms by dominating in both above-ground growth and roots. Bright sunshine and continued moisture stress in June and early July badly affected the growth of *Leymus chinensis*, the major dominant plant of this community. This was very evident in 1997, when the summer was exceptionally hot.

TABLE 4.6
Assessment of effect of treatments on the bioproductivity of individual plants at Site 3 (Khusluurt).

Treatment	*Leymus chinensis*			*Bromus inermis*		
	Length of vegetative shoots (cm)	Plants per m^2	Fresh weight of individual plants (gram)	Length of vegetative shoots (cm)	Plants per m^2	Fresh weight of individual plants (gram)
Control	25.7	280.5	0.50	21.5	225	0.47
Dung	29.1	343.5	0.59	25.7	305	0.60
Dung + NP	31.1	462.5	0.76	25.3	168	0.76
Ice Irrigation + NP	33.4	367.5	0.77	28.0	137	0.80

CART DESIGN

Transporting and spreading dung is one of the hardest tasks. Dung is not always available close to suitable hay sites, and has to be transported from the shelters. For this, simple mechanization is necessary. The compacted dung has to be broken up to allow even spreading. Wooden ox-carts of traditional design, with wooden wheels, are widely used in the area; wood is relatively plentiful in the mountain zone, mainly from larch (*Larix dahurica*) forests, but the carts are easily damaged when hard dung is broken in them. An improved version was built and tested wherein the parts where dung is crushed for spreading were made of steel. Initial tests showed that metal is much more resistant and more suitable for heavy work. Two carts were built and used in 1998. Their use greatly simplified work and reduced by 47 minutes the time required to spread dung on one hectare, although much slower than spreading from lorries. Ox-carts have the great advantage that no fuel is required and the herders are well used to handling them. Spreading from carts was estimated to be cheaper by tugrik 690/tonne of dung (≈US$ 0.8 at 1998 prices) compared with spreading using a motor lorry.

Three training sessions were held in 1997 for local administrative staff, researchers and herders. Field training sessions were followed by a broad discussion of what had been seen and observed; this took most of one day. Based on the major findings and preliminary conclusions of the two years of field work, a small booklet was printed, describing the technical aspects of hay improvement using locally available materials – *Practical recommendations on hay and pasture in Khangai High Mountain Area* – and distributed to those who had participated in training, as well as to other interested herders.

CONCLUSIONS

The yield of the control plots was generally very low and would have led to difficulties in handling so thin a hay crop. Even under drought conditions, ice irrigation along with dung can raise hay yields, and the costs of so doing are low. No doubt in "normal" years the effect would be greater. The technique of developing ice-sheets and then spreading by ditches the water from their melting in spring has proved to be relatively simple and costs little other than labour. Mineral fertilizer, of course, gives large responses, as is usual on grassland, but price and non-availability are likely to rule out its use by subsistence herders.

There are indications that the treatments, along with closing sites to grazing to allow haymaking, does lead to changes in the botanical composition of the sward.

Longer study would be necessary to determine the full effects of treatments on plant communities.

The sites have had a valuable demonstration effect, familiarizing herders with simple animal-drawn equipment and manual techniques. Some have taken to producing hay on their own initiative; this may spread if better weather improves the availability of herbage suitable for mowing.

Chapter V
China's pasture resources

Zizhi Hu and **Degang Zhang**

SUMMARY

This chapter has been condensed from a much more detailed *Country Fodder/Pasture Resource Profile*, which can be found on the FAO website (Hu and Zhang, 2001). China's pastoral areas are concentrated in six provinces and autonomous regions – Inner Mongolia; Xinjiang; Tibet; Qinghai; Sichuan; and Gansu – where extensive stock raising is the main agricultural enterprise. Mixed farming, on relatively small family farms, is the agricultural system of the rest of the country, where livestock are still important, but are mainly fed on crop residues, some sown pasture and limited rough grazing if available. Since China spans a latitude range from below the tropics to areas with permafrost, and from sea level to great plateaus above 5 000 m, there is a great diversity of pasture types; these are defined and described along with the animal production systems that have developed on them. A range of forages and pasture plants have been developed to suit the various zones; some forages, such as lucerne (*Medicago sativa*), which is of very ancient cultivation in northern and western China, and *Astragalus sinicus,* which is rotated with rice as a fodder-*cum*-green-manure, are widespread. Now *Lolium multiflorum* is becoming increasingly used in southerly rotations. The main forages, their adaptation and use are described, including several aquatic fodder crops.

The pastures of family farms still belong to the state and families pay according to a *Long-term Grassland Use Contract* with the government. The livestock belong to the family. In the past decade, the government has put the *Long-term Grassland Use Contract system* into force, with great effort. Under this system, grassland productivity is improved by subdividing pastures and allocating long-term grazing rights to individual families, based on the number of family members, with fencing, homestead and barn, establishing artificial grassland and building infrastructure for water and electricity supply. This has been basically completed nationwide. Contracting of pastures simplifies their administration and gives families incentives for their better management and improvement, but does restrict mobility in semi-arid areas of traditional transhumance. Pasture degradation is a major problem, currently increasing by about two percent annually, but some parts – Xinjiang, Inner Mongolia and Heilonjiang – are worse than the average, and it is hoped that grassland allocation will allow this trend to be slowed or reversed.

In the agricultural areas, farm size is small, so sown pastures and forages are generally cut and carried to feed livestock. In intensive systems, forage is fed to monogastric stock as well as to ruminants. Several specialized, non-pasture, fodders are grown, including aquatic forages, in suitable, mostly subtropical, zones. There has been considerable innovation in the livestock and forage sector in recent years and the livestock sector is now much more market oriented, and its subsistence component relatively small. *Lolium multiflorum* is now widely used as a winter forage in rotation with rice. Increasing use is being made of crop residues, and ensiled maize stover and ammoniated straw are widely used in commercial fattening and overwintering of cattle and sheep.

Three case studies are presented in subsequent chapters: two from Xinjiang Uigur Autonomous Region – one on transhumance allied to irrigated haymaking and the other on lucerne breeding – form Chapters VI and VII, with a detailed study of the pastures and animal husbandry of Tibet Autonomous Region in Chapter VIII.

INTRODUCTION

China covers about 9 600 000 km², and its territorial waters cover 4 730 000 km². It has land borders with fourteen countries and maritime borders with five others. The country is divided into 34 provinces, autonomous regions, municipalities and special administrative regions. The population – 1 205 000 000 – is 22 percent of the human race. Han account for 94 percent of the population, but there are 56 other ethnic groups. Chinese is spoken throughout the country.

Based on economic development and geography, China is divided into three parts: west, central and east. The east includes Liaoning, Tianjin, Hebei, Shandong, Jiangsu, Shanghai, Zhejiang, Fujian, Guangdong, Hainan, Hong Kong and Macao. The centre includes Heilongjiang,

FIGURE 5.1
East, Central and West parts of the People's Republic of China.

Jilin, Shanxi, Henan, Anhui, Hubei, Jiangxi and Hunan. The west includes Guangxi, Sichuan, Chongqing, Guizhou, Yunnan, Shaanxi, Gansu, Ningxia, Qinghai, Xinjiang, Inner Mongolia and Tibet.

Cultivated land and forests are mainly in the east and centre; grassland is in the west. The east is dominated by farming and the west by grassland husbandry. Inner Mongolia, Xinjiang, Tibet, Qinghai, Sichuan and Gansu are the six main pastoral areas.

China's topography is in three great terraces: highest in the west and lowest in the east. The terrain is generally mountainous, with a very high mean altitude: 33 percent is mountains and only 12 percent plains. The area below 500 m almost equals that above 3 000 m: both are around a quarter of the total. The natural conditions and agriculture of the three terraces are very different:

- the first terrace is that of the west: the Qinghai-Tibet Plateau, with an average altitude over 4 000 m;
- the second terrace extends from the northern and eastern edges of the Qinghai-Tibet Plateau, and ends in Daxinanlin, Taihang, Wushan and Xuefengshan Mountains. It is highlands, with basins, at altitudes between 1 000 and 2 000 m; and
- the third terrace is east of the above areas, and extends to the eastern continental shelf. Its landform is mainly plains and hills.

Most water systems run from west to east, and drain to the Pacific, except for those rising on the southern Qinghai-Tibet Plateau, which run from north to south and drain into either the Pacific Ocean or the Indian Ocean from the barrier of the Hengduanshan Mountains.

SOILS

China's soil types are complex. The zonal soil types in the East Monsoon Zone are – from south to north – latosol, lateritic red soil, red soil, yellow soil, yellow-brown soil, burozem and drab soil, dark brown forest soil, and podzolic soil. Zonal soil types from northeast to northwest are chernozem, chestnut soil, brown soil, sierozem, grey brown desert soil, and brown desert soil. On the Qinghai-Tibet Plateau, the soil types from east to west are alpine meadow soil, alpine steppe soil, alpine desert soil and alpine frozen soil. Because there are many mountains, the vertical zonal pedigree of a soil type appears widely. There are different soil pedigrees on the different mountains. Influenced by a long history of cultivation, there are also many agricultural soil types, including paddy soil, oasis soil and *lou* soil (stratified old loessial soil).

Soil fertility is, as everywhere, a limiting factor in grassland production. China's soils are generally low in phosphorus; potash is low in many of the better watered southern and eastern areas, but high in many northern and western semi-arid zones. There are few national sources of phosphate and potash, and, because of long transport routes, farmers do not have easy access to these fertilizers. Fertility recycling is stressed, with use of manure, compost, etc., together with green manuring, including using legumes and Azolla.

Soil degradation (Plate 22) is the most important constraint for China's ecological conservation and economic development. Desertified (i.e. degraded soils in the arid, semi-arid and subhumid areas) land accounts for 27.32 percent of the total area. Of this, 61.3 percent was caused by wind, 7.80 percent by water,

Plate 22.
*Land cleared for crops and then abandoned gives poor grazing in Guizhou, China.
Once the forest cover was removed, the shallow soils were soon eroded to expose the
underlying rock.*

TABLE 5.1
Agricultural land use characteristics in PR China.

Land Use	Area ('000 ha)	Percentage of Total
Cultivated land	120 040	13.53
Forest	158 940	16.56
Inland water	17 470	1.82
Grassland	400 000	41.67
of which usable grassland	313 330	32.64
Other	253 550	26.41

8.89 percent by salinization, 13.85 percent by frost and 8.16 percent by other factors. The area of degraded grassland – 1 052 300 ha – is increasing by two percent annually. The area of degraded arable land in the arid, semi-arid and non-humid regions is 7 744 900 ha, or 40.6 percent of all arable land. See also Tables 5.1 and 5.9.

VEGETATION

According to the system used in Vegetation of China (Wu Zhengyi, 1980), 10 vegetation type groups cover 29 vegetation types and 560 formations: (1) Coniferous forest, (2) Broad-leaf forest, (3) Shrubs and shrub-meadow, (4) Steppe and savannah, (5) Desert, (6) Tundra, (7) Alpine sparse vegetation, (8) Meadow, (9) Marsh, and (10)

Aquatic vegetation. Vegetation types in the East Monsoon Zone have a latitudinal zonal distribution; from south to north they are: tropical rain forest and monsoon forest; subtropical evergreen broad-leaf forest; warm-temperate deciduous broad-leaf forest; temperate broad-leaf and coniferous mixed forest; and subtemperate coniferous forest. Vegetation types in northern China have an obvious longitudinal distribution; from east to west they are: forest; steppe; and desert. Vegetation type distribution on the Qinghai-Tibet Plateau is characterized by both horizontal and vertical zonal features. With increasing altitude and decreasing rainfall from southeast to northwest, the vegetation types are: mountain forest; alpine shrub; alpine meadow; alpine steppe; and alpine desert. All types (forest, steppe and desert) are present. Subtropical evergreen broad-leaf forest is widely distributed through the impact of the monsoon; a complete and unique vertical distribution spectrum of alpine vegetation is found on the Qinghai-Tibet Plateau.

CLIMATE

Despite its vast territory and the effects of topography and atmosphere circulation, there are only three climatic zones: East Monsoon; Northwest Arid and Semi-arid; and the Qinghai-Tibet Alpine Zone. Regional capitals, even Lhasa, are usually in relatively clement sites. Climate is further discussed below in relation to grassland zones.

The East Monsoon Zone

It occupies 45 percent of the land; north and northwest winds are common in winter, and southeast, south and southwest winds in summer. Rainfall varies seasonally

according to wind and coincides with high solar radiation. Drought, waterlogging, wind disaster and cold snaps are frequent in the east because of the protean monsoon, typhoon and cold waves. Eastern China can be divided into three climate zones from south to north: Tropical; Subtropical and Temperate. Temperature differences are quite large in winter, but small in summer. The major vegetation in the East Monsoon area is various types of forest.

The western arid and semi-arid area

This area in inner Eurasia has a continental climate all year round. Precipitation decreases gradually from east to west, from 400 mm to less than 100 mm. Steppe and desert dominate the landscape. Vertical variation of climate in the Qinghai-Tibet Alpine area is very significant, characterized by low temperature, strong solar radiation, wind and uneven rainfall. Precipitation declines from southeast to northwest on the plain of the plateau; the natural landscape varies accordingly from forest, through alpine shrub and alpine steppe, to alpine desert.

FEATURES OF AGRICULTURAL ZONES

The most important difference in agricul-tural zonation is between east and west; water is the main determining factor. China can be divided into three natural zones: the monsoon zone in the east, which accounts for 45 percent of all land; the arid inland zone in the northwest, with 30 percent; and the Qinghai-Tibet Plateau inland zone in the southwest, accounting for 25 percent of all land. The eastern monsoon zone is agricultural; the northwest and southwest are pastoral.

The northeast
This is a vast plain with fertile land for crops and forests with plenty of water but low solar radiation. Industry and communications are developed, the population engaged in agriculture is low, and farming is comparatively large scale. It is the main production area for cereals, soybean and sugar beet. Forestry is also developed, with the largest natural wood production. There is little development of animal husbandry, which is dominated by stall feeding.

Inner Mongolia and along the Great Wall
With a temperate climate, low precipitation and scarce water, there is less arable and forest, but vast grasslands. There is frequent drought, windy weather and increasing desertification. Livestock is the main agricultural sector: crops and animal husbandry are intermixed. Animal production is traditional nomadic or semi-nomadic (herders have fixed houses in winter and early spring, but travel at other seasons) and its commercial economy is undeveloped.

Yellow River, Huai River and Hai River
The climate is temperate monsoon, with rainfall at the season of high solar radiation; water is relatively scarce. With vast plains, well-equipped agricultural machinery, good communications, a long history of cultivation and a high proportion of arable land, it is an important area for wheat, cotton, maize, groundnut and fruit. The development of animal husbandry and aquaculture is relatively good.

Loess Plateau
The topography is characterized by plateaus and hills covered by loess; soil erosion is very severe. Solar radiation is plentiful but water scarce. Agriculture is primarily rainfed grain production. The commodity economy is undeveloped, but the potential for developing grassland farming and fruit growing is high.

Middle and lower reaches of the Yangtze River
Solar radiation, temperatures and water are all favourable. Water is abundant, the arable area is large and fertile. City density is high and industry is well developed. Agriculture is highly developed, with a high total yield of a variety of agricultural products. It is the main integrated agricultural production area and the centre for rice, cotton, oil crops, tea, silk, swine and fish.

The southwest
The climate is warm and humid. The terrain is dominated by hills; flat land is scarce. Agriculture is poor, extensive and low yielding; grain production is for subsistence. It is the production centre for tobacco, rape seed, silk, tea and fruit. The dominance of commercial swine production is remarkable. There are many forest and speciality products.

South China
This part is hilly, with scarce arable land and a long coastline. Most is subtropical with plenty of precipitation; it is the only area suitable for tropical crops. The position is advantageous, and favours export-oriented industries. The rural economy is well developed. Staple agricultural products are vegetables, fish, swine and poultry. Grain production exceeds local needs. The difference in development between coastal and hill areas is very marked.

Gansu and Xinjiang

There are vast areas of low-quality land; much is natural grassland, with little forest and arable. Solar radiation and thermal resources are abundant, but water is very scarce. Desertification and salinization are very severe and the agricultural environment is very fragile. Energy and mineral resources are abundant. Communications are poor. Scattered oases are the main crop production mode. Grain and oil resources per capita are high. Cotton, sugar beet, fruit and melons yield well. Grassland husbandry is well developed. Livestock are raised in both crop and pastoral areas, but output is quite low.

Qinghai-Tibet

This zone is characterized by rarefied air, high altitude, strong solar radiation and low temperatures. Natural grassland covers the largest area, forest takes second place. Arable land is rare and patchily distributed. Water is plentiful but unevenly distributed. It is a sparsely populated, vast land in a remarkable landscape. Communications are very difficult. Agriculture, forestry and animal husbandry have features in common with all alpine areas. Livestock, crops and trees are adapted to low temperature and low oxygen concentration, and their potential for productivity is quite high. Livestock herding on natural pasture is the major agricultural sector. Grain production per capita is half of the national average. Management of agriculture and livestock is extensive and production levels low. The commodity economy is undeveloped and backward.

RUMINANT LIVESTOCK PRODUCTION SYSTEMS

Livestock production has developed rapidly since 1949. At the end of 1999,

livestock numbered 670 020 000, of which 430 198 000 (64 percent) were pigs. Grazing livestock and the pastoral industry are concentrated in six regions and provinces: Inner Mongolia Autonomous Region, Xinjiang Uigur Autonomous Region, Tibet Autonomous Region, Qinghai Province, Sichuan Province and Gansu Province. These have 70 percent of sheep, all the camels, 25 percent of cattle and goats, 44 percent of horses and 39 percent of donkeys (see Table 5.2a). Of the total livestock, 2 461 300 are kept by state-owned farms (3.67 percent of the total, including 2.54 percent of swine). Production of meat and milk (see Table 5.2b) has increased greatly. Average annual growth rates of meat and dairy output from 1980 to 1998 were 8.7 percent and 9.9 percent, respectively. National production of meat and wool took first and second places, respectively, in the world in 1999. Meat availability per capita is 47.3 kg – above average world level – but the per capita availability of milk and wool is still low. The proportion of animal product value in total agricultural production increased from 12.4 percent in 1949 to 28.5 percent in 1999. Until recently, livestock production was mostly not commercial and the supply of livestock products inadequate; now it has moved from the subsistence to the commercial economy and the proportion of animal products consumed domestically is very small.

FARM TYPE AND SIZE

China is a country of small, family farms; small farm size in agricultural areas has a marked effect on choice of forage management systems, which often makes grazed pasture impractical, so sown pastures and fodders are usually cut and

TABLE 5.2A
Livestock population changes in the pastoral provinces⁽¹⁾ of PR China (in thousand head).

Year	Cattle & buffalo	Horses	Donkeys	Mules	Camels	Swine (year end)	Goats (year end)	Sheep (year end)
1996	110 318	8 715	9 444	4 780	349	362 836	123 158	114 125
1997	121 757	8 912	9 528	4 806	350	400 348	134 801	120 956
1998	124 419	8 981	9 558	4 739	335	422 563	141 683	127 352
1999	126 983	8 914	9 348	4 673	330	430 198	148 163	131 095
Six pastoral provinces and regions (1999)	29 608	3 907	3 637	1 502	329	63 952	38 032	91 454
Proportion of pastoral provinces in total (1999)	23.32%	43.83%	38.91%	32.14%	99.70%	14.87%	25.67%	69.76%

NOTE: (1) The pastoral provinces and regions include Inner Mongolia Autonomous Region, Xinjiang Uigur Autonomous Region, Tibet Autonomous Region, Qinghai Province, Sichuan Province and Gansu Province.
SOURCE: National Bureau of Statistics, 2000.

TABLE 5.2B
Output of livestock products of China.

Year/ Region	Meat ('000 tonne)			Milk ('000 tonne)		Sheep wool (tonne)			Goat fibre (tonne)	
	Pork	Beef	Mutton	Total	Cow milk	Total	Fine	Semi-fine	Wool	Cash-mere
1996	31 580	3 557	1 810	7 358	6 294	298 102	121 020	74 099	35 255	9 585
1997	35 963	4 009	2 128	6 811	6 011	255 059	116 054	55 683	25 865	8 626
1998	38 837	4 799	2 346	7 454	6 629	277 545	115 752	68 775	31 417	9 799
1999	40 056	5 054	2 513	8 069	7 176	283 152	114 103	73 700	31 849	10 180
Pastoral⁽¹⁾ (1999)	5 476	814	959	2 228	2 084	172 336	71 694	33 629	9 914	5 971
Share⁽²⁾ (1999)	13.67%	16.11%	38.16%	27.61%	29.04%	60.86%	62.83%	45.63%	31.13%	58.65%

NOTES: (1) Production from the six pastoral provinces and regions, which are Inner Mongolia Autonomous Region, Xinjiang Uigur Autonomous Region, Tibet Autonomous Region, Qinghai Province, Sichuan Province and Gansu Province. (2) The proportion from the six pastoral provinces and regions in national total production.
SOURCE: National Bureau of Statistics, 2000.

carried. There are two types of holdings: family farms and state-owned farms. The pasture of family farms still belongs to the state and families pay according to a Long-term Grassland Use Contract with the government; the livestock belong to the family. In pastoral areas, a family farm usually has 5–6 people, 40–80 ha of pasture and 100–150 sheep units of livestock. In eastern agricultural areas, animal production at family level is small due to land scarcity. According to the sample survey of rural households, a family had

only 1.48 swine, 0.47 sheep and 0.05 cattle on average in 1999, and the output of beef, milk and wool were 0.40 kg, 12.74 kg and 0.73 kg, respectively. Some family farms specialize in livestock (pigs, sheep or cattle) and their scale is much larger than common family farms. Some sell more than 100 fat beef cattle annually.

State farms are mainly for breeding. Those in crop growing areas, for swine and poultry, are usually small; those in pastoral areas are normally larger, with 30 000–50 000 ha and 20 000–30 000 head of stock (in sheep units). The largest state-owned farm covers 150 000 ha. These farms are mainly for breeding sheep and cattle, with a very few for horses and goats. The state ranches of ancient China were to supply war horses. In the late 1970s, most military ranches switched to sheep, cattle or mixed farming.

LIVESTOCK SPECIES AND BREEDS

Livestock in China can be classified into four lineages, according to origin and distribution:

- Mongolian (horse, cattle, sheep and goat) in the north;
- Kazakh (horse, cattle, sheep and goat) in the west;
- Tibetan in the western Qinghai-Tibet Plateau; and
- Central Plains in the central and southeast.

China has a great range of livestock breeds, famous for their prolificity, flavour and adaptation to extensive management, cold tolerance, load carrying and suitability for specific regions. There are excellent special breeds in each typical grassland type. Breeds have been described by species (Editorial Board of Cattle Breeds of China, 1988; Editorial Board of Sheep Breeds of China, 1989).

Cattle

Bos taurus and Bos indicus, called Huang Niu (Yellow Cattle) in Chinese, are found everywhere below 2 000 m. There are 55 recognized breeds. Based on their adaptation to ecological conditions, cattle fall into three ecogeographical groups: Northern Cattle, Central Plains Cattle and South China Cattle. Cattle breeds have been described by Chen Youchun (1990).

The representative breed of Northern Cattle is the Mongolian, adapted to grazing in the Temperate Zone Steppe and Temperate Zone Meadow. Excellent breeds are Wuzhumuqin Cattle, Kazakh Cattle and Sanhe Cattle, all dual-purpose breeds.

Central Plains Cattle are found in the flat agricultural tracts of the Temperate Zone Deciduous Broad-leaf Forest and are mainly stall fed, with some grazing. There are many excellent breeds, such as the Qinchuan, Nanyang, Luxi and Bohai Black. These are famous draught animals, and their raising depended, historically, on lucerne cultivation.

South China Cattle are in the hilly tropical and subtropical zones, and include Hainan Cattle, Guangxi Cattle and Yunnan Cattle.

Yak (*Bos grunniens*)

This, the "ship of the plateau", is typical of the Qinghai-Tibet Plateau, at 3 000–5 000 m. There are 15 million yaks in China (in Qinghai, Tibet, Sichuan, Gansu, Xinjiang and Yunnan), around 90 percent of the world total. They were domesticated from Bos grunniens mutus, which is still found in remote mountains of Tibet (Zhang, 1989). Yak are raised for draught and meat; milk, hide and hair are also important products. As "green food" (from less polluted plateaus), yak meat is very popular in cities. Nomadic herding is the main management system and yak have probably been kept on the Qinghai-Tibetan Plateau for 4 000 years. Herders drive their yak from low (cold season pasture) to high mountains (warm season pasture). Chinese yaks can be classified into two groups: Valley and Plateau.

Valley Yaks are mainly found in the alpine region of the Hengduan Mountain range of the southeastern Qinghai-Tibet Plateau, including the eastern part of Tibet, the southern part of Qinghai, the southwestern part of Sichuan and northeastern Yunnan. The altitude is 4 000–5 000 m. Annual precipitation is more than 600 mm; the climate is frigid and subhumid. Grassland in this region is mainly alpine shrub meadow and the growing period is about 150–180 days. Yak of this type are big, hardy, have high meat productivity and high yield of hair and undercoat. Both sexes have wide and rough horns. Yak × cattle hybrids (see Plate 23) are common at the altitudinal interface between the two species.

Plateau Yaks are mainly found in the centre of the Qinghai-Tibet Plateau, which covers most of Qinghai, Tibet and parts of Sichuan and Gansu. Their habitat is mountainous and difficult of access. There are many marshes, semi-marshes and hilly grasslands with broad valleys, open topography and gentle slopes. Plateau yaks

have therefore a wide range of geographical types, with various hair coats, a high proportion of polled animals, and different horn shapes. Generally, plateau yaks are good milkers, with high fat content milk.

Buffalo (*Bubalus bubalis*)
These are of the swamp type, and are kept in humid tropical and subtropical areas. They are stall fed and mainly kept for draught and meat, although milk and hide are also important.

Sheep (*Ovis aries*)
These are the main grazing stock in China, and are kept in temperate areas between 30°–50° N and 75°–135° E.

Kazakh is an ancient coarse-wool breed in the desert areas of Xinjiang. It was used as the female parent of Xinjiang Fine-Wool sheep, which is a very adaptable breed and has been successfully introduced to many

Plate 23.
Yak × cattle hybrids. These are common, and productive at the altitudinal interface between the two species. Gansu, China.

places. Tibetan sheep are suited to extreme alpine climates, but cannot adapt to warm areas. Gansu Alpine Fine-Wool sheep and Qinghai Fine-Wool sheep are excellent breeds with Tibet sheep as the female parent. Tan sheep, famous for their pelt with long curled hair, are raised in desert and semi-desert areas.

Central Plains sheep are kept in warm temperate and subtropical areas under semi-stall feeding. Hu sheep, the southernmost sheep breed, can live under subtropical humid conditions. Xiaoweihanyang sheep and Hu sheep are very prolific: each lambing can give 2–6 young (so artificial feeding is always needed). Daweihanyang sheep have very fat tails.

Goats (*Capra hircus*)

These are the most widely distributed livestock in China, since they can adapt to many climates and pastures. There are 35 recognized breeds. One special breed is the Zhongwei goat, with fur like that of the famous Tan sheep. The Tibetan Turi goat is famous for its cashmere. Since 1999, government has advised farmers to switch goats from grazing to stall feeding to assist grassland rehabilitation.

Horse (*Equus caballus*)

Horses are the traditional draught animals below 4 000 m. There are four major ecogeographical groups (North Grassland horse, Xinjiang Mountain Grassland horse, Qinghai-Tibet Plateau horse and Southwest Mountain horse), with 70 breeds. In pastoral areas, horses are used for riding and grazed on natural grassland. Herders in Inner Mongolia and Xinjiang also drink mare milk.

In agricultural areas, horses are pack and draught animals, mainly for ploughing, and kept in stables or even the farmers' yard. Normally, Chinese do not eat horsemeat. Special breeds include Haomeng horse (natural pacer), Chinese Mini Debao pony, Erlunchun Forest horse, and anoxia-tolerant Tibetan horse and Yunnan horse (adapted to stony mountain terrain).

Camel (*Camelus bactrianus*)

Camels are important in temperate deserts. There are some single-humped (dromedary) camels in south Xinjiang but the great majority are two-humped Bactrian camels. There are three breeds: Xinjiang, Alashan and Sunite. The Sunite lives in the steppe and is the largest since forage is better. Camels, which are kept as pack animals and for wool, are raised on natural pasture, with winter supplementation.

Swine (*Sus scrofa domestica*)

China has some 60 recognized swine breeds. Most are stall fed. The Tibetan pig is a grazing breed, grazing on natural grassland as a mixed drift of 60 to 80 head (mixed adult and young, male and female). The Tibetan pig grows slowly because of poor forage; its adult liveweight is around 35 kg. However, its meat is very lean and is excellent for preserved pork and roast suckling pig. Xinjiang Yili White pig is another grazing breed, but its numbers are few; they graze along rivers or in woodland, but are housed in winter.

FEEDING SYSTEMS
Extensive grazing system

Feeding systems in the north differ from those in the west. Inner Mongolian grasslands are flat and the environment is simple; pastures can be grazed at any season if water is available; and animals are moved rotationally following a certain range and routine. In desert areas of Xinjiang there are two seasonal grazing belts: basins and mountains. Animals graze in the basins in winter, move in transhumance to mountains in spring, and to high mountains in summer, returning to basins in late autumn. This is a strict seasonal grazing system and animals spend 1–2 months travelling from winter to summer pasture. On the Qinghai-Tibet Plateau, animals graze above 3 000 m, but pastures are still divided into seasonal pasture belts: low cold-season and high warm-season. Summer pasture can only be used for 1–2 months. Recently, the system has been changing to one where animals receive supplementation in winter.

Tethering
Animals are tethered so the grass can be completely used, but it is used primarily for saddle horses, high yielding milk cows in pastoral areas and for small pieces of pasture in agricultural areas.

Uncontrolled grazing
This is not planned and animals are herded from place to place over a large area. This system existed when the grazing rights were not defined and the grassland was sufficient. Once the Long-term Grassland Use Contract System was completed, this system has been gradually replaced by rotational grazing and only exists in remote summer pastures or open pasture. However, some researchers consider that if nomads still follow this system it is proof of its rationality and the efficacy of many aspects of traditional pastoral practices as means to convert forage from cold, arid rangelands into animal products in an environment where crop growing is not possible. The survival of pastoral nomads indicates that many strategies of animal

husbandry and grassland management developed centuries ago are well adapted to the spectrum of environment conditions (Miller and Craig, 1997).

INTEGRATION OF LIVESTOCK INTO FARMING SYSTEMS
In the past two decades, ruminant livestock husbandry has been successfully integrated into farming systems. The rationale of the approach is that since holdings are small, grazed sown pasture is not practicable, so stall feeding with cut-and-carry is usual for ruminants, using crop residues, wild herbage and cultivated fodder.

Since 1983, the government has encouraged farmers to grow fodder and raise livestock. Agricultural experts and extension services applied a "three components growing" model (cereals, cash crops and forages in rotation). Both farming structure and production efficiency improved under this model. Practices vary according to region.

In pastoral areas, farmers are encouraged and assisted to establish some artificial grassland for hay.

In northern warm-temperate agricultural areas, farmers are encouraged to use some, or even all, arable land to grow high quality forages such as lucerne, or to grow Vicia sativa for high quality hay after the wheat harvest and use it to raise swine and poultry.

In southern subtropical paddy areas, farmers use the fallow paddy field to grow Lolium multiflorum for swine, dairy cows and rabbits: a rotation of rice and ryegrass. Annual ryegrass is sown in November and cut every 10 days from December to March (8–10 times). The fresh yield is 60–70 tonne/ha, and its crude protein content is 20–26 percent. This farming system has been extended to more than 2 million hectares in southern subtropical paddy areas.

Beef production with maize stover

In the Central Plains (including Henan, Hebei, Shandong and Anhui Provinces), maize stover was used as fuel or thrown away. Since the mid-1980s, silage technology has been the subject of an extension campaign. With the help of the Livestock Technical Extension Service, farmers can easily get beef cattle through artificial insemination with imported frozen semen, and now fatten them with maize silage supplemented with some concentrates. This is a high profile initiative. The central government, starting in 1992, established demonstration counties at national level for cattle fattening using maize stover; as well as counties for raising sheep with ammoniated straw. There are now many large-scale beef cattle farms in this area and the Central Plains has become the main beef production area, supplying around half of national beef needs. This activity is expanding rapidly as cereals are relatively abundant and the demand for beef is rising.

Sheep production with ammoniated straw

In northern agricultural areas, wheat straw was fed untreated to draught animals. More and more farmers use machines and huge amounts of straw were not utilized. In the last decade, ammoniated straw technology was extended to increase the nitrogen content in straw, and improve palatability and feeding value. Animal production in this area has greatly improved. The central government started, from 1995, to establish demonstration counties. It strongly promotes roughage utilization and animal production. Rations are based on ammoniated wheat straw, supplemented with concentrates.

SOCIO-ECONOMIC CONDITIONS
Legislation

Since the Open Door and Reform Policy of 1979, legislation development in the animal husbandry sector has made great progress. It started with the By-law on Livestock and Poultry Epidemic Prevention in 1985, and since then 13 laws relating to grassland and animal production have been promulgated, including Law on Grassland, Law on Animal Epidemic Prevention, By-law on Animal Remedy Management, By-law on Breeding Animal and Poultry, Law on Quarantine Inspection of Imported and Exported Plants and Animals and By-law on Fodder and Fodder Additive Management. Over 100 detailed rules and regulations have been made and local governments have made local regulations accordingly. Usually, the local Grassland Station or Animal Production Station is responsible for seeing that regulations are observed.

Extension and veterinary services

China has a complete animal husbandry technical extension service network (including grassland technical services) at four levels: National, Provincial, Prefectural and County. There are more than 50 000 service points in the country, with more than 400 000 staff. Additionally, around 500 000 village extension workers are involved. Some workers at grassroots level were lost around 1990 when funds were reduced. In 1998, the 46 249 Animal Husbandry and Veterinary Medicine

Stations (or Grassland Stations) at township level were declared government-sponsored institutions, and of them, 30 989 stations are totally sponsored, employing 67 percent of the total 295 407 staff.

Market constraints

Animal products had a sellers market before the 1990s and supply was insufficient. Thereafter, animal production was dramatically promoted and farmers now have to face furious competition in a buyers market. To make market mechanisms more active, and favour animal production, government strengthened information exchange between producers and consumers. Government also established a Milk Plan for Students and Breakfast Revolution to increase milk consumption. To improve fine-wool production, a Society of Fine-Wool Producers has been set-up in Xinjiang Uigur Autonomous Region. Meanwhile, shows, sales and auctions of breeding sheep and wool have been held in Inner Mongolia Autonomous Region. These two regions produce most of the sheep wool in China.

PASTURE AND FORAGE RESOURCES

In China, grassland is defined as "land mainly covered by herbaceous vegetation, or with sparse shrubs or trees concurrently present in the community". It can provide food for livestock and wildlife; it also provides a pleasant environment, organic products and other functions for humans. Land sown to forages is defined as artificial grassland.

Area and distribution of grassland

China takes third place after Australia and Russia in grassland area, with a total area of 392 832 633 ha in 1994. This was 11.82 percent of the world's grassland. The usable grassland is about 330 995 000 ha, or 35 percent of the national mainland area. Most grassland is in the northern arid and cold zones. The six major pastoral provinces for grassland and livestock – Tibet, Inner Mongolia, Xinjiang, Qinghai, Sichuan and Gansu – account for 75 percent of national grassland and around 70 percent of grazing livestock.

GRASSLAND CLASSIFICATION

Because of its huge territory, complex terrain, diverse climate and long history of grassland use, China has many grassland types; this has led to in-depth research on their classification. Currently, there are two systems of grassland classification, with more than 40 years of research behind them.

The Vegetation-habitat Classification System

This was created by Professors Liao Guofan, Su Daxue, Xu Peng, Liu Qi and Zhang Zutong, and is a compendious and non-numerical system based on the subjective judgement of the surveyor. It was used for the national survey of grassland resources from 1980 to 1990 (Animal Husbandry and Veterinary Medicine Division, 1994, 1996). Most of the data cited in this document are from that investigation. The system has four grades:

- First grade: Class. Grassland is classified into nine Classes based on thermal parameters and the vegetation features (see Table 5.3).
- Second grade: Subclass. This is the further division of Class, based on features of climate or vegetation. Some Classes, such as marshes, are not further divided (see Table 5.3).

TABLE 5.3
Areas of different grassland classes.

Grassland Class and Subclass	Total Grassland Area		Usable Grassland Area		Rank[1]
	Area (ha)	percent	Area (ha)	percent	
Temperate Steppe Class	74 537 509	18.98	66 247 465	20.01	1
Temperate Meadow-Steppe	14 519 331	3.7	12 827 411		[8]
Temperate Typical Steppe	41 096 571	10.46	36 367 633		[1]
Temperate Desert-Steppe	18 921 607	4.82	1 705 421		[5]
Temperate Desert Class	55 734 229	14.19	39 745 057	12.00	4
Temperate Typical Desert	45 060 811	11.47	30 604 131		[3]
Temperate Desert Steppe	10 673 418	2.72	9 140 926		[11]
Warm Shrubby Tussock Class	18 273 058	4.65	15 627 185	4.72	7
Warm Tussock	6 657 148	1.69	5 853 667		[14]
Warm Typical Tussock	11 615 910	2.96	9 773 518		[10]
Tropical Shrubby Tussock Class	32 651 615	8.31	25 506 997	7.71	6
Tropical Tussock	14 237 196	3.62	1 141 999		[9]
Tropical Typical Shrub Tussock	17 551 276	4.47	13 447 569		[7]
Tropical Savannah	863 144	0.22	639 429		[15]
Temperate Meadow Class	41 900 414	10.68	35 942 515	10.87	5
Lowland Meadow	25 219 621	6.42	21 038 409		[4]
Mountain Meadow	16 718 926	4.26	14 923 439		[6]
Alpine Meadow Class	63 720 549	16.22	58 834 182	17.75	2
Alpine Steppe Class	58 054 911	14.77	149 202 826	14.87	3
Alpine Meadow-steppe	6 865 734	1.75	6 011 528		[13]
Alpine Typical Steppe	41 623 171	10.59	35 439 220		[2]
Alpine Desert Steppe	9 566 006	2.43	7 752 078		[12]
Alpine Desert Class	7 527 763	1.92	5 592 765	1.69	8
Marsh Class	2 873 812	0.73	2 253 714	0.68	9
Total	392 832 633	100.00	330 995 458	100.00	

Note: (1) Numbers in [brackets] denote rank of subclass.

- Third grade: Group. This level divides the economic groups of grasses based on the grassland Type. For example, Tall Herbaceous Group, Medium Herbaceous Group, Short Herbaceous Group.
- Fourth grade: Type. This is the basic unit and divided according to the features of the dominant species in community and habitat. Types are named according to the dominant species. Grasslands in China are divided into 276 Types.

The Comprehensive and Sequential Classification System

This was developed by Professors Ren Jizhou, Hu Zizhi, Zhang Degang, Long Ruijun and Dr Gao Caixia (Ren, 1985; Ren, Hu and Zhang, 1999). It can be used for grassland classification worldwide within a unified system, and its features are:

- the basic unit, Class, is divided on the basis of humidity grade and thermal grade. This method enables quantitative classification and computer retrieval; and
- the Classification index chart can visually indicate the different classes, sort order of classes, the grassland development relation and zonal features among classes.

There are four levels in this system:

- First level: Class Group. After the Class is determined, the Classes can be

TABLE 5.4
The Thermal levels and the corresponding thermal zones.

Thermal Level	Accumulated temperature>0°C	Thermal Zone
Frigid	<1 300°C	(Alpine) Frigid Zone
Cold Temperate	1 300 to 2 300°C	Cold Temperate Zone
Cool Temperate	2 300 to 3 700°C	Cool Temperate Zone
Warm Temperate	3 700 to 5 300°C	Warm Temperate Zone
Warm	5 300 to 6 200°C	North Subtropics
Subtropical	6 200 to 8 000°C	South Subtropics
Tropical	>8 000°C	Tropics

TABLE 5.5
The Precipitation categories and their associated natural landscapes.

Humidity category	K Value[1]	Typical natural landscape
Hyper-arid	<0.3	Desert
Arid	0.3 to 0.9	Semi-desert (Desert steppe, Steppe desert)
Semi-arid	0.9 to 1.2	Typical Steppe, Xerophytic Forest, Savannah
Subhumid	1.2 to 1.5	Forest, Forest Steppe, Meadow Steppe, Savannah, Meadow
Humid	1.5 to 2.0	Forest, Tundra, Meadow
Per-humid	>2.0	Forest, Tundra, Meadow

NOTE: (1) $K = r/(0.1\sum\theta)$, where K is humidity, r is annual rainfall (mm), and $\sum\theta$ is >0°C annual accumulative temperature (°C).

merged into Class Groups according to cumulative temperature or humidity.

- Second level: Class, divided in terms of thermal and moisture conditions. Thermal category is determined with >0°C accumulative temperature (see Table 5.4). Humidity category is determined with humidity (Table 5.5). Classes are named consecutively on the basis of thermal category, humidity category, and representative zonal climax vegetation.
- Third level: Subclass, divided according to land condition, including soil and terrain. Soil type is used in flat areas and terrain type in hilly areas. Subclass is named on the basis of the soil or terrain.
- Fourth level: Type, divided and named after the dominant species in the plant community.

Grassland types
According to the Vegetation-habitat Classification System, grassland in China can be divided into nine classes and 268 types. The names of classes and subclasses and their areas were shown in Table 5.3. There are 69 types in the Temperate Steppe Class, 39 types in the Temperate Desert Class, 25 types in the Warm Shrubby Tussock Class, 39 types in the Tropical Shrubby Tussock Class, 51 types in the Temperate Meadow Class, 24 types in the Alpine Meadow Class, 17 types in the Alpine Steppe Class, 4 types in the Alpine Desert Class and 8 types in the Marshes Class.

Index of grass yield
Herbage yield varies greatly among different classes. The dry grass yield is 911 kg/ha on average, with the highest at 2 544 kg/ha, from the Tropical Shrubby Tussock Class, and the lowest at 117 kg/ha, from the Alpine Desert Class (see Table 5.6). Carrying capacity is shown in Table 5.7.

Grassland protection
Many factors can ruin grassland. Apart

TABLE 5.6
Dry Herbage yield of different grassland classes in China.

Grassland Class	Yield (kg/ha)	Rank	Total yield (kg)	Percentage of total
Temperate Steppe	888.9	5	$5\ 888 \times 10^7$	19.55
Alpine Steppe	272.5	8	$1\ 006 \times 10^7$	4.45
Temperate Desert	360.3	7	$1\ 432 \times 10^7$	4.75
Alpine Desert	117.0	9	65×10^7	0.22
Warm Shrubby Tussock	1 740	3	$2\ 718 \times 10^7$	9.02
Tropical Shrubby Tussock	2 544	1	$6\ 490 \times 10^7$	21.56
Temperate Meadow	1 697	4	$6\ 090 \times 10^7$	20.26
Alpine Meadow	882	6	$5\ 189 \times 10^7$	17.24
Marshes	2 183	2	492×10^7	1.63
National Average	911		$3\ 009 \times 10^7$	100.00

TABLE 5.7
Carrying capacity of different grassland classes.

Grassland class	Carrying capacity (ha/ sheep unit/year)	Theoretical carrying capacity (million sheep unit)	Percentage of total	Rank
Temperate Steppe	1.42	46.734	14.6	4
Alpine Steppe	3.73	13.259	4.1	6
Temperate Desert	3.67	10.016	3.3	7
Alpine Desert	9.27	0.603	0.3	9
Warm Shrubby Tussock	0.45	34.682	10.8	5
Tropical Shrubby Tussock	0.33	77.401	24.2	1
Temperate Meadow	0.51	70.350	22.0	2
Alpine Meadow	0.98	60.132	18.8	3
Marsh Class	0.39	5.730	1.8	8
Total	0.93	318.907[1]	100.0	

NOTE: (1) 13 million sheep units on fragmented grassland are not included.

from overgrazing, these include rodents, pests, diseases, toxic plants, harmful plants and fire. Of these, rodents and pests are most important. The area of grassland destroyed by rodents ranges from 1.7 to 2 million hectares, and pests damage 6.5–7 million hectares annually. Disease management systems for China are discussed by Nan (2000).

Grassland nature reserves

The establishment of grassland nature reserves began in the 1980s, and eleven have been set up, with a total area of 2 068 968 ha. The Xilingol Steppe Nature Reserve in Inner Mongolia is one of the internationally recognized sites designated as an International Biosphere Reserve. However, the number of grassland reserves is very low compared to the 85 forest reserves. The government plans to create another 17 grassland reserves, of which five are under way.

DOMINANT PLANTS OF THE MAIN GRASSLAND ZONES

Many plants play an important role in forming a grassland community in terms of coverage and herbage yield over large grassland areas and with various grassland types. The most important species in different grassland classes are listed below.

Dominant plants of the Temperate Steppe

Leymus chinensis, Stipa baicalensis, S. grandis, S. krylovi, S. bungeana, S. breviflora, S. glareosa, S. klemenzii, S. capillata, Festuca ovina, Cleistogenes squarrosa, Filifolium sibiricum, Artemisia frigida, A. halodendron, A. ordosica, A. intramongolica, Thymus serpyllum var. *mongolium* and *Ajania fruticulosa.*

Dominant plants of the Alpine Steppe

These are cold resistant, mainly from the Gramineae and Compositeae. The most important are *Stipa purpureum, S. subsessiflora, Festuca ovina* subsp. *sphagnicola, Orinus thoroldii, Carex moorcroftii, Artemisia stracheyi* and *A. wellbyi.*

Dominant plants of the Temperate Desert

These are super-xerocole shrubs and sub-shrubs. The most important are *Seriphidium terrae-albae, S. borotalense, Artemisia soongarica, Salsola passerina, S. laricifolia, Sympegma regelii, Anabasis salsa, Reaumuria soongarica, Ceratoides latens, Kalidium schrenkianum, Potaninia mongolica, Nitraria sphaerocarpa, Ephedra przewalskii, Haloxylon erinaceum* and *Haloxylon persicum.*

Dominant plants of the Alpine Desert

The ecological environment of this class is the harshest. The dominant plants have outstanding ability to resist cold and drought. The most important are Rhodiola algida var. tangutica, Seriphidium rhodanthum and Ceratoides compacta.

Dominant plants of the Warm Shrubby Tussock

These are mainly grasses of medium height and some forbs. The most important are Bothriochloa ischaemum, Themeda triandra var. japonica, Pennisetum centrasiaticum, Spodiopogon sibiricus, Imperata cylindrica var. major and Potentilla fulgens.

Dominant plants of the Tropical Shrubby Tussock

Almost all in this class are hot-season grasses. The most important are Miscanthus floridulus, M. sinensis, Imperata cylindrica var. major, Heteropogon contortus, Arundinella setosa, A. hirta, Eremopogon delavayi, Eragrostis pilosa, Eulalia phaeothrix, E. quadrinervis and Dicranopteris dichotoma.

Dominant plants of the Temperate Meadow

These are mainly perennial temperate and medium-humid mesophytic grasses. Some are halophytes or forbs. The most important are Achnatherum splendens, Arundinella hirta, Agrostis gigantea, Calamagrostis epigeios, Bromus inermis, Deyeuxia angustifolia, Deyeuxia arundinacea, Poa pratensis, P. angustifolia, Miscanthus sacchariflorus, Phragmites communis, Brachypodium sylvaticum, Festuca ovina, Carex duriuscula, Potentilla anserina, Sanguisorba officinalis, Iris lactea var. chinensis, Suaeda spp. and Sophora alopecuroides.

Dominant plants of the Alpine Meadow

These are mainly cold-resistant perennials. Most are Kobresia spp. and forbs. The most important are Kobresia pygmaea, K. humilis, K. capillifolia, K. bellardii, K. littledalei, K. tibetica, Carex atrofusca, C. nivalis, C. stenocarpa, Blysmus sinocompressus, Poa alpina, Polygonum viviparum and P. macrophyllum.

TABLE 5.8
Grassland types by use.

Grassland Type	Area (million ha)	Proportion (percent)
Grazing pasture, of which	264.2	75.3
Warm season pasture	117.5	33.5
Cold season pasture	64.1	18.3
Year-round pasture	82.6	23.5
Grazing and hay dual purpose pasture	67.3	19.2
Grassland difficult to use	19.6	5.6
Total usable grassland	351.1	100.0

NOTE: Figures are not exact due to rounding.

TABLE 5.9
Overgrazing and grassland deterioration in major pastoral regions (percentage).

Region	1990		1999	
	Overgrazing rate	Deteriorated grassland	Overgrazing rate	Deteriorated grassland
Tibet	-	14	30	15
Inner Mongolia	-	40	32	60
Xinjiang	-	-	60–70	65
Qinghai	-	17	31	39
Sichuan	-	24	13	28
Gansu	-	40	35	50
Heilongjiang	-	30	124	65

Dominant plants of Marshes

These are mainly Cyperaceae and Gramineae. The most important are Carex meyeriana, C. muliensis, C. appendiculata, C. stenophylla, Scirpus yagara, S. triqueter, Phragmites communis and Triglochin palustre.

OPPORTUNITIES FOR PASTURE IMPROVEMENT
Grassland use

Most grassland in China is in the arid, semi-arid or alpine areas, where the climate is harsh, communications poor and the economy backward. Grassland within agricultural and agropastoral areas is scattered in remote places, and its use is extensive, mainly uncontrolled, grazing. Utilization methods are based on natural geographic conditions and grassland productivity. Natural grassland can be divided into three types according to their use (see Table 5.8).

Grassland deterioration and control strategies

Grassland deterioration – a worldwide problem – is severe in China. According to data published in 1994, the area of degraded grassland was 68 million hectares at the end of the 1980s – over a quarter of the usable grassland. It has increased significantly in the past decade. Now 90 percent of grassland shows signs of deterioration, of which moderately degraded grassland is 130 million hectares (32.5 percent of the total), and it is accelerating by 20 million hectares annually (Liu, 2001). Grassland deterioration in major pastoral regions is shown in Table 5.9.

Symptoms of grassland deterioration are drifting sand, salinization, patch-like distribution and hammada. Its major causes are severe overstocking, long-term uncontrolled grazing, improper land reclamation and abandonment, climate change, and collecting fuelwood and traditional medicinal herbs. It not only results in decline of productivity, but also in environmental damage, water and soil erosion, sand and dust storms, and desertification. The government is paying great attention to this. As one of its most important targets, ecological environment rebuilding has been covered in the West Development Plan of 2000. In agricultural and agropastoral areas, this target will be achieved through returning arable land on slopes of >25° to forest and grassland, and reducing the number of grazing livestock. Severely degraded pasture will be closed for recovery. Stock numbers at pasture will be reduced by yard feeding so that the vegetation and environment can recover rapidly.

Grassland improvement

According to the Planning Programme for National Ecological Environment Construction and the Outline of the Fifteenth Ten-Year Plan, the following should be achieved by 2010:

- increase artificial grassland and improved grassland by 50 million hectares;
- improve 33 million hectares of degraded grassland and 20 million hectares of desertified land;
- control 600 000 ha of water- and soil-eroded land; and
- return 6.7 million hectares of crop land (on slopes >25°) to forest and grass.

These objectives show the resolve to improve degraded grassland and the environment. There are temporary and permanent solutions for grassland improvement: the latter is to establish artificial grassland.

Closure

This is to protect grassland, or strictly control grazing pressure, through fencing, so that the land has a chance to recover. Herbage yield increases rapidly in the humid and subhumid areas, but the effect declines with time; closure should not exceed three years. In western China, where the grassland is severely degraded, a large area has been closed since 2000 and many animals culled or stall fed.

Reseeding

Reseeding involves oversowing degraded grassland to improve sward composition and productivity. Manual methods are used on small areas, but aerial seeding should be used on large areas. The cost–benefit ratio is 1:2–4, and investment can be recouped in two years. The following require attention during aerial seeding operations:

- the area should exceed 350–650 ha, of which the target area should be more than 80 percent;
- seed should be pre-treated by coating and de-awning, with scarification as appropriate and with legumes inoculated;
- the land should be smoothed with a heavy harrow, with burning and weeding, prior to seeding; and
- after aerial seeding, treading by livestock can improve the establishment rate.

Surface tillage

Shallow tillage (with a cultivator) has a positive effect on yield in pasture dominated by rhizomatous grasses such as *Leymus chinensis* and *Phragmites communis*, and those that form a dense sod (dominated by *Kobresia* spp.). Shallow tillage improves air and water permeability of the soil and by cutting rhizomes enhances vegetative propagation. The yields of grasslands dominated by Leymus chinensis, Kobresia spp. and Agropyron cristatum could be increased by 50 to 200 percent. Seed yields of Leymus chinensis and Agropyron cristatum can be increased by 180 percent to 1 500 percent.

Burning

Burning is an old, practical method of grassland improvement, but is no longer used in northern China because the grassland is so severely degraded. It is, however, still widely used in the shrub grassland and swamp grassland in southern China.

Forage grasses and artificial grassland

Artificial grassland combines pastoralism with agronomy. China was one of the earliest countries to grow Medicago sativa, since at least 126 BC along the Yellow River, where it was rotated with wheat. Apart from improving crop yields and soil fertility, this system contributed to forming livestock breeds such as Qingchuan cattle, Jinnan cattle, Zaosheng cattle, Nanyang cattle, Guanzhong donkey and Zaosheng donkey (donkeys are less important now because of mechanized cultivation and transport). The regional distribution of cultivated forage is described by Hong Fuzeng (1989), and Chen Baoshu (2001) describes fodder cultivation.

The area of artificial grassland is small. In 1995 it was 13.8 million hectares (3.4 percent of all grassland). It increased to 15.48 million hectares in 1997 (3.8 percent) and 20 million hectares in 2000 (4.8 percent). Aerial seeding has been important for establishment; it began in 1979, and the area aerially seeded was almost 2.5 million hectares; by the end of 1998, the established

area was almost 1.5 million hectares. The artificial grassland area in Inner Mongolia, Gansu, Xinjiang, Shaanxi and Sichuan is large: over 2.5 million hectares in Inner Mongolia and close to 1 million hectares in Gansu. Priority is given to lucerne in all provinces except Sichuan. The lucerne area in Gansu is close to 400 000 ha, which is 34 percent of the national total.

There are over 100 species of cultivated forage in China, mostly legumes and grasses, and over 30 are sown on more than 10 000 ha (excluding mixed sowing – see Table 5.10).

Forage cereals

Avena sativa (oats) is the most important fodder in the north and alpine areas, generally sown pure; the area has increased rapidly in recent years because it is easy to grow and harvest. Its seeds do not ripen on the Qinghai-Tibet Plateau.

Hordeum vulgare (barley) has a cultivated area just less than forage maize. It is sown countrywide, both in the north (spring barley) and south (winter barley). Naked barley is the Tibetan staple food.

Secale cereale (rye), introduced from Russia in the 1940s, is widely cultivated in northern and alpine areas.

Setaria italica (foxtail millet), an annual, is indigenous to China and has been grown for more than 6 000 years. It is widely sown in the north as a cereal. The nutritive value, palatability and digestibility of its straw are higher than those of wheat and rice. It can be made into high quality hay (retaining the grain) by dense planting.

Sorghum bicolor has been cultivated in China for 4 000 years, but its area is much less than Sorghum sudanense, which has been increasing in recent years.

Zea mays (maize) is the most important

TABLE 5.10
Major forages and sown area (thousand hectares; 1998).

Forage	Area	Life form
Medicago sativa	1804.7	Perennial
Astragalus sinicus	1686.9	Perennial
Caragana koshinskii	1108.7	Shrub
Astragalus huangheensis	653.2	Perennial
Zea mays (forage)	570.5	Annual
Leymus chinensis	403.7	Perennial
Hordeum vulgare	358.7	Annual
Elymus sibiricus	230.3	Perennial
Lolium multiflorum	183.2	Annual
Avena sativa	155.7	Annual
Elymus dahuricus, E. excelsus	138.6	Perennial
Vicia villosa	123.9	Biennial
Avena nuda	118.7	Annual
Vicia sativa	98.9	Annual
Setaria italica (forage)	80.0	Annual
Sorghum sudanense	77.2	Annual
Onobrychis viciifolia	65.2	Perennial
Trifolium repens	31.7	Perennial
Artemisia sphaerocephala	55.3	Sub-shrub
Oxytropis coerulea	28.7	Perennial
Trifolium pratense	28.2	Perennial
Stylosanthes guianensis	26.9	Perennial
Bromus inermis	22.5	Perennial
Melilotus alba, M. officinalis	20.7	Biennial
Secale cereale	20.1	Biennial
Lolium perenne	17.6	Perennial
Raphanus sativus	17.0	Biennial
Agropyron cristatum	14.4	Perennial
Dactylis glomerata	13.7	Perennial
Amaranthus paniculatus	10.5	Annual

forage, sown countrywide in a long, narrow belt from northeast to southwest. It was used as human food before 1980, but is now mostly used for livestock.

Grain legumes as forage

Cicer arietinum (chickpea) is a dual-purpose crop. Introduced from Russia in the 1950s, it is cultivated in both the north and the south. Its grain is a very nutritious concentrate.

Glycine max (soybean) is indigenous to northeastern China, and the forage variety is a primitive form. Both green chop and grain are good feed, with high protein content.

Pisum sativum (white flowered pea) and Pisum arvense (purple flowered) have been cultivated for 2 000 years in China and are sown countrywide for their cold tolerance and they are better than Vicia sativa in admixture with oats.

Vicia faba (broad bean) is a dual-purpose crop and has been cultivated for 2 100 years in China, where its cultivated area is the greatest in the world. A forage cultivar introduced in 1960, it is cold resistant, with high yield and high quality.

Root tuber, stem tuber and melon forages

Beta vulgaris is widely grown in the north for sugar (main purpose) and fodder.

Brassica rapa, a biennial, is an old crop. It was mainly grown on the Qinghai-Tibet Plateau in early times and now has been extended to the whole country as succulent fodder.

Cucurbita moschata gives high yields and high quality, succulent fodder. The levels of carotene, vitamin A, B and C in flesh and fruit are 100 times higher than in cereals.

Daucus carota is grown countrywide as a succulent fodder.

Helianthus tuberosus has leaves, stem and tuber that can be used for livestock feed.

Other cultivated forages

Amaranthus paniculatus, an annual herb, is a high quality fodder for swine, poultry and cattle, and is of ancient cultivation in China, where the area is the largest in the world.

Calligonum mongolicum, a super-xerocole shrub, is a plant for sand fixation and for gravel deserts, with tolerance to drought and cold. It is used for aerial seeding.

Ceratoides latens, a shrub important in the temperate zone and alpine desert, with tolerance to drought and cold, is adapted to sandy and rocky soils.

Kochia prostrata, a creeping sub-shrub, is good forage in desert and semi-desert, tolerating drought, salt and poor soil. It is suitable for establishing rainfed grassland.

Lactuca indica, a biennial herb indigenous to China, is grown countrywide for swine and poultry.

Silphium perfoliatum, a perennial herb in the Compositeae, was introduced in the 1980s and is cultivated nationwide as fodder for cattle, swine and rabbits.

Symphytum peregrinum, a perennial herb introduced in the 1970s is widely cultivated between the Great Wall and Yangtze River for swine and cattle.

Aquatic forage crops

Alternanthera philoxeroides, a perennial herb of the Amaranthaceae, was introduced from Brazil in the 1920s. It is cultivated in both the north and south for swine, poultry, cattle, sheep and fish. Its dry matter content is less than 5 percent.

Aneilema keisak, an annual herb of the Commelinaceae, has been cultivated in subtropical China for a long time. Its dry matter content is around 5 percent. It grows fast and is used for swine, cattle and rabbits.

Azolla imbricata, a floating fern of the Azollaceae and widely distributed in tropical and subtropical zones, has been cultivated in China for 500 years. It forms a fern-algal symbiosis with blue-green alga (Anabena azolla, Cyanophyta) and can fix atmospheric nitrogen. Its yield is as high as 300–500 tonne/ha, with 16–18 percent of crude protein (DM basis). It is high quality fodder for swine, poultry and fish, and a good green manure. There is a detailed FAO publication (Van Hove, 1989) available in French and English which gives details on Azolla cultivation and its use as both a green manure and fodder.

Eichhornia crassipes, a floating herb of the Pontederiaceae, is a high yielding forage indigenous to South America. It is cultivated in the Warm Temperate Zone in China. Its dry matter content is around

Plate 24.
Trifolium fragiferum *in Xinjiang. China has a very wide range of indigenous pasture plants. This, usually Mediterranean, clover is growing on the floodplain of the Ertix.*

5 percent and it is used for swine, poultry, cattle, sheep and fish feed, or as green manure.

Pistia stratiotes, a floating herb of the Araceae, is a high yielding forage in tropical and subtropical zones. It has been extended to the watershed of the Yellow River. The dry matter content ranges from 5 to 6 percent. It is mainly fed to swine, poultry and fish, or as a green manure.

Zizania caduciflora is a perennial temperate and subtropical grass, long cultivated in southern China. Its height is 1–2.5 m and it is high quality fodder for cattle, horses and fish, with 14 percent crude protein.

CULTIVARS AND SEED PRODUCTION

The selection and breeding of forage grasses in China began in early times. Farmers selected many native forages (Plate 24), but modern grass breeding began quite late. In the 1950s, two cultivars of Medicago sativa were bred: Gongnong No. 1 and Gongnong No. 2. Breeding has speeded up since 1980. The National Examining and Approval Committee for Forage Cultivars, affiliated to the Ministry of Agriculture, was set up in 1987 (National Examining and Approval Committee for Forage Cultivars, 1992). China's forage plant genetic resources have been described by Chen Shan (1994).

A set of laboratories and experimental stations was set up. In 1986, the National Crop Germplasm Store in the China Agricultural Academy (based in Beijing) was set up and is responsible for long-term conservation of crop genetic resources (including forages). In 1989, a Forage Germplasm Store was set up in the Grassland Institute of the Agricultural Ministry. Its storage capacity is 40 000 samples and it is responsible for medium-term conservation and supply of forage germplasm. Meanwhile, five Resource Gardens of perennial forages were set up in Hohhehot, Beijing, Wuhan, Nanning and Kunming for field conservation, propagation and supply of germplasm. In 1998, the nationwide Testing Centre for Forage Seeds was established. All these units, based on the Forage Germplasm Store, combined with the National Crop Germplasm Store and Resource Gardens, make up a national network for conserving, supplying and evaluating forage germplasm.

Seed production

China has very long history of grass seed production, but seed supply is still a bottleneck because of weak breeding work. Although a set of centres for foundation seed production was set up in the 1980s, the output of commercial seed is very low. China currently cannot produce sufficient seed of Medicago sativa, Astragalus huangheensis, Melilotus alba, Vicia sativa, V. villosa, Leymus chinensis, Puccinellia tenuiflora, P. chinampoensis, Elymus sibiricus, E. nutans, E. dahuricus and Sorghum sudanense to meet national demand. Seeds of other grasses and forages cannot be produced commercially, including seed of Lolium perenne, Dactylis glomerata, Festuca arundinacea, Trifolium repens, T. pratense and the cold-season turf grasses Poa pratensis, Festuca elata, F. tenuifolia (syn. F. capillata), Agrostis stolonifera, so supplies are almost totally reliant on imports. Although large amounts of seed of Zoysia japonica and Cynodon dactylon could be produced in China, they would have to be exported for cleaning and then re-imported for end use because of lack of seed cleaning technology and equipment.

DEFINING ECONOMIC ZONES OF GRASSLAND AGRO-ECOSYSTEMS

Herbivorous livestock, based on a properly functioning grassland agro-ecosystem, can use both native and introduced forages in a large range of varying ecological environments, so grassland adaptability to natural conditions is wider and more flexible than field crops and forestry. Considering the regional characteristics of grassland in relation to natural, social and economic conditions, the zonation for sustainable development is based on the following criteria:

- similarity of ecological conditions, particularly precipitation and temperature;
- similarity of grassland types and landscape;
- similarity in grassland production and its structure;
- consistency between grassland ecosystems and economic systems;
- consistency between grassland policy and critical technology adopted; and
- consistency of grassland zones and administrative divisions that enables practical regional programming for grassland development.

Grassland zones

Based on the above criteria, China's grasslands can be divided into seven ecological-economic zones:

- Zone 1: Inner Mongolia-Ningxia Arid Grasslands, including the Ningxia Huizu Autonomous Region, the bulk of the Inner Mongolia Autonomous Region, and Hebei Province north of the Great Wall.
- Zone 2: Northwest Desert-shrublands, including Tibet Autonomous Region, the Hexi Corridor of Gansu, and Alashan Meng of Inner Mongolia

Autonomous Region.

- Zone 3: Qinghai-Tibet Alpine Shrublands, including Tibet Autonomous Region, Qinghai Province, the southern part of Gansu Province, the western part of Sichuan Province and the northwest of Yunnan Province.
- Zone 4: Northeast Forests, including Heilongjiang Province, Jilin Province, Liaoning Province and the northeast of Inner Mongolia Autonomous Region.
- Zone 5: Loess Plateau and Huang-Hai Plain, covering Shanxi Province, Shandong Province, Henan Province, Beijing and Tianjin Municipalities, the north of Shaanxi Province, the east of Gansu Province, that part of Hebei province to the south of the Great Wall and the parts of Anhui Province and Jiangsu Province to the north of the Huaihe River.
- Zone 6: Southwest Karst Shrublands, including Guizhou Province, Chongqing Municipality, the east of Sichuan Province, the southeast of Yunnan Province, the bulk of the Guangxi Zhuang Autonomous Region and the west of Hunan Province and Hubei.
- Zone 7: Southwest Evergreen-broadleaf forests-shrublands, including Zhejiang Province, Jiangxi Province, Fujian Province, Guangdong Province, Hainan Province, Hong Kong and Macao, the Sichuan Basin, the south of Shaanxi Province, Tianshui Prefecture of Gansu Province, the east part of the Guangxi Zuang Autonomous Region, the parts of Anhui Province and Jiangsu Province to the south of the Huaihe River, and the eastern parts of Hubei Province and Hunan Province.

Statistical data on local natural and social conditions and agricultural production in each Zone are given in Tables 5.11 and 5.12. Agricultural production by zone is shown in Table 5.13.

CURRENT GRASSLAND SITUATION AND PROPOSED STRATEGY FOR EACH ZONE
Inner Mongolia–Ningxia Arid Grassland Zone

This is one of the most important pastoral areas (Plate 25). Grassland types change from northeast to southwest with decreasing precipitation, from meadow grasslands to typical grasslands, then to desert grasslands. The environment is fragile due to severe desertification caused by a combination of frequent gales, coarse soils, overgrazing and poor management. Deserts and desertified lands make up 11 percent and 18.4 percent of the land, respectively, of the zone. The rich grassland resources have high primary productivity and stocking capacity (Plate 26). Typical grasslands in Hulun Beir Meng and Jirem Meng in the east of the zone are among the best grasslands in China, with annual hay yield as high as 900–1 500 kg/ha (Plates 27 and 28) and stocking capacity of 0.7–1.2 sheep unit/ha. Desert grassland types occur in the Ulanqab Meng, on the Ordos Plateau and in the areas to the east of the Helan Mountain Range, with Stipa spp., Salsola collina and Artemisia frigida as dominant species. Annual hay yields are 400–600 kg/ha and stocking capacity is 0.25–0.40 sheep unit/ha.

Winter grassland is only 30–60 percent of the warm-season grassland, so these areas are heavily grazed, usually lasting for five months, and longer than on warm-season grasslands. Significant annual variation in precipitation causes great differences in forage production, which can be as much as a factor of four between a year of good

TABLE 5.11
Major climate data of each grassland zone.

Zone	Annual accumulated temperature ≥0°C (°C)	Annual precipitation (mm)	Humidity (K) (mm/°C)
1	2000–3000	250–400	0.5–1.4
2	4000–5700	< 250	0.1–0.9
3	2000–1600	500–700	0.1–4.4
4	1700–3500	500–1000	1.6–3.3
5	3000–4800	500–900	1.1–2.1
6	4000–7000	1000–2000	1.2–3.5
7	4500–7500	2000–2500	1.6–2.7

NOTE: $K = r/(0.1\sum\theta)$, where K is humidity, r is annual rainfall (mm), and $\sum\theta$ is annual accumulative temperature ≥0°C (°C).

TABLE 5.12
Major socio-economic data for each grassland zone (1995 data).

Zone	Land area (×10³ km²)	Population (million)	Arable land (ha)	Grassland (ha)	Theoretical NPP[1] of grassland (10⁶ tonne DM/year)
1	697.7	20.4	4 886 700	54 045 500	255.60
2	2 223.3	20.0	4 078 100	88 547 800	214.29
3	2 209.5	9.2	1 082 500	135 626 200	810.09
4	965.6	102.1	17 153 600	21 537 800	122.38
5	979.6	324.0	32 430 600	26 107 600	164.71
6	835.0	111.9	7 494 600	31 340 700	371.42
7	1 684.8	550.8	27 499 000	35 891 800	436.33
All	9 595.5	1 138.4	94 910 200	393 097 400	2 374.82

NOTE: (1) NPP is net primary productivity, calculated by the formula of Li, Sun and Zhang (1998) and Zhou and Zhang (1996).

TABLE 5.13
Agricultural production in each grassland zone (RMB×10⁸; 1995).

Zone	Crops	Forestry	Livestock	Fisheries
1	149.60	8.65	95.2	2.82
2	289.57	7.35	89.87	2.34
3	42.30	2.89	46.58	0.16
4	977.70	33.87	485.38	86.05
5	2 720.49	129.17	1 357.90	3.27
6	710.24	82.22	340.75	18.74
7	4 200.10	346.39	2 253.84	861.56
All China	9 169.22	611.07	4 671.99	1 298.19

rainfall and a dry one. Crop growing has been expanding to the north, taking over more and more grasslands, resulting in increased conflicts in the local society.

Nomadic extensive management prevails. With rapid growth in livestock numbers and slow development in estab-lishing artificial pastures, the grasslands have deteriorated seriously under heavy grazing. Shortage of pasture and frequent natural disasters cause heavy losses of livestock: loss, sale and domestic consumption by local herders each account for up to a third of the total animal production annu-

Plate 25.
Herder with sheep. Inner Mongolia, China.

Plate 26.
Pastoral scene in July near Hailar City, Inner Mongolia, China.

Plate 27.
Hay being carried to the homestead near Xilinhot, Inner Mongolia, China.

ally. In this zone, crop production should be restricted and development focused on livestock, with grassland protection, establishment of artificial pastures and integration of crops with feedlots. Feed processing and mechanization of forage production should have a high priority in development planning.

The Northwest Desert-shrubland

This is the largest zone in terms of area. It is arid and semi-arid desert, most of which has annual precipitation of less than 250 mm, with a lot of solar radiation, between 2 600 and 3 400 hours annually. An extremely arid climate, frequent wind and sparse vegetation are features of this fragile environment. Sand storms often cause serious damage to grassland. It is estimated that desertification and salinization have affected 486 000 km² and 1 730 700 km², respectively (21.6 percent and 47.5 percent

of all affected land in China).

The zone has 676 continental rivers, fed by snowmelt and glaciers in the Tianshan, Kunlun, Altai and Qilian Mountains, which allowed the development of local oasis agriculture over thousands of years. Nowadays, the Yili, the Ertix and Shule Rivers maintain their supply to the increasing population, but the other rivers are seriously short of water. Meanwhile, the area of arable land affected by secondary salinization has reached 14.7 percent in Xinjiang and 31.1 percent of the Hexi Corridor of Gansu.

The dry matter yield of native grassland is 300 kg/ha in mountain areas, and 300–1 200 kg/ha from sown pastures. This indicates the great grassland potential of this zone. Livestock production is mainly in the mountains, where serious seasonal imbalance between forage supply and requirement is a major constraint. Very often, in

Plate 28.
Hay being stored ready for the winter near Xilinhot, Inner Mongolia, China.

spring, livestock die in large numbers due to fodder shortage. The fodder resources of crop-producing areas in the zone are not used efficiently as there could be a combination of grazing and crop production.

As measures of improvement, artificial pastures should be widely and intensively established in mountain areas to protect against natural disasters. Rotational grazing needs to be adopted and measures taken to protect water sources. In desert areas, stocking rates should be strictly controlled, while feed and fodder production needs to be expanded in oases. Livestock can be transferred from mountain areas to oases for fattening, which would greatly improve the overall production system.

Qinghai-Tibet Alpine Shrublands Zone

This is the least populous zone, while the area of natural grassland is the largest.

Due to its high altitude, averaging more than 3 000 m, solar radiation is 50 percent higher than in neighbouring zones, but heat resources are less.

Water resources are unevenly distributed. Annual precipitation is 1000–2000 mm, reaching as high as 3000–4000 mm in some places on the southern slopes of the Himalayas and in the southeast of the Hengduan Mountains. At the other extreme, precipitation is only about 50 mm in the Qaidam Basin and the northwest of the Qiangtang Plateau. Precipitation is 500–700 mm in other areas. Many rivers rise on the Plateau.

The primary productivity of native natural grasslands is low. Forages from alpine meadow are palatable and nutritious, but those from sparse wood and shrub grasslands are of poor quality. Due to the long cold season, windy weather, frequent snow disasters and drought, the imbalance between fodder supply and livestock requirement is great, and so the system has difficulty in resisting natural disasters. Long-term overgrazing has turned many places on grasslands into Black-Soil Patches or Sandy Lands (Liu, Zeng and Cai Rong, 1999; Ma and Li, 1999).

The offtake of marketable animal products is the lowest in China. Measures for improvement include strictly controlling the stocking rate, breed improvement, rotational grazing, establishing artificial pastures and accelerating the development of markets for animal products. The problems of transport, poor adoption of new technology and lack of funding for development should be given high priority. The zone is one of the least polluted regions in the world, so there is the potential to produce "green" food to meet the increasing demand for such on the world market.

Northeast Forests Zone

This zone is characterized by adequate rainfall, but low temperatures. The major grassland types are meadow grassland, typical grassland, alpine meadow and marsh. The dominant species are Leymus chinensis, Stipa baicalensis and Dendranthema maximowiczii, with the Leymus chinensis meadow being the most important type. Annual dry matter yield is 1 000–1 500 kg/ha, and remains quite stable from year to year. The stocking capacity is 1.5–2.0 sheep/ha.

Dairy cattle and milk production in this zone takes first place in China, and grassland is integrated with crop production to use more efficiently fodder and feed resources such as crop residues and maize. The strategy for development in the zone is to establish large-scale production

centres with increased input and establish close cooperation between agricultural sectors for efficient utilization of resources. Ecologically healthy animal products should be the main output of production.

Loess Plateau and Huang-Huai-Hai Plain Zone

This area has the longest history of agriculture in China. There are many fine native breeds and rich feed resources. In addition to concentrates, silage and urea-treated maize stover have been widely adopted in recent years in beef feedlots, which have become a profitable enterprise. To meet the demand for fodder, lucerne (Medicago sativa) cultivation is expanding rapidly. In Gansu and Shandong, farmers grow Medicago sativa (cultivars Gannong No. 2 and Gannong No. 3, and other native or imported cultivars) for hay or sale to processing companies for pellet production, and farmer income can be increased by more than 15 percent compared with cereal growing.

The climate is humid or subhumid monsoon, with high consistency between rainfall and biologically active accumulated temperature. However, variation in rainfall between years is large and drought is a major problem (Hou, Li and Zhang, 1991). Surface and underground water is insufficient to meet agricultural demand. Average runoff per capita is only about 500 m^3, a fifth of the national average. The Loess Plateau is seriously eroded, while the Huang-Huai-Hai Plain is dominated by soils of poor quality for agriculture, such as shajiang black saline soil and heavy sandy soil.

The zone is a major area for forage seed production. The forages include Medicago sativa, Melilotus spp., Onobrychis viciifolia,

Plate 29.
Astragalus adsurgens. *This species has promise for northern areas, but has fallen out of favour lately because of high water needs and problems with persistence.*

Sorghum sudanese, Astragalus adsurgens (Plate 29) and Zoysia spp. Erosion control and conversion of arable to woodland and pastures should be the major measures for sustainable development. Pasture establishment can be integrated into plans for small-catchment management. In the Huang-Huai-Hai Plain wastelands, beaches of rivers can be used to grow pastures for fodder and soil improvement. Based on established pastures and crop by-products, beef and dairy cattle, sheep and goats can be raised to expand the livestock sector of the local agriculture.

Southwest Karst Shrubland Zone

There are 48 ethnic minorities; half of the poverty-stricken people in China live in the zone (Research Group on Sustainable Agricultural Development in Karst Regions of China, 1999). The karst landforms have widely distributed limestone cliffs and bare stone deserts caused by irrational cultivation, overgrazing and deforestation of hillsides. It is estimated that the area of stone deserts has quadrupled in the past 50 years in Guizhou and Yunnan. This trend has been accompanied by serious water loss and soil erosion and general deterioration of the environment (Research Group on Sustainable Agricultural Development in Karst Regions of China, 1999).

Natural grassland is distributed in scattered patches in mountainous areas and usually difficult to manage. There are many poisonous plants, with palatable species accounting for only 30–60 percent. Native forage legumes are scarce, but the leguminous shrubs that exist in great number have not yet been utilized. Both overgrazing and under-utilization of local fodder resources co-exist.

Although water resources are adequate and the temperature regime is fair, there is not enough sunshine for seed production (Hou, Li and Zhang, 1991). Cereals yields and quality are low. Climatic conditions are suitable for improving natural grasslands and establishing artificial pastures vegetatively (Ren, Hu and Zhang, 1999). Sown pastures can have 3–4 cuts, even 6 cuts in some places, annually. Some forages, such as Lolium spp., Stylosanthes spp., Trifolium repens, T. pratense and Dactylis glomerata grow well. Annual hay yield is 3 400–4 500 kg/ha from natural grasslands and 8 000–10 000 kg/ha from sown pastures; on some it was more than 10 000 kg/ha, with 2 133 ha of pastures carrying 12 000 sheep that produced 2.5–3.0 kg clean wool each in a year (Jiang, Mu and Cheng, 1996).

Southeast Evergreen Broadleaf Forest-shrubland Zone

This zone has the largest population, the most developed economy and the best climatic conditions (Hou, Li and Zhang, 1991). Grassland is secondary after tropical and subtropical forest is cleared. Annual hay yield is 2 000–3 000 kg/ha, but quality is usually poor. Productivity could be increased by 5–8 times if improvement measures are applied (Yang et al., 1997a, b).

Traditionally, green manure is grown, so it is easy to establish a new rotation between paddy rice and commercial fodder in the zone to realize better economic, ecological and social benefits. According to a study by Yang et al., (1997a, b) in Guangdong Province, rotation of Italian ryegrass (Lolium multiflorum) and rice increased the content of OM, total N, available N, biomass of micro-organisms and enzyme activity in the soil. These, in turn, increased the yield of early and late rices by 10 percent and 7 percent, respectively. In addition, the annual forage production

was worth RMB 15 000. The current area of forage can be expanded within existing farming systems with available techniques. Processing needs to be developed for producing high-quality animal products with high added value.

This economic zone of the grassland agro-ecosystem is a kind of integrating system between pasture use, crop production and forestry. It is a multicomponent complex of ecosystems over a large geographical area, involving many economic and social activities. The theory of combining systems can be used to guide in planning and implementation of development programmes in suitable zones to achieve sustainable economic, social and environmental benefits.

RESEARCH AND EDUCATION

There are 23 organizations related to grassland and grass research in China, of which six national institutes are affiliated to the China Agricultural Academy and China Academy. Out of 36 agricultural universities, 16 provide four-year undergraduate education in grassland science. Gansu Agricultural University, Inner Mongolia Agricultural University, Xinjiang Agricultural University, China Agricultural University and China Agricultural Academy are authorized to provide a PhD programme. The top-level technical extension organization for grassland management and fodder production is the Animal Husbandry and Veterinary Medicine Station of China's Agriculture Ministry. Each province has a Grassland or Forage Grass and Forage Crop Extension Station. Each county has an Animal Husbandry and Veterinary Medicine Station, or a Grassland Station where the pastoral area is large.

Chapter VI
China case study 1: Studies on traditional transhumance and a system where herders return to settled winter bases in Burjin county, Altai prefecture, Xinjiang, China

Wan Lin Wang

SUMMARY

Burjin, in the extreme northwest of China, about 48°N, has a cold, arid to semi-arid continental climate. Grazing lands are between 300 m and the summer snowline at 3 500 m. Stock rearing is the main land use and herders follow a traditional transhumance pattern. The long winter, when feed supply is a very serious problem, is spent on the desert fringe. Cattle, horses, sheep and goats are kept, with some baggage camels. Grazing rights are leased to households, which are responsible for the proper management of the pasture on a thirty-year basis; this can be revoked in case of mismanagement. Transit routes are defined officially and cannot be used as grazing; moving is organized to space out households on the trek routes. During the 1980s, a large area was developed for irrigated fodder, in rotation with crops, and selected households were allocated holdings for hay and crop production. These households have built houses as family bases, but continue to send stock on transhumance in the grazing season. The transhumance patterns of two groups, one with irrigated land and permanent housing and the other traditional nomads, were studied, together with their socio-economic conditions. There is ample summer pasture for 75–90 days. The highest pastures are just below 3 500 m, with winter grazing on the desert fringe between 300 and 1 000 m. The transhumance circuit can be up to 400 km. Families with irrigated land and hay had far higher incomes. Their herds are increasing and risks low; they also have good access to medical, educational and other facilities and are investing in production equipment and household goods. Lucerne yields are very low, far below their potential, largely because herders are unwilling to provide inputs. Winter weight loss in sheep has been converted to weight gain through shelter and feeding hay; such flocks can be mated earlier and lambs brought to slaughter weight in their first year. Nomadic families have lower incomes, little access to services and own what they can carry in their baggage train; their sheep still lose weight through winter and lamb late, so that many have to be kept through a second summer.

INTRODUCTION

Xinjiang Autonomous Region is in the extreme northwest of China; Altai Prefecture is in the extreme northwest of Xinjiang, and Burjin County ["County" is used interchangeably for the whole administrative area and the county seat] is in the extreme northwest of the prefecture (see map – Figure 6.1) to the north of Junggar Basin, and southwest of the Altai Mountains, at 47°22´–49°11´ N and 86°25´–88° 06´ E. The distance from north to south is 200 km and from west to east it is 49–82 km. Its total area is 10 540 km².

A large programme of provision of irrigated land for fodder in rotation, to supply hay for winter feed as well as allowing settlement of nomadic families,

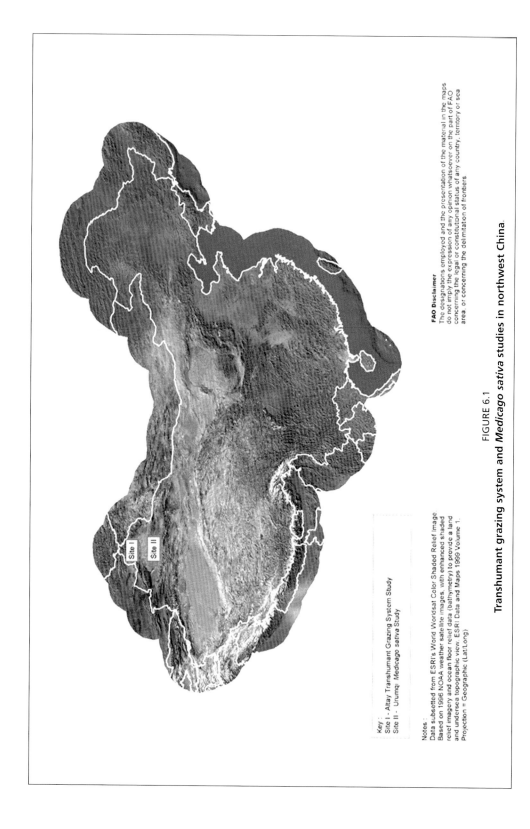

Key :
Site I - Altay Transhumant Grazing System Study
Site II - Urumqi *Medicago sativa* Study

Notes :
Data subsetted from ESRI's World Worldsat Color Shaded Relief Image
Based on 1996 NOAA weather satellite images, with enhanced shaded
relief imagery and ocean floor relief data (bathymetry) to provide a land
and undersea topographic view. ESRI Data and Maps 1999 Volume 1.
Projection = Geographic (Lat:Long)

FAO Disclaimer
The designations employed and the presentation of the material in the maps
do not imply the expression of any opinion whatsoever on the part of FAO
concerning the legal or constitutional status of any country, territory or sea
area, or concerning the delimitation of frontiers.

FIGURE 6.1

Transhumant grazing system and *Medicago sativa* studies in northwest China.

Source: Li-Menglin, Yuang and Suttie, 1996.

FIGURE 6.2
Location of the project's fodder sites in Altai Prefecture, China.

while maintaining transhumant production systems, has been undertaken in Altai Prefecture. The effects of settlement on herders were studied in comparison with households that still followed the traditional, fully nomadic life style.

FODDER PRODUCTION AND PROJECT 2817

In the 1980s, the Animal Husbandry Bureau developed 25 000 ha of irrigated land for hay production on sandy-gravelly soils unsuited to arable cropping (Li, Yuang and Suttie, 1996). Project 2817 was assisted by the World Food Programme (WFP);

work began in 1988, the scheme was in production by the end of the decade, and completed in 1995. One Project site was in Burjin County, others were in Fuhai and Altai City (see Figure 6.2).

Irrigated units of several hectares are managed by herders' families; the herds follow their usual transhumance, but some of the family stay behind during summer to irrigate the crops and make hay. The settlers were provided with loans so that they could build houses as winter quarters; social services, including medical facilities and schools, have also been made available – facilities otherwise inaccessible to families with no fixed winter base. Sown forage for hay is the basis of cropping. Lucerne (*Medicago sativa*) is the main crop, rotated with wheat, maize, sunflower and soybean. The lucerne activities of the Project – selection for cold-resistance – are discussed in Chapter VII. Trees are a project component for shelter, windbreaks, timber and forage. The main trees are poplar (*Populus* spp.), willow (*Salix* spp.), Siberian elm (*Ulmus pumila*) and Russian olive (*Elaeagnus angustifolia*). The irrigated holdings are leased to households. Development of the scheme required a great deal of training, from senior technical staff to herders, who previously did not cultivate crops. The Burjin project area now has six primary schools, a clinic, twelve shops, a water and forestry management station and a breeding station. Four out of five villages have electricity. Some herders in villages without electricity have solar energy devices. Living and production conditions for herders have improved greatly, and a purely livestock economy has been turned into a diversified one.

The Burjin Project site is 30 km from town, between the Burjin and the Ertix rivers [places and geographical features often have several names in this region: the Ertix is also shown on maps as Irtich and Erqis – it flows into Kazakhstan and joins the Ob system, which drains to the Arctic Ocean]. Site altitude is 520 m; it is 16 km from south to north and 18 km from east to west, on mainly brown-calcium and sandy soil. The developed area is 16 667 ha. Irrigation is from the Burjin river and it drains to the Ertix. The annual average temperature is 4°C, with a short frost-free period (135 days). Winter is cold and long. It is windy all year round,

with 40 very windy days above Force 8. Annual average precipitation is 120 mm.

Burjin borders Kazakhstan and Russia to the northwest and Mongolia to the northeast. It has six townships, one town and 59 administrative villages. Its population of 68 000 includes 19 ethnic groups. All Burjin's 17 635 herders are Kazakhs, one of China's ethnic minorities, who form 57 percent of Burjin's population. They are Muslims who speak a Turkic language, and are the main ethnic group in neighbouring Kazakhstan; they are also present in Mongolia, especially in Bayan-Ölgii *aimag*, which borders Altai prefecture. They have moved into Xinjiang since the 1860s; traditionally they are perpetual, transhumant, nomads who live in circular felt tents on a collapsible frame – like the *gers* of the Mongols and similar to those of other Turkic herders, like the Kyrgyz. Because of their lifestyle, they neither cultivate crops nor keep poultry. Most continue with traditional transhumance: those of the Project have permanent housing and irrigated land for hay but when taking the herds to summer pasture they still use traditional tentage.

Stock rearing is Burjin's major industry. The crop area is 19 800 ha, the area of grassland is 818 000 ha and the area of usable wasteland is 126 700 ha. There are two river systems, the Ertix and the Burjin, with an annual flow of 7.45×10^9 m^3. Topography is varied: the highest elevation is 4 374 m while the county headquarters is at 479 m. Water resources are plentiful in some areas, whereas lower areas are almost desert. The main land types and their soils are summarized in Table 6.1.

The climate is continental; precipitation, mainly as snow, varies from under

TABLE 6.1
Land types in Burjin County.

Type	Area (km²)	Percentage	Soil
Glacier	704	6.68	Tundra soil
Alpine and subalpine meadow grassland	1 788	16.97	Alpine and subalpine meadow soils
Coniferous forest—meadow grassland	2 239	21.24	Grey forest soil, chernozem
Forest	702	6.66	Grey forest soil, chernozem
Semi-dry grassland in hilly land	1 482	14.06	Chestnut soil, brunisolic soil
Semi-desert grassland on plains	1 653	15.68	Brunisolic soil, meadow soil
Plains forest	71	0.67	Brunisolic soil, meadow soil
Farm land	216	2.05	Chestnut soil, brunisolic soil
Desert	333	3.16	
South desert grassland	1 231	11.68	Sandy soil, brunisolic soil
Water	93	0.88	
Town and other land	28	0.03	
Total	10 540	100.00	

100 mm/year in the plains to over 600 mm in the high pastures. Cold waves, with high winds and snow, can cause heavy losses. In the mountains it is much colder; the higher pastures are open for less than three months. Stock rearing is based on transhumance of the traditional, vertical type. The division of grazing periods is: Spring – early April to end of June – about 90 days; Summer – end of June to late September – about 83 days; Autumn – mid-September to end of November – about 70 days; and Winter – about 121 days.

In 2000, the annual average temperature was 5.1°C, with a minimum of -37°C. The coldest period is late December and early January. The first snow was on 18 October; the last on 10 March. Snow depth was 117 cm. The frost-free period was 143 days, and annual sunshine was 2 721 hours.

There are four major vegetation zones:
* alpine snow and rock, of little use for grazing; the snow line is at about 3 500 m;
* summer grazing lands above 1 300 m provide rich grazing for 75 to 95 days per year. These are the fattening pastures and, in season, are capable of carrying more stock; they also have important forest resources;
* spring and autumn pastures are transition routes and show serious signs of overgrazing. Due to lack of winter feed, herds linger on these pastures in autumn and go on to them too early in spring. The irrigated areas are in the drier, southern fringe of this zone; and
* winter pastures (plains, desert, low meadows and marshland), which are inadequate for the number of stock carried. The provision of winter feed through irrigated haymaking was identified as the most effective way of improving the overall production system and reducing pressure on the winter and transitional pastures. Desert grazing is controlled by snowfall: if there is no snow as a source of drinking water livestock cannot use the zone; sudden thaws or deep snow can be disastrous.

LIVESTOCK

Cattle, sheep, goats, horses and camels are all part of the production system. Sheep are the most important numerically, with cattle a close second. In terms of livestock units, however, sheep account for 30–40 percent, about the same as cattle.

The Kazakh horse

This is a dual-purpose breed with both Central Asian and Mongolian blood. It is strong, with a thick hair coat. The main colours are bay and black. It is the main saddle and pack animal for herding and for draught in agricultural areas. It is capable of carrying heavy loads, working at least eight hours a day and travelling 40–50 km. The average liveweight of a mare is 328 kg, carcass weight 152 kg and dressing-out percentage 37 percent. Breeding age for both sexes is three years. The main breeding season is May–June.

Kazakh cattle

These are an old Xinjiang line of Yellow cattle. Because of widespread cross-breeding, they are now rare. The average liveweight of a bull is 365 kg and of a cow 274 kg. Their lactation period is 140–180 days at pasture and 240 days with supplementary feed. They are very hardy and disease resistant, and the basic breed for upgrading. Altai white-head cattle are another old breed of Yellow cattle, reared by Mongolian herders in Kumu township and found throughout the prefecture. Lactation at pasture is 150–200 days; average daily milk yield is 4.5–6.0 kg. Carcass weight at eighteen months is 138 kg and at three years, 286 kg. Xinjiang brown cattle are an improved breed, with some Brown Swiss, Alatau and Kesiteluomu blood. They are dual-purpose, medium-sized animals and account for 25 percent of the county's cattle.

Kazakh sheep

They are coarse-wool, dual-purpose, meat and fat, fat-tailed animals, which are good long-distance walkers in mountain terrain. An adult ram weighs 60 kg and an ewe 46 kg. They are shorn twice, in spring and autumn; wool yields are 2.6 kg per ram and 1.38 kg per ewe. The Altai fat-rump is a branch of the Kazakh sheep, with a characteristic body form and high yield of hair and fat. An adult ram weighs 93 kg and an ewe 68 kg. An eighteen-month wether has a liveweight of 50 kg with a carcass weight of 27.5 kg including the fat tail, which weighs 4.3 kg; they fatten well on summer pasture. They are sheared in spring and autumn, yielding 2 kg per ram and 1.5 kg per ewe. Altai fat-rump is the main breed of Burjin; fine-wool sheep account for 35 percent. Xinjiang fine-wool sheep were developed by introducing merino and other fine-wools. They are white-woolled, with a fleece yield of 4.5 kg and a staple length of about 10 cm. Adult, shorn rams weigh 94 kg and ewes 48.3 kg.

Others

Local black goats produce high quality cashmere. Bactrian camels, which are kept as pack animals, also produce fine wool.

NATURAL PASTURE MANAGEMENT

The government has for some time been acutely aware of the problems associated with the management of extensive grazing lands: in 1980 an act was passed whereby such lands would be allocated under a family responsibility system, making households responsible for the good management of the pasture allocated to them.

Natural pasture belongs to the state; government officers manage and allocate it. They contract with herders and provide them with grazing certificates. Herders own grazing rights, pasture protection rights and pasture improvement rights, valid for thirty years, so long as they manage their grazing correctly. They pay taxes according to the number of livestock owned. Allocation and registration is now complete for all Altai Prefecture. Natural grazing throughout the transhumance system, apart from stock routes, is allocated to family groups. Families are allocated land in each seasonal grazing zone. The system, dealing as it does with a transhumant system, is of necessity complex, but the population, traditionally used to complex systems, copes with it.

Transhumance routes are defined and may only be used for transit, not grazing. It is forbidden to keep stock on the route unless weather is very bad, when herds will be allowed to stay for one or two days. The moving schedule is arranged in advance; flocks move along the route household by household in an endless stream, at intervals of about 500 m.

The Herders Management Office, which is both an administrative and service organization, is responsible for organizing production activities and resolving major problems on summer pastures. Their responsibilities include: deciding on moving time; resolving pasture disputes; regulating pasture management; providing weather forecasts; livestock mating; control and treatment of animal disease; marketing livestock products; disseminating family planning information; protecting forests and providing fire control; organizing recreational activities; and receiving visitors. Scientific and technical training are organized by the government. Common livestock ailments are controlled and treated. Measures, such

as dipping, quarantine and vaccination have been adopted. For breed improvement, herders are required to cull males not qualified as stud stock and introduce superior sires in their place.

In 1999, livestock products did not sell well and prices were low; prices of fat-rump sheep and cattle improved slightly in 2000. September and October is the main season for selling stock, but prices are lower then. Only small numbers of livestock and products are sold locally; most are sent to larger markets, such as Urumqi and Kelamayi.

THE GROUPS STUDIED
The Treatment Group
Nine herder households with irrigated land and settled winter bases were selected in the project area; these are referred to as the Treatment Group. There were three subgroups of three households each. For convenience, households of a subgroup lived close to one another. One subgroup was selected from each of three administrative villages of three townships.

The Control Group
According to the natural herding practice of nomadic groups, nine households were selected. Three households from one location formed a group. Study methods included interviews, field investigation and documentation.

STUDIES ON THE TREATMENT GROUP (PROJECT HOUSEHOLDS)
The population breakdown of the group is shown in Table 6.2.

With government assistance and loans, all settled and semi-settled herders in the project area have built permanent houses: some in brick and wood, others are earth

TABLE 6.2
Population of the Treatment Group.

| | | Treatment Group | | | Total | Percentage |
		1	2	3		
Group size, comprising		20	20	24	64	100
males		10	9	11	30	47
females		10	11	13	34	53
of which,	aged	–	1	–	1	1.6
	students	9	6	11	26	40
	workers, comprising	7.5	9.5	10.0	27	42
	crop workers and	5.5	6.5	8.0	20.0	31
	livestock workers	2.0	3.0	2.0	7.0	11

NOTES: Workers are both full and part time. Students are from school and university. Livestock workers go on transhumance; crop workers stay at settlement sites, they feed animals in winter.

and wood. The housing area per household is 90–180 m²; all have electricity and domestic electrical appliances. Livestock sheds include cattle sheds, sheep sheds, lamb sheds and plastic-film warm sheds. Some of them have built permanent warm sheds with brick, steel windows and glass. The advantages of these sheds are that:

- they are warm inside in winter as there is plenty of sunshine. Milk yield of livestock is high;
- they save fodder;
- they reduce animal disease; and
- they develop winter lamb and early spring lamb production.

Coal is generally used in winter – about five tonnes per household, and all households in the Treatment Group bought coal. Some still used wood and sheep dung for heating and cooking. The project settlement site is the base for herders; old people, children, women and the ill generally live there all year round. Settled families are busy from seed time to harvest, with the women working with the men. From 1 April to 30 September is the "golden season", when they must work very hard to make money, have a good harvest and ensure livestock safety for winter and

spring. Some workers stay at the site to manage crops, while others take the stock to the high pastures. Some families hire others to herd their stock. At the end of autumn and onset of winter, stock move back to the settlement and families are reunited. Some activities, such as slaughtering, visiting relatives and friends, betrothals, weddings and circumcision, take place in November and December, when herders and their families are together and have time and money from sale of livestock and agricultural products.

Crop production by the Treatment Group

All households grew crops (Plate 30), with a total area of 69.1 ha: 7.7 ha per household on average and 1.08 ha per capita. The area of lucerne was the largest, at 31.7 ha, 45.8 percent of the total. Details of 1999 cropping are shown in Table 6.3. The 2000 cropping pattern was similar, but the soybean area increased and sunflower decreased.

Lucerne yields were very low, the potential is much higher. At the outset of Project 2817, large-scale pilot plantings were developed, on farmers' fields, for demonstration

TABLE 6.3
Cropping by the Treatment Group in 1999.

Crop	Area (ha)	Sowing date	Grain yield (kg)		Straw and hay (kg)	
			Unit yield	Total yield	Unit yield	Total yield
Wheat	19.3	4–10 May	3 073	593 089	1 459	28 159
Maize	2.5	1–10 May	4 410	11 025	18 520	46 300
Lucerne	31.7	1 April–18 August	–	–	3 815	120 396
Soybean	7.1	2–28 May	2 077	14 747	1 554	11 033
Sunflower	8.3	5–28 May	813	6 748	747	6 200
Vegetables	0.2	–	–		–	–
Total	69.1	–	–	625 609	–	–

and training. When the project was evaluated by WFP in 1991, these pilot farms had hay yields (Plate 31) of 5–8 tonne/ha or greater. The reasons for low yields are lack of maintenance fertilizer, infestation with dodder (*Cuscuta* sp.) and poor husbandry, especially faulty land levelling. Herders are unwilling to invest inputs for a "grass" which they consider should grow naturally. Much training has been carried out and a series of fertilizer demonstrations during the 1990s showed that phosphate has a highly positive effect, but still herders refuse to take proper care of their lucerne. They do, however, buy fertilizer for their other field crops. Another promising fodder crop is *Lotus corniculatus* (Plate 32).

Households also planted trees; about 18 090 on 6.7 ha. Leaves and twigs are fed

Plate 30.
Altai crops include maize, which is grown on irrigated land and used for silage.

Plate 31.
Haymaking in Altai from a thin crop of lucerne on irrigated land.

Plate 32.
Lotus corniculatus *is a promising fodder crop for poorer soils. Forage diversification trials in Altai; plot of* Astragalus adsurgens *in background.*

TABLE 6.4A
Livestock of the Treatment Group in 1999 (head).

Species	Number at start of year		Fate			Number at year end
	Total	of which females	Weaned offspring	Killed for home use	Sold	
Cattle	126	61	34	14	25	121
Horses	68	19	11	–	2	74
Camels	24	10	1	–	–	25
Sheep	834	714	667	89	460	952
Goats	62	29	27	5	1	83
Total	1 114	836	740	111	488	1 255

TABLE 6.4B
Livestock of the Treatment Group in 2000 (head).

Species	Number at start of year		Fate			Number at year end
	Total	of which females	Weaned offspring	Killed for home use	Sold	
Cattle	121	47	45	11	34	136
Horses	74	13	10	2	12	74
Camels	25	4	4	–	1	24
Sheep	952	637	634	119	408	1 055
Goats	83	37	40	14	13	99
Total	1 255	736	733	146	468	1 388

to stock. The yield of leaves and twigs was 54 tonne, or 3 kg/tree on average.

Animal production by the Treatment Group.

Livestock numbers and the time spent in the project area in winter vary. Herders retain some winter pasture and decide how many livestock it can support and how long they should stay, according to the weather, forage availability and the state of the herbage. Situations differ from household to household. Generally stock graze first, then move to the project area when it is cold, or before lambing. Herders with winter pasture move stock into the project area in December or January, and leave about 20 April, staying about 120 days. Some herders feed cattle and horses in the project area in winter, but herd their sheep and camels at pasture. The livestock holdings

of the Group are shown in Tables 6.4a and 6.4b.

For overwintering, herders calculate stock numbers according to their experience and available fodder. About 50 m³ of fodder per household should be left in a good year. Livestock must graze if fodder is insufficient in a bad year. By the end of 1999, the nine households had 1 255 head, and total daily hay consumption was 3 904 kg. The yield of lucerne, straw, tree leaves (Plate 33) and other forage was 370 612 kg, enough to feed 1 255 livestock for 95 days. So stock fed in the project area for 80 percent of winter. The principle is grazing first, then supplementation and feeding in sheds when it is impossible to graze. When stock are stall-fed, fodder is crushed and fed in troughs. Feeding priority is sheep and horses, then cattle; camels usually graze and browse.

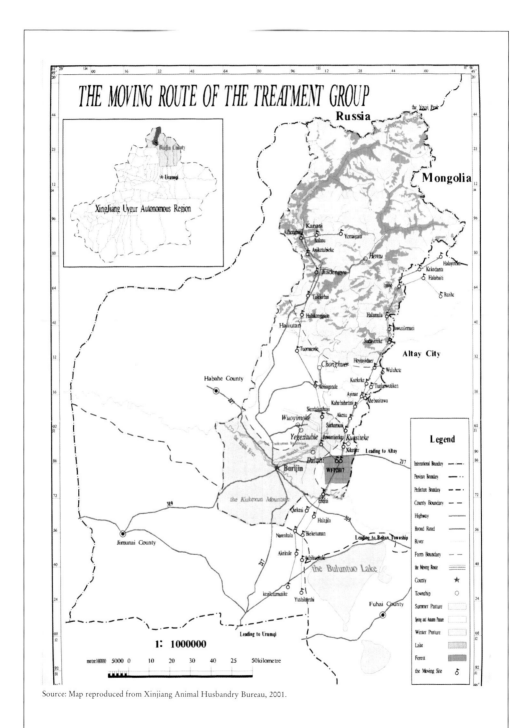

Source: Map reproduced from Xinjiang Animal Husbandry Bureau, 2001.

FIGURE 6.3
Livestock movements and pasture utilization by the treatment group in 1998/99.

SEASONAL PASTURE AND LIVESTOCK MOVEMENT

Livestock movements and pasture use in 1998–1999 (see map, Figure 6.3), were:

- Stock grazed at Shawur Mountain and Qian Mountain in the project area from 1 December 1998 to 31 March 1999 (120 days) and moved four times.
- They moved from Shawur Mountain to spring pasture between 1 April and 15 May (45 days) and moved four times.
- They were at spring pasture (Tuohenyekekaile and Kekeke) from 16 May to 20 June (35 days) and moved four times.
- They were at summer pasture (Sumudayierke, Kekejiaote and Baziher) from 21 June to 11 September (80 days) and moved five times.
- They were on autumn pasture (Alasu, Kekeke and Tuohenyekekaile) from 11 September to 10 October (30 days) and moved four times.
- Winter pasture was at Kuosidake and the WFP Project 2817 area from 11 October to 30 November (50 days) and moved four times.

The total annual transhumance was 500 km and livestock were moved 25 times. Five of the nine households asked others to herd livestock for them and remained in the project area to do farm work.

Burjin has a large area of pasture, but the areas for different seasons are not in balance. At summer pasture, grass quality is high with a variety of species and high yield, but can be used for only 80–90 days. Salt is fed to livestock on the summer pasture to supplement mineral matter and increase feed intake. Spring and autumn pastures are poor, with sparse desert vegetation, but livestock must stay there

Plate 33.
Riparian willow and poplar forest along the Ertix provides valuable winter grazing.

for 150–160 days. Winter pasture is very poor yet stock stay there for 120 days. Forage is plentiful in summer, scarce in spring and autumn and seriously lacking in winter.

In 1998–1999, spring and summer rainfall was less than usual and locusts caused serious damage to the natural pastures, but in the project area it was worst on spring and autumn pasture; 500 locusts/m^2 at most and at least 20 50 locusts/m^2. A plague of Italian locust (*Calliptamus italicus*) appeared in April and was most serious in May; it covered 400 km^2 and was serious over 300 km^2. During the 80 days from October to the end of 2000, there was snow for more than 60 days; the depth of snow was 117 cm and the lowest temperature was -37°C. Traffic was stopped throughout the Prefecture. Such snow had not been seen for 50 years.

Winter pasture

The winter pastures are at Salebur Mountain, Shawur Mountain and the mountain valley of Kukexun. Sawur Mountain is in Hefeng County, Tacheng Prefecture, where, because of extreme shortage of winter pasture in home areas, Burjin has grazing rights. The elevation of winter pasture is 800–1 900 m, and is cold in winter and cool in summer. The annual average temperature is 3.6°C; it is coldest in

January, with an average temperature of -12°C. Annual precipitation is 200–300 mm, annual evaporation is 2 300–2 400 mm; the frost free period is about 105 days. The period of snow cover is 180 days (October to March). Snow depth in the study period was 13 cm, but is usually less than 10 cm. The productivity of winter pasture is poor, yielding 800 kg/ha fresh weight.

Water is scarce: people and stock drink melted snow. The weather was unusual in 1999; snow was 20 days later than usual, so people and livestock could not move to winter pasture, which put pressure on the autumn pasture.

The main species in pastures with an elevation of 1 200–1 900 m include *Festuca ovina*, *Stipa pillata*, *Agropyron cristatum*, *Cleistogenes squarrosa*, *Carex liparocarpos* and *Artemisia frigida*. The main species on desert and semi-desert pasture include *Stipa glareosa*, *S. sareptana*, *Cleistogenes squarrosa*, *Agropyron desertorum*, *Allium polyrrhizum*, *Seriphidium gracilescens*, *Nanophyton erinaceum*, *Anabasis* spp. and *Ceratoides lenensis*.

The winter pasture is used from December to March (3–4 months). Up to half of Burjin's winter pasture is also used by neighbouring counties. Salebur Mountain is the winter pasture of Burjin County, and the spring and autumn pasture of Hefeng County; the plains around

TABLE 6.5
Pasture utilization by the Treatment Group.

Pasture type	Area (ha)	Unit yield (kg)	Total yield (kg)	Period of use	Grazing days	Stocking rate (SSE[1]) Theoretical	Actual
Winter	445	844	375 580	1 Dec.–31 Jan.	62	3 575	1 700
				1 Feb.–31 Mar.	59		
Spring–Autumn	722	1 860	1 343 920	1 Apr.–20 June	81	4 796	2 221
				12 Sep.–30 Nov.	80		
Summer	275	2 837	780 175	21 June–11 Sep.	83	5 573	2 221
Total	1 442		2 499 675		365		

NOTES: (1) SSE = Standard Sheep Equivalent.

the Shawur Mountain are the winter pasture of Burjin County and the summer pasture of Hefeng County.

Livestock move to spring pasture at the end of March and in early April, when snow is melting on the winter pasture. With the snow melting from plain to upland, livestock are moved to summer pasture and arrive there in mid-June when grass is growing and the climate is cool, without flies and mosquitoes.

Winter pastures are close to townships and villages, within easy travelling distance (10–30 km. The area between Yushikershi and Erqis used as the spring and autumn pasture for the group requires a journey of 80 km.

Spring and autumn pastures

Spring and autumn pastures are in the Ertix valley in front of the Altai Range and its foothills, between 490 m and 1 400 m. The yield of fresh grass is about 1 200 kg/ha. The rainfall is about 110 mm, evaporation is very high, and sunshine is full. With increasing altitude the vegetation changes from plains lowland meadow, to plains gravel desert, and to plains sandy desert.

The vegetation of spring and autumn pasture is open, with a simple structure and much bare ground. Xerophilous dwarf shrubs predominate, such as *Anabasis* spp., *Salsola collinna, Suaeda glauca, Reaumuria soongarica, Seriphidium terrae-albae, Kochia prostrata, Agropyron monglicum, Ceratocarpus arenarius, Artemisia arenaria* and *Leymus secalinus.* The vegetation cover is 20-40 percent.

Shearing is in May, and the animals are moved to summer pasture in June (Plate 34). Spring and autumn pasture

Plate 34.
Horses of a family group moving to Altai top summer pastures.

Plate 35.
Altai – front summer pastures, with camps in the valley.

Plate 36.
The back summer pastures in Altai. These mountain areas have only a short growing season, but are highly productive. Lake Hanas in the foreground.

is plains or hilly land, close to towns or villages, which is convenient for herders. Autumn pasture is at 800–1 400 m. Rainfall exceeds 200 mm, but evaporation is ten times the precipitation.

Summer pasture

Summer pastures – in the mid-alpine zone and alpine zone, at 1 800–3 200 m – are under snow for about 270 days (September to May). Annual precipitation is about 600 mm, plant height is 15–60 cm, and vegetation cover is 80–90 percent. The yield of fresh forage is 1 500–4 000 kg/ha. There are two kinds of summer pasture, according to climatic condition and their season of use.

Front summer pasture is used from mid-June to mid-July (Plate 35). The temperature in the alpine zone (above 2 300 m) is low, snow melt is late and vegetation growth is slow, so flocks graze the mid-alpine (front) zone between 1 400-2 300 m.

Back summer pasture From mid-July to mid-August, as temperatures rise, the herds move to the alpine (back) zone (Plate 36). In mid- to late August, temperature in the alpine zone starts to fall and it snows as well; herders return to the front summer pasture.

The weather in the front summer pasture is mild and delightful; most herders and families stay there (Plate 37). Many activities take place: shearing, dipping, livestock counts, tax paying and making dairy products (red sweet cheese, white sweet cheese and sour cheese) (Plate 38). There are recreational activities, such as Aken singing parties, horse races, sheep catching and other social activities. There are posts where skins and wool can be

Plate 37.
A Kazakh family in their ger *on summer pastures in Altai.*

Plate 38.
Drying curd on summer pastures.

Plate 39.
High pastures for grazing and valley areas for haymaking. Near Lake Hanas, Altai.

sold, and shops where herders can buy daily necessities. In autumn, when flocks return from the back summer pasture, traders arrive and livestock trading begins.

Rainfall in the front summer pasture may amount to 600 mm. There are large areas of forest, mainly *Larix* and *Picea*. The soils are meadow soil and paramo soil, which is rich in organic matter and fertile. The main pasture plants are *Festuca sulcata, Poa annua, Phleum phleoides, Stipa pennata, Helictotrichon hookeri* subsp. *schellianum, Bromus inermis, Achillea millefolium, Galium verum, Polygonum alpinum, Phlomis alpina, Dracocephalum ruyschiana, Medicago falcata, Vicia sepium, Fragaria vesca, Spiraea media* and *Rosa oxyacanta*. Plant height is 20–30 cm and vegetation cover is 80–90 percent. The yield of fresh forage is 3 400–4 500 kg/ha, and some hay may be made (Plate 39).

The back summer pasture, above 2 300 m, is in the alpine zone; plants are low-growing, plant structure is simple and the growth period short. Annual precipitation is about 400 m. The annual average temperature is below 0°. The soil is alpine meadow soil. The main plants are bunch type dwarf grasses and associated forbs: *Festuca kurtschumica, F. kryloviana, Poa alpina, Anthoxanthum alpinum, Ptilagrostis mongolica, Carex stenocarpa, Carex melanantha, Kobresia*

bellardii, Polygonum viviparum, Alchemilla bungei, Ranunculus japonicus, Gentiana algida, Thalictrum alpinum and *Potentilla gelida*. Plant height is 10–15 m and the vegetation cover is 80–90 percent. The yield of fresh forage is 2 300–3 200 g/ha. The climate of the summer pasture is cool, with an excellent environment and beautiful scenery. There are no schools or hospitals, but doctors and veterinarians move from household to household and are welcomed and respected.

STUDIES ON THE CONTROL GROUP (NOMADIC HOUSEHOLDS)
The population of the Control Group
The nine households comprised 61 people (31 males and 30 females). There were 35 workers (20 male and 15 female). Of the 61 people, the education levels were 5 above senior school, 23 middle school, and 13 primary school.

The pastures of the Control Group
They have only their allocated pastures and must feed their herds on natural grazing throughout the year, using their herding skills to have stock fat enough in autumn to survive through winter and early spring. The area of pasture allocated to the nine households was 1 245.8 ha. The general situation is described in the following paragraphs, and the pattern of natural pasture use is summarized in Table 6.6.

TABLE 6.6
The pastures of the Control Group.

Pasture type	Area (ha)	Season of use	Days grazed	Yield of green matter Unit (kg/ha)	Total (kg)	Number of livestock
Winter	469.1	1 Dec.–15 Mar.	105	899	421 720	1 249
Spring and Autumn	388.3	16 Mar.–1 July	105	2 790	1 083 357	1 527
		13 Sep.–30 Nov.	80			
Summer	388.4	2 July–12 Sep.	70	3 060	1 188 504	1 644
Total	1245.8		365		2 262 274	1 721

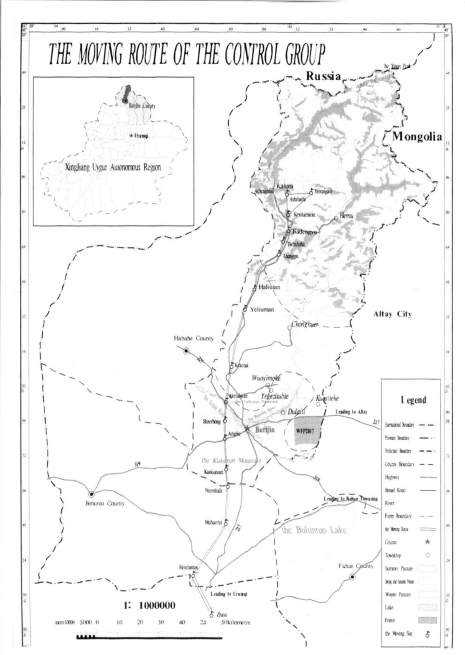

FIGURE 6.4
Map of the traditional transhumance routes of Burjin, northwest China.

Winter pasture This is in Hasenhamur and Shawur regions, 100 km from Burjin at 460 m; annual precipitation is 206 mm. The frost-free period is 101 days and the annual average temperature is 3.6°C. The main vegetation is *Stipa pillata* and *Carex* spp. Plagues of locusts and mice often occur in this area. The vegetation cover is 60 percent, with a unit yield of 899 kg/ha. There are no schools or houses; women, children and old people live in a village in winter. Strong herders tend flocks in winter. Necessities have to be bought from town, 100 km away. Sheep and cattle manure is used as fuel. Life on the winter pasture is hard.

Spring pasture is at Jialipahetasi and Kekebai, 40 km from Burjin, at 550 m. The frost-free period is 153 days. Annual rainfall is 119 mm, with snow cover for 120 days, the depth of snow averages 20 cm. The average annual temperature is 4.1°C. The vegetation cover is 40–50 percent, with a yield of 730 kg/ha. Wild animals include wolves, foxes and rabbits. This is the lambing pasture, where flocks stay for 50 days in spring.

Spring and autumn pastures are in the region of Ahonggaiti, 90 km from Burjin, at 1 370 m. Annual precipitation is 289 mm, with 142 frost-free days. The average annual temperature is 2.7°C. The depth of snow is 60 cm, with a covered period of 140 days. The soil is chernozem; pasture is upland meadow. The vegetation cover is 90 percent with a yield of 2 790 kg/ha. Wild animals include wolves, foxes, marmots, squirrels and rabbits. Herders get drinking water from mountain springs or streams. Dung or branches are used as fuel. Herder children can go to primary school at the pastures, and to middle school at the township. There are mobile medical services for people and animals. Flour, food and daily necessities can

be bought from a mobile shop. Ahonggaiti and Haliutan are the main places for recreational activities and festivals in spring and autumn. This area is also a trading site.

Yegamaiti summer pasture is 150 km from Burjin, at 2 300 m, beside the famous Hanas Lake. It is upland meadow on soil rich in organic matter. This is the largest summer pasture in the county; parts are mown for hay (Plate 39), with a yield of 3 060 kg/ha. The precipitation is 600 mm, the average annual temperature is -3.7°C and the frost-free period is 100 days. Snow depth averages about 150 cm, laying for 180 days. There are large areas of original forest, mainly coniferous, on the shady slopes. There are many wild animals, including brown bears, snow leopards, wolves, foxes, snow chicken, deer, wild duck and squirrels.

The basic transhumance pattern of the Control Group

The routes of the transhumance cycle are shown on the map (see Figure 6.4).

Moving times and distances

The distance from Shawur (Zhaya) winter pasture to Yemaigaiti summer pasture is 320 km (240 km by road), with 16 moves of about 20 km each. Times and distances are similar when the flocks return. Flocks moved 33 times in a 640-km journey. Horses, camels, cattle and carts are used for transport. In 2000, the movement times of the three Groups were similar. Group 1 moved 26 times, spending 41 days on the move. Group 2 moved 25 times, spending 37 days on the move, and Group 3 moved 27 times, taking 42 days.

Moving from Winter to Summer Pasture

In 1999, herders left Hasenhamur on 15 March and arrived at Biesikuola on the first day, Muhurtai on the second, Narenkala on the third, Kekexun on the fourth, Artuobieke on the fifth, Sharhong on the sixth and Aketuobieke on the seventh day, having moved seven times in seven days (15–22 March). They stayed at Aketuobieke for 8 days, then moved to Kekebai spring pasture (1 day) and stayed for 50 days (1 April–20 May). Their ninth stop was Yeliuman (1 day). They took one day to reach the tenth stop: Haliutan and Ahonggai, then stayed there for 30 days (22 May–22 June, with spring shearing). They took one day each to move to Tielishahan (the eleventh stop), to Jiadengyu (the twelfth stop), Kexitubieke (the thirteenth stop), Ashibashi (the fourteenth stop), Kadinger (the fifteenth stop) and finally to Yemaigaiti summer pasture, where they grazed for 70 days (2 July–12 September). When they left on 12 September they had grazed for 177 days.

Moving from Summer to Winter Pasture

The return started on 13 September; the first six one-day stops were at Kadinger, Ashibashi, Kexituobieke (a day), the fourth stop was Jiadengyu (a day), the fifth stop was Tielieshahan and then Halahongai, where they stayed for 20 days (19 September–9 October). The seventh stop was Ahongai and Haliutan (20 days – 10–30 October). The eighth stop was Yeliuman (a day), and the ninth was Kekebai (one day), where they stayed for 18 days (2–20 November). The tenth move was to Aketubieke (a day), with a three-day stay, then a move to Sharhong on 24 November. The twelfth to sixteenth stops of one day each were at Artuobie, Kekexun, Narenkala, Muhurtai, and Biesikuola. Flocks arrived at Zhaya winter pasture on 1 December and remained till 15 March (183 days).

Plate 40.
Moving gear to the summer pastures, Altai. Bulls are widely used as pack animals.

Moving from Winter to Spring Pasture, then to Summer from Spring Pasture

In 2000, herders started to move from the regions of Hasenhamur and Sawur on 15 March. They moved seven times in seven days (15–22 March). They stayed at Aketubieke for 8 days, then moved to Kekebai spring pasture and stayed there for 50 days (1 April–20 May). Nomadic herders cannot produce lambs in late winter or early spring because of lack of feed and hay, so lambing is timed for late spring, with lamb sales in the autumn, but usually in the following year. There is a simple lambing shed for each household. Herders always take a bag with them when they graze sheep in the day so as to put lambs in as soon as they are born. The ninth stop was Yeliuman (21 May) and the tenth stop was Hailiutan and Ahongaiti, where they remained for 30 days (22 May–22 June). The eleventh stop was Tielieshahan (started on 23 June), the twelfth stop was Jiadengyu, the thirteenth stop was Kexituobieke, the fourteenth stop was Ashibashi, the fifteenth stop was Kadinger, the sixteenth stop (the last stop) was Yemaigaiti summer pasture (Plate 40), where they grazed for 70–80 days (2 July to 12–20 September). From 15 March to 12 September was 177 days in total.

Moving from Summer to Winter Pasture

Moving started on 13 September, taking six one-day stages: Kadinger – Ashibashi Kexituobieke – Jiadengyu – Tielieshahan – Halahongai, where they stayed for 20 days (19 September – 9 October). The seventh stop was Ahongai (one day) and Haliutan, where they stayed for 20 days (10–30 October). This period is generally the best period for livestock selling. Herders will sell lambs that were born around 15 April in the year and with an age of 6–7 months.

The liveweight of lambs is about 35–45 kg and the carcass weight is about 17–22 kg. From 1 November, the eighth and ninth stops were Yeliuman and Kekebai (one day each), staying at Kekebai for 18 days (2–20 November). The tenth stop was Aketubieke (one day), with a three-day stay, then a move to Sharhong on 24 November. The twelfth to sixteenth stops (each one-day moves) were Artubieke, Kekexun, Narenkala, Muhurtai and Biesikuola. Finally, on 1 December, flocks were moved to the seventeenth stop: Zhaya winter pasture.

Livestock production of the Control Group

The livestock numbers of the group for the two seasons are given in Tables 6.7a and 6.7b.

LIVESTOCK PRODUCTION OF THE TWO GROUPS

While the Treatment Group had slightly more stock than the Control, the differences were not large. Since the project began over a decade ago, this would seem to indicate that the Treatment Group is not intent on increasing numbers but may be more interested in maximizing offtake (Tables 6.4a,b and 6.7a,b). The Treatment Group sold more stock than the Control. The two most important sales were: cattle – Treatment Group, 20 percent (1999) and 28 percent (2000); Control Group, 16.5 percent (1999) and 22 percent (2000); sheep – Treatment Group, 55 percent (1999) and 43 percent (2000); and Control Group, 40 percent (1999) and 44 percent (2000). These are not great differences, apart from sheep in 1999. As noted below, the main difference is that the Treatment Group can sell more of their lambs in the first year, and at a greater weight.

TABLE 6.7A
Livestock of the Control Group in 1999 (head).

Species	Number at start of year		Fate			Total number at year end
	Total	Females	Weaned offspring	Killed for home use	Sold	
Cattle	121	57	51	8	20	144
Horses	74	19	11	5	4	76
Camels	26	12	7	–	1	32
Sheep	670	459	452	64	269	789
Goats	108	66	64	27	16	129
Total	999	613	585	104	310	1 170

TABLE 6.7B
Livestock of the Control Group in 2000 (head).

Species	Number at start of year		Fate			Total number at year end
	Total	Females	Weaned offspring	Killed for home use	Sold	
Cattle	144	49	46	7	32	153
Horses	76	12	12	4	3	70
Camels	32	1	1	–	–	24
Sheep	789	501	494	90	346	735
Goats	129	90	94	28	37	155
Total	1 170	653	647	129	418	1 127

AGRICULTURAL INCOME AND EXPENDITURE

The agricultural incomes from livestock and crops and the associated production expenses of the two groups are summarized in Tables 6.8 and 6.9.

The Treatment Group, with crops and livestock, had, of course, a far higher income than the Control, but they had a considerably higher income from livestock in both years although herd numbers were not very different (compare Tables 6.4a,b and 6.7a,b). The Treatment Group's livestock income exceeded that of the Control by 60 percent in 1999 and 65 percent in 2000. This was mainly due to a much greater sale of sheep, presumably because they were able to get lambs to saleable weight in autumn, whereas the Control Group had to keep them for a second year. The stock of the Treatment Group were on average heavier than those of the Control (Table

6.10). A five-year survey on winter sheep weight, 1989–1993, showed that sheep in the project area gained 5–6 kg during winter. Sheep on natural pasture lost 1.2–1.5 kg each during winter. In addition, the sheep in the project area were mated in August–September and lambed in February; their average slaughter weight by the end of September was 45 kg and the heaviest reached 65 kg. Control sheep were mated at the beginning of November and lambed in April–May; their slaughter weight was 30–34 kg by the end of September.

The Treatment Group earned more from crops than it did from livestock. The crop component was 55 percent of their total in 1999 and 60 percent in 2000.

The production costs of the groups also differed greatly (Table 6.9). The Treatment Group expended far more on livestock production, notably in herding labour, electricity and water, and fodder;

TABLE 6.8
Agricultural income of both study groups (RMB).

	Control Group		Treatment Group	
	1999	2000	1999	2000
Livestock Sales	98 642	133 680	126 150	170 950
Milk	1 900	33 800	22 176	23 260
Skins	–	6 340	620	3 050
Wool	–	10 155	11 778	3 250
Subtotal Livestock	100 542	120 803	160 724	200 510
Other	57 058	10 950	9 900	33 180
Crop sales	–	–	61 584	126 464
Fodder	–	–	47 860	129 469
Straw	–	–	29 059	–
Machinery hire	–	–	45 200	10 500
Total	157 600	194 925	354 327	500 123
Per household	17 511	21 658	39 370	55 569

TABLE 6.9
Production expenses of both study groups (RMB).

Item	Control Group		Treatment Group	
	1999	2000	1999	2000
Moving and transport	2 120	7 850	3 700	700
Herding by others	970	5 000	11 868	17 228
Animal health	5 420	5 338	4 024	7 851
Salt	980	870	1 276	2 730
Pasture fee	1 358	1 564	631	1 030
Fodder	2 860	10 500	71 887	86 202
Other	3 320	16 740	100	370
Water and electricity	2 799	2 144	19 668	14 780
Construction	1 650	–	7 130	3 000
Machinery and tools	–	2 180	2 200	1 060
Subtotal livestock and general	21 477	52 186	122 484	134 951
Ploughing and harvesting	–	–	22 197	22 040
Fertilizer and pesticides	–	–	27 349	21 997
Seed	–	–	21 193	12 969
Total	21 477	52 186	193 223	191 957

TABLE 6.10
Slaughter weight of livestock (kg).

	Treatment Group	Control Group
Male cattle	280	270
Female cattle	270	260
Fat rump – two-year-old	60	50
Fat rump lamb	45	30
Goats	35	32
Horse	380	380

570 percent of the Control costs in 1999 and 258 percent in 2000. In 2000, the Control Group bought more fodder and had higher unspecified production costs.

The net agricultural incomes (Table 6.11) of the Groups were, of course,

TABLE 6.11
Per capita income of both study groups (RMB).

	Control		Treatment	
	1999	2000	1999	2000
Total income	157 600	194 925	354 327	500 123
Number of persons	61	59	59	61
Per capita income	2 583	3 303	6 005	8 198
Income per household	17 511	21 658	39 369	55 569

markedly different – that of the Treatment Group being roughly twice that of the Control.

Household expenditure (Table 6.12) reflects the differences in income, and perhaps also access to goods. The Control Group, however, expended a greater proportion of its net income on household needs than did the Treatment Group.

Differences in economic status

All households of the Treatment Group have acquired fixed assets of two types: productive and non-productive. Productive fixed assets are land, agricultural machinery, tractors, grass harvesting machines, rakes, sprayers, greenhouses, sheds, etc. Non-productive fixed assets consist of houses, furniture, family electrical equipment, motorcycles, etc. There are almost no fixed

assets in the control households; all of their belongings have to be carried on the back of camels throughout the year. Economic state decides living standards. Herder life in the Treatment Group is improving, but there is little change in that of the control.

PROJECT ACHIEVEMENTS

The development objective of Project 2817 was "To improve the income and living conditions of nomadic herders through increased forage production and settlement, at the same time retaining the transhumant system of grazing." This it certainly has done. Selected herding families have been settled and are obviously thriving; their herds continue to use natural pastures according to the transhumant system, but also benefit from increased availability of winter feed and shelter. The

TABLE 6.12
Household expenses of both study groups (RMB).

Item	Control Group		Treatment Group	
	1999	2000	1999	2000
Food and basic commodities	52 183	51 468	89 299	133 510
Clothing	17 900	17 000	29 500	28 040
Marriages and funerals	14 000	11 200	15 100	26 250
Tuition	15 496	8 440	26 650	20 300
Medical	5 630	9 650	17 270	4 460
Various fees	–	8 036	–	5 860
Fuel	–	–	–	6 570
Building and repair	13 060	–	18 580	–
Other	10 200	5 986	1 052	2 240
Total	128 469	111 780	197 451	227 230
Expenses per household	14 274	12 420	21 939	25 248
Expenses as proportion of net income	67%	43%	35%	32%

feed production component, however, is disappointing since yields are less than one-third of their potential; the crop component in contrast is now the source of more than half the household agricultural income. These improvements in feed and shelter have allowed lambs to be marketed at a far earlier age than previously – that and reduction of grazing in winter should have reduced pressure on the grazing lands, but it is not clear whether this has had much effect since there is a far larger number of non-scheme stock in the area. The benefits of fixed, well constructed housing with access to social and other facilities is obvious, and will probably have an even more marked effect on the Treatment Group in the long term.

This is an imaginative use of available irrigation water and of land too light for sustained annual cropping. Almost all the available area in Altai has now been developed. Whether the model can be replicated elsewhere under similar conditions is not known. A considerable investment per household has been made, but no information is available on how that compares to the increased incomes of project households.

Chapter VII
China case study 2: Cold-resistant lucerne (*Medicago sativa*) for northern Xinjiang

Jichun Min

SUMMARY

Large areas of lucerne have been developed for hay at Altai, near Burjin, in the north of Xinjiang – an arid region with very cold winters. Only one cultivar (a local landrace) was in use and it was deemed desirable to have a wider genetic base. Introduced supposedly cold-tolerant cultivars failed to overwinter. Local selection has produced an improved cultivar, registered by the Chinese Herbage Cultivar Registration Board as 'Xinmu No. 3'. It is well adapted to the area and is more productive than the cultivar already in use. A system of seed multiplication and maintenance of mother seed has been installed. Improvement of lucerne to suit local conditions is obviously feasible, and this work should have application to areas of similar ecology within the subregion. Uptake of new cultivars has been slow in the Project that was the main target of the work; partly because of lack of training and experience on the part of the herders involved, who still use the cheapest seed available. It may, however, be more readily accepted by more experienced communities. Field testing and experience in the project has shown that there are many constraints other than genetic ones in the production of lucerne: correct field levelling, use of clean seed and field hygiene to control *Cuscuta*, general careful husbandry and adequate fertilizer are all necessary if reasonable crops, adequate to cover the costs of infrastructure and water, are to be attained.

INTRODUCTION

The area of World Food Programme (WFP) Project 2817, for which this work was mainly carried out, is described in Chapter VI. Lucerne, *Medicago sativa*, is a crop of very ancient cultivation in the irrigated areas of Xinjiang. It was probably introduced when improved horses were imported from Central Asia. The oases of Xinjiang lie on the ancient Silk Route, which led through the original homeland of lucerne, in the historical region of Media and adjacent lands in Asia Minor. Several landraces have developed over the centuries, with notable differences between those from the colder northern areas of the Djungar basin and those from the Tarim basin, which is south of the Tien Shan

Range and where winters are less harsh. Several wild relatives of lucerne occur in the better-watered areas of Xinjiang's mountains, notably *M. falcata*.

In the 1980s, the Animal Husbandry Bureau developed 25 000 ha of irrigated land for hay production on sandy-gravelly soils unsuited to arable cropping (Li, Yuang and Suttie, 1996) in Altai Kazakh Prefecture in the extreme north of the Region, under Project 2817. The work was assisted by the World Food Programme (WFP) and technical inputs were funded by the United Nations Development Programme (UNDP) and executed by the Food and Agriculture Organization of the United Nations (FAO). The scheme was in production by the end of the decade.

The livestock activities of the Project were described in an earlier chapter. For a map of the Project area, see Figure 6.2.

While the currently used cultivar, 'Beijang', was admirably adapted to the local conditions, reliance on a single cultivar of one species over so large an area gave rise to some concern. The Project covered four areas (Altai, Fuhai, Dure and Burjin), and formerly lucerne had been cultivated in scattered fields. In addition, cv. Beijang is susceptible to some fungal diseases and this was exacerbated by imperfections in the micro-levelling of the newly-formed irrigated fields; plants in tiny depressions where water lay longer were frequently attacked by fungi, often giving rise to a "little leaf" effect through proliferation of many weak stems caused by damage to the crown. A literature search was carried out (by R.W. Brougham, FAO consultant under the UNDP/FAO project) to identify cold-tolerant, disease-resistant lucernes, and a large number of samples, mostly from North America, were introduced for screening. Their testing was undertaken by the Xinjiang Agricultural University, with the main site at the Altai part of the scheme.

The initial growth of many of the introductions was impressive and their first year performance far outstripped the local control (cv. Beijang). Next spring, however, none of the introductions survived at Altai – only the control was alive! The project sites, on the desert fringe, have little or no snow cover in winter so the young plants had no protection; perhaps they had been selected in areas with snow cover. It later transpired that earlier introductions from Russia had failed in a similar way. There was, therefore, no easy way to diversify and improve the lucernes in use by importation of commercially available cultivars. After discussions with the fodder specialists of Xinjiang Agricultural University, the Grassland and Pasture Crops Group of FAO/AGPC agreed to provide some support so that the University's ongoing work on breeding and selection of lucerne could be intensified.

TESTING SITES

Although the climate at Urumqi (see maps, Figures 6.1 and 6.2) is very harsh, it is less so than that of the project production sites. Urumqi, 43°47' N, 85°37' E, at 919 m altitude, has an annual mean temperature of 7°C and a January mean minimum of -20°C; precipitation is 302 mm. Long-term data from project sites are not available. The nearest site for which data are available is at Fuyun, which is higher than the irrigated areas and receives more precipitation: project sites receive less than 100 mm annually. Fuyun is at 46° 59' N, 85°43' E, at 1294 m altitude; its mean annual temperature is 3.5°C, January average minimum is -26°C; precipitation is 198 mm. The temperature and precipitation at the two sites are shown graphically in Figures 7.1 and 7.2.

The main field testing was carried out at Altai, with breeding and other work at Urumqi to facilitate access to facilities and specialized staff.

Development of 'Xinmu no. 3' lucerne

In 1995, when they greened up in spring, 33 plants were selected from a four-year-old plot of cv. Spredor 2 lucerne at Urumqi. Spredor 2 is a cultivar released by Northrup King in 1974. Its parentage is Travois, Rambler and Vernal, which

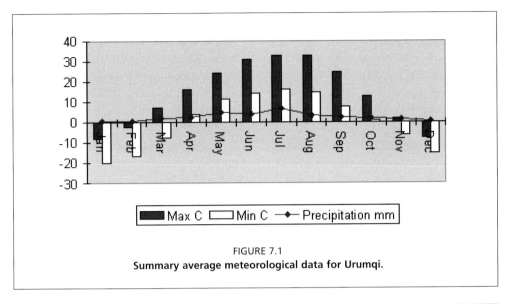

FIGURE 7.1
Summary average meteorological data for Urumqi.

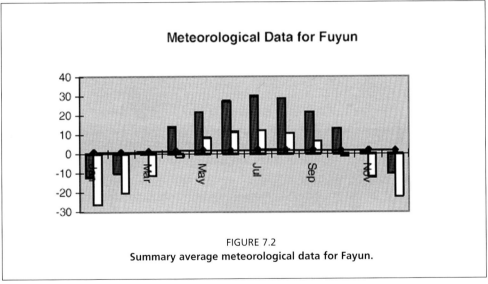

FIGURE 7.2
Summary average meteorological data for Fayun.

are cold-tolerant cultivars with Ladakh, *M. falcata*, Siberian and Cossack among their parents. Spredor 2 has variable flower colour; it is highly resistant to bacterial wilt and moderately resistant to verticillium wilt and fusarium wilt. The Spredor 2 at Urumqi had been sown in 1990 and grown unprotected through the subsequent winters; the selection was made among the

survivors. These were open pollinated and the seeds mixed to form line 9501. Some stems were taken as cuttings and taken to 183 Farm, Beitun, Altai (hereafter referred to as Altai) in August for cold tests. Splits of twelve mother plants were grown in a greenhouse to speed up seed production; seed was harvested in November, 1995.

Some survivors (at Urumqi) from the

FAO introductions were crossed with the local standard cv. Xinmu No 1, but, since rapid results were required to assist the Altai Project 2817 scheme and the work would have required at least 11 years, this was not followed-up under FAO financing.

Four cultivars were chosen for testing at Altai and Urumqi from 1996: line 9501, Beijang, Xinmu No. 1 and Spredor 2. These were sown in randomized blocks (Plate 41) with three replications at both sites in plots of 5.63 m² with a 30 cm row spacing and a seed rate of 3 kg/ha. Harvest was at early flowering (2–3 percent) with two-and-a-half cuts at Urumqi and two at Altai. The last cut was taken one month before growth was expected to stop. For dry-matter estimation, 500 g samples were air-dried. The trials received five to six weedings, three to four hoeings and five to six irrigations annually. Yield data are given in Tables 7.1 and 7.2.

Line 9501 was the highest yielder throughout the trials at both sites. In both cases, second-year yields were much higher than those of the seedling or third year – this may be due to the lack of maintenance fertilizer – normal practice for the area.

Testing for cold resistance was done at both sites. Surviving and dead plants were counted after greening-up each year; with three counts made, since some plants that were injured by low temperatures, but had not died, greened-up 3 to 20 days later than normal plants. Plants that had not greened up at the first counting were marked; if they greened up at the second or third counting, they were added to the survivors; those which had not greened up by the branching stage were counted as dead. Results for the two sites are given in Table 7.3. Survival was very good throughout; as all entries in the trial were, of course, known to be adapted to local conditions. Survival of Spredor 2

Plate 41.
Lucerne trial plots in Urumqi.

TABLE 7.1
Yield trial at Urumqi over three years (yield in t/ha of air-dry material).

Cultivar or line	1996	1997	1998	Total
9501	7.54	15.82	9.15	32.52
Xinmu No. 1	6.65	12.54	6.02	25.21
Spredor 2	7.22	13.63	4.22	25.07
Beijang	6.21	12.96	5.77	24.94

TABLE 7.2
Yield trial at Altai over three years (yield in t/ha of air-dry material).

Cultivar or line	1996	1997	1998	Total
9501	8.13	31.52	19.50	59.15
Xinmu No. 1	6.58	24.96	16.17	47.71
Spredor 2	6.73	28.03	16.68	51.44
Beijang	6.37	23.42	13.56	43.35

TABLE 7.3
Comparison of winter survival rate (percent).

Cultivar or line	Urumqi		Beltun/Altai	
	1997	1998	1997	1998
9501	100	97.51	100	93.90
Xinmu No. 1	100	86.28	100	91.00
Spredor 2	100	77.06	100	88.06
Beijang	98	79.06	100	91.04

TABLE 7.4
Effect of removing snow cover at Urumqi, 1997.

	9501		Spredor 2		Beijang	
	Snow cover removed	Control	Snow cover removed	Control	Snow cover removed	Control
Density before winter (plants/m^2)	17.15	13.55	20.57	16.28	19.46	16.07
Winter survival (percent)	96.67	100	94.40	100	97.20	100
Date of greening	13 April	5 April	15 April	5 April	9 April	5 April
Single plant weight (gram)	518	649	348	348	400	358
Yield (tonne/ha of green matter)	85.9	87.9	67.7	56.7	75.8	58.5

and Beijang at Urumqi in the third year was much poorer than that of line 9501 and Xinmu No. 1, but at Altai all survival rates were similar.

The effect of removal (by brushing) of any snow cover from the third replicate was studied between November and April of the establishment year (Table 7.4). Snow removal delayed greening-up by a few days and caused a small decrease in survival.

Overwinter survival, of course, reflects more than cold tolerance: disease susceptibility is also involved. For both, line 9501 was superior. Snow removal led to a mortality of between three and six percent, with no difference in winter survival between line 9501 and Beijang (Table 7.4).

As part of the characterization of the new cultivar for registration, phenological data (Tables 7.5 and 7.6) and information

TABLE 7.5
Growth stages of line 9501 in Urumqi.

Stage	Germination or greening	Budding	Early flowering	Flowering	Ripe	Growth season
Seedling year	5 May	24 June	9 July	18 July	24 August	115 days
Second year	10 April	24 May	5 June	13 June	23 July	94 days

TABLE 7.6
Comparison of plant height, Urumqi 1998 (cm).

	13 April	20 April	27 April	4 May	11 May	18 May	25 May	1 June	8 June
9501	10.1	13.2	16.9	24.5	39.8	54.0	67.6	85.2	104.5
Beijang	5.8	9.4	11.3	17.5	32.6	47.0	59.2	74.2	89.6

TABLE 7.7
Proximate analysis of line 9501 and cv. Beijang (percentage of dry matter).

Cultivar or line	Crude protein	Ether extract	Crude fibre	NFE[1]	Ash	Phosphate	Calcium
9501	18.68	2.81	31.47	36.81	10.24	0.286	1.93
Beijang	17.34	2.22	33.36	36.73	10.35	0.292	1.63

NOTE: (1) NFE = Nitrogen-Free Extract

TABLE 7.8
Field-scale yields at two sites (yield in t/ha of air-dry material).

Cultivar or line	Urumqi		Beitun/Altai
	1997	1998	1998
9501	9.50	16.18	25.33
Beijang	7.95	11.46	18.12

on the approximate forage composition (Table 7.7) were collected. Line 9501 (Xinmu No 3) has at least as good a feeding value as Beijang.

As formal testing advanced, field-scale trials were installed at Beitun/Altai and Urumqi, under conditions similar to those used by herders, to see how the selection performed as a possible commercial cultivar. As shown in Table 7.8, line 9501 performed well at both sites.

STUDIES ON OTHER CULTIVARS

A few plants of other FAO introductions had survived at Urumqi; these were studied in observation plots at Urumqi from 1996 to 1999, with Xinjiang Diaye as control. None were really promising (see Table 7.9). Recently (2002), some new cultivars from Montana, USA, have been introduced

and are currently being assessed at Xinjiang Agricultural University in Urumqi.

SEED MULTIPLICATION

Seed production of line 9501 was a priority from the outset in order to provide enough for proper testing; once the line showed promise, provision of breeder's and foundation seed was organized so that these could be supplied to producers. Since isolation, protection from livestock, avoidance of volunteer plants and access for supervision are all necessary on seed production plots, suitable sites were limited and small, but, starting from the few plants grown in the greenhouse in 1995, over 10 kg of breeder and foundation seed was produced in 1997, and a total of 35 kg by 1998. The improved cultivar 9501 has

TABLE 7.9
Comparison of introduced material (t/ha green matter).

Cultivar or line	1996	1997	1998	Total
Xinjiang Diaye (control)	31.73	62.14	43.51	137.38
5262	38.04	68.84	36.86	143.69
Meteor	40.49	52.51	29.93	122.93
Skriver	19.18	55.00	32.33	106.51
K4	34.06	64.34	41.00	139.40

been registered by the Chinese Herbage Cultivar registration Board as cultivar Xinmu No. 3. Following another FAO project (FAO/TCP/CPR 0065), Xinjiang Agricultural University started (2002) multiplying seed on various seed farms, and large quantities were expected to be available in 2003 or 2004.

Lucerne seed production in Altai has been a problem for a long time. Seed production bases were set up there in the 1970s, but the level of technology was low, cultural practices were unsuitable for good seed production, and infestation with dodder (*Cuscuta* sp.) became serious. Unfortunately, much of this seed was used in the initial years of the Altai scheme and much of the land is now contaminated with dodder. The dodder infestation occurred because there was no scientific seed production and no attempt to eliminate dodder systematically. *Cuscuta* seeds can survive for twelve years in the soil and can be spread by irrigation water, as well as through animal droppings. The seed production base at Dulati had to be closed in the early 1990s. For Project 2817, following the advice of Dr Brougham, a seed production base for Xinmu No. 1 was established in the early 1990s and nearly 2 tonne of seed harvested, but this base was closed because of lack of funds.

Lucerne seed is not an attractive crop in Xinjiang. Yields are low, about 150 kg/ha is common on commercial farms (although Xinjiang Agricultural University farm has regularly been achieving seed yields of 600–700 kg/ha, and yields in excess of 1000 kg/ha are expected), and farmers are unwilling to pay for quality. The cultivar Xinmu No 1 was released in 1987; since then, seed has been provided to more than forty farms for multiplication but only two farms have produced seed and multiplied the cultivar, and total extension has been only 100 000 ha. The main reason is that field crops – cotton, oilseed rape, sugar beet and cereals – are easier to grow and more profitable.

It has now become necessary for a well supervised three-step production system (breeder seed ⇒ foundation seed ⇒ certified seed) to be used for future lucerne seed production. Clean, dodder-free, healthy seed of adapted varieties is the key to sustainable, high yielding lucerne production in Altai. Farmers are now buying cheap seed from other parts of China, but that seed is of cultivars that are not sufficiently cold-tolerant, and the seed is not clean. A greater extension effort will be required by Project 2817 authorities, together with the re-opening of their base for seed multiplication, if the problems associated with poor seed are to be overcome. The herders of the project had no experience of crop and fodder production before the project's inception; they were transhumant stock rearers. Every aspect of cultivation is new to them, and it is unfortunate that they have not yet appreciated the importance of proper choice of cultivars and maintenance of clean healthy seed. Even more so since the importance of animal breeding and health is well understood by them.

To assure long-term preservation of the seed base for Xinmu No 3, sixteen lines have been planted in isolation at stations throughout Xinjiang. Production of breeder seed is undertaken at five sites, including Chanji and Hami. This also facilitates the introduction of the new cultivar to other parts of the region: Xinjiang covers about 1 600 000 km² and distances are vast. Recent efforts by Xinjiang Animal Husbandry Bureau and especially by Xinjiang Agricultural University should ensure that adequate quantities of seed will become available in 2003–2004.

DISCUSSION

The very cold, arid areas of northern Xinjiang pose a problem when broadening the genetic base of lucerne cultivation, especially since introduction of cultivars from elsewhere does not succeed. Earlier work (development of cvs Xinmu No 1 and Xinmu No 2) showed that considerable progress can be made by working with local material. The work described above shows that introduced material can have a very positive role in lucerne improvement, at least insofar as material with some *M. falcata* in its background is concerned. The cultivar Xinmu No 3 has shown itself to be superior in yield to the landrace currently in use, and well adapted to the conditions and methods of husbandry used locally. It may well prove to be valuable over a much wider area in the colder, arid tracts of northern China and northeastern and central Asia.

The practical application of the work, however, shows clearly that there are major factors limiting lucerne production in Project 2178, other than the cultivars in use. The main factors are associated with proper husbandry and irrigation:

- lack of care with seed quality at the outset of the scheme has led to serious infestation with *Cuscuta*. This will be very difficult to control, and impossible unless a clean seed supply is assured and strict crop hygiene insisted upon;
- correct land levelling and in-field water management is essential to assure an even stand and lessen the challenge from fungal disease;
- it is likely that maintenance dressings of phosphatic fertilizer should be used to prolong the productive life of the crop and avoid the drop seen after the second year; and
- the poor uptake of seed of improved cultivars means that the majority of herders still use unimproved, and probably unclean, seed because it is cheapest.

These omissions are particularly serious in irrigated farming, where high yields per unit of area are desirable in order to pay for water and maintenance of infrastructure. The herders, who have never cultivated before, have made great progress in haymaking, but there is still a great deal of training to be done if they are to make good, sustainable use of the irrigation infrastructure and of the well adapted cultivars now available to them.

It is still too early to say how the new cultivar might be accepted in other lucerne-growing areas of the region. While uptake of new cultivars has been very slow among the inexperienced growers of Project 2718, there may be better reception in the more traditional lucerne-growing communities.

Chapter VIII
China case study 3: Pastoral systems, change and the future of the grazing lands in Tibet

Tashi Nyima

SUMMARY

Tibet's vast grasslands are not only grazing land, they are of prime ecological importance for their great biodiversity and as the upper catchments of most of Asia's main rivers. Before 1950, both human and livestock populations were low, and probably in equilibrium with grazing resources. Once the industry was collectivized and modern health care for man and beast introduced, both human and animal populations rose extremely steeply, overgrazing became widespread and the fragile grasslands suffered and their yield dropped.

Decollectivization only defined rights to livestock ownership, not grazing rights, so subsequently there has been no rational grazing management and even less investment in grazing infrastructure. Widespread attempts at introducing crop production to zones manifestly unsuitable for it have resulted in the sterilization of large areas of the best grazing. Instead of trying to get stock, and people dependent on stock rearing, into equilibrium with pasture production, the authorities are trying to intensify so that stock output meets urban demand. They are also following a policy of sedentarization, which is totally unsuited to very extensive stock rearing in so harsh a climate. Implementation of this policy worries many pasture ecologists. In the areas where crops can be grown, mixed farming is increasingly important. Since the output of pastoral areas is static or declining, improvement of meat and milk production from agricultural and agropastoral zones is likely to be the main way of reducing the urban areas' reliance on imports from elsewhere in China.

INTRODUCTION

The Tibetan plateau occupies an eighth of China; its average altitude is about 4 000 m. Tibet Autonomous Region, a major part of the plateau, which covers 1 200 000 km², is one of China's largest, but least developed and least populated, provinces. More than 2.5 million Tibetans live in this subregion. Crops and forests are limited to a few areas because of the short growing season, and pastoralism is widespread. For most highlanders, livestock is the only means of sustaining their food security and livelihood.

There are two systems, pastoral and agropastoral. Pastoral systems are nomadic – the Tibetan plateau is one of the largest nomadic pastoral areas in the world – and are usually at altitudes above 4 200 m (Plate 42); agropastoral systems are below 4 200 m, where crops can be grown. Profound changes in both systems are taking place, with both negative and positive impacts on the fate of the grazing land, including:

• promotion of infrastructure to improve herders' access to services and markets; re-structuring to encourage a market-oriented pastoral system;

- policies to settle nomads and allocate pasture to families, which will change the interaction of nomads with their environment, and limit their mobility;
- expansion of natural reserves, such as Changtang natural reserve, which limit the areas of grazing and mobility of herders;
- promotion of crop production in areas which were previously good pastoral land; this encourages stationary herding or agropastoralism where previously it was nomadic; and formation of new markets, through improvement of transport networks and capabilities; and
- climatic change, such as decrease in rainfall and increased temperature, as well as increasingly frequent natural disasters such as snowstorms and drought.

All these changes will alter the future fate of Tibet's grazing lands and affect herders' way of life and the ecosystems on which their livelihood depends.

This paper describes Tibet's grazing lands and livestock production systems, discusses their history briefly, and the changes that have taken place in the last 20–50 years in terms of systems, and finally gives suggestions on the scope for exploring opportunities for sustainable development of pastoral systems.

TIBET AUTONOMOUS REGION

The Tibet Autonomous Region (hereafter referred to as Tibet) is in the southwest of China, from 26°50'N to 36°53'N (2 000 km) and from 78°25'E to 99°06'E (1 000 km). It has borders with the provinces of Qinghai and Xinjiang in the north, Sichuan and

Plate 42.
Much of the grazing land is high, cold and of low productivity. A pass above 5 000 metres on the Lhasa to Namco road.

Yunnan in the southeast, and with India, Nepal and Bhutan in the southeast. In the southwest, near Nepal, is the highest and most magnificent mountain range in the world, the Himalayas. In the northeast is vast, open pasture (Changtang means "the vast land in north") where nomads live by yak rearing. Central Tibet, with valleys and mountains between 3 500 and 4 500 m, is a land of barley farming, where the majority of Tibetans live, eating barley as their staple food. Tibet has six prefectures: Shigatse, Shannan, Naqu, Changdu, Ali and Linzhi; and one municipal city, Lhasa. There are 71 administrative counties, 900 townships and more than 7 000 villages.

The total area of usable land is about 760 300 km^2, 63 percent of the territory. The area of arable land, grazing land, forest lands and barren land by prefectures and their proportions are shown in Table 8.1.

There are about 64.8 million hectares of grazing land, of which about 55.6 million are usable; nearly 80 percent is in Naqu and Ali Prefectures (Table 8.2). By 1995, there was 5 420 000 ha of fenced pasture for winter grazing and protection; about 4 170 000 ha of it was in Naqu. There were 4 400 000 ha of irrigated pasture, mostly in Shigatse. In recent years, there has been major progress in promoting fenced and irrigated pasture, but, with increasing livestock numbers, overgrazing is common and serious.

LIVESTOCK AND LIVESTOCK PRODUCTION

The common large animals are yak, cattle, *zo* (a cross of yak and cattle), donkey, horse and mule; there are also sheep, goats, swine

TABLE 8.1
Distribution of land resources in Tibet ('000 ha).

Prefecture	Arable land		Forest land		Natural pasture		Barren land	
	Area	%	Area	%	Area	%	Area	%
Lhasa	55.53	15.40	101.33	0.80	2 117.79	3.27	502.24	1.36
Changdu	72.18	20.02	2 976.70	23.53	7 061.07	10.90	2 886.00	7.80
Shannan	63.74	17.68	3 059.49	24.18	3 187.51	4.92	1 188.25	3.21
Shigatse	135.52	37.59	219.97	1.74	12 617.14	19.47	4 208.52	11.37
Naqu	6.02	1.67	220.90	1.75	20 858.08	32.19	16 602.11	44.87
Ali	1.76	0.49	0.00	0.00	16 906.76	26.09	9 084.19	24.55
Linzhi	25.80	7.16	6 073.61	48.01	2 048.38	3.16	2 531.72	6.84
Tibet in total	360.56	100.00	12 651.98	100.00	64 796.72	100.00	37 003.03	100.00

SOURCE: Land Management Bureau of Tibet Autonomous Region, 1992.

TABLE 8.2
Area of usable, fenced and irrigated grazing land, by prefecture ('000 ha).

Prefecture	Total area	Area usable	Area fenced	Area irrigated
Lhasa	2 117.79	1 112.0	12.7	75.3
Changdu	7 061.07	4 965.3	4.7	5.3
Shannan	3 187.51	1 731.3	14.0	26.0
Shigatse	12 617.14	4 331.3	29.3	309.3
Naqu	20 858.08	26 041.3	416.7	0.0
Ali	16 906.76	17 324.7	0.0	0.0
Linzhi	2 048.38	115.3	64.7	23.3
All Tibet	64 796.72	55 621.3	542.0	439.3

SOURCE: Land Management Bureau of Tibet Autonomous Region, 1992.

and poultry. In 1999, the total livestock was 23 000 000 head, of which there were about 5 790 000 large animals (3 000 000 yaks, 400 000 horses and 130 000 donkeys), 16 900 000 small stock (11 000 000 sheep and 5 890 000 goats) and 230 000 swine. Goats are mostly in western and sheep in northwestern and central zones. Tibet currently produces about 150 000 tonne of meat, of which about 83 000 tonne is beef (yak and cattle) and 57 000 tonne is mutton and goat meat. There are 1 150 000 milk cattle; milk production was 210 000 tonne in 1999. With the promotion of livestock in crop-dominated areas and increasing demand for dairy products, cattle have become very profitable. Wool, cashmere and leather are the main non-food livestock commodities. At present, Tibet produces 9 400 tonne of wool (sheep and goat) and about 640 tonne of cashmere. Cashmere is largely exported; wool is processed locally.

BIOPHYSICAL ENVIRONMENT

The great variations of topography, with elevations ranging from 500 m to 8 848 m, and the vast extent of the plateau, lead to obvious vertical zonation and horizontal patterns of climate, soil and vegetation. The Chinese Academy of Sciences in 1992 classified Tibet into seven physiogeographical units, more natural-vegetation-oriented than an exclusively topographic classification (Leber, Holawe and Hausler, 1995), namely:

- Southern slope of the Himalayan zone of rainforest and montane evergreen broad-leaf forests, mainly about and below 2 500 m and down to 500 m, with tropical and subtropical monsoon types of moist climate, mean monthly temperature of 18°–24°C, annual mean temperature above 10°–18°C and annual

precipitation of 800–2500 mm. This region, which borders northeastern India along the lower reaches of the Yalongtsangpo river, includes most of Chayu, Metok and Cuona counties.

- Ranges and gorges of the East Tibet zone of montane coniferous forests, characterized by plateau temperate monsoon type semi-moist climate, with annual mean temperature ranges from 3°–9°C, and some of the area can reach 8°–12°C, with total precipitation of 400–1000 mm. This region is mostly steep mountain and cut from north to south by several rivers, such as Nujiang, Lancangjiang and Jinshajiang. A vertical differentiation of above 1000 m in gorges can be found in this region. Most of Changdu Prefecture lies in this region.

- Nakchu and upper reaches of Nujiang zone of montane shrubby steppe, mostly covered by alpine meadow in the south and alpine shrubby steppe and meadow in the west, generally with an annual mean temperature range of -3°C to +1.5°C, and precipitation varying from 400 mm in the west to 700 mm in the east of the region. This is a typical plateau cold monsoon subhumid climate. Counties in Nakchu Prefecture, such as Baqing, Nirrong, Biru and Suoxian, belong to this region.

- Broad valleys and basins of the south Tibetan zone of montane shrubby steppe, which is the main producer of grain and crops. Most of the population is concentrated here, along the Yalongtsangpo, Lhasa and Niachu rivers. It is characterized by plateau cold monsoon semi-arid climate, with mean temperature of 1°–7.5°C. Annual precipitation ranges from 200 mm in the northwest to 500 mm in the southeast, and is concentrated between June and September, which accounts for about 90 percent of the total. Major parts of Shigatse prefecture, Lhasa and Shannan Prefecture are in this region.

- Changtang plateau zone of alpine steppe, which is now largely a protected natural wildlife reserve. The annual mean temperature is only about 0° to -3°C, with total precipitation of 150–300 mm. This region is a very typical region of plateau cold monsoon semi-arid climate. It consists of much of the eastern part of Ali prefecture and western part of Nakchu Prefecture.
- Mountain and basin of Ali zone of montane steppe and desert, with annual mean temperature of 0°C and annual precipitation only 50–200 mm. This region is very dry and cold. It falls into the plateau sub-cold monsoon arid climate. Counties of Ge'er, Zhada and Ritu belong to this region. Despite the dry and cold climate, perhaps also because of it, this region is the largest producer of cashmere.
- Kunlun Mountain and basin zone of alpine desert steppe and desert. Most of this region is uninhabited, with a mean annual temperature about -4°C, and precipitation only 100–150 mm. It is mostly in the Changtang Natural Preserved Area for Wildlife. This region belongs to the plateau cold monsoon type arid climate. The far northern part of Nyima county of Naqu Prefecture and northern Gaize and Ritu counties of Ali Prefecture are in this region.

SOIL, VEGETATION AND MAJOR TYPES OF GRAZING LAND

There are grazing lands throughout Tibet with a great diversity in structure

and composition, ranging from cold, steppe-like lands, dominated by *Stipa*, to mountain desert shrub lands with shrubs such as *Ceratoides*, *Artemisia* and *Ajania*, with a sparse cover of grasses, to alpine valleys in the Himalayas with a diverse flora, and to temperate conifer and deciduous forests where forest meadows provide valuable grazing for transhumant herds (Miller, 1995). These types of grazing are determined by soil, topography and climate.

There are nine major soil types in the grazing lands: Alpine meadow soils; Subalpine meadow soils; Alpine steppe soils; Subalpine steppe soils; Mountain shrubby-meadow soils; Alpine desert soils; Subalpine desert soils; Alpine marsh-land meadow soils; and Taupe and Brown soil. These soils developed under different types of vegetation and conditions, such as steppe, meadow, shrubby meadow, shrubby steppe, wetland and desert, as well as a few of them under forest.

Alpine meadow soil

This is one of the more widespread and better soils, found between 4 600 and 5 200 m, developed under cold, semi-humid conditions, with annual mean temperatures of -6° to -0°C and average annual precipitation of 350–550 mm. *Kobresia pygmaea* and *K. humilis* are the major plants, with combinations of *Carex* spp., *Polygonum macrophyllum*, *Leontopodium* spp. and *Anaphalis* spp. Soil depth varies from 4 to 20 cm, with average organic material (OM) content of 3.7–27 percent. Soil pH is 6.1–7.2. There are three major subtypes: alpine steppe-meadow soils; alpine marshland-meadow soil; and alpine shrubby-meadow soils. Alpine steppe-meadow soil is often in the transition area of meadow to steppe, where plants such as *Stipa* and *Artemisia* dominate, and average OM content is less than 5 percent. Alpine marshland-meadow soil is in low areas where water accumulates. Meadow grass dominates, and the soil is rich in organic matter, with an average content of over 20 percent. Alpine shrubby-meadow soils are usually on north-facing slopes, with shrubs like *Rhododendron* spp., *Dasiphora fruticosa* and *Salix* spp., with soil OM content of about 10 percent.

Subalpine meadow soil

This is widespread and of good quality. It is found in between 3 900 and 4 600 m where the average annual temperature is about -2° to -4°C and annual precipitation 400–700 mm. Vegetation is very variable, but *Kobresia* spp. and *Carex* spp. are common. Other plants, such as *Potentilla* spp., *Pedicularis*, *Anemone*, *Roegneria* spp., *Ptilagrostis mongolica* and *Poa* spp., are found in many areas. Shrubs are typically *Rhododendron*, *Dasiphora fruticosa*, *Salix* and *Caragana*. The OM content is about 12 percent and the soil is highly acid.

Alpine steppe soil

This is the most widely distributed and largest in area, with several subtypes – see Table 8.3. It is found in northwestern Tibet, and at altitudes between 4 400 and 5 300 m throughout Tibet. It develops under the alpine cold semi-dry climate with annual

mean temperatures of 0°–6°C and annual precipitation of 200–300 mm. The soil is frozen for more than five months of the year and the vegetation is cold-tolerant species, such as *Stipa* spp., and accompanied by *Festuca ovina*, *Oxytropis*, *Astragalus*, *Orinus*, *Carex moorcroftii*, *Androsace* sp. and *Arenaria* sp. In drier western Tibet, *Stipa glareosa* and *Artemisia* spp. are common. In some parts, *Ceratoides compacta* grows. The OM content of the soil is often 2 percent, and some has less than 0.4 percent; the pH averages more than 8.0. With high elevation and cold climate, biological and chemical soil weathering is very slow, so there is a high gravel content, often more than 10 percent.

Subalpine steppe soils

These are found in central Tibet between 4 100 and 4 700 m, under temperate semi-dry climatic conditions with an annual mean temperature of 0°–3.7°C and annual precipitation of 230–350 mm. *Stipa capillacea*, *Pennisetum flaccidum* and *Aristida triseta* are the most common plants, accompanied by *Festuca ovina*, *Oxytropis*, *Astragalus*, *Potentilla chinensis* and *Stellera chamaejasme*. The OM content is usually about 2 percent, with a pH of 7.5–8.9. There are five subtypes: typical subalpine steppe soil; subalpine meadow-steppe soil; subalpine desert-steppe soil; subalpine shrubby-steppe soil; and subalpine alkalized-steppe soil.

TABLE 8.3
Subtypes of soil under alpine steppe soil.

Subtypes of soil	OM content (%)	Vegetation	pH
Alpine meadow-steppe soil	1.5 – 3.5	*Stipa purpurea*, *Kobresia* spp., *Carex* spp., etc.	7–8
Alpine desert-steppe soil	< 0.8	*Orinus*, *Stipa* spp.	> 9
Alpine shrubby-steppe soil	1.5 – 2.0	*Stipa purpurea*, *Stipa glareosa*, etc.	7–8
Alpine alkalized-steppe soil	1.4	*Kobresia* spp., *Poa annua*, *Trikeraia hookeri*, etc.	7–8

SOURCE: Land Management Bureau of Tibet Autonomous Region, 1992.

Mountain shrubby-meadow soil

This is found in central Tibet at elevations of 3 400–4 200 m under a temperate semi-dry climate with annual mean temperature of 4°–9 °C and annual precipitation of 300 – 500 mm. Vegetation such as *Sophora moorcroftiana, Caragana spinifera, Artemisia, Pennisetum flaccidum, Aristida triseta* and *Orinus thoroldii* is found, with *Cotoneaster* spp. and *Rosa* spp. near the forest line. The OM content is usually about 2 percent and can be up to 3 percent, with pH values of 6–7.

Alpine desert soil

This is found in the far north, along the Kara-Kunlun Mountains, above 4 800 m, where the climate is cold and dry, with annual mean temperature of -8°C and low annual precipitation. *Ceratoides compacta, Stipa glareosa, Carex moorcroftii* and *Oxytropis* spp. are the only plants that survive. The OM content of the soil is less than 1 percent and pH is around 8.6.

Subalpine desert soil

This is found in far western Tibet, in Rutob and Zhada counties, where the altitude is 3 600–4 500 m. It developed under a temperate, dry climate with annual mean temperature of 0° to -3°C and annual precipitation of 50–150 mm. Only a few cold- and drought-tolerant plants grow, such as *Ceratoides* sp., *Ajania fruticulosa, Ptilotrichum canescens* and *Ephedra* spp. The OM content of the soil is less than 0.5 percent, with strong alkalinity at the surface.

Meadow soil and marshland soils

These two types, the best for grazing and mowing, are in low valleys and basins. Vegetation varies depending on soil moisture. On meadow soil, *Kobresia* spp. and *Carex* spp. are the common species. In marshland, there are plants such as *Ranunculus, Hippuris* and *Potamogeton*, in addition to *Kobresia* spp. and *Carex* spp. Meadow soil has 7 percent of organic matter, on average, and marshland soil has more than 10 percent and up to 20 percent. The average pH range in both types is 6–8.

Taupe soil and Brown soil

These are found in southeastern forest zones. Taupe soil is found between 3 600 and 4 200 m and brown soil below 3 700 m. Taupe soil is found under temperate and semi-humid climates with average annual temperature of 2°–5°C and annual precipitation of 400–700 mm. Trees such as *Populus davidiana, Betula platyphylla, Picea likiangensis* var. *balfouriana* and *Sabina tibetica* are common, as are shrubs like *Sabina wallichiana,* and *Spiraea* sp. Grass-like species such as *Kobresia* spp. and *Carex* spp. are common, as are *Potentilla* spp. Brown soil is found in warm semi-humid climatic condition with average annual temperatures of 7°–13°C and annual precipitation of 350–600 mm. Both shrubs and grass are common. The common shrubs are *Sophora viciifolia, Ceratositgma minus, Caragana* sp., *Lonicera thibetica* and *Rhamnus* sp. The OM contents of taupe soil and brown soil are 6 percent and 5 percent, respectively.

Nutrient and mineral contents of major soil types

Alluvial calcium soil and alluvial non-calcium soil are the major soil chemical types in grazing lands. Alluvial calcium soil is distributed in the lower elevations of river valleys and alluvial non-calcium soil is mainly in the higher elevations of mountains. Both can be found in alluvial fans. In most soils, the humus layer is very thin and humus content low because of slow decomposition of organic material due to low temperature and dryness. In general, meadow types of soil have high contents of OM, N, P and K (Table 8.4).

Iron (Fe), zinc (Zn), molybdenum (Mo), copper (Cu), boron (B) and manganese (Mn) are the main minerals required for plant growth and development. Among the different types of soil, alpine desert soil is very low in mineral content, while in meadow soil there is relatively adequate mineral content (Table 8.5).

Major pasture types

Pasture types are determined by soil, climate and vegetation. From southeast to northwest, pasture type varies from tropical and subtropical to warm and temperate to cold, and from humid and subhumid to semi-arid to extreme dry types. In general, 17 different types of grazing land have been classified (Tibet Bureau of Land Management, 1994). Figure 8.1 illustrates the major types.

Cold highland steppe is the largest in area and the most widely distributed type. It is mostly found in Ali Prefecture and Naqu Prefecture. Cold highland meadow is second largest in area and is found in all parts of Tibet. Cold highland desert

TABLE 8.4
Nutrient status and fertility of major soil types of grazing lands in Tibet.

Soil type	OM (%)	N (%)	P (%)	K (%)
Alpine meadow soils	10.8	0.484	0.182	1.90–2.43
Subalpine meadow soils	12.5	0.530	0.210	0.21
Alpine steppe soils	1.78	0.157	0.102	1.89–2.88
Subalpine steppe soils	2.04	0.108	0.122	0.079–0.196
Mountain shrubby-meadow soils	2.33	0.125	0.067	2.2
Alpine desert soils	1.00	0.040	0.062	1.6
Subalpine desert soils	0.32	0.029	0.042	2.0
Meadow soil	15.60	0.598	0.126	2.24
Marshland soils	16.30	0.661	0.158	2.17
Taupe soil and Brown soil	4-7	0.252	0.192	2.54

SOURCE: Land Management Bureau of Tibet Autonomous Region, 1992.

TABLE 8.5
Mineral content of major grazing land soil types in Tibet (in ppm).

Major grazing land soil type	Fe	Zn	Mo	Cu	B	Mn
Alpine meadow soils	20-200	1-3	< 0.1	> 0.2	> 1	5-15
Subalpine meadow soils	30-100	> 2	0.1	1-2	> 1.0	7.0
Alpine steppe soils	10-40	0.5-1.0	0.1	0.2-1.0	> 1.0	18
Subalpine steppe soils	< 10	0.5-10	< 0.15	0.3-0.6	0.5-2	< 10
Mountain shrubby-meadow soils	20	1-3	< 0.1	1-1.8	1-2	11-15
Alpine desert soils	5	1.0	0.12	0.006	0.4	3.8
Subalpine desert soils	> 20	1.93	0.16	0.74	0.5	15.9
Meadow soil	> 20	3.0	< 0.1	2.0	2-10	5-12
Marshland soils	> 20	> 3.0	< 0.1	> 1.8	> 2	15-30
Taupe soil and Brown soil	> 20	1.19	0.15	1.45	0.5	37.9

SOURCE: Land Management Bureau of Tibet Autonomous Region, 1992.

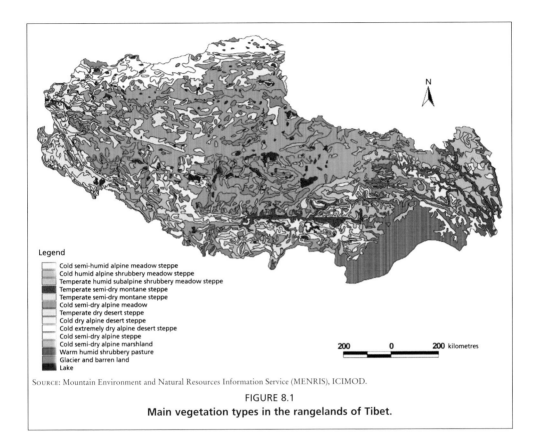

Legend
- Cold semi-humid alpine meadow steppe
- Cold humid alpine shrubbery meadow steppe
- Temperate humid subalpine shrubbery meadow steppe
- Temperate semi-dry montane steppe
- Temperate semi-dry montane steppe
- Cold semi-dry alpine meadow
- Temperate dry desert steppe
- Cold dry alpine desert steppe
- Cold extremely dry alpine desert steppe
- Cold semi-dry alpine steppe
- Cold semi-dry alpine marshland
- Warm humid shrubbery pasture
- Glacier and barren land
- Lake

200   0   200 kilometres

SOURCE: Mountain Environment and Natural Resources Information Service (MENRIS), ICIMOD.

FIGURE 8.1
Main vegetation types in the rangelands of Tibet.

steppe is the third largest in area, but is only found in Ali and Naqu Prefecture. There are warm and tropical pasture types, but they are limited to Linzhi Prefecture, where it is lower elevation and humid (details are given in Table 8.6).

Among the 17 pasture types, seven – Cold highland steppe; Cold highland meadow; Cold highland desert steppe; Cold meadow steppe; Cold desert steppe; Temperate steppe; and Mountain meadow – comprise some 98 percent of the total. Their area and percentages of the total are shown in Table 8.7.

Agro-ecological zones

There are seven agro-ecological zones in Tibet (see Figure 8.2).

There is a hot humid agroforestry zone in the southeast, in a mainly forest area, where livestock depend on forage cut from the forest, with grazing in the warm, tropical shrub pasture. Yak, cattle, swine and goat are common. Shifting cultivation is seen in many villages. It has distinct dry and wet seasons, affected by the monsoon. Most of the crops are rainfed. Winter wheat, winter barley, maize and even rice are the major crops.

The warm semi-humid agroforestry zone is where major rivers such as Jingsha Jiang, Lancangjiang and Nujiang flow south out of Tibet. Moisture comes through the river valley and the climate is affected by the monsoon. Shrub pasture is the main resource for stock raising. Yak

TABLE 8.6
Proportion of different pasture types in the seven Prefectures of Tibet.

Type of grazing land	Lhasa	Linzhi	Changdu	Shigatse	Ali	Naqu	Shannan
1. Temperate meadow steppe		10.09	73.26	7.87		7.78	
2. Temperate steppe	17.95	1.56	17.63	34.52	2.16		26.18
3. Temperate desert steppe					100.0		
4. Cold highland meadow steppe	1.89			20.28	2.38	72.66	2.82
5. Cold highland steppe	0.36			15.62	39.74	43.05	1.23
6. Cold highland desert steppe					44.55	55.45	
7. Temperate steppe desert					100.0		
8. Temperate desert					100.0		
9. Cold highland desert					42.92	57.08	
10. Warm pasture		100.0					
11. Warm brushy pasture		30.29	69.71				
12. Tropical pasture		100.0					
13. Tropical brushy pasture		100.0					
14. Lowland meadow	19.51	20.11		60.38			
15. Mountain meadow	0.41	7.6	81.28	3.35		3.36	4.0
16. Cold highland meadow	6.12	6.8	16.09	22.17	7.69	32.69	7.9
17. Marshland and wetland	9.61			64.03	26.36		

NOTE: Because of rounding errors, some types do not total exactly 100%.
SOURCE: Land Management Bureau of Tibet Autonomous Region, 1992.

TABLE 8.7
Area of major pasture types and their proportion of the total area in Tibet.

Pasture type	Area ('000 ha)	%
Cold highland steppe	31 588.60	38.5
Cold highland meadow	25 367.33	30.9
Cold highland desert steppe	8 678.67	10.6
Cold meadow steppe	5 938.67	7.2
Cold desert steppe	5 441.33	6.6
Temperate steppe	1 786.00	2.2
Mountain meadow	1 254.67	1.5
Total	80 062.27[1]	97.6

NOTE: (1) This higher figure for pasture (Table 8.1 has 64 796.72 thousand hectares) reflects the inclusion here of areas of barren land, unusable areas, and even disputed border lands.
SOURCE: Land Management Bureau of Tibet Autonomous Region, 1992.

is a predominant animal in livestock production. Many temperate crops are grown (not rice or warm-climate types).

The warm semi-dry agricultural zone comes with increasing altitude. It is a crop-dominated, livestock-crops mixed agricultural zone. More than 70 percent of the livelihood of farmers depends on crops. Barley, wheat and rape are the main crops; cattle, yak, sheep and goats are the main animals.

The cool semi-dry agropastoral zone is transitional between crop and pure pastoral zones. Fields of barley, rape and pea are found. Crop cultivars are early maturing and drought resistant. Cattle, sheep and yak are the main animals.

The cold semi-arid pastoral zone is the largest, and is known to Tibetans as Changtang ("the vast northern plateau").

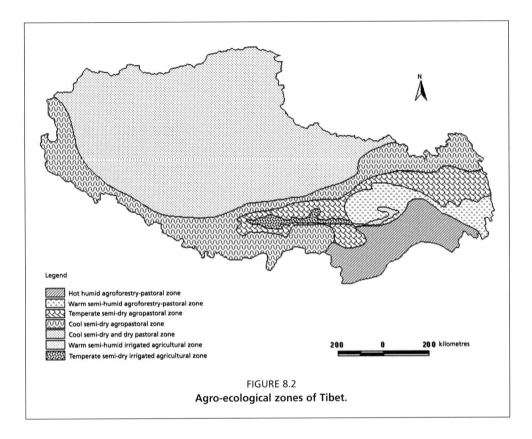

FIGURE 8.2
Agro-ecological zones of Tibet.

Legend
- Hot humid agroforestry-pastoral zone
- Warm semi-humid agroforestry-pastoral zone
- Temperate semi-dry agropastoral zone
- Cool semi-dry agropastoral zone
- Cool semi-dry and dry pastoral zone
- Warm semi-humid irrigated agricultural zone
- Temperate semi-dry irrigated agricultural zone

Because of low temperatures and a very short growing season, crop production is not possible. Nomadism is the main production system of the people, who migrate following availability of pasture and water. The north of the zone is very dry, with less than 200 mm of annual precipitation; it can be divided into a cold dry pastoral zone and a cold semi-dry pastoral zone. Yak, sheep and goats are the main livestock. In the east there are more yak, while sheep and goats predominate in the west. Cashmere goats in particular are found in the far west, adjacent to Nepal and India.

LIVESTOCK PRODUCTION SYSTEMS
There are four broad livestock production systems (see map – Figure 8.3):
- Crop-based livestock production in central areas, with 18 counties.
- Pastoral systems in northern Tibet, with 17 counties.
- Between these is the agropastoral production system, with 27 counties.
- An agrosilvipastoral mixed production zone covers 9 counties in the southeast.

There is great variation within production systems, particularly in the crop-based livestock system. Most households, except purely pastoral ones, grow crops, keep livestock and diversify activities to generate income and ensure food security.

The area of grasslands in each system is illustrated in Table 8.8. Generally, there is only a little grazing land in crop-based livestock systems, but they have a larger proportion of sown grassland. More

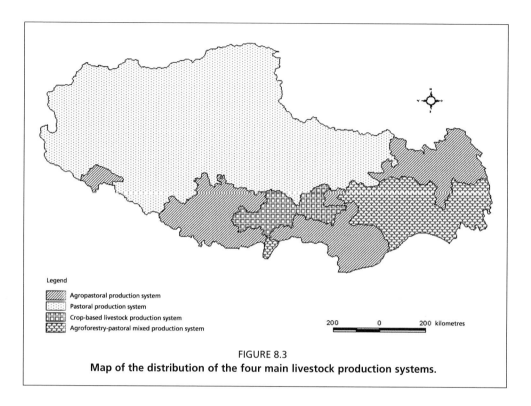

FIGURE 8.3

Map of the distribution of the four main livestock production systems.

TABLE 8.8
Grassland resources in the four livestock production systems in Tibet.

Grassland type	Total ha	Crop-based		Agropastoral		Pastoral		Agrosilvipastoral	
		ha	%	ha	%	ha	%	ha	%
Natural grassland (total)[1]	64 303 965	4 161 198	6.5	15 696 757	24.4	41 004 485	63.8	3 441 525	5.4
Of which									
Cold season	11 917 980	239 151	2.0	2 304 255	19.3	9 137 122	76.7	237 452	2.0
Warm season	36 756 100	2 316 363	6.3	10 135 116	27.6	21 653 426	58.9	2 651 195	7.2
Non-seasonal	8 799 213	1 538 396	17.5	2 442 007	27.8	4 458 605	50.7	360 205	4.1
Grazing-mowing	18 922	454	2.4	17 682	93.4	122	0.6	664	3.5
Temporary grassland	4 399 364	2 857	0.1	243 822	5.5	4 119 223	93.6	33 462	0.8
Degraded grassland	2 412 402	63 983	2.7	553 882	23.0	1 635 991	67.8	158 546	6.6
Improved grassland	3 864	541	14.0	2 688	69.6	0	0.0	635	16.4
Sown grassland	5 349	3 712	69.4	293	5.5	1 016	19.0	328	6.1

NOTE: (1) Depending on the source of the data, the total grassland area varies between 64.3 million hectares and 64.8 million hectares.
SOURCE: Land Management Bureau of Tibet Autonomous Region, 1992.

degraded land is found in the pastoral system, while most improved grassland is in the agropastoral zone (see Table 8.8).

Crop-based livestock production system

This includes the majority of Lhasa Municipality and some counties of Shigatse and Shannan Prefectures. It

Plate 43.
In the lower Lhasa river valley, yak × cattle hybrids are widely used. Yaks and their hybrids are easily trained for draught and as pack animals.

occupies the river valleys of the middle reaches of Yalongzangpo (Brahmaputra) River and its two tributaries, Lhasa Stream and Nyachu Stream (known locally as One River, Two Streams). The main production is cereals and rapeseed. Average altitude is 3 800 m. Precipitation in this zone is unevenly distributed, both spatially and seasonally: 90 percent occurs during June to September, with 80 percent falling at night. Spring and winter are dry, with annual average relative humidity of 43 percent. Strong sunshine and wind, especially during the spring, lead to high annual evaporation – 2 425.5 mm, almost six times the level of precipitation. Crops are prone to drought in spring and waterlogging in autumn. In higher areas, crops are damaged by both spring and autumn frost, and by hail in late summer and early autumn.

Over half the arable land and half the urban areas are in the crop-based system, which accounts for over 56 percent of grain and 70 percent of rapeseed. Although crops dominate the economy, the area still has 16 percent of the animals, 16.1 percent of meat production and 22 percent of the milk production of the whole of Tibet. Pasture has relatively low productivity, as rainfall is low. Stock raising depends on crop residues and by-products, especially in spring and winter. Yak and zo are the main draught animals (Plate 43). In lower valleys, milk is mostly from cows; higher up it is from yak and zo. In this zone, people mostly eat grain, little meat, and milk as butter tea. In terms of energy intake, barley makes up over 77 percent for farmers. In urban areas, wheat and rice consumption is increasing and accounts for 35 percent of energy intake.

Agropastoral production system

This system includes northern Changdu, northwestern Shigatse and southern Shannan Prefectures. It is in the upstream valleys of the Yalongzangpo, Cuona, Longzi, Nujiang, Lancangjiang and Jinshajiang Rivers. The system is spread over the cold semi-arid highlands, with a few cool semi-arid areas at 4 000–4 500 m. The climate is similar to the crop-based system, but spring temperatures rise more slowly, autumn temperatures fall earlier and the frost-free period is shorter. This zone suffers from gales, frost, hail and snow, which severely restrains development of agriculture. Because of cold and the high altitude, most land is for grazing or barren; large amounts have been cultivated in lower valleys. In a few counties in lower areas, some apples and peaches are grown. Crops and livestock (cattle, sheep) have equal importance in farming.

Barley is the main cereal, making up over 65 percent of total crop area. In lower parts, spring wheat is grown where possible. Pea (*Pisum sativum*), the only pulse, is important as a source of protein for both man and animals. Sown area and production of grain is 30 percent of that in Tibet as a whole. Peas, usually grown mixed with barley or rape, are mostly used for human food, usually mixed with barley, but are also used as animal feed, particularly horses; pea haulm is considered locally to be the best animal feed; mixing barley straw with pea haulm is common. Potatoes and small areas of vegetables, both in greenhouses and outside, are also grown. Cattle, yak, sheep, goat and chicken are the main livestock. The number of animals, production of meat and production of milk are 47 percent, 45 percent and 40 percent, respectively,

of Tibet's output. Small quantities of barley are imported or exchanged with other areas for meat and animal products. Barley and mutton are the main sources of energy for farmers.

Pure pastoral production system

Changtang, the vast open land of the northern Tibetan Plateau, including the entire territory of Naqu Prefecture, most of Ali Prefecture and Dangxiong County of Lhasa Municipality, is a vast pastoral area covering altogether 17 counties. It is surrounded geographically by the Kunlun Mountains in the northwest, Himalayas in the west, the Gandisi Mountains in the southwest, the Nianqingtanggula Mountains in the southeast and the Tanggula Mountains in the east. It occupies almost 60 percent of Tibet, with a total area of 711 000 km². Stock rearing accounts for over 95 percent of agricultural output. Barley and rape have been cultivated since the 1960s in the lower river valleys of the south.

Biophysically, this area is cold semi-arid or arid, with an average elevation above 4 600 m (most is between 4 600 and 5 100 m). Annual average temperature is below 0°C, with an average of 7.3°C in the hottest month and -7.5°C in the coldest. Cropping is impossible in most of this zone, and even animal husbandry is limited by harsh natural conditions; disasters such as wind storms, hail and frost are frequent, and nomads, in particular, often suffer from snow calamities. Heavy snow in 1997–1998 nearly caused the collapse of the livestock production system, as about half of the livestock died. Many nomads were plunged into poverty despite being rich before.

Livestock depend on grazing; there is little forage and hay. In the east, grassland is dominated by highland meadows and swampy meadows, which are relatively productive and can support large grazing animals; the yak predominates (Plates 44 and 45).

Over 80 percent of livestock, in sheep equivalent units, is yak, which provides almost 80 percent of meat and milk and 70 percent of the nomads' income. In the west, pasture is mainly alpine steppe and alpine desert steppe, which cannot support large ruminants, but local sheep and goats are well adapted to the conditions.

In the last few decades, particularly during the 1960s and 1970s, crops have been grown where possible. It was hoped to solve the problem of shortages and avoid the heavy cost of transport. Many attempts failed as there were no suitable crop cultivars, and herders did not know how to grow crops. A few farmers succeeded in growing crops in favourable

microclimates in lower river valleys and on the bank of lakes.

Those who gained knowledge and experience in growing crops later went to other counties to reclaim land. The crop area in both eastern and western parts increased rapidly during the 1970s, but decreased considerably after the 1980s. One important lesson learned was that this cold and fragile land often cannot maintain its productivity when cultivated, because decomposition of organic matter is difficult. Large amounts of farmland were abandoned and became useless for both cropping and grazing. Recently, with new cultivars of barley, adapted to local conditions, and improvements in crop management, attempts to achieve food grain self-sufficiency have been increasing in areas such as the counties of Ge'er, Suoxian, Biru and Geji. However, food grain and oilseed production in this

Plate 44.
Yak breeding station on the high plateau at over 4 500 m.

zone have never reached 1 percent of that in Tibet as a whole. This zone currently supplies over 36 percent of meat, 47 percent of milk, 56 percent of sheep wool and 40 percent of sheepskins of Tibetan production.

Livestock products are commonly exchanged for agricultural products through private traders. People eat considerable amounts of barley and wheat, which forms 83 percent of their energy intake. Nomads generally only feel comfortable when they have at least 12 yaks or 50 sheep, or 60 sheep equivalent units per person in the family, and enough *tsangpa* (flour of roasted barley).

Agrosilvipastoral mixed production
This prevails in the middle valleys of the Nyiyang, Nujiang and Lancangjiang Rivers, including the entire Linzhi Prefecture, and Mangkang and Zuogong Counties of Changdu Prefecture – nine counties altogether. In more favourable environments, crops, livestock and forestry co-exist and are fundamental to ensuring food and livelihood security.

Affected by topography and the monsoon from the Indian Ocean, the climate varies horizontally and vertically. Vertical differentiation of climate and vegetation are much more marked than horizontal differentiation, and greater than in the other three systems. Climatic variation ranges from hot humid in the south to warm humid in the middle range, and to temperate semi-humid in the north, and even to cold arid in the higher altitudes. The livestock production system has developed over a long time, typically incorporating different resources through cropping, livestock raising and forestry.

Plate 45.
A warm welcome at the yak breeding station at 4 300 m in Linzhou county, 70 km from Lhasa, Tibet.

Farmers here are much better off than elsewhere in Tibet. Most are self-sufficient in both livestock and crop-based food production. There is a more balanced intake of food in this zone than in others.

LIVESTOCK PRODUCTION POTENTIAL

The carrying capacity of grazing land has been studied from different perspectives (Liu, 1992; Yang, 1995; Tibetan Bureau of Land Planning, 1992b). The supporting capacity of crop straw as animal feed has also been analysed (Yang, 1995; Tibetan Bureau of Land Planning, 1992b). Xiao (1994) attempted to analyse the capacity of agricultural by-products to support livestock production. However, livestock production potential and quantities of meat and milk produced still remain largely unknown. In this report, production potentials for meat and milk were calculated based on an analysis of carrying capacity of pasture, and potential capacity for raising livestock using crop residues and agricultural by-products.

Pasture carrying capacity

Over the last thirty years, animal numbers have increased, from 17 million in 1965 to 23 million in 1999. Total production of meat and milk has reached 103 000 tonne and 185 000 tonne, respectively (Zhang, 1997). However, growth has been at a cost, in terms of overgrazing, in particular, and degradation of livestock productivity. There has been a lack of input to the grazing land; output has always exceeded input. This lack of sustainable utilization has caused overgrazing (57 percent overstocking in Naqu Prefecture), degeneration (49 percent of Naqu) and declining productivity (20 percent fall since the 1980s). The situation is becoming worse (Ling Hui,

1998). Carrying capacity has decreased by 20–40 percent compared to the 1970s (Bai, 1995). Desertification, salinization, increases in poisonous plants and increasing damage from rodents and insects are common. They lead to degradation of the grazing environment and lowered productivity (Bai, 1995; Ling, 1998).

Sustainable use of pasture is crucial to livestock development. In the early 1990s, the total carrying capacity of pasture land was 40–60 million sheep-equivalent units (SEU), where 1 yak = 5 SEU, (Liu, 1992; Bai, 1995); it dropped to 34.2 million SEU (Yang, 1995), and it is now estimated that carrying capacity is less than 30 million SEU, or about 40 SEU per 100 ha. These estimates differ from each other, but the overall tendency is that the carrying capacity of Tibet's pastures is declining due to steady grassland degradation.

The spatial distribution of potential carrying capacity does not match the actual distribution of grazing land, being limited by biophysical conditions and socio-economic development. In the pastoral production system, where livestock have high priority, there is little room to increase livestock numbers and production. In contrast, in the south, where carrying capacity is considerably higher, increases in livestock are limited by lack of grazing land, steep topography and low priority for livestock.

Moreover, carrying capacity is not only unevenly distributed spatially but also between seasons. The difference of carrying capacity between summer and winter is about 50 percent (Bai, 1995). There are tremendous differences in stocking rate between cold and warm seasons, where the Stocking Rate = [(Number of livestock - Carrying Capacity) / Carrying

Capacity)] × 100. Numbers of livestock in cold and warm seasons were based on the numbers of livestock in December and July, respectively. In the warm season, most of Tibet is understocked, but in the cold season, almost all areas are overstocked; there are only a few counties in the far south that possess some potential to keep more livestock. Large parts of the north and centre are overgrazed by the existing numbers of animals.

Overstocking in the cold season is high in all systems. In the pastoral system, there is great overstocking in the cold season and slight overstocking in the warm season. In the crop-based livestock system, there is substantial overstocking in both seasons.

The ratio of carrying capacity in warm season to cold season is more than 2.73, while the ratio of numbers of livestock in the warm and cold seasons is only 1.09. There is great potential to raise livestock in the warm season (about 13 million SEU), but in the cold season there is 15.6 million SEU of overstocking (Table 8.9). Culling and marketing stock in late autumn or early winter for cash and for other necessities may make livestock production more profitable and reduce overstocking on winter grazing.

Overstocking is exacerbated because conservation and rehabilitation of grazing land is largely ignored; improvement and development of artificial grassland has made little progress. The total area of rehabilitated pasture by re-seeding, irrigation, fencing and artificial grassland is only 0.02 percent of the grazing area. Over 20 percent of grazing land in Naqu and 18.8 percent of pasture in Shannan is seriously degraded. There is a lack of effort in developing fencing, irrigation systems, controls for disease and rodent damage, eradication of poisonous plants, and replanting and fertilizing of grassland. The proportion of poisonous plants has increased from 15 percent to 45 percent in some areas. The area for grass-cutting and winter grazing is decreasing year by year. Production of grass has decreased by 60 percent since 1960. There is no established forage reserve of hay to reduce livestock loss and preserve body weight in winter.

Herd structure is often unbalanced, with a large proportion of small, old, unproductive animals in the flock. The proportion of productive animals is 23 percent on average. The reason herders give is the high death rate of animals in winter, compelling them to keep

TABLE 8.9
Carrying capacity and stocking status of grazing land (million SEU).

Production System	Warm season			Cold season			Ratio of carrying capacity in warm to cold season	Ratio of No. of livestock in warm to No. in cold season
	Carrying capacity	No. of livestock in July	Over-stocking	Carrying capacity	No. of livestock in December	Over-stocking		
Crop-dominated	6.43	8.53	2.10	2.78	5.65	2.87	2.31	1.51
Agropastoral	22.26	13.03	-9.23	7.93	12.73	4.80	2.80	1.02
Pastoral	13.92	12.69	-1.23	5.52	12.69	7.17	2.52	1.00
Agrosilvipastoral	7.18	2.74	-4.44	2.00	2.74	0.74	3.59	1.00
Tibet in total	49.79	36.99	-12.80	18.23	33.81	15.58	2.73	1.09

SOURCES: Dr Liu Yanghua of the Institute of Geography, Chinese Academy of Sciences, provided data for carrying capacity of natural pasture. The Bureau of Statistics of Tibet Autonomous Region provided livestock numbers.

more livestock. The production system exhibits a vicious cycle of high death rate, more livestock kept over winter, low offtake rate, leading to poor economic performance and poor livelihoods for herders.

There is a lack of scientific management and improved livestock. While traditional stock are very hardy, currently neither traditional pure breeds nor improved ones are increasing production. Several investigators have reported declines in productivity of local yak and sheep breeds. Efforts have been made to improve yak, sheep and cattle, and extension of these improved breeds on a large scale is limited by their limited economic capability and biological adaptability. On a per area or per animal basis, production of milk and meat is still among the lowest in China, mainly because of lack of good feed, particularly over the winter, lack of proper veterinary services and poor feeding strategies. With the growth in the population and the need to sustain the livelihoods of nomads, more livestock products are needed. However, the low productivity of individual animals means that this can only be attained by increasing stock numbers. Without improvement in the carrying capacity, this leads to overgrazing.

Inconsistencies between livestock ownership and grazing tenure remain unsolved. The commune system ended and implementation of the responsibility system of agricultural and livestock management began in 1980. Each person was allocated a fixed number of animals so that everyone had equal assets. However, grazing rights were not allocated to individuals and still belong to the government. When livestock is owned privately and pasture public, there is no incentive for herders to conserve, improve or use it sustainably. This leads to overgrazing and degradation.

The commercialization rate of livestock products is low. The more livestock a herder has, the wealthier he feels in nomadic society. Over the past several decades, this has not changed. The average offtake rate is only 18-30 percent, of which over half is consumed by the herders themselves. Few livestock products, particularly meat and milk, are sold outside nomadic society.

Potential of crop residues as animal feed

Straw is an important source of feed in the crop-dominated and agropastoral systems, and is the only feed available in winter and spring. In Linzhou County, Lhasa, in 1996, over 85 percent of the winter and spring feed was straw; a similar situation was found in Shigatse County. Over 89 percent of straw is barley, which has on average 48 percent total digestible nutrients (TDN) and 4.3 percent crude protein (CP) in the dry matter, compared to wheat straw with 41 percent and 3.6 percent, respectively (Christensen, 1999). Pea haulm is also an important feed in the agropastoral systems; in many high areas, peas may not mature for grain, but are grown with barley for forage. A promising trend is the growing of lucerne (*Medicago sativa*) and other green forages in central Tibet. Many herders plant fodder oats and barley. Nevertheless, straw is an irreplaceable source of feed.

Straw production was estimated at 1.2 million tonne in 2000, based on 1 million tonne of grain production. Cereal straw includes pea straw; rapeseed residues are hardly used as feed. Barley straw accounts for 76 percent; in the crop-based livestock production systems, winter wheat straw accounts for more than 50 percent. Current management of straw is not good: its rate of use for feed is about 26 percent. Farmers in most cases simply pile straw beside the house or on the roof. There is rarely further processing, such as application of ammonia or micro-organisms to ferment straw. There is no facility for feeding straw, such as troughs or racks; it is simply spread on the ground, so large amounts are wasted. In some villages, straw is used as fuel.

In recent years, the introduction of fermentation, together with troughs and chopping, has been successful for fully utilizing straw. In Tsedang Township and Gongga County of Shannan Prefecture in 1997 and 1998, many farmers adopted the combined package of fermentation of straw, chopping, and feeding with troughs. Local extension staff and farmers feel that this approach could enhance the utilization rate by up to 60 percent. Another approach adopted by farmers in Dazi County of Lhasa is mixing chopped barley straw with wheat or corn flour, as well as forage from lucerne. The total utilization rate improved by up to 62 percent. Assuming that the utilization rate of straw reaches 60 percent, more than 360 million SEU can be additionally supported, based on an estimate of 200 kg of barley straw for one sheep as a supplement to grazing. This is calculated based on number of SEU animal supported by straw feeding = total production of straw (1.2 million tonne) × ratio of utilization of straw as feed for animal (60 percent) / estimated amount of straw needed for one SEU (200 kg/SEU).

Feed-production potential

To increase livestock production by promoting improved livestock and developing intensive production, high quality feed will be required. Currently, over 173 000 ha of wasteland are available for developing forage, haymaking and silage production. If 40 000 ha of this land were cultivated for forage and grass, then after three years, an additional 1 500 000 SEU could be supported (Hu, 1995).

Expansion of the area of winter barley is now possible with multiple-cropping systems in central Tibet. A crop of green forage of alfalfa, turnip or rape could be taken after harvesting winter barley; about 30–60 tonne/ha of fresh forage could be produced. With expansion of winter barley to 10 000 ha, more than 35 000 grazing SEU could be supported. Besides these opportunities, with an increase in crop production, more than 100 000 tonne of cereals could be used for livestock feed. In addition, there are over 243 000 tonne of agricultural by-products, such as bran, oilseed meal and lees, which are not properly used as animal feed and are wasted.

To summarize, with the existing carrying capacity of grassland, full utilization of barley and pea straw, substantial use of wasteland to produce feed, development of forage and adequate use of agricultural by-products, 30 percent more livestock could be sustained on average. Based on this assumption, total carrying capacity in Tibet was estimated at 38 680 000 SEU at current production levels (Table 8.10). Comparing this capacity with the existing numbers of animals, the limit has been reached. At the existing level of livestock production, population structure and rate of offtake, 140 000 tonne of meat and 230 000 tonne of milk can be produced.

TABLE 8.10
Total potential supporting capacity and stocking status of grazing land in Tibet (million SEU).

Farming and food production system	Total supporting capacity			Supporting capacity of natural pasture		
	Total supporting capacity	Ratio of overstocking in warm season	Ratio of overstocking in cold season	Supporting capacity of natural pasture	Ratio of overstocking in warm season	Ratio of overstocking in cold season
Crop-dominated system	9.52	13.31	45.46	3.39	32.59	49.49
Agropastoral system	13.42	-68.73	35.73	12.21	-41.46	60.44
Pastoral system	11.76	-13.96	81.43	10.02	-8.85	319.26
Agrosilvipastoral mixed system	3.95	-89.55	14.93	2.99	-61.77	11.93
Tibet in total	38.67	-33.98	41.34	28.63	-25.70	85.28

SOURCES: Dr Lui at the Institute of Geography, Chinese Academy of Sciences, provided data for carrying capacity of rangelands. The author estimated total supporting capacity of livestock production in Tibet.

Further increases in meat and milk production will depend not only on improved livestock productivity by breeding, but also on improving pasture, increasing utilization rate of straw, developing forage, processing agricultural by-products for feed, re-structuring livestock populations and increasing rates of offtake.

Potential for livestock breed improvement

In 1999, the average offtake rate of sheep and goats was 26 percent, and 15.2 percent of yak and cattle. Total meat and milk production was 146 000 tonne and 208 800 tonne, respectively. Average per capita consumption of meat and milk in rural areas was 14.32 kg and 112.37 kg respectively.

Stock numbers are currently being controlled, so to increase production, local government is looking at possibilities of increasing productivity per unit or per animal. The potential productivity of improved breeds to intensify output and re-structure livestock populations is crucial to increasing livestock output.

In terms of new breeds, it was reported that both milk and meat production of yak, in most areas, can be increased by 30 percent through cross-breeding among the main breeds of Pali Yak, Sibu Yak, Jiali Yak and Dandxiong Yak. Local cattle are well adapted to the harsh conditions; most are tolerant of coarse feed and are well suited to grazing, but their productivity is low. Improvement through cross-breeding with external large-framed cows increased milk production more than five times and body weight by 46–57 percent (Hu, 1995). Improved cows, however, need better quality and larger quantities of feed. A 40 percent increase in wool, meat and milk production of sheep was achieved by similar cross-breeding. Up to 1996, there were only 15 000 improved yaks, 15 000 crossbred sheep, 40 000 improved cattle and 35 000 improved goats.

In the latter half of the 1990s, breed improvement has been one of the four important technologies (improved breeds, micro-organic fermented straw as feed, artificial grassland and disease prevention) promoted to increase the profitability of livestock in Tibet. Nevertheless, the number of improved animals has not increased substantially and the proportion of improved and crossbred livestock is still small.

In general, there are large numbers of yak and sheep, and a large proportion of old and small animals. It is advisable that, in the crop-based production systems, promotion is focused on cow and zo, while in the agropastoral and pastoral production system, on yak, sheep and goats. Increasing female yak and sheep to a proportion of 50 percent and 60 percent, respectively, would increase milk production (Hu, 1995). In general, livestock production can only be sustained when it fits local biophysical conditions and where there is a market for its products.

Changing trends of pastoral systems and livestock production in Tibet

Livestock raising comprises more than 50 percent of gross agricultural output and is fundamental to ensuring food security. Historically, the number of livestock was about 10 million head. Socio-economic changes in the 1950s and 1960s resulted in stock numbers increasing rapidly. Livestock systems are in transition, driven by increasing demand for livestock products, particularly meat and milk, due to human population increase, income growth, and changing lifestyles and food preferences.

The number of livestock: quantitative increase towards qualitative improvement

The total number of livestock has had three distinct development stages: fast-growing, steady-growing, and stagnant. Figure 8.4 illustrates this trend.

- **Fast-growing stage** Before 1960, livestock numbered about 10 million head. It increased rapidly following liberalization, land reform and democratic reform. By 1967, after just nine years, it had doubled, to 20 million head. The average annual growth rate was 9.47 percent during this period.

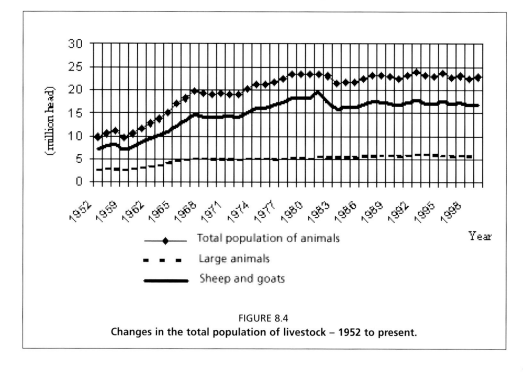

FIGURE 8.4
Changes in the total population of livestock – 1952 to present.

- **Steady-growing stage** During 1968–1980, the average growth rate was about 1.4 percent. By 1980, the number of livestock had reached 23.4 million head. While numbers had increased, livestock development stagnated; it was devastated following the transformation of large areas of productive grazing into cropland. There was greater emphasis on cereals than livestock. By the late 1970s, there was hardly any growth in livestock numbers.
- **Stagnant period** After 1980, the total number of livestock was between 22 and 25 million. The average growth rate was about 0.12 percent. In recent years, there has been slow growth, but it has not reached the level of 1978.

Overall, during the 1960s, the average growth rate was more than 10 percent. There was a slow increase in the 1970s, at an average rate of 2.16 percent. During the 1980s, there was stagnation, decreasing at -0.16 percent. In recent years there has been a slight increase in the livestock population. Particularly with increasing demand for pork in recent years, the number of pigs has increased at a rate of 6.6 percent annually, after a large decrease during the 1980s.

The total number of livestock has reached an alarming level compared with the carrying capacity of the pastures. Actions have been taken by local government to control livestock numbers. Guidelines for sustainable use of grazing lands and livestock development in the pastoral production system have been prepared, and a series of official documents have been formulated. One is the Pasture Law. It is laid down in the law that the number of livestock should be based on the area and productivity of the grazing land. In the implementation

of this statement, certain measures have been taken, including fixing the number of livestock – particularly numbers of yak, cow and sheep – according to area of grazing land in each administrative village, and encouraging herders and farmers to improve the unit productivity of livestock. Guiding herders to focus on the profitability and unit yield of livestock instead of seeking increase in number has been the focus of re-orientation and re-structuring of livestock production systems. In addition, traditionally, livestock numbers are perceived as the symbolic wealth of the household. Now herders and farmers are encouraged to produce what the market wants, using local resources. General principles for future development of livestock production were set as: stable development of pasture-based livestock production; vigorous development of crop-based livestock raising; and accelerated development of peri-urban intensified livestock production. The main aim of this is to boost total livestock production without burdening the grasslands.

PASTURE MANAGEMENT: TOWARDS A RESPONSIBILITY SYSTEM

Overall reform of the rural economy and agricultural development policies in Tibet began in 1978. The household responsibility system was formulated and introduced after the First Central Government Symposium on Tibetan Development, in 1980. Actions have been based since then on two 'long-term steadiness' policies. One has been long-term stability of cultivated land allocated to household use and self-determination of management. The second has been long-term stability of animals allocated to households for raising and owning privately, and self-determination of management. The landholding system for crops was changed from communes to household responsibility. However, that for grazing land has remained a state-owned or government-controlled system. Incentives for herders and farmers and mechanisms to conserve, sustainably use and better manage the grasslands by themselves are lacking. This is one of the factors that has led to degradation and overgrazing year by year.

To tackle this, most of the counties and prefectures have emphasized putting the household's responsibility and ownership of grazing land into effect in recent years. The intention is to make herders and farmers aware of long-term sustainable use and management of pastures. However, some ecologists suggest that this will create problems by restricting the mobility of nomads and their herds, which is the nomad strategy developed over centuries, to use and manage vast but fragile grazing land effectively on the high and cold Tibet plateau. Local policy-makers and pasture management specialists are aware of this, and some degree of flexibility has been given, such as the village responsibility system, collective responsibility system and household responsibility system, which were being adopted where appropriate. Meanwhile, different levels of government have been working on the expansion of irrigated pastures, artificial grassland and fenced pastures. Responsibility for carrying out these developments and post-management operation responsibilities were given to each village or household, and government takes responsibility for allocating minimal funds. The fundamental idea and expectation behind these activities is to increase pasture productivity so as to increase the unit supporting capacity of grazing toward the actual number of livestock.

GRAZING LAND DEVELOPMENT: TOWARDS INTENSIFIED MANAGEMENT

Under the general conditions of low carrying capacity, lack of feed in winter and spring, and shortage of winter grazing, one of the last hopes of promoting and reinforcing grazing-based livestock production systems in Tibet is now considered to be to develop fenced, irrigated, fertilized and planted pasture wherever possible. Both fenced and irrigated pasture are, however, currently limited, and development has not progressed much. For example, the area of fenced pasture during 1980–85 was about 308 000 ha; in 1996, it was 546 000 ha. The average irrigated pasture area during 1980–85 was about 122 400 ha, and in 1996 it was 153 000 ha. Thus fenced pasture increased by only 238 000 ha and irrigated pasture by 30 600 ha. This is too small to support productive and profitable livestock raising.

In recent years, especially since the huge disaster due to heavy snow in the 1997–98 winter and early spring, efforts have been made to increase the productivity of the grazing lands through developing fenced, irrigated and sown grasslands in pastoral areas. In 1999 alone, 20 000 ha of pasture were fenced for winter grazing. Application of fertilizer to pasture is also increasing. Almost all counties are speedily popularizing the technologies of fencing, irrigating, fertilizing and eliminating insects, mice and weeds from the pasture, and planting grass. Meanwhile, local government is focusing on settling nomads. Great efforts have been made in building sheds or shelters for stock in winter. In 1999 alone, 1 220 000 m² of sheds or shelters were built.

MEAT PRODUCTION: HOPE FROM INCREASING THE OFFTAKE RATE OF LIVESTOCK

The demand for meat and milk is increasing, but, as noted earlier, pasture production and feed supply have not been improved, neither have offtake rate nor unit output per animal. Thus, the increase in production has been mainly attributed to increases in the number of animals during the last 15 years. Land which was already overgrazed and degraded has been further burdened, to an alarming point, so it is necessary to increase the offtake of livestock.

Locally, great attention has been paid to increasing the offtake rate. Total offtake of yak and cattle increased to 690 500 head during 1995–1999, from 411 400 head in the late 1980s (Table 8.11). In 1999, total offtake of large animals was 774 900 head, from a total herd of more than 5.7 million. Total offtake of small animals ranged from 4.1 million head to 4.5 million head out of a total flock of more than 17 million. The average rates of small animal offtake and large animal offtake in 1999 were about 26.3 percent and 15.2 percent, respectively. Nonetheless, the offtake rate of most animals has, by and large, been the same during the past 15 years (Figure 8.5), except for pigs.

TABLE 8.11
Changes and trends in offtake of livestock.

Period	Yak and cattle		Swine		Sheep and goats	
	Average offtake ('000 head)	Average offtake rate (%)	Average offtake ('000 head)	Average offtake rate (%)	Average offtake ('000 head)	Average offtake rate (%)
1980–1985	303.2	6.22	51.5	31.08	2 678.4	15.45
1985–1990	411.4	7.67	71.8	48.22	3 399.8	20.06
1990–1995	540.9	9.32	93.6	51.82	3 595.0	20.98
1995–1999	690.5	12.98	127.6	58.57	3 956.5	23.18

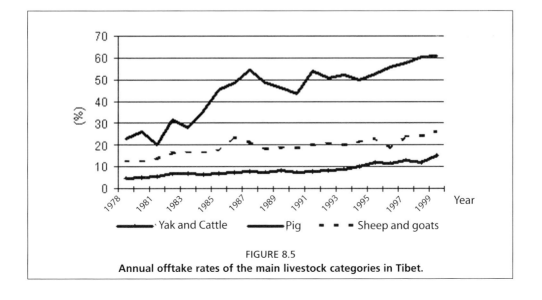

FIGURE 8.5
Annual offtake rates of the main livestock categories in Tibet.

MILK: INCREASING MARKET DEMAND BUT STAGNANT PRODUCTION LEVELS

Tibetan food preferences have been changing very rapidly. Urban cereal consumption has been declining, whereas in the rural population it is still increasing slightly. Both in rural and urban areas, the use of barley as a staple has fallen significantly in recent years. Most urban households now use wheat and rice as staples. Just 10 years ago, *tsangpa* was the main cereal. Consumption of meat, milk, eggs and vegetables have increased very rapidly since 1990. In particular, urban populations now prefer low calorie but high protein food. In rural areas, richer households consume more rice, wheat and vegetables. Consumption of meat and butter tea are increasing with the improvement of living standards.

There is a trend that once farmers become rich and have economic capacity to buy imported cereals, which are more palatable, local barley and wheat are replaced. The lifestyle and food preferences in urban areas are now similar to other provinces of China. Traditionally, tsangpa (roasted barley flour) has been the staple cereal; butter tea and *chang* (beer from barley) the drink; dried (or cooked) sheep and yak the meat; and potato and radish the vegetables. Though overall food preference is changing, butter tea is now the only distinct and common Tibetan drink in most households, both rural and urban, and butter consumption (Plates 46 and 47) is increasing with rising living standards. Tibet is highly deficient in butter: in 2001, this study estimated

Plate 46.
Dairy products are important for domestic consumption. Milk pails and churns on sale in Lhasa.

TABLE 8.12
Growth rate of meat and milk production (percent).

Period	Meat Production				Milk Production	
	Total	Pork	Beef	Lamb and mutton	Total	Cattle and yak milk
1980–1985	4.38	6.54	7.47	2.49	8.53	12.67
1985–1990	7.97	11.78	8.95	6.93	7.32	6.47
1990–1995	3.64	8.62	4.74	1.91	-0.34	-0.20
1995–1999	7.07	7.11	7.92	5.97	4.55	4.50

that there was a shortfall of at least 7 000 tonne.

The growth of meat and milk production has been slowed by the limitation of stock numbers since the 1980s. The average annual growth rates of meat and milk production were 4.38 percent and 8.53 percent, respectively, during 1980–85, but in 1990–95, they were 3.64 percent and -0.34 percent, respectively (Table 8.12). Since 1994, both meat and milk

production have been steadily increasing, but the growth rate of milk production still has not reached the level of the early 1980s. The growth rates of per capita meat and milk production also decreased during the 1980s and early 1990s, although again increasing in the late 1990s (Figure 8.6).

In general, total production of meat is still increasing, while the production of milk has stagnated (Figure 8.7). By using linear regression analysis (1978–1999) for

Plate 47.
Spiritual values are important in Tibet and butter has many religious uses. Butter lamps in Johang Temple.

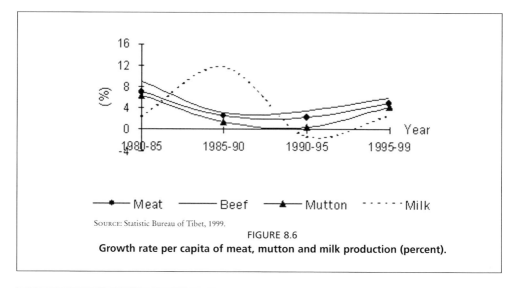

SOURCE: Statistic Bureau of Tibet, 1999.

FIGURE 8.6
Growth rate per capita of meat, mutton and milk production (percent).

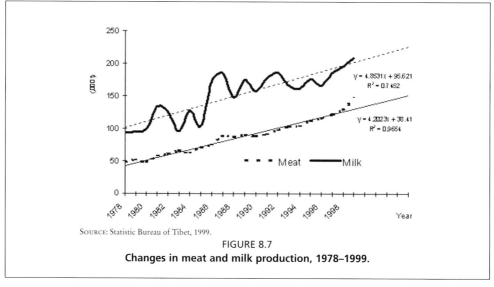

SOURCE: Statistic Bureau of Tibet, 1999.

FIGURE 8.7
Changes in meat and milk production, 1978–1999.

total production of meat and milk with the equations $Y_{mt} = 4.2023x + 38.41$ [$R^2 = 0.9654$] and with $Y_{mk} = 4.8531x + 95.621$ [$R^2 = 0.7452$], total production of meat was expected to be 140 000 tonne and production of milk would fluctuate around 210 000 tonne by 2001, which would be far from meeting the rapidly increasing demands for meat and especially milk.

MEAT AND MILK PRODUCTION: THE DRIVING FORCES OF THEIR GROWTH

There are many factors driving meat production to increase. Generally, it depends on the number of livestock and the rate of offtake, and the area of grazing land, its quality, feed production and climatic conditions, particularly drought. Time series data during the 1990s for these major factors were used to analyse the relevancy and correlation between meat production and those factors. The results are shown in Table 8.13.

Table 8.13 shows that:

- The offtake rate of yak and cattle is the main factor affecting meat production. Increase in the rate of offtake will facilitate an increase in meat production.
- Increasing the offtake rate and number of pigs also has great potential to boost meat production.
- Meanwhile, there is a close correlation between meat and cereal production. Increase in cereal production may provide more scope for producing stock feed. It also suggests that crop-based livestock production has major potential for increasing meat production.
- Area of grazing land does not have a major effect on meat production, but improvement of the grazing land does, particularly an increase in the area of irrigated pasture.
- The total number of livestock has not increased meat production much compared with other factors. This is because when the total population of animals is relatively stable, the rate of offtake and per unit yield are the main factors that affect meat production.

- This analysis shows that there is negative correlation between drought ranking and meat production. The degree of drought does not have much effect on meat production. However, drought itself has been a constraint on livestock development and meat production.

The same approach was used to analyse milk production, with factors such as the total number of yak and cattle, numbers of sheep and goats, total cereal production, total area of grazing land, total usable area, area of fenced pasture, area of irrigated pasture and ranking of drought. The results are presented in Table 8.14.

It was concluded that the total number of yak and cattle has the greatest effect on milk production, followed by the total number of sheep and goats. Again, correlation between cereal production and milk production is very close. But there is less effect from the area of pasture, and area of irrigated and fenced pasture. It might be because there is just a small area and also because of little change in area of fenced and irrigated pasture. Moreover, at current levels of socio-economic development, there could be considerable expansion of fenced and irrigated pasture. Increases in both total number and per

TABLE 8.13
Major factors affecting total meat production.

Factor	Degree of relevancy	Coefficient of correlation
Population of livestock	0.79	0.65
Cereal production	0.90	0.89
Cattle and yak offtake	0.94	0.95
Pig offtake	0.92	0.96
Sheep and goat offtake	0.84	0.68
Total area of grazing land	0.90	0.70
Total usable grazing land area	0.85	0.13
Area of fenced grazing land	0.68	0.23
Area of irrigated grazing land	0.80	0.68
Ranking of drought	0.70	-0.39

TABLE 8.14
Major factors affecting milk production.

Factor	Degree of relevancy	Coefficient of correlation
Number of cattle and yak	0.86	0.77
Number of sheep and goats	0.85	0.75
Total grain production	0.91	0.66
Total area of grazing land	0.91	0.61
Total area of usable grazing land	0.86	0.00
Area of fenced grazing land	0.64	0.39
Area of irrigated grazing land	0.76	0.37
Ranking of drought	0.75	-0.19

unit yield of cattle, yak, sheep and goat could be achieved through development of cereal production. It is important to suggest that milk production could be increased through developing specialized small-scale dairy cattle raising in cropping areas, and improvement of feed quality and feeding strategies.

MEAT AND MILK PRODUCTION: WHERE ARE THEY GOING?

Throughout Tibet, almost every household produces meat and milk for domestic use. The great variation in carrying capacity of grazing land – its area, biophysical conditions and socio-economic development of counties and regions – means that there is corresponding variation in meat and milk production. Per capita meat and milk production were estimated for each county of Tibet, and then compared. In most counties in the north and northwest, per capita meat production is more than 60 kg; in central parts, it is under 30 kg. Per capita milk production follows the same pattern.

In order to examine where meat and milk production are going, the data for the last 15 years were taken and the growth rates of meat and milk for each county during that period were calculated (see Figures 8.8 and 8.9). Two main conclusions were drawn.

First, there has been a large increase in meat production, particularly where cropping is possible. In most of central and southern Tibet, total meat production increased annually by more than 3 percent on average (see Figure 8.8). By and large, areas where cropping is possible recorded the largest increase. The crop-based production system increased by 11.8 percent per annum and the agropastoral area by 9.7 percent per annum. In pastoral systems, meat production increased by only 1.97 percent per annum.

Second, milk production is declining in the pastoral system, while it is increasing in the crop-based system. Figure 8.9 shows that milk production has decreased at a rate of more than 2 percent per annum in most of the north and northwest counties. In the counties where cropping is possible, milk production has grown at more than 2 percent per annum. Milk production in pastoral systems has declined by 1.8 percent per annum, whereas in both crop-based production systems and agropastoral systems it has increased by more than 16 percent per annum.

In general, meat and milk production bases are shifting towards central Tibet. Reinforcement of crop-based livestock production systems is desirable for further increasing both meat and milk pro-

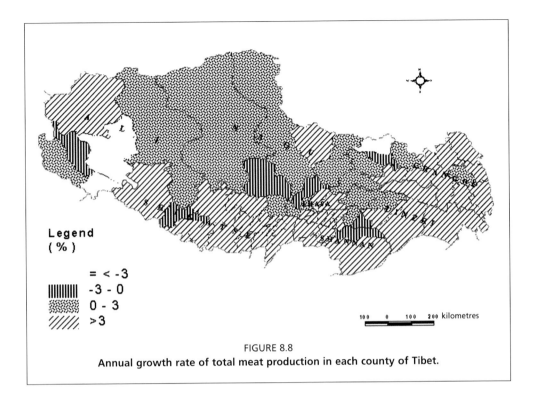

Legend
(%)

	= < -3
‖‖‖‖‖	-3 - 0
░░░	0 - 3
//////	>3

100 0 100 200 kilometres

FIGURE 8.8
Annual growth rate of total meat production in each county of Tibet.

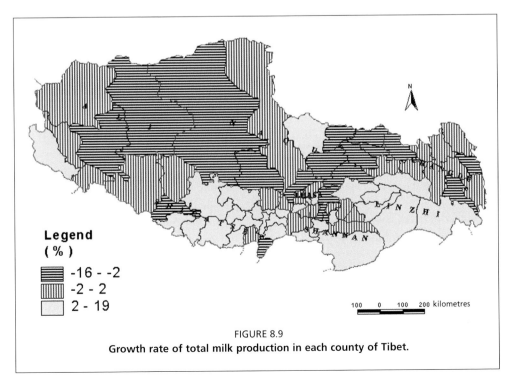

Legend
(%)

▤	-16 - -2
▥	-2 - 2
☐	2 - 19

100 0 100 200 kilometres

FIGURE 8.9
Growth rate of total milk production in each county of Tibet.

duction. In the pastoral system, increases in per unit yield of meat and milk production are needed.

The above analysis indicates that in the crop-based production system and regions where cropping is possible, both meat and milk production have been increasing, while in pastoral areas they are declining. This reflects the limitations of further development of the livestock sector, not only because of the low carrying capacity of grazing land, but also from difficulties in improving unit yield. Grazing-based livestock production may not have much growth in the near future unless there is radical improvement in grazing land production conditions. In the cropping areas, there is great potential for livestock production through utilizing crop straw and agricultural by-products as animal feed, devoting marginal land to forage production, producing forage through promotion of multiple cropping, and developing silage production. In other words, there is greater potential for biomass production in the lower river valleys of the cropping areas than in the pastoral system.

FUTURE GRAZING LAND (RANGELAND) NEEDS FOR FEEDING THE INCREASING POPULATION

The total area of grazing land (rangeland) is about 80 million hectares, making up 71 percent of Tibet and over 20 percent of total rangeland in China (Tibetan Bureau of Land Planning, 1992a). In yield terms, 49 percent of usable pasture yields 750 kg/ha of fresh grass. This yield is very low compared with other regions of China, but the area with this yield level is almost half of the usable rangelands in Tibet. The area yielding 750-1 500 kg/ha of fresh

grass accounts for 28 percent. However, the area yielding more than 4 500 kg/ha of fresh grass comprises only 1 percent, and is mostly distributed in non-livestock-dominated areas in southeastern Tibet (Tibetan Bureau of Land Planning, 1992a). Middle and low-grade rangeland accounts for 44 percent (Tibetan Bureau of Land Planning, 1992a). In Tibet, the carrying capacity of natural grazing is 1 SEU per 2.13 ha, compared to 1 SEU per 0.7 ha in Qinghai Province, 1 SEU per 0.75 ha in Inner Mongolia and 1 SEU per 0.41 ha in the United States of America. Production per animal is extremely low. For example, production of sheep wool in Tibet is about 0.5 kg/head, which is one-third of Qinghai production levels, and only one-eighth of average production in the United States of America.

How in the next 20 years could such low yielding grazing land sustain the increasing population with rapidly rising living standards and a changing food preference towards meat and milk? A simulation model was developed to calculate the demand for grazing land by year 2020, based on various assumptions for milk and meat demand, and unit yield of milk and meat production. Figure 8.10 illustrates the procedure.

The basic concept is that for different assumptions of population growth rate (1.3%, 1.5% and 1.7%) and its meat and milk consumption levels (Meat: MT1 = 18 kg/head; MT2 = 23 kg/head; MT3 = 30 kg/head. Milk: MK1 = 68 kg/head; MK2 = 72 kg/head; MK3 = 86 kg/head), the total demand for meat and milk in each county of Tibet can be calculated. Based on the current production of meat and milk, and area of grazing land in each county, yield per hectare of both milk and

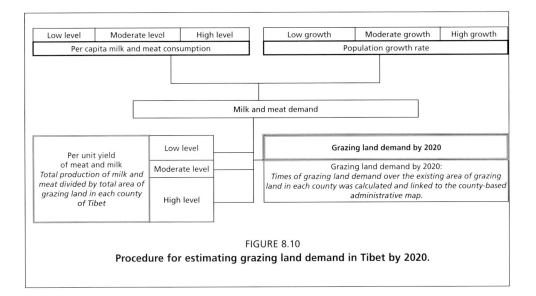

FIGURE 8.10
Procedure for estimating grazing land demand in Tibet by 2020.

meat can be estimated. These estimates for unit grazing land yield also include the yields contributed by agricultural by-products, forage produced from farmland, and straw from cereal crops. Thus the calculated demand for grazing land should be seen as equivalent to a certain amount of feed production for supporting the production of milk and meat. It cannot indicate the exact actual demand for grazing land, but it can be seen as an indicator of pressure on rangelands from increasing demands for milk and meat. Different assumptions of yield growth rate were used (0%, 15% and 25%). In all, 27 scenarios were generated.

On average for all Tibet, total demand for grazing land at different assumptions of milk and meat demand and population growth rate could be 1.5 times the total existing area. Were population growth to stabilize at the lowest growth rate, the demand for grazing land would be less than the current area, and – particularly if yields increase – grazing needed for different levels of consumption would be far less than Tibet's current resources.

However, the situation differs from county to county. Especially when all the estimated demands for grazing land are aggregated into the different production systems, adjusted for the size of population and area of grazing land, the estimated demand for grazing land compared with the current level becomes very different. For example, in the crop-based livestock production system, where population is concentrated and there is less pasture, the demand for grazing land under different scenarios is more than twice the current area, especially the *Low Yield + High Population Growth + High Consumption* scenario (No. 2 in Figure 8.11), where demand would be 4.46 times current resources. In contrast, in the pastoral area, because of smaller population and large areas of grassland, the future demand for grazing land compared to current resources is lower. For instance, under the *High Yield + Low Population Growth + Moderate Consumption* scenario (No. 5 in Figure 8.11), future demand could be expected to be less than current levels.

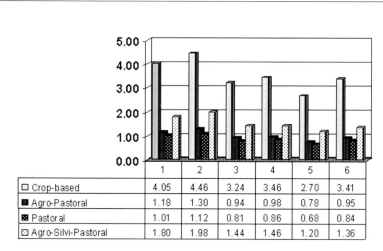

FIGURE 8.11

Level of demand for grazing land in 2020 compared with current availability (present = 1.00), based on six scenarios:
1. **Low yield increase + low population growth + moderate consumption.**
2. **Low yield increase + high population growth + high consumption.**
3. **Moderate yield increase + low population growth + moderate consumption.**
4. **Moderate yield increase + moderate population growth + moderate consumption.**
5. **High yield increase + low population growth + moderate consumption.**
6. **High yield increase + high population growth + high consumption.**

When the various scenarios are superimposed on the county-based administrative map, the spatial distribution of future demand for grazing land can be visualized. Taking the examples of Scenario 4 (*Moderate yield increase + moderate population growth + moderate consumption*) (Figure 8.12a) and Scenario 1 (*Low yield increase + low population growth + moderate consumption*) (Figure 8.12b), it can be visualized that there will be increasing pressure on the grazing land or demand for animal feed production in central Tibet, where the majority of the population is concentrated. In other words, there is going to be increasing demand for milk and meat in these areas, which will not be available locally, so it will have to be brought in, transferring the grazing pressure to more distant areas.

RECOMMENDATIONS

Livestock production cannot be sustainably increased unless there is productive and sustainable use of grazing land. The area available, soil quality, production of forage and its quality, regeneration, and environmental conditions directly affect the development of healthy and productive livestock.

Using the niches of the unique grazing lands and their biodiversity

Using the niches of the unique pastoral biodiversity to promote income generation for the herders is the essence of poverty alleviation in pastoral areas. The Tibetan

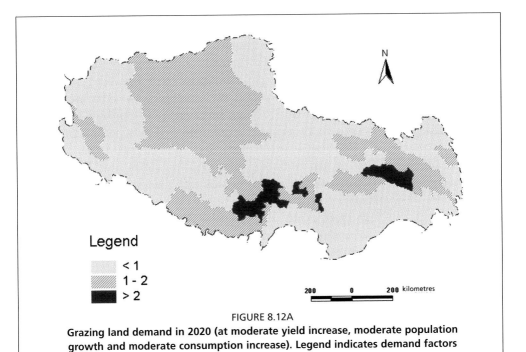

FIGURE 8.12A

Grazing land demand in 2020 (at moderate yield increase, moderate population growth and moderate consumption increase). Legend indicates demand factors compared to present, where present = 1.

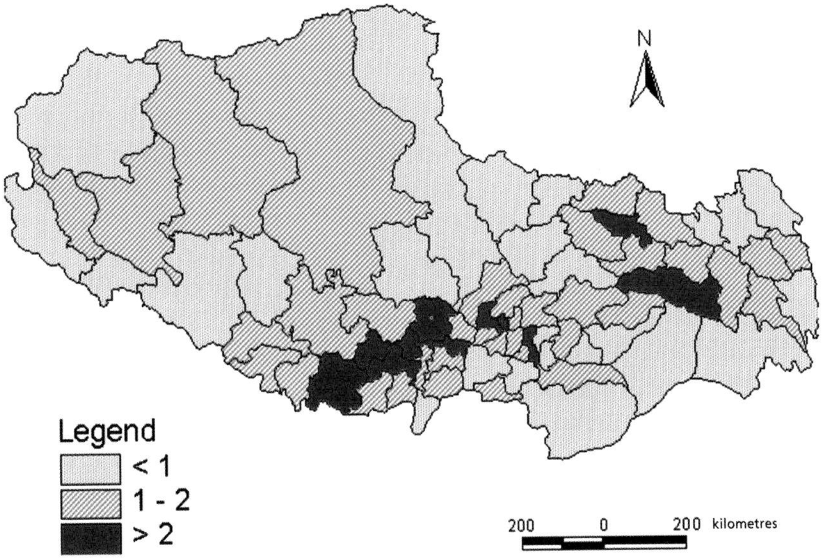

FIGURE 8.12B

Grazing land demand in 2020 (at low yield increase, low population growth and moderate consumption increase). Legend indicates demand factors compared to present, where present = 1.

Plateau has been recognized as the water tower of Asia, providing almost one-fifth of freshwater resources. It has been called the ecological fountain or riverhead of the region (Luobsang Linzhiduojee, 1995). However, the fragility and marginal nature of Tibet's grazing land ecosystem demands respect for its limitations, so care is needed in its development, with full awareness of the increased time and cost implicit in rehabilitation for livestock production compared with more clement areas. Environmental destruction and degradation, particularly of the grazing land, has a direct impact downstream. This should be realized in the formulation of law and policies. Legislation should be considered so that the local people are financially compensated for any conservation and rehabilitation of grazing lands on these very important catchment areas that will benefit peoples downstream. Unless there is much greater concern about, and concomitant care for, Tibet's grazing lands, with active conservation and rehabilitation, further destruction and degradation of the environment will occur, and the knock-on effect will alter the fate of much larger populations downstream.

Biodiversity in the grazing land is unique and of great value. There are over 3 100 species of plants (Sun Shangzhi, 1994) of which about 2 670 are edible (Tibetan Bureau of Land Planning, 1992a). Collection of high-value plants, such as saffron, *aweto*, fritillary bulb and lotus flower, is a major local income source. Vast areas of grazing land provide habitat for many rare and endangered species of animal, such as musk deer, wild yak, black-necked crane and wild ass or kiang (*Equus kiang*, sometimes referred to as a subspecies of *E. hemionus*). The nutritive

quality of forage is also reasonable. Many grasses have high protein and fat content, and low fibre (Tibetan Bureau of Land Planning, 1992a). However, productivity is low. Sustainable use and conservation of grazing land biodiversity and grazing land ecosystems is the essence and fundamental base for poverty alleviation in pastoral areas and improving livelihoods of the herders and nomads.

Accelerating the development of livestock production in the crop-based systems

Overstocking has led to grassland degradation and production stagnation in pastoral systems. Increased crop and cereal production holds scopes for raising livestock in crop-based production system where equal priority can be placed on increasing feed production, livestock improvement and marketing of livestock products. Farmers in this area need improved forage production technologies associated with cropland, such as seeding, irrigating and harvesting. It is also necessary to promote the use of forage crops such as oats, peas and lucerne. Multiple-cropping systems for forage production and the use of barley and wheat straw for livestock feed are yet to be fully promoted, but there is potential. Increased crop production and improved unit yield of cereal crops also provide opportunities for livestock feed from agricultural by-products and production of hay. Sufficient cereals mean sufficient concentrated feed. Productive cropland means marginal land can be devoted to the development of artificial grasslands and the cultivation of perennial forage crops. Feed production and the development of a market for livestock products should receive priority for developing livestock production in crop-based production systems.

Promoting integrated stable development of livestock production in the pastoral system

Increasing production without raising the number of stock is the major thrust in development of animal husbandry in Tibet. Increasing numbers leads to serious overgrazing and further pastoral deterioration. Controlling and rehabilitating degraded grazing land has been given great attention by local authorities. During the late 1990s, a comprehensive study of the grassland degradation and desertification in Naqu Prefecture showed that degraded grazing land in the area made up almost 50 percent of the total area of pasture; in some counties, such as Shenzha County, it reached 70 percent. It also indicated that the production of fresh biomass in various types of grazing land has decreased by more than 50 percent compared with the level recorded in the 1960s (Liu Shuzhen, 1999). This indicates that grazing land cannot sustain and support livestock as it did in the 1960s. However, recent increases in meat and milk production are not attributed to the area of grazing land and improvement of productivity, but rather to increases in stock numbers. Most counties have tried to increase stock numbers and there has been considerable growth in order to maintain total production of meat and milk. Thus, total production of livestock could be reduced for the sake of preserving and rehabilitating the degraded land, but this could lead to hunger and poverty among the nomads and herders. The only way to overcome this is to increase the yield of meat and milk per animal, while rehabilitating and improving productivity.

Speeding up development of urban and peri-urban intensified livestock production

Rapidly increasing the production of poultry, pork and milk, to satisfy the increasing urban demand, is a great opportunity to develop livestock production near urban areas. The per capita annual purchases of pork, poultry and eggs in 1999 were 13.2 kg, 4.8 kg and 4.6 kg, respectively. Taking the total urban population of Tibet as 660 000 in 1999, the demands for pork, poultry and eggs were more than 8 700 tonne, 3 100 tonne and 3 000 tonne, respectively; more than 70 percent of this is currently imported. Milk and butter are much in demand by the urban population, reflecting the improvement in their living standard, but most of the butter in the market comes from Qinghai and Gansu, or even from Inner Mongolia. Specialized and intensified livestock production in urban and suburban areas has great potential. Feed processing and supplying concentrate feed and forage is the essence of further development of livestock production in this area. Currently, there is no feed processing plant that can produce and supply large quantities of concentrates, forage or hay. Special attention should be paid to the possibility of developing scattered, small household-based small dairy farms, poultry farms and pig farms near urban areas, which are linked to the urban market. Development of greenhouse vegetable production near urban areas is developing rapidly. Combining greenhouse vegetable production with poultry and swine production for small-scale farmers has been successfully promoted.

Chapter IX
The western Himalaya

SUMMARY

This zone includes the Himalaya in India to the west of the Nepalese border; the Himalaya in Pakistan, with the foothills of the Karakoram and the uplands of Balochistan; the Hindu Kush in Afghanistan; and other mountain ranges to where they run down to the Turkestan plain. The transhumance systems are similar throughout in that they are of the classical, vertical type, where stock overwinter in warmer zones, the plains, foothills or the desert fringe, moving upwards as the weather warms until they reach mountain or alpine pastures in summer. Overwintering in the lowlands gives herders access both to markets and to opportunities for seasonal employment. Small stock are the basis of most systems, although the Gujars in Pakistan and India migrate with buffalo and cattle; camels are important in Balochistan and Afghanistan.

Herders generally belong to minority tribes, except in Afghanistan, where Kuchis are part of the Pushtun majority. Herders' diets are generally based on dairy products and purchased cereals. Most groups have no fixed homes and the whole family travels; the Gaddi described in the Indian case study are an exception. Migration routes have to traverse settled areas where increasing population pressure and land development make the passage of herds increasingly difficult and where disputes can occur.

Three related case studies are presented. The Indian study (Chapter X) describes traditional Gaddi migration, where they have fixed homes and a little crop land, usually in the hills, and only some family members migrate with their herds of sheep and goats. Two case studies from Pakistan are presented in Chapters XI and XII. The first describes a migratory system in the NWFP, where alpine pastures are used in summer both by migratory herds and those of settled communities from nearby valleys. The second describes how private afforestation and land development in Swat has disrupted nomadic grazing systems by obstructing traditional routes and has made herding more laborious. Stock have to be kept out of plantations and away from crop land.

INTRODUCTION

The western Himalaya (see Figure 9.1) lies in Pakistan and India as far east as the Nepalese border but, from a herding point of view, the zone extends beyond the Himalaya, northwards through the foothills of the Karakoram to the Hindu Kush and most of Afghanistan's mountains to the shoulder of the Pamirs; in the west of Pakistan it includes the Balochistan uplands; the Karakoram is too steep and desolate to be used even by the hardiest herders. The north of Afghanistan is on the edge of the Turkestan plains. Transhumant herding is common throughout this region; there are two main situations: full-time herders who follow a transhumance cycle between high pastures and lowlands throughout the year; and settled farmers, within reach of high pastures, who send their stock there in summer.

Herders and herding ethnic groups tend to specialize in either small or large ruminants, in contrast to the multispe-

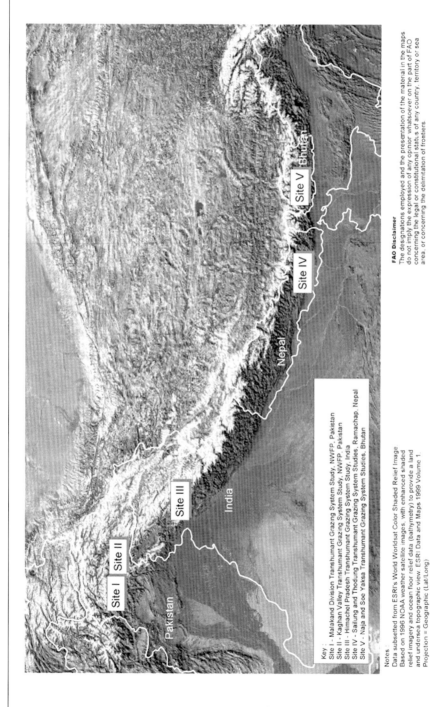

Key :
Site I - Malakand Division Transhumant Grazing System Study, NWFP, Pakistan
Site II - Kaghan Valley Transhumant Grazing System Study, NWFP, Pakistan
Site III - Himachel Pradesh Transhumant Grazing System Study, India
Site IV - Sailung and Thodung Transhumant Grazing System Studies, Ramachap, Nepal
Site V - Naja and Soe Yaksa Transhumant Grazing System Studies, Bhutan

Notes :
Data subsetted from ESRI's World Worldsat Color Shaded Relief Image
Based on 1996 NOAA weather satellite images, with enhanced shaded
relief imagery and ocean floor relief data (bathymetry) to provide a land
and undersea topographic view. ESRI Data and Maps 1999 Volume 1
Projection = Geographic (Lat/Long)

FAO Disclaimer
The designations employed and the presentation of the material in the maps
do not imply the expression of any opinion whatsoever on the part of FAO
concerning the legal or constitutional status of any country, territory or sea
area, or concerning the delimitation of frontiers.

FIGURE 9.1

Locations of Himalaya–Hindu Kush transhumant grazing system studies in Bhutan, India, Nepal and Pakistan.

cies herds of northern Asia. Horses are relatively unimportant, although some ponies are used for baggage. Yak occur in a few very high places in Afghanistan, Pakistan and Ladakh in India, but are not as important as they are in the Eastern Himalaya, Mongolia or the Tibet-Qinghai Plateau. Camels are not used by herders on high-altitude pastures in India, but are important in Afghanistan and Pakistan's Balochistan grazing areas, where nomads breed Arabian camels, which are also used as transport to highland grazing. Herders' diets are mainly of cereals, bought with the proceeds of livestock sales, and dairy products, meat being reserved for special occasions.

Overwintering in the lower areas has several advantages, apart from climatic ones; herders may buy crop residues, grain and fodder, or graze stubbles in winter; some do seasonal work on farms in return for straw and crop wastes. The winter areas are also mostly close to markets. Upland farmers who send their flocks to summer pasture rely on straw and stover for winter feed. Transhumant herding is carried out by minority ethnic groups who must herd their stock through or between agricultural or forest lands to reach their seasonal pastures.

Grazing areas, transhumant groups, stock routes and grazing rights are well documented in India and Pakistan from the time of the land settlement in the late nineteenth century, and many of these accounts and records are still available. Regulations concerning forest grazing, stock numbers, seasons for various pasture areas as well as grazing fees were all codified at and after settlement; with increasing population and political pressure, these rules may not always be observed and fees have not been increased for a very long time.

Many of the upland pastures and hay fields of the subregion are exceedingly steep, and trekking routes often very difficult. Haymaking is common in the better watered areas that receive the monsoon. Designated areas are usually closed to grazing throughout the monsoon period and the hay is made – from overmature herbage – once the rains are over; the product is of poor quality and low feeding value, but is highly prized by both settled and transhumant stock owners.

AFGHANISTAN

Afghanistan is at the junction between Central Asia and the Himalayan zone. Transhumant herding is very important. The overall pasture situation in the country is described by Thieme (2000). It is essentially semi-arid to desert and most crop production is limited to pockets of irrigable land, with some rain-fed areas in the north and at high-altitudes. Crops cover less than 10 percent of the total land area; most of the rest is extensive grazing, desert or high mountain and permanent ice. By far the greatest part of the surface is extensive grazing – desert, semi-desert or high or steep mountain; only about 40 percent is said to be suitable for winter grazing. From satellite imagery it has been estimated that more than 70 percent is rough grazing.

Afghanistan is at the convergence of several vegetation types: the Mediterranean, the Tibetan, the Himalayan, and, towards the Pakistan border, is influenced by the monsoon. Its great altitude range also adds to diversity, but, for the vast majority of the grazing lands, low precipitation, with winter incidence, means that the main grazing vegetation type is Artemisia steppe.

Artemisia steppe is by far the predominant grazing vegetation; there is high-quality pasture in the upper alpine zones, for a short season. There are variations towards Pakistan, where there are effects of the monsoon, and the great deserts of the west and southwest are allied to the flora of Iran and Balochistan. The mainstay of this vast area is Artemisia; the plant of the extensive grazing lands is generally referred to as A. maritima as it is in Pakistan; this may merit further investigation, since the altitude range of the Artemisia steppe is from about 300 to 3 000 m. In neighbouring Turkmenistan and Uzbekistan, A. herb-alba, A. turcomanica and A. maikara are mentioned. Throughout most of its range, Artemisia is associated with the viviparous grass Poa bulbosa (Plate 48); Stipa spp. are frequent. There is a very short flush of annuals in spring, but these dry off quickly. Other sub-shrubs associated with Artemisia include Acanthalimon (Plumbaginaceae), Cousinia (Compositeae), Acanthophyllum (Caryophyllaceae), Astragalus spp. (Leguminoseae), and Ephedra sp. (Ephedraceae).

In eastern areas close to Pakistan, Laghman, Kunar, Nangarhar and Paktia, where rainfall is adequate, Cymbopogon, Chrysopogon (Plate 49), Heteropogon, Aristida and other grasses of the monsoon areas occur, often associated with Acacia modesta and Olea cuspidata.

In the warmer areas of Mediterranean climate, including Farah and the Northern Plain, the leguminous sub-shrub Alhagi is a widespread colonizer on disturbed land and provides useful browse for small stock and camels; around Balkh it is made into hay.

Trees are often taken as sound indicators of ecological zoning. Afghanistan's

Plate 48.
Camels in spring on Artemisia–Poa bulbosa *pasture. Ghanzi, Afghanistan.*

forests have long been sparse and in recent years they have suffered destruction either by local populations desperate for fuelwood, or where there is valuable timber, through uncontrolled logging. In the central mountains below 2 000 m, degraded Pistacia atlantica [this pistachio has many names: P. khinjuk and P. cabulica occur frequently in local literature] forest is widespread, but often degraded to the extent of an occasional vestige. North of the Hindu Kush, on deep loess hills and plains, Pistacia vera is common between 600 and 1 600 m, with Amygdalis buharica and Cercis griffithii. These pistachio forests are a valuable source of high-quality pistachio nuts, but have been heavily exploited for fuelwood. In the east and south, between 1 200 and 2 000 m, Quercus baloot and Amygdalis kuramica occur. At low elevations in the east, Acacia modesta is frequent and, with adequate moisture, Olea cuspidata (Plate 50). In Paktia, towards the Pakistan-Waziristan border, the dwarf palm Nannorhops is locally important and is exploited for fibre. Between 2 200 and 2 500 m, Pinus gerardiana and Betula sp. occur. From 2 500 to 3 100 m has been deodar (Cedrus deodara), forest, but large parts have been severely exploited and have been replaced by stable Artemisia communities. From 3 100 m to the tree line at about 3 300 m, Picea smithiana and Abies webbiana occur in areas of higher precipitation, while Juniperus spp. are in the drier zones, often heavily used for fuelwood.

There are two main divisions in livestock production systems: those of sedentary villagers, and the transhumant (Kuchi) systems; Karakul sheep production is a third, specialized, subsystem in

Plate 49.
Goats on a Cymbopogon–Chrysopogon *pasture in Laghman, Afghanistan. Degraded forest eroded to rock, with grasses in fissures.*

the north of the area, which is out of the mountain masses and on the Turkestan plain and continues over the border in Uzbekistan.

Kuchi herders who practice vertical, seasonal migrations between the dry plains and the summer pastures in the mountains exploit much of the pasture on a seasonal basis. Sedentary communities also use many of these grazing lands, and often there is friction between the two systems. Overgrazing is probably mainly caused by the sedentary stock, since the Kuchis only graze for a short season (and rested the land in their traditional system), whereas farmers' stock graze every day unless there is snow cover.

The country has undergone much trouble and civil war over the past twenty years; its pasture situation has to be seen in the context of these events. A communist coup in 1978 ousted the then government, and Islamic guerrillas fought the regime, which had military support from Russia. Millions of the rural population became refugees in Pakistan and the Islamic Republic of Iran. The Russians withdrew in 1988, and many rural refugees returned to their farms in 1992 when the Najibullah government fell. Much international aid was supplied for the returnees, but serious civil war followed and more refugees fled when most of the country fell into the hands of local commanders. The Taliban fundamentalist movement took over most of the west, south and southeast of the country progressively from 1994; they have now been deposed with strong external involvement, central government is in the process of being restored, but a large

Plate 50.
Degraded Olea–Acacia modesta *forest. Lagham, Afghanistan.*

number of refugees are still in Pakistan and the Islamic Republic of Iran. Severe drought for several years has seriously affected transhumant livestock and many herders are said now to be destitute.

Pre-war migrations systems are well documented. Migrations were disrupted by the war, but many have been re-established, although where the Kuchis had used the lands of other ethnic groups as summer pasture, these rights have not been re-established. Under present circumstances it is unlikely that the problems of management of extensive grazing systems by the traditional pastoralists can be addressed.

While the Kuchis of Pathan origin are by far the most important, numerically and economically, of the transhumant livestock raising ethnic groups, they are not alone. In the extreme south there are Baloch and Braoui (of ancient Dravidian origin), and in the northeast there are *yurt*-dwelling groups with Altaic affinities.

At the height of the disturbance, livestock numbers fell drastically as farmers and herders became refugees and some Kuchi stock moved to other countries. According to anecdotal evidence, the grazing land (hard grazed for a very long time) recovered rapidly and there was excellent pasture. This situation did not last long: the stock numbers of both communities rapidly regained their former levels, through purchase and natural increase once the refugees returned, and now most pastures are as sorely overgrazed as before. The herds suffered greatly during the severe drought of 1999–2000, which was broken by severe floods in November 2000, and losses up to 80 percent have been reported.

The resurgence of the herding industry in Afghanistan is remarkable in that it had to start from a desperate situation, had no support from the administration, and yet regained a flourishing status in a few years. Marketing has been dealt with by local methods: stock are trekked to external markets, mainly in Pakistan, and the traditional cashmere and carpet traders deal with these products.

As might be expected in so mountainous a country, there are many systems of transhumance routes between alpine or mountain pastures and the lowlands and the desert fringe. Some from southwestern Afghanistan overwinter in Pakistan. Many Kuchi families have rights, attested by papers from the rule of the kings, to specific summer grazing. Transhumant herders are blamed for pasture degradation by villagers, but the greatest damage is done by the sedentary stock who graze for as long as the land is snow free; the Kuchis only graze in season and move on.

INDIA

India's temperate pastures are mainly in the Himalayas and adjacent chains; they form a narrow strip on the country's northern and northeastern border. Most are in the west of the country since the central part of the Himalaya is largely in Nepal and Bhutan and the extreme east is forest rather than grazing land. The Indian-administered part of Kashmir has great areas of grazing, much of it exploited by transhumant systems, but up-to-date information from there is not available. The Himalayan pastures are notable for the extreme steepness of the transit routes and much of their grazing land, as well as their very great altitude range.

Of India's twenty agro-ecological regions, only one has a cold climate:

AER-1: Western Himalayas (cold-arid climate; limited cultivation of millets, barley and wheat). Misri (2000), in the Country Pasture/Forage Resource Profile, indicates that temperate-alpine grasslands are spread across altitudes higher than 2 100 m and include the temperate and cold arid areas of Jammu and Kashmir, Himachal Pradesh, Uttar Pradesh, West Bengal and the northeastern states. The deterioration of Indian pastures, grasslands and other grazing lands may be ascribed to the large bovine population, free grazing practices, lack of management, and natural constraints like extremes of temperature, steepness of slopes, variable precipitation, and scarcity of moisture in arid and semi-arid situations. The situation in Himalayan pastures is even more alarming due to the severe pressure of the sedentary, semi-migratory and migratory graziers. Overgrazing has caused the near complete loss of edible species. Weeds such as *Stipa, Sambucus, Aconitum, Cimicifuga, Adonis,* and *Sibbaldia* have heavily infested these pastures (Misri, 1995).

The transhumant system is prevalent in the Himalayas, where there are several nomadic tribes, such as the Gujars, Bakarwals, Gaddis and Changpas, who rear sheep and goats under this system. The animals are moved to subalpine and alpine pastures during summer, while during winter they are grazed on adjoining plains. The scale of this enterprise is widespread and is practised by a variety of farmers, including landless and marginal farmers, who have adopted this profession for earning a livelihood. Sale of wool and live animals for meat is their only source of income. The transhumant system is practised in order to locate the best herbage resources from pastures and grasslands. There are also well recognized pastoral tribes who practise a complete transhumance, moving from one place to another on traditional migratory routes. The dates of migration have traditionally been fixed. Even grazing rights rest with the migratory graziers by traditional usage, though they do not hold proprietary rights over the land. The transhumant system is prevalent in the Himalayan region. However, this system still exists in some states situated in the plains, such as Rajasthan, Madhya Pradesh, Tamil Nadu, Gujarat and Uttar Pradesh.

Transhumant stock rearing is widespread in two forms insofar as temperate pastures are concerned: hill farmers taking their stock to high summer pastures, and full-time herders who use high pastures in summer but overwinter in the foothills or far into the agricultural tracts of the plains. Itineraries are of the classic vertical kind, spending the hottest months on alpine pastures; the altitude range is usually large. In addition to following availability of good quality feed, this allows stock to avoid the summer heat of the plains. Heat is stressed in the case studies, but the humidity of the monsoon, which follows the hottest season, is probably even more dangerous for small stock since the conditions are very conducive for the proliferation of internal parasites.

The Indian case study describes one of the important herding groups, the Gaddis, who are specialized in small ruminants, especially sheep. A second very important group are the Gujars, who are present in both India and Pakistan and are mentioned in all the case studies. The Gujars are an ancient race; they are essentially lowland people who go to high pastures for a short period in summer. Drew (1875) states:

> Unlike the Gaddis, who are really hill people, and only for a short time visit lower parts, the Gujars have their homes below; they are only summer visitors to the mountains... ...These Gujars are a set of people who are found scattered from Delhi to the Indus. Though holding some land they do not depend on it chiefly for subsistence, for they are a migrating, pastoral people... . Wherever I have met Gujars I have found them to be possessors of herds of buffaloes.

Christina Noble, then resident in Himachal Pradesh, followed Gaddi herds for a summer season. Her Over the High Passes (1987), although basically a travel book, gives much information on Gaddi herding, lifestyle and problems. She describes (p. 144 et seq.) how at the time of land settlement Gaddis paid fees for their pastures to the state, thus becoming titleholders and state tenants, while Gujars had to pay fees to the local villagers. Also around the time of settlement, Gaddis had the foresight to purchase land down in Kangra, which gave them a winter base and also rights to grazing on "waste land" of the village. Gaddi herders had capital; local people were mostly subsistence farmers who might earn some cash by labouring, but they lacked the capital that flock-owners could raise for land purchase. Now many Gaddis have lowland bases.

Misri (1996), at a meeting of the Temperate Asia Pasture and Fodder Working Group, described the Gujars of Jammu and Kashmir and indicated that they are increasingly becoming settled and giving up the nomadic lifestyle; those who can, acquire land and engage in agriculture while keeping livestock and trading in milk, milk products and cat-

tle. Gujars are not limited to Himalayan transhumance, nor to herding in India: they are also found in the lowlands of Rajasthan and Punjab.

In Pakistan, Gujars are still very much involved in herding and are mentioned in both case studies. They are also very important in peri-urban dairying and in milk and buffalo trading; in the irrigated tracts they often work for crop and horticultural producers to obtain straw and crop residues, but that is under subtropical, not temperate, conditions. The city of Gujranwala near Lahore was founded by and named after them, and they are widespread on the Punjab plains. Many others continue to take their herds to mountain pastures in summer, often with buffaloes on surprisingly steep slopes for such clumsy looking beasts. Some Gujars have settled and made their homes in higher areas, while still using mountain pastures in summer. Drew (1875: 110) states that "Gujars are found in Kashmir if not beyond" and Ehlers and Kreutzman (2000), discussing pastoralism in the Karakoram area, state that Gujars settled in the Nanga Parbat region around 1910, while other areas may have been visited much earlier; some have become shepherds for the local elite. Some Gujars graze in Balochistan.

The disputed territories of Kashmir are traditional areas of transhumance but, because of security problems of long duration, little information is available. Some routes that crossed present frontiers have probably changed since partition. The high lands of Leh and Ladakh are the edge of the Tibet-Qinghai plateau and yak are important; they are also visited in summer by herders with small stock.

India's Himalayan pastures are bisected

by Nepal; those to the east differ from the dry western pastures in being in a moister, more southerly climate. The plains are much more humid and probably less suited to the small-ruminant migration that is so common in the west. Some pastures are at very high altitudes and are contiguous with those of Tibet. Large ruminants, including yaks, are much more important.

PAKISTAN

The overall pasture situation in the country is described by Dost (1999). Transhumant herding is common to the alpine pastures of the mountains that flank Pakistan's eastern and northern limits, from Azad, Jammu and Kashmir (AJK) through Punjab, the NWFP and the Northern Areas that border Afghanistan and China. Generally,

the pattern is followed of upland farmers sending stock to high pastures, with full-time nomads moving between the foothills or plains and the high pastures.

The uplands of Balochistan, to the west, which border on Afghanistan and the Islamic Republic of Iran, are largely grazing land, mostly dominated by Artemisia, with Chrysopogon and Cymbopogon grasslands at the eastern edge where there is some influence from the monsoon. These lands are largely used by Baloch and Braoui herders, who raise small stock and camels; they are also winter grazing for Afghan herders, some of whom transit as far as the lowlands of Punjab and Sindh. The troubles in Afghanistan, and recent severe drought, have periodically caused refugee flocks to move into Pakistan, both in the Himalayan pastures

Plate 51.
Mountain landscape in autumn in the Hunza Valley, Pakistan, with terraced slopes and villages on alluvial fans and the mountain pastures already under snow.

and Balochistan.

As has been noted above, Gujars are one of the most important herding and stock owning groups; they were discussed under India since they are found in Rajasthan, throughout the area from Delhi westwards, and Himalayan grazing lands.

It is not clear whether migration patterns have been modified since partition. Bakarwals in Azad Kashmir still use the high pastures near the cease-fire line and have found good markets for fresh meat with high-altitude military posts, as well as employment for their ponies as mountain transport.

Until the opening of the Karakoram Highway in 1978, a large part of the Northern Areas had only very tenuous transport links with the outside world.

Stock rearing was important and based on using high pastures in summer (Plate 51); through the long, cold winter stock have to be housed and fed as well as possible. Small areas of the valley bottoms are irrigated, but mainly for orchards and crops (Plate 52). In the rain shadow of the Himalaya, valley bottoms are desert with little grazing. Some of the steep slopes have Artemisia scrub (Plate 53), but the only good grazing is high up on the alpine pastures.

The opening of the highway has had a noticeable effect on both the agriculture and the animal husbandry of the area. The road link permitted easy transport of cereals from the plains, sometimes subsidized; this has led to an increase in fodder cultivation for winter feed (Plate 54). How improved fodder technology has been

Plate 52.
Crops, lucerne (Medicago sativa) *and orchards on irrigated terraces in the Hunza Valley, Pakistan.*

Plate 53.
Artemisia *pastures in the Indus valley below Gilgit, Pakistan.*

Plate 54.
*Lucerne (*Medicago sativa*) hay drying for winter feed for livestock on their return from the summer pastures. Hunza Valley, Pakistan.*

taken up by the population is described by Dost (1996; 2001). Introduction of improved lucerne (Medicago sativa) cultivars to replace old, winter-dormant landraces was especially successful. In recent years there have been many inputs to development in the area, as well as intensive improvements in education, much funded by the Agha Khan Foundation. Now many youths have received education, and are no longer interested in herding. The present situation has been studied in detail and is described by Ehlers and Kreutzman (2000); the local population is now making less use of high pastures although there is some anecdotal evidence that other groups may be taking an interest in them.

Chapter X

Migratory goat and sheep rearing in Himachal Pradesh, India

Misri Bimal

SUMMARY

Transhumant stock rearing is very common throughout the Himalaya; various nomadic groups, such as Gujars, Bakarwals and Gaddis, keep sheep, goats and even buffaloes under such systems. With changing times there has been a considerable decline in the number of pastoral nomads, but this is still the only occupation of a large Himalayan population. Gaddis are a distinct pastoral tribe found in the state of Himachal Pradesh. Himachal Pradesh is flanked by Jammu and Kashmir on its northwest, Uttar Pradesh on its east and Punjab on its south. The Gaddis in all probability derive their name from their native land, the Gadheran, situated on both sides of the Dhauladhar ranges, which begin on the right bank of the Beas river and extend up to Chamba and Kangra districts. These ranges have several peaks as high as 5 500 m, although the average altitude is about 2 500 m. In the northeast, the Dhauladhar range leads to the higher Himalaya, while to the south they reach the Shiwaliks – the lesser or outer Himalaya – which merge into the plains. This continuity from the high Himalayan ranges to the plains offers excellent migration routes for the Gaddis.

INTRODUCTION

High altitude pastoral systems are integral to natural resource utilization, management and production in the Himalaya. There are different systems in different altitudinal and administrative zones. Although these systems have existed since times immemorial, few detailed studies have been undertaken on them. This study, in the state of Himachal Pradesh, is confined to Gaddi herders, who rear sheep and goats under a well defined migratory system. This small Himalayan state (total geographical area: 55 673 km²) is in the northwest of India, flanked by Jammu and Kashmir on its northwest, Uttar Pradesh on its southeast and Punjab on its south. More than 80 percent of the population is engaged in agriculture, but for climatic and economic

reasons arable agriculture is not very remunerative. All farmers keep animals to generate extra cash, so livestock and crops complement each other .

Migratory pastoralism is very common in the Himalaya, where several nomadic communities are found. Although with changing times a considerable decline has taken place in the number of pastoral nomads, this system is still the only occupation for a large number. Gaddis form a distinct tribe of pastoralists found in Himachal Pradesh; they, in all probability, derived their name from their native land, the Gadheran, which lies on both sides of the Dhauladhar range, reaching as high as 5 500 m above sea level, though the average altitude is about 2 500 m. In its northeast, the Dhauladhar range leads to the higher Himalaya, to its southwest it touches the Shiwaliks – the lesser or outer Himalaya – that merge into the plains. This continuity from the plains to the higher Himalayan ranges offers excellent migratory routes, where herbage is available at different periods of the year.

In this study of the Gaddis (Site III in Figure 9.1), observations were recorded at every tenth stopover of the migration, but (mostly at higher altitudes) the requirement of tenth stopover could not always be adhered to because of the logistics of migration. At higher altitudes, valleys get very narrow and the grade of the slope increases, so graziers do not find suitable resting places. There are no flat places to rest nor gather the flock, so they continue their climb non-stop.

Since the whole southwest boundary of Himachal Pradesh adjoins the plains, there are numerous migratory routes, which are selected by various families according to their grazing rights and which have been established through very long-term usage. A significant feature is that the grazier's home is on their route. The study route was chosen since the homes of the graziers involved are around Palampur, which facilitated data recording about the family and their sedentary activities.

While data were recorded from all graziers encountered, three families were selected for continuous observation, the households of Singhu Ram, Balak Ram and Jagdish Chand.

The observations recorded were both visual and actual. For determining botanical composition and biomass, 1×1 m replicated quadrats were clipped and weighed, then separated by species and recorded. Representative samples were oven dried to determine dry weight, and later analysed for nutritional parameters. Representative soil samples were collected from various altitudes for the determination of soil characteristics. For other observations, field interviews were conducted with the graziers.

THE PEOPLE AND THEIR MIGRATION ROUTES

Gaddis are a distinct people, wearing a characteristic and striking costume; they are an exogamous union of castes of Rajputs, Khatris, Ranas and Thakurs. They differ from other nomads in having a permanent house; while herds are on migration, the elders and the women of the family stay at home. Gaddi habitations are situated on the Dhauladhars between 1 000 and 2 500 m. Of late, some Gaddis have migrated to other districts of the state, but the majority still lives in Bharmour region of Chamba. Out of a total population of 76 859, some 76 037 lived in the region, with only 827 are recorded as living in nine other districts. While 30 percent of the Gaddis are still fully migratory, 70 percent have adopted a sedentary or semi-migratory mode of life. Many have shifted to other professions, like government jobs. Another major migratory pastoral tribe found in the area is the Gujar. They number 26 659 and differ from Gaddis in their ethnicity, livestock rearing practices and migratory patterns (Anonymous, 1995).

The Gaddi community is very small, socially very well knit although spread over a large area of Himachal Pradesh. They have a very rich history of ruling the Gadheran, and the mention of their erstwhile Kings is very common in their folk tales and songs. Most historians have traced their origin to Delhi and Lahore.

Gaddis are superstitious, god fearing, kind, honest and hard working people and have Hinduism as their religion. Only 18 individuals practising Islam have been reported from Bilsaspur (13) and Shimla (5) districts.

Gaddis follow a patriarchal and patrilineal family system. The father, as the head of the family, is responsible for looking after the interests of each family member, but mother is equally responsible and works hard, to some extent harder than the father, in the fields and the household. Because of their liberal approach, nuclear households are very common. After 2–3 years of marriage, a son is encouraged to start his own household; 75 percent of families are nuclear while only 25 percent, mostly migratory, are extended. Though most of the families are nuclear, they are woven in genealogically defined social bonds. They are grouped in *Tols* (Groups or Clans). Each *Tol* consists of 2–3 generations of the same ancestry. Every village is headed by an elder known as *Pradhan* and everybody abides by his decisions. A group of villages is organized into a *Panchayat*, the local governing body. Local disputes are settled at the level of Pradhan, whereas disputes between villages are settled by the local Panchayat.

Gaddis generally have small families. Those studied were Singhu Ram and wife, with three sons, all over 16 years (5 in total); Balak Ram and wife, his mother and father, two sons aged 11 and 9, and one daughter aged 6 (7 in total); and Jagdish Chand and wife, his mother and father, one brother, and two sons, both over 16 years (7 in total).

Overall in the community the literacy percentage is 30, against a State average of over 60 percent. Of late, following the introduction of social welfare schemes like free education, books, uniforms, lunch and cash incentives for Gaddis and other weaker sections of the society, the situation is expected to change significantly.

Male members are exclusively responsible for the care of migratory flocks. As far as the sedentary agricultural activities are concerned, the land is ploughed and sown by the male members. Clod breaking and weeding is done by the women, while harvesting is done jointly. Tree fodder is collected by men, whereas the livestock rearing, both grazing of animals and collection of forage from forest areas, is done by women, who also collect fuelwood.

MIGRATION, MANAGEMENT AND LAND TENURE

Before the mid-nineteenth century there was no legislation on the use of forests and grazing land, but as increasing pressure became a threat to their existence a national Forest Law was passed in 1865, giving the government powers to regulate most of the forests and pastures. A major outcome of the law was the regulation of grazing in forests to allow tree regeneration. Land settlement, carried out in Kangra between 1865 and 1872, led to the promulgation of the 1878 Forest Law, which introduced a system of reserved and protected forests. The settlement earmarked grazing areas for each Gaddi family, and herd size was fixed, as were the migration routes for each family, and it was stipulated that each flock would move at least five miles daily, spending one night at each stopover; the Gaddis did not appreciate these controls. Goats were identified as a major threat and in 1915 farmers were asked to pay a higher herding fee for goats than for sheep; even sedentary stock came under this regulation. Later, the deterioration of the forests was the subject of discussion and evaluation by many experts, and, acting on a 1920 report on the degradation of pastures in Kullu, the local forest settlement, a ban was proposed on grazing by local flocks, but migratory flocks were exempted from the ban.

After Independence, two Himachal Pradesh Commissions on Gaddis reported, in 1959 and 1970 (Verma, 1996). The second recommended a freeze on flock size. In 1972, the State Government again issued orders regulating flock size, but due to political pressure these decisions have never been implemented strictly. At present, the allocation of grazing lands and migration routes made in 1865–1872 are adhered to; the herders do not own the land but by usage they have the grazing rights, which pass on by inheritance in the family. Graziers have to renew their permits annually, paying a grazing fee of Rs 1 for a sheep and Rs 1.25 per goat [At the time of writing, 40 Indian Rupee (Rs) = US$ 1]; the permits contain details of the flock, grazing area and the route to be taken.

The migratory routes are well defined bridle paths which begin in the plains and, after passing through the Shiwaliks, where the dominant vegetation is scrub forest, cross the middle Himalaya, which has open grazing areas and coniferous forests, and end in the subalpine, alpine and arctic zones, where the dwarf vegetation is treeless and comprises mostly grasses and a few legumes. Migratory routes are for transit purposes only; the flocks stay for most of the time either in the lower hills, plains or in the alpine pastures. The journey from the plains or outer hills to the alpine areas takes about three months;

the time is highly variable and depends on the distance. A flock covers 7–8 km/day, starting at 6 a.m. and travelling until 6 p.m. At three night stops, the flocks stay overnight, but at the fourth stop they stay for two nights to graze, and rest the livestock and herders. Even the choice of stay for two nights is elastic, and at times it may not be the fourth stop but where relatives or a friend of the grazier live, or better fodder and groceries are available. This could mean a longer stay of 2–3 nights. The three flocks studied, however, spent two nights at every fourth stopover. This pattern of night camping continued to Palampur, where the families stayed for fifteen days (1–15 March).

The preferred movement to the middle hills is always through river valleys; river sides provide flat ground and an easily accessible water resource. In case of inclement weather, the river sides provide some shelter in the form of overhanging rocks. Besides, the travel is not as tiring as on hill slopes. The graziers always carry a few aluminium cooking utensils and a *Tawa* (steel pan) to make chapattis. At stopovers a frugal meal is cooked that includes chapattis, chutney (ground leaves of *aaonla* (*Emblica officinalis*), tamarind, green chillies and salt) and goat milk. Occasionally, goat milk is made into cheese, normally at a stop where they stay for two nights. At times, vegetables may also be purchased from villages. Ninety percent of graziers do not carry camping kit but sleep in the open under blankets. On colder nights, fires may be lit.

This pattern of movement continues till the middle hills; above them the slope becomes as much 70 percent and there are no suitable places to camp. A brief stop is made for a meal or a rest, otherwise the movement is continuous till the flat pastures of the subalpine or alpine regions are reached.

Migration is essentially associated with finding forage. In winter – late October-early November to late February-early March – the flocks stay in the outer hills or the plains, which locally are known as Kandi Dhar. These areas are also known as Ban, and in Kangra district these areas are claimed by Gaddis as *warisi,* i.e. inheritance. These areas were granted by local kings as gifts to Gaddi families and the grazing rights are still maintained by the heirs. The holder of grazing rights is known as *Mahlundi,* and in the old days he would pay tax to the King and in turn collect fees from the Gaddis who graze their flocks in his area. However, a Gaddi is free to let others graze their animals in his area against the payment of a fee, which may be in cash or kind. In these areas, owners of the cultivated land often offer their fallow to the flocks to graze the aftermath of the last rice crop. The flocks in the process provides natural fertilizer to these lands and the landowners pay a fee to the flock holder.

The upward movement starts in February or March, depending upon the length of the route. In this study, they started their upward movement on 10 February.

With small herds, the owner and some family members always accompany the flocks. Medium sized flocks are also accompanied by the owner, but sometimes contractual graziers, known as *puhals,* are engaged. The owners of large flocks always stay at home and puhals are engaged to take the flocks on migration. Puhals may be friends or natives of one's own village; they have to be provided with food in the form of maize flour and other essentials. For this an advance payment is made, or, in case of large flocks, adequate rations and other supplies are provided, which are carried by the horses that accompany the flocks. In this study, each herder had two assistants with him and the flocks had the following composition. Singhu Ram – 270 sheep and 163 goats; Balak Ram – 203 sheep and 157 goats; and Jagdish Chand – 302 sheep and 187 goats.

On leaving the outer hills the flocks travel into the middle hills across ridges and through river valleys; roads are always avoided. On the way the flocks are managed by herders and dogs. All three flocks dispersed to different sides during the day but assembled at prearranged stopping places overnight. Each flock is led by a herder, another follows at the rear and the youngest of the three runs here and there to keep animals from straying. The flock has to be prevented from trespassing on reserved and closed forest areas. *Radhari* check points, originally established by the erstwhile rulers and now managed by the Forest Department, are established on the migration routes to regulate grazing numbers and collect taxes.

Managing the flocks on migration is very hard work. The routes pass through very thick bush cover, particularly *Lantana camara.* Graziers have to work hard to keep their flocks together, and have to be most careful when passing villages to avoid damage to the cultivated fields. In the event of damage, they have to stay at an unscheduled stopover, wait for the village elders to gather and consider the dispute, assess the damage, and a suitable compensation is paid by the erring flock's owner.

By 10 March, the graziers had reached their homes at Palampur, and it was a great time to rejoice. The flocks are put on fallow land to fertilize it; the major reason for a long stay at home. A goat was slaughtered to celebrate the home coming. Meanwhile, the graziers prepared for travel to colder places, mending their clothes or even getting new ones. Essential repairs are done to houses and all other matters relating to family affairs are settled. This is also when marriages of the young ones are solemnized.

The journey to the alpine pastures is harder; there are very few stopping places and the steep slopes are difficult to traverse. After reaching the alpine pastures, it is time to rest and organize the daily routine.

In alpine pastures, the grazing lands are defined, though there are no marks on the ground; the Gaddis know their boundaries; trespassing on each others areas is always avoided and this is ethically adhered to. However, in case of dispute, the entire community gathers to resolve it.

The downward journey faces the same problems and follows the same routines. The time of commencing upward or downward journey is related to marketing. In March, traders come to the graziers and strike deals for the purchase of animals; during downward movement, the traders arrive again in September. The process of migration is very tough and has unique problems. En route there are frequent attacks on the flocks by wildlife, particularly leopards. Gaddi dogs are very brave and always have a spiked collar around their necks to avoid lifting by a cheetah. In spite of dogs and a constant vigil by the graziers, up to 10 percent of

the flock may be destroyed by predators and accidents. In case of natural death of an animal, the flesh is cut into slices and dried to be eaten later.

Crops only play a minor role. Gaddis own some land at their permanent residences and grow crops like maize, rice, wheat and oilseed. Holdings are small, at 0.25–1 ha per family.

GRAZING LAND

Of the total geographical area of 5 567 300 ha of Himachal Pradesh, 1 223 500 ha have been classified as permanent pastures and grazing lands (Anonymous, 1995). However, it is very difficult to ascertain the actual area available for grazing. Besides the areas classed as pastures, other land is used during migration and heavily grazed, including open forest (3 334 982 ha), unclassified forest (86 848 ha), non-Forest Department forest (94 770 ha), fallow land (55 700 ha), cultivable waste land (126 400 ha) and uncultivable waste land (190 600 ha).

The grazing area is spread over three zones, with distinct pasture types: subtropical grazing of the lower hills; subtemperate–temperate pastures of the middle hills; and alpine pastures of the high hills. The altitude ranges between 300 and 4 500 m. The area is spread over undulated, sloping and hilly terrain, with slopes of 30–70 percent.

The soil characteristics of the three zones are:

- **Subtropical ranges of the lower hills**
  The soils are alluvial-loamy, shallow on the slopes; deficient in available nitrogen; and low to medium in available potassium. The soil reaction is neutral and texture varies from loamy sand to sandy loam.

- **Subtemperate–temperate ranges of the middle hills** The soils are grey brown, podzolic brown; shallow to deep; and neutral to highly acidic. Available nitrogen varies from medium to high; phosphorus is low to medium; and potassium availability is medium.
- **Alpine pastures** These soils correspond to alpine humus and mountain skeletal soils, which are rich in organic matter. The texture is generally sandy loam to fine sandy loam. Available nitrogen, phosphorus and potassium are high, while the soil reaction is neutral to acidic.

The three distinct zones support diverse vegetation. The outer hills have scrub forests of *Lantana camara*, *Acacia* spp., *Adhatoda vesica*, *Dodonaea viscosa*, *Carissa*, etc. Herbaceous vegetation is very scarce and mostly comprises grasses like *Cynodon dactylon*, *Bothriochloa pertusa*, *B. intermedia*, *Imperata cylindrica* and *Saccharum spontaneum*. At higher elevations the arboreal element is dominated by *Pinus longifolia*.

In the middle hills, *Pinus longifolia* is replaced by *Cedrus deodara*. Other shrubby plants are *Cotoneaster racimiflora*, *Daphne oleoides*, *Desmodium tiliaefolium*, *Indigofera heterantha*, *Parrotiopsis jacquemontii*, etc. The ground vegetation is dominated by grasses like *Agrostis stolonifera*, *Andropogon tristis*, *Chrysopogon echinulatus* and *Dichanthium annulatum*. Common trees are *Quercus incana* and *Rhododendron* spp.

The highest zones support dwarf, mat-like vegetation, including *Poa triandra*, *Chrysopogon echinulatus*, *Andropogon ischaemum*, *Festuca alpinum* and *F. rubra*. A few trees of *Betula utilis* may be found. The bushy vegetation mostly comprises *Viburnum foetens*, *Sambucus wrightiana*, etc.

The climate of the study area varies from hot summer to severe cold winter. The outermost Himalaya, in the south of the state, experiences as hot a summer and as mild a winter as the plains; it also receive monsoon rains and the total annual precipitation is 1 500–1 750 mm. The maximum summer temperature reaches 40°C, while the minimum winter temperature goes down to 10°C. The climate of the middle hills is moderate; both summers and winters are mild. The summer temperature may rise to 30°C while the minimum winter temperature may go down to an average of 5°C, though sometimes the temperature may go down to freezing levels. The annual precipitation, including occasional light snowfall and monsoon rains, ranges between 750 and 1000 mm. The higher hills have a typical cold climate; the maximum temperature during summer rarely exceeds 20°C and during winters the minimum temperature may go down to -20°C; the precipitation declines in these regions, becoming 300–500 mm per annum, progressively decreasing with increasing altitude.

BOTANICAL COMPOSITION

The biological diversity of the Himalaya is vertical; between the altitudinal zones it is very common to find some ecological niches. The data collected on the botanical composition are massive and it is only summarized here. The percentage composition of grazing areas (which did not support bushes and trees) or *ghasnis*, as these are locally known, from three zones is presented in Table 10.1, which gives a general pattern. In reality, the vegetation is very degraded in the lower and middle hills.

TABLE 10.1
Botanical composition of ghasnis (grasslands) of the three hill zones in Himachal Pradesh.

Zone	Species	Percentage composition
Lower Hills	*Arundinella nepalensis*	7
	Bothriochloa pertusa	11
	Cynodon dactylon	6
	Chrysopogon gryllus	13
	Dichanthium annulatum	7
	Eragrostis spp.	8
	Imperata cylindrica	18
	Saccharum spontaneum	22
	Other grasses like *Themeda*	8
Middle Hills	*Agrostis stolonifera* and *A. gigantea*	13
	Alopecurus myosuroides	7.6
	Chrysopogon echinulatus	39.4
	Dactylis glomerata	5
	Dichanthium annulatum	4
	Eragrostis spp.	3
	Festuca rubra	1
	Imperata cylindrica	10
	Pennisetum orientale	9
	Poa pratense	2
	Trifolium repens	2
	Lotus corniculatus	1
High Hills	*Agropyron* spp.	6.3
	Agrostis stolonifera	10.5
	Andropogon ischaemum	10.5
	Alopecurus myosuroides	4.2
	Dactylis glomerata	15
	Festuca alpina	6.5
	Festuca rubra	9
	Lotus corniculatus	8
	Pennisetum flaccidum	13
	Poa alpina	7
	Phleum alpinum	6
	Trifolium repens	4

Although the botanical composition of the higher hills seems to be inadequate for the flocks, the weight gains shown by sheep and goats in these areas suggest otherwise. The degradation of the vegetation in the lower hills may reach stage 3–4 on a scale of 1 to 4.

The commonest weeds of the lower hills are *Ageratum conyzoides*, *A. houstonianum*, *Lantana camara* and *Parthenium hysterophorus*. The grasslands in the middle hills mostly have noxious weeds like *Eupatorium adenophorum*, *E. odoratum* and *Erigeron canadensis*. The high hill pastures have a predominance of *Aquilegia*, *Cimicifuga*, *Aconitum*, *Viburnum*, etc.

FORAGE PRODUCTION

Biomass production varies a great deal. The estimations for the present study were made after laying out quadrats of

1×1 m, replicated three to five times; the frequency of replication depended upon the area of study. In case of larger grazing areas, 5 quadrats were used, while smaller areas were scored by 3 quadrats. Herbage estimations were made only from areas dominated by grass or herbaceous vegetation. The observations were recorded at stopping places or about 2 km short of them. This was because stops are the most convenient place to encounter graziers.

The mean figures on biomass production and its nutritive value are representative and generalized (Tables 10.2 and 10.3). The values vary a great deal. Since the alpine pastures were the priority area of study, observations were recorded during the actual stay of the animals there. In case of middle and lower hills the observations were recorded during the monsoon and post-monsoon period, which is the most productive season. In March–June these areas are absolutely dry and production is very low. Estimations of the standing biomass during this period in lower and middle hills have been made by Misri and Sareen (1997) and are presented in Table 10.4. During October – February, the winter months, all the grasslands are dormant and growth is arrested. During this period the migratory flocks depend

TABLE 10.2
Herbage production of grasslands (tonnes of dry matter per hectare).

	Lower Hills	Middle Hills	High Hills
July	4.9	5.02	7.06
August	3.44	3.98	4.51
September	1.67	2.40	2.58

TABLE 10.3
Nutritive value of pasture herbage (percentage in dry matter).

Parameter	July	August	September	Mean
		Lower hills		
Crude protein	4.32	4.87	3.91	4.36
NDF	69.25	70.29	75.62	71.72
ADF	43.12	46.22	48.12	45.82
Calcium	1.32	1.12	1.31	1.25
Phosphorus	0.13	0.16	0.14	0.14
		Middle hills		
Crude protein	8.27	10.22	10.13	9.54
NDF	71.32	71.76	74.27	72.45
ADF	37.33	38.46	41.12	38.97
Calcium	1.29	1.47	1.63	1.46
Phosphorus	0.11	0.17	0.16	0.15
		High hills		
Crude protein	10.10	9.78	10.32	10.04
NDF	58.32	62.51	67.11	62.65
ADF	35.10	34.70	42.12	37.31
Calcium	0.83	0.91	1.13	0.96
Phosphorus	0.19	0.13	0.17	0.16

KEY: NDF = neutral detergent fibre. ADF = acid detergent fibre.

TABLE 10.4
Biomass production on lower and middle hill grazing areas in March–June (tonne/ha).

Month	Fresh weight	Dry weight
	Lower hills	
March	3.24	0.83
April	3.10	0.83
May	2.75	0.66
June	1.76	0.44
	Middle hills	
March	1.59	0.30
April	3.08	0.47
May	6.62	2.20
June	1.36	0.35

TABLE 10.5
Leaf yield of important fodder trees.

Tree	Age at lopping (years)	Fresh yield (kg/tree)
Bauhinia variegata	8–10	15–20
Dendrocalamus hamiltonii	8–10	30–40
Grewia optiva	8–10	8–10
Quercus incana	10–12	8–10
Robinia pseudoacacia	6–8	10–15
Terminalia arjuna	8–10	40–50

on the scrub vegetation of the forests and tree leaf fodder.

The reactions of flock owners to the question of availability of herbage were very interesting. In spite of the low levels of biomass production in the alpine pastures, they were more than satisfied with the production levels and the species composition of the pastures. Goats and sheep gained 8–12 kg of weight in the alpine pastures and the Gaddis attribute it to *Neeru* grass (*Festuca gigantea*). They were also happy with the available forage resources *en route* during migration. They were only worried about their winter abode, i.e. the outer hills and adjoining plains, where they stay during winter. The closure of forest areas and low levels of forage production in river valleys were a matter of concern for them. They would

like the planting of grasses, fodder bushes and trees in this area and would like the government to open more forest areas for their flocks.

FODDER TREES

Trees provide a major proportion of livestock feed in the middle hills, with 84 major fodder trees and 40 shrubs reported to be of very high forage value in the Himalayan region (Misri and Dev, 1997). Migratory graziers do not own trees; however, they use tree leaves wherever available. Trees in open forests and road sides are regularly lopped; illicit lopping is done in reserved forests as well. At times, tree leaf fodder is purchased from adjoining villages during migration. The tree fodder is either fed at stopovers or during the winter stay in the outer hills. The leaf biomass

TABLE 10.6
Crude protein percentage and farmers' scoring of trees.

	Crude Protein	Score
Ficus benghalensis	10.30	1
Albizia lebbek	18.90	2
Grewia optiva	20.00	3
Dendrocalamus hamiltonii	18.70	4
Cordia dichotoma	12.40	5
Bauhinia vahlii	12.80	6
Quercus incana	11.42	7
Ficus glomerata	13.90	8
Robinia pseudoacacia	20.45	9
Bambusa nutans	14.10	10
Litsea glutinosa	14.60	11
Cedrela toona	14.80	12

production of some important trees is presented in Table 10.5, and nutritive value and farmers' scoring for preference of some important fodder trees of the region are presented in Table 10.6.

LIVESTOCK

The livestock population of Himachal Pradesh at the time of the study comprised 2.1 million cattle, 700 000 buffaloes, 1.1 million sheep, 1.1 million goats and 14 000 horses. Data on Gaddi herds are not maintained separately at state level. Of the 1.1 million sheep and 1.1 million goats, as much as 70 percent may be migratory – only small ruminants and a few ponies for transport are in transhumant systems. Migratory herds are classified in three categories. Small Flocks are up to 100 animals; Medium Flocks consist of 300–500 animals; while the Large Flocks comprise 1 000–1 500 animals. The average composition of flocks is the same, with 60 percent sheep and 40 percent goats. Each flock has two or three dogs and large ones have four or five pack ponies. The main products sold are wool and live animals. Gaddis owning 250 and more animals are generally considered to be well off.

There are two breeding seasons annually. Mating begins in September and the stock have a comfortable stay in winter quarters before lambing at the end of February or early March. It can extend up to April. After the upward journey starts, mating is repeated, and graziers prefer to start their downward journey after the second lambing is completed on the alpine pastures. The twinning percentage is only 10 percent. Lamb mortality is 5 percent on the high pastures and 3 percent in the outer hills.

Veterinary care is available up to the middle hills, but is out of reach while the flocks are on the summer pastures. The commonest ailment is poisoning: animals bloat after eating *Eupatorium* and *Ageratum,* and become drowsy after eating *Lantana.* Traditional cures are used. In case of death, meat is sliced, salted and dried. Salt is given weekly at 3 kg per hundred animals. No other supplement is fed.

The major livestock products and their production pattern are considered below.

Wool

Sheep are shorn thrice yearly, in January (yield ca. 500 g), April-May (yield ca. 800 g) and September (yield ca. 1 500 g), for a total of 2 800 g per sheep. The wool is sold to traders who know the routes and shearing times and where to buy. Prices are fixed by the government; the present rate is Rs 6.5/kg of mixed wool. Black wool is in high demand but, following sheep improvement programmes, most is white or shades of white. Black sheep, like black wool, fetch higher prices. About **5** percent of the wool is woven domestically.

Meat

Live beasts are sold at the beginning of upward and downward movements. The mother stock is maintained to the age of 8 years. Lambs and kids aged 3–6 months are sold in the plains or outer hills in March: 3-month-old lambs fetch Rs 350 (US$ 7.6) while a 6-month-old may fetch Rs 700 (US$ 15.2). Kids of the same age fetch Rs 250–350 (US$ 5.43–7.60) more since goat is preferred for meat. At this age the body weight of lambs and kids is 9–12 kg. The second sale is in September, when downward migration starts, by which time lambs and kids are fully grown and weigh between 20 and 22 kg. Traders go up to the subalpine and alpine areas to buy the animals. Sheep fetch Rs 650 (US$ 14.13) each, while goats may fetch Rs 750–850 (US$ 16.30–18.47). Herders sell 40 percent of their sheep and 70 percent of their goats every year. Gaddis are very reluctant to reveal their income, but a fair estimate would be the following:

- A 100-animal herder selling 50 animals @ Rs 500 (US$ 10.86)/animal/year (average) would have a total income of Rs 25 000 (US$543.47) annually.
- A 350-animal herder selling 100 animals @ Rs 500 (US$ 10.86)/animal/year (average) would have a total

income of Rs 50 000 (US$ 1 086.95) annually.
- A 1000-animal herder selling 300 animals @ Rs 500 (US$ 10.86)/animal/year (average) would have a total income of Rs 150 000 (US$ 3 260.86) annually.

Expenditure is only Rs 1.00 (US$ 0.02) per sheep and Rs 1.25 (US$ 0.02) per goat as grazing fee. Ten percent of animals are lost due to wildlife or accidents.

Sale of goat milk is considered unethical by Gaddis; goat milk is never sold, it may be given to acquaintances. The only use of this milk is consumption by the graziers and making cheese for their own use. Since it is not a marketable commodity, graziers spend a lot of time preventing kids from overfeeding.

Besides grazing, the only supplement provided to the animals is salt (at 3 kg/100 animals), which is fed once a week by spreading it over the rocks at stopovers.

In case of death of an animal, the flesh is sliced and separated from bones; salt is rubbed over and it is dried for future consumption. Hides are not sold, but turned into bags to store and carry food items.

Animal sacrifice is common on religious occasions, family celebrations or before crossing a pass in the hills. The animal for sacrifice (it is always a male goat) is first given a bath, then the priest applies a paste of flowers and rice to its head and says prayers. A third person, not connected with the rearing of this animal, slaughters it. The priest takes the hide, head and a leg, the rest of the carcass is eaten by the family and friends. The important occasions for sacrifice include putting a new field to the plough; improving a field so that it can grow wheat; laying the foundation stone of a house; celebrating births, reunions and marriages; the 12th and 14th day after a death in the family; before the start of a journey; and before crossing a mountain pass.

HERDERS' OPINIONS

Gaddis, being busy with their own affairs, of a quiet disposition and suspicious of government officials, were apprehensive about the study. With the help of local contacts from the research centre's sub-stations, three families were persuaded to participate in the study. The following major points came out of contacts with the Gaddis:

- They are happy with their present life style.
- They are hesitant to reveal their economic status.
- They feel that forage availability at lower altitudes is dwindling and that winter feed availability is a priority area for improvement.

- They were unaware that pasture productivity could be improved through better management or, eventually, other interventions.
- They would not agree to any raising of grazing fees, but are willing to participate in improvement activities provided that all inputs are provided by government.

Some now have periodic exposure to electronic media and this is increasing the demand for schooling and medical facilities.

CONCLUSIONS

The Gaddis' transhumance system has gone on for centuries and will continue so long as it is profitable; this involves hard work, seasonal separation from the family, and an uncertain future.

Chapter XI

Pakistan case study 1: Agropastoral production systems of high altitude pastures of the upper Kaghan Valley, North West Frontier Province, Pakistan

Muhammad Rafique Sardar

SUMMARY

High altitude grazing lands in the Himalayan region are important for many reasons, including as water catchments and wildlife habitat; they are mainly a source of livelihood for herders, both fully transhumant and local. The study involved two distinct herder groups using the same summer pastures: local farmers who take their herds to the high pastures in summer, and herding nomads with no settled homes who move between the high pastures and the foothills in Punjab and North West Frontier Province (NWFP). The nomadic groups itinerary is such that they spend most of the year in fairly clement climates, escaping the summer heat by going to the hills and overwintering in the subtropical plains and foothills, where they are also close to markets and opportunities for casual employment. Gross management faults have led to widespread pasture degradation, mostly associated with lack of control of grazing pressure and grazing continually from the first growth in spring. Since graziers are often not the landowners, they have little incentive, or possibility, to improve management. Some regulation of land use, probably community based with government backing, might allow improvement. It is hoped that the studies will provide information toward community-based interventions to improve both vegetative cover and household incomes.

INTRODUCTION

Pakistan's alpine pastures are between the snow and tree lines, above 3 000 m. They cover 1 050 000 ha, one percent of the area of the country, including Azad Jammu and Kashmir (AJK). Some 700 000 ha are in the Northern Areas [a territory administered by Pakistan, comprising the disputed territories other than Azad Jammu and Kashmir – the old Gilgit Agency], 270 000 ha in the North West Frontier Province (NWFP) and 80 000 ha in AJK (Sardar, 1997). Subalpine pastures lie between the temperate humid and alpine zones at the southern latitudes and are treeless; further north they are an ecozone between temperate forests and the alpine zone, as subalpine forests,

grasslands, shrub-grasslands and meadows (Khan, 1971).

The study deals with two distinct areas: the summer, high altitude pastures in the Kaghan Valley, and winter pastures in the subtropical foothills. Two groups of graziers are involved on the summer pastures: local residents who take their flocks to the alpine grasslands in summer, and nomadic groups who graze there in summer but move to lower, milder areas in winter.

THE KAGHAN VALLEY

The area of alpine grazing in the Kaghan Valley (Site II in Figure 9.1) is about 12 000 ha (Hussain, 1968). The alpine grazing of Hazara Division can be divided into subalpine and alpine, based on vegetation. They are grazed by two groups: sedentary stock owners who live in neighbouring valleys, and nomadic sheep and goat herders, Bakarwals and Gujars, who come there at the beginning of summer, moving upwards as the snow melts, almost to the permanent snow line, and return in autumn to lower altitudes in the foothills or plains.

The four types of alpine vegetation in the Kaghan valley are, from high to low: alpine stony deserts; alpine meadows; alpine scrub; and alpine forest. Plant cover, cumulative cover and soil protective cover were 90.8, 119.3 and 97.8 percent, respectively. Average forage production was 700 kg/ha, range condition was determined as "Low Good" or "High Fair" (Hussain, 1968). The valley is surrounded by roughly parallel ranges which rise to 5 291 m at Malika Parbat; it is drained by the Kunhar river, which flows from Lulusar lake to the Jhelum. Saif-ul-Maluk is east of Naran town, at 3 267 m. The valley is a deep gorge about 96 km long and hardly more than 24 km wide, covering 945 km². Major land uses are grazing (55 percent), forest (24.6 percent), agriculture (2.6 percent) and the rest is built up, roads or barren land. Every available piece of land is cultivated, from terraces built with great labour on hillsides, to rich irrigated valley bottoms.

Almost all the valley is subject to grazing of varying intensity and frequency.

In 1901, the total population of the then Tahsil Mansehra was 18 396, of which Gujars (aborigines) were 9 200 (Anonymous, 1908). By 1981, the population had increased to 154 602 (Anonymous, 1981), a density of about 164 persons/km².

Grazing is heavy and uncontrolled (Plate 55), with no concept of pasture management. The land tenure system exacerbates the problem as graziers are not landowners and both they and the landowners want to extract maximum income without maintenance or other inputs. Hussain (1968) estimated that 147 941 animals used the pasture. A count by the Forest Department in 1998 at Bunja checkpoint indicated that 139 024 head (Table 11.1) visited the alpine pastures. Both figures are underestimates: livestock coming from the Northern Areas are not counted and not all graziers use the main roads, where the counts were made.

Four representative sites were selected in the Upper Kaghan Valley (see map – Figure 11.1), one each in Burawai, Jalkhad, Besal and Gittidas. All were main camping-settlement points of graziers. At each site, five paired plots were laid out, representing typical slopes and micro-aspects. Each pair of plots were close to each other, about a metre apart.

TABLE 11.1
Forest Department estimates of stock using the Kaghan pastures in 1998.

Livestock type	Number	AU[1]	Conversion factor
Cattle and buffalo[2]	21 680	24 498	1.13
Sheep	74 738	14 947	0.20
Goats	42 606	8 521	0.20
Total	139 024	47 966	

NOTES: (1) AU = Animal Units. (2) Cattle and buffalo were not distinguished in the count.

This distance was kept for ease in passage of grazing animals. One was fenced, the other open to grazing. Each fenced plot was 1.5 × 1.5 m and its clipped area was 1 m²; the ungrazed plot was 1 m². The corners of clipped areas were marked by wooden pegs.

The second study area was Saif-ul-Maluk (see map – Figure 11.1), which was similar to other pastures but, due to its accessibility, was more seriously degraded. No study has evaluated traditional use, but Hussain (1968) assessed range condition. The present study to evaluate natural productivity and management systems followed on from that of Sardar (1997). A preliminary vegetation survey was done in June–July 1996; the productivity and utilization of the pasture was explored using a paired-plot system. Socio-economic data were obtained through questionnaires and interviews. The extreme north was chosen for studies on pastures of the alpine and subalpine ecozones, between 2 925 and 4 184 m. Access is by a jeep track, which is open from June to September. Saif-ul-Maluk area was selected because it is accessible, is one of the highest pastures, and is valuable to graziers and tourists alike. In the last week of June 1996, about 80 percent was snow covered. A preliminary vegetation survey was carried out after 15 June. The forage production and utilization trial was laid out in mid-July and continued till October 1997.

For winter (foothills) pastures, two sites – Dara in Khanpur (NWFP) and Thatha Khalil in Taxila (Punjab) – were selected, with grassland-scrub in the dry subtropical zone. These were winter grazing areas of nomads. At each site, three transect lines, one 20 paces above

Plate 55.
Heavy, uncontrolled grazing (and natural erosion) causes degradation on steep slopes in the Upper Kaghan Valley, NWFP, Pakistan.

S. RAFIQUE

the bottom, a second in the middle, and a third 20 paces below the top or ridge were laid out. On each line, 20 quadrats each of 1 m² were laid out 200 paces apart. Sixty quadrats were studied at each site by the weight-estimate method.

In 1996 and 1998, paired-plots species cover was estimated visually; the current growth of vegetation was clipped in all plots; herbaceous vegetation was clipped to 2.5 cm above ground level, and any current growth of shrubs was clipped. The material was separated into grasses, forbs and shrubs; weighed; air-dried for a week; and re-weighed. Soil protective cover values for litter, cryptogams and bare rock were estimated. Soil samples to 16.5 cm were taken. In the first years of paired plots (1996 and 1998), data was recorded from August to mid-September; in the second years (1997 and 1999), data was collected monthly from June to mid-September. Collection of socio-economic data continued throughout the working period. In the foothills, data on species cover, protective cover, forage production and availability were collected in 1999. Material from foothill and alpine sites was analysed for nutritive value.

THE GRAZIERS

The Kaghan valley is home to people of diverse tribes or castes. Sayeds and Swatis, and to some extent Awans, are influential landowners; others are either tenants or tenants-*cum*-landowners. Gujars have been recorded as aborigines who were pushed aside by powerful tribes like the Sayeds and Swatis; they were herders – sedentary or nomadic – and are still traditional graziers.

Sedentary graziers are subsistence farmers, their stock are stall-fed in winter on crop residues and hay from field boundaries and hillsides; residues and hay are often bought locally; they keep livestock for domestic use; some stock and produce may be sold. Nomads live mainly by the sale of livestock; dairy products are consumed domestically. They make no hay but move following fodder availability seasonally and graze foothill ranges in winter, and they may buy green fodder and hay and use leaves of *Olea, Acacia* and other shrubs in time of scarcity.

Nomads are stock owners; most settled farmers prefer to be called *Zamindar* (landowner – cultivator) and have small-holdings; all earn money as casual labourers, especially in winter. Subsidiary occupations include hiring ponies to tourists, acting as trekking guides, day labouring and teaching. Most live in one household as an extended family: 68 percent of the settled group and 53 percent of nomads were thus. Sons of some settled families work as labourers. Both groups had large families (11 persons) of whom 3–4 were adult males, 2–3 adult females, one was aged, and 4–5 under sixteen. Earners were all males. There were two schoolchildren, of sedentary graziers. Almost all nomads are illiterate; the lack of educational facilities in their shanty hutments is obvious. Only 20 percent of the settled group were educated to middle-school level.

Socio-economic information was collected from both sedentary and transhumant graziers using a questionnaire with 36 main questions, and interviews, covering movements, livestock management, mode of grazing, and involvement in grazing land management. An accidental sampling system was used: graziers who were at a camping site, on the road or visited a specific locality were interviewed. In alpine areas, huts are far apart

TABLE 11.2
Types of land and ownership of graziers (ha).

Land use category	Sedentary	Nomads
Cropped – Irrigated	0.44	–
– Barani	0.16	0.36
Uncultivated – Grassland	0.49	–
Forest and plantations	0.12	–
Total – all types	1.21	0.36

and herders are not near them during the day; during the working seasons, only 43 household heads were interviewed: of these 29 were sedentary and 14 nomads. Of the sedentary group, 9 were Gujars, 5 were Awans and the others were Sayeds, Swati, Quresh, Mughal, Rajput and Pathan; of the nomads, 13 were Gujars.

Nomads live in tents and or *kacha* (mud) houses, mostly rented; 84 percent of sedentary graziers live in kacha houses (Plate 56), which they own. Sedentary

graziers own or rent about 1.25 ha of land per household. Land rented by nomads averaged less than 0.5 ha (Table 11.2). Maize, wheat, potato and peas are the major crops; straws and haulms are fed to cattle and buffaloes.

The average annual income per household of sedentary graziers was PRs 21 600 (1 US$ = 51 Pakistan rupees (PRs)) and non-crop income was PRs 12 230. Nomads' non-crop income was only PRs 23 856, which hardly covers daily expenses.

Plate 56.
Subalpine pastures at Suri Paya, Kaghan Valley, Pakistan, with the earth-roofed dwellings (kacha) *of the herders. There is evidence of considerable deforestation.*

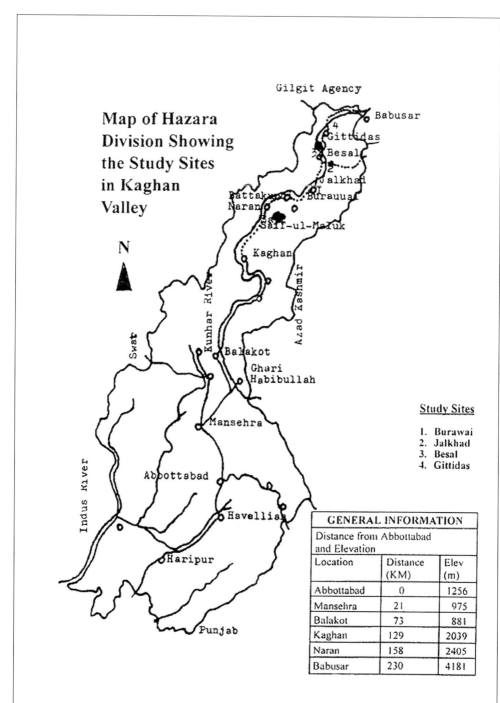

Map of Hazara
Division Showing
the Study Sites
in Kaghan
Valley

Study Sites

1. Burawai
2. Jalkhad
3. Besal
4. Gittidas

GENERAL INFORMATION		
Distance from Abbottabad and Elevation		
Location	Distance (KM)	Elev (m)
Abbottabad	0	1256
Mansehra	21	975
Balakot	73	881
Kaghan	129	2039
Naran	158	2405
Babusar	230	4181

FIGURE 11.1
Study sites in the Kaghan Valley and Saif-ul-Maluk.

PRODUCTION SYSTEMS

The concept of community could not be used since the graziers come from several areas and are of two types: those who live permanently in Kaghan or adjacent valleys and take their stock to high pastures in summer, hereafter referred to as "sedentary graziers", and nomadic transhumant herders (Plates 57 and 58), hereafter referred to as "nomads", who move between alpine pastures in summer, transiting through forest areas in spring and autumn and overwintering on foothill sites. Nomads have no permanent settlements and are always on the move in search of forage. Afghan herders also use these pastures temporarily. Nomads overwinter around Khanpur, Haripur, Hassanabdal and Taxila. Sedentary graziers come from towns and villages of Kaghan valley, such as Phagal, Ghanool, Balakot and Kohistan.

GRAZING LANDS
Saif-ul-Maluk

The upper watersheds are permanently snow covered. At three to five places, permanent glaciers are a continuous source of melt water, which flows onto the main valley floor and renders it unproductive for grazing. Saif-ul-Maluk covers about 4 614 ha, of which 91 percent is grazed, 8 percent is under glaciers and rocks and 1 percent is the lake.

Upper Kaghan Valley

The valley covers 66 898 ha, of which 64 238 ha (96 percent) is grazing, 855 ha (1.3 percent) is forest (subalpine forests), 220 ha (0.3 percent) is cultivated land and the rest (2.4 percent) is glaciers, natural lakes and river beds. Valley bottoms in Burawai and Jalkhad are cultivated; elsewhere all possible spots are converted

Plate 57.
Transhumant herders and their livestock on the way to summer pastures. Upper Kaghan Valley, NWFP, Pakistan.

into sloping fields and planted with crops in late May or early June and harvested in September. Crops are irrigated using snow melt. Farmers get good yields, particularly of peas, and a good variety of potatoes is grown. These crops fetch good prices in big city markets, particularly out-of-season peas.

There are sparse subalpine forest trees on the side slopes of the main valley, particularly northwestern aspects around Burawai and Jalkhad. Fir, blue pine, birch and junipers are the main species. On old maps (published 1930) patches of forests are shown, but there is now only scattered to very open wooded grazing; forests are on the verge of extinction through heavy grazing and wood collection. On right bank slopes, occasional trees of blue pine and junipers, with a relatively thick scrub layer of *Artemisia,* are found near

Burawai. Around Jalkhad, trees are absent on this slope. In Besal and Gittidas ranges there are no trees.

Jalkhad and Burawai ranges are mostly used by farmers who bring their livestock in summer, stay and grow crops. Nomads are found in huts or tents scattered in distant areas on the slopes. Besal receives graziers of many origins: Afghan refugees with sheep; nomads; and Kaghan valley residents. In Gittidas, graziers from Chilas in the Northern Areas exclusively graze the range. They have 5–8 temporary settlements, each of 50 or more huts in the valley. They bring all types of stock.

Saif-ul-Maluk valley's altitude varies from about 3 350 m up to 5 490 m. Side slopes are very steep and most peaks have bare rock, while others are covered by ice-caps or glaciers.

S. RAFIQUE

Plate 58.
Transhumant herders carry hay (as head loads) to feed livestock during transit to summer pastures. Upper Kaghan Valley, NWFP, Pakistan.

The main valley has undulating, rolling topography. Elevation increases from Burawai up to Gittidas and in side mountain valleys. The valley bottom elevations are 2 955 m at Burawai, 3 080 m at Jalkhad, 3 161 m at Besal and 3 600 m at Gittidas; side slopes are much steeper. The Babusar pass, near Gittidas, is at 4 184 m. The main ranges run more-or-less parallel to the valley, which is oriented northeast to southwest. Side valleys are dendritic and dissect the main aspects. Accordingly the aspect of the left bank is northwest–southeast. Along the right bank, the side valleys have no pattern, running in all directions. The paired plots at range sites were laid out to represent all possible aspects. The slopes of these points were moderate to steep. Very steep slopes were avoided.

The soil of Saif-ul-Maluk is calcareous, pH 7.3, predominantly sandy loam, and the soluble salts are within safe limits. It has adequate OM, phosphorus and potassium. Average soil moisture content was 31.9 percent in July 1996; it was very low and plants were showing stress. Twenty soils were analysed for physico-chemical properties and 20 oven dried and their bulk density calculated (Table 11.3).

Soil bulk densities at all sites were much higher than normal, indicating heavy compaction, due to continuous seasonal overgrazing, which badly affects the water infiltration and storage capacity of their upper layers. Moisture contents in July – a potential growing season – varied from 7.1 percent in Jalkhad to 13.4 percent in Gittidas, which was too low.

VEGETATION ZONES

Subalpine and alpine are the two major ecozones of the study sites. The subalpine ecozone is between temperate forests and the alpine zone; its vegetation has both temperate and alpine elements. Species well represented in the subalpine are blue pine, fir and birch among trees; and *Juniperus, Rosa, Berberis, Salix* and *Cotoneaster* among shrubs. Many grasses, grass-like forbs and other plants are also found. Scattered trees of the above species are present around Burawai and Jalkhad. The climax grazing vegetation in the alpine zone is meadows; tropical grasses are mostly absent. The major pasture types are meadows, shrub-meadows and shrubs (Khan, 1971). In the study area, 16 grasses and grass-like herbs, 49 forbs, 5 shrubs and 4 trees were recorded and identified. Vegetation covered 60–90 percent of the soil (Table 11.4), with forbs having the highest share (46 percent in fenced plots, 33 percent in open ones), with grasses (35 and 25 percent) second.

Saif-ul-Maluk is in a rain shadow (Champion, Seth and Khattak, 1965), so

TABLE 11.3
Physico-chemical analysis of soils from study sites.

Site	CaCO₃ (%)	Organic matter (%)	Major elements			pH	EC (×10³)	TSS (%)	Soil size separates (%)			Texture
			N (%)	P (ppm)	K (ppm)				Clay	Silt	Sand	
Burawai	5.10	2.51	0.135	17.3	1836	6.70	0.09	–	8.8	35.2	56.0	Loam
Jalkhad	7.10	2.01	0.096	19.9	704	7.56	0.07	0.022	13.2	38.2	49.2	Loam
Besal	4.70	2.31	0.155	9.8	961	5.98	0.08	–	9.4	50.0	40.6	Silt loam
Gittidas	4.35	3.02	0.151	29.2	308	6.26	0.13	0.041	13.6	36.6	49.8	Loam

KEY TO COLUMNS: EC = electrical conductivity. TSS = total soluble salts.

TABLE 11.4
Vegetation ground cover (percentage) at alpine sites, averaged over two years.

Vegetation	Burawai		Jalkhad		Besal		Average	
	Fenced	Open	Fenced	Open	Fenced	Open	Fenced	Open
Grass	36.2	24.3	30.2	21.5	39.6	28.1	35.3	24.6
Forbs	49.7	39.1	40.4	26.1	47.1	34.7	45.7	33.3
Shrubs	8.5	7.4	11.0	7.1	6.4	2.0	8.6	5.5
Total	94.4	70.8	81.6	54.7	93.1	64.8	89.7	63.4

does not receive enough precipitation in the monsoon. Winters are very cold, with snow from November to April. Summers are mild and pleasant. In summer, after noon, strong winds blow southeast to northwest and produce local cyclones of mild intensity. In 1997, a telemetry observatory was established by the Water and Power Development Authority (WAPDA) as part of the Pakistan Snow and Ice Hydrology Project. August is the hottest month, with a mean temperature of 12.2°C, and the coldest is January, with a mean temperature of -6.9°C. Five months (December to April) remain below 0°C. Probably it receives about 7600 mm annually, mostly in autumn. The cumulative depth of snowfall may be more than 6 m. Figures are reported for Naran (2 438 m) by Champion, Seth and Khattak (1965).

The Upper Kaghan Valley study areas are in the subhumid boreal and semi-arid climatic zones, with long, frozen winters and short, cold summers; in early autumn, chilly winds bring temperatures down. Precipitation is rain in spring–summer and snow in autumn–winter. Relative humidity varies from 42 to 84 percent. Mean minimum monthly temperatures recorded for three years were -8.9°C in January. Mean maximum monthly temperature was 24.6°C both for July and for August. Monthly temperature range was 17.5°C (lowest) for August to 26.0°C

(highest) for October. Temperatures are below zero from November to March. The mean minimum is below 5°C for 9 months, so the growing period is 3 months.

A diurnal mean temperature of 6°C and above defines the growing season for agriculture. During this period, mean temperature varies between 9° and 13°C (Arsvoll, 1995). Lunnan (1985) has defined growing seasons as the period between mean minimum temperature of 5°C so the growing seasoning in Saif-ul-Maluk is from July (11.8°C) to September (10.9°C), which agrees with observations on the ground. At the end of June 1996, about 80 percent was snow covered; about 50 percent was covered in mid-June 1997 and growth had begun in uncovered areas.

BOTANICAL COMPOSITION

In Saif-ul-Maluk, grasses and grass-like plants, other forbs and shrubs are found in different groups, patterns, frequency, cover percentage and composition. Micro-topographic features and morphological and physiological characteristics of the vegetation give rise to patterns which vary in size and are found intermittently. For example, *Juniperus communis* is prostrate with spreading aerial parts, so its compact patches are found all over the pasture, but particularly on rocky ridges. *Salix* occupies depressions on cooler aspects. Species of *Polygonum* have extensive rhizomes and several patterns are usually visible in the pasture. *Iris* form more or less compact patches distributed all over the area, giving the impression of pure stands. *Potentilla–Astragalus* type vegetation is present. Though 7 grasses and grass-like plants, 46 other forbs and 10 shrubs were recorded and identified, most were very rare. Some species are at risk of disappearance due to overgrazing. Those that are locally abundant perform well due to their better morphological and physiological characteristics. Patchy distribution, due to the different patterns and grouping, rendered the step–toe method ineffective, as most of the rare species could not be intercepted on transect lines. Some were only present in protected or sheltered sites. The frequency of intercepted species was low compared to that in plots.

The large number (63) of species indicates the richness of floral diversity. Prevailing conditions suggest that more palatable (decreaser) species have disappeared due to heavy grazing. Most (17 species) forbs have poor palatability (increaser species); two are unpalatable and poisonous. Most shrubs were not browseable. However, woody species are a good source of fuelwood and thatch. Dry branches and stems of *Juniperus communis* and *Salix* are collected for fuel. Besides feed for livestock, some forbs have medicinal values, and locals use them to treat both humans and livestock. Fresh leaves or branches of some are used as food.

All four sites in Upper Kaghan Valley showed minor variations in species composition (cover percentage) and frequency. At Burawai, an *Agrostis–Trifolium* community was recorded. Frequency of *Trifolium repens* was 80 percent as com-

pared to 40 percent of *Agrostis gigantea*. At Jalkhad, an *Alopecurus–Taraxacum* community was found, with 60 percent *Alopecurus* and 40 percent *Taraxacum*. At Besal, an *Agrostis–Cerastium–Trifolium* community was recorded with frequencies of 100, 90 and 100 percent, respectively. At Gittidas, a *Polygonum–Taraxacum–Carex* community was recorded with frequencies of 100, 80 and 80 percent respectively.

Hussain (1968) noted that range conditions were Low Good to High Fair. Visual estimates for this study indicated range conditions of "Fair to Poor", with a downward trend. A few unpalatable and less-palatable species were observed. Among grasses, *Stipa* spp. were unpalatable, while *Anemone speciosa*, *Aconitum heterophyllum*, *Gentiana tianshanica*, *Rhazya stricta* and *Verbascum thapsus* were unpalatable forbs. Among shrubs, *Ephedra procera* and all trees were unpalatable. Many forbs were of low palatability, but none were toxic.

For the alpine sites, 16 grasses and grass-like species were recorded, but of these only *Agrostis gigantea* (20 percent in fenced and 15 percent in open plots) and *Poa alpina* (10 percent in fenced and 7 percent in open plots) reached over 2 percent of total cover. Forb species were much more numerous, at 48; *Trifolium repens* (20 percent in fenced and 11 percent in open plots) was present at all sites and had the greatest ground cover; others exceeding 2 percent were *Potentilla sibaldii*, *Polygonum plebejum* and *Taraxacum officinale*. Five shrubs were recorded, of which *Astragalus candolleanus* (5 percent in fenced and 2 percent in open plots) and *Artemisia vulgaris* (4 percent in fenced and 5 percent in open plots) had some importance.

TABLE11.5
Seasonal forage production of high alpine pastures (kg/ha air-dry material).

Month	Grasses	Forbs	Shrubs	Total
June	11	21	8	40
July	94	242	44	380
August	106	251	36	393
September	72	187	28	287
Total for season	282	701	116	1 100

TABLE 11.6
Annual forage production at Saif-ul-Maluk (kg/ha air-dry material; average of two seasons).

Month	Grasses	Forbs	Shrubs	Total
June	20	110	6	136
July	62	560	17	639
August	64	961	15	1 040
September	58	392	2	462
Total for season	204	2 023	50	2 277

Due to close grazing and heavy snow in winter no herbage remains at the start of the grazing season (June). Only fresh growth after snow melt is grazed by livestock, which move upwards as snow melts, so measurement of forage production was only possible in caged plots. The estimated natural production potential of the Saif-ul-Maluk pasture was 2 277 kg of dry matter per hectare per annum (or season). Of this 45.7 percent (1 040 kg/ha) was produced in August, 28.1 percent (639 kg/ha) in July and 20.3 percent (462 kg/ha) in September. The lowest production – 6.0 percent (136 kg/ha) – was in June (Table 11.6). Average seasonal (June–mid-September) yield in Upper Kaghan Valley was 1 100 kg/ha air-dry material. In June, the yield was 40 kg/ha; during July, 380 kg/ha; during August, 393 kg/ha; and, in September, 287 kg/ha. Forage availability in Saif-ul-Maluk and Upper Kaghan Valley was lowest in June and highest in August (Tables 11.5 and 11.6).

Estimation of carrying capacity is based on available forage for well-nourished grazing animals. A proper use factor of 0.5 was applied, to leave enough stubble for soil protection or amelioration and for carry-over effects (start of growth next year). Both are important for sustained pasture productivity.

A mature cow of 400 kg is taken as the standard livestock unit (LU), for which the feed requirement is 8 kg DM/day, or 2 percent of its body weight (ICIMOD, 1995). This indicates that 1 LU requires 240 kg DM per month, and for the 90 days (mid-July to mid-September) of the growing season it will require 720 kg DM. The theoretical stocking rate each month varies according to the availability of forage. It is estimated at 2.2 LU/ha in August, 1.3 LU/ha in July and 1 LU/ha in September. This is possible only under proper use (50 percent utilization) and proper pasture management. However, the actual grazing intensity is very different from this estimated value.

FORAGE UTILIZATION

Average monthly and seasonal yield in caged and open plots were measured by clipping. The difference between caged

TABLE 11.7
Pasture utilization (percent) during grazing season, Kaghan Valley.

	Grasses	Forbs	Shrubs	Cumulative
June	21	17	32	20
July	68	70	62	66
August	74	73	60	71
September	67	73	63	69

TABLE 11.8
In vitro **digestibility of the forage from alpine pastures (percent).**

Location and month		Grasses	Forbs	Shrubs
Besal	July	74.88	76.31	–
	August	67.25	71.87	80.84
	September	60.88	34.77	–
	Average	67.67	60.98	80.84
Jalkhad	July	–	42.59	–
	August	40.29	41.64	62.57
	September	44.79	44.84	–
	Average	42.54	43.02	62.57
Gittidas	July	50.27	49.36	–
	August	46.72	43.45	–
	September	45.07	79.01	–
	Average	47.35	57.27	–
Burawai	July	62.07	63.89	63.32
	August	51.12	69.81	71.39
	September	50.52	64.80	57.57
	Average	54.57	66.16	64.09

and open plots yield was used to calculate forage utilization. Saif-ul-Maluk pasture utilization is very high due to overstocking. The highest cumulative utilization was estimated for August, as was the highest utilization of forbs. The estimated cumulative utilization (83 percent) for July to September was 33 percentage points higher than the recommended proper utilization (50 percent) (Table 11.9). The monthly and seasonal utilizations of Upper Kaghan Valley Pastures were 20, 66, 71 and 69 percent for June, July, August and September, respectively (Table 11.7).

Percentage dry matter, percentage ash and crude protein on a dry matter basis were determined. Grasses had the lowest ash content, forbs had the highest. Crude protein was highest in forbs, except at Gittidas.

In vitro dry matter digestibility was determined separately for grasses, forbs and shrubs (harvested leaves), but not sorted into species; all grasses were put together, as were forbs and shrubs. In grasses, digestibility was highest in July and lowest in September. Forbs and shrubs showed no set pattern (Table 11.8). On a seasonal basis, digestibility varied from site to site and vegetation type to vegetation type.

Herd movements coincide with sowing and harvesting of crops. Sedentary graziers start to move after sowing summer crops, and return for harvest. They go upwards from the second week of May to the third week of June, and start downwards in the third week of September, reaching home in the first week of October, the time of

TABLE 11.9
Pasture utilization (percentage) during grazing, Saif-ul-Maluk.

	Grasses	Forbs	Shrubs	Cumulative
June	35	11	–	14
July	75	80	68	81
August	63	89	63	88
September	50	80	55	75
Total for season (July–September)	62	85	63	83

TABLE 11.10
Timing of arrival and departure on pastures.

	Sedentary Graziers	Nomads
Departure upwards	12 May – 15 June	2 May – 1 June
Arrival on alpine pasture	20 May – 21 June	25 May – 21 June
Stay on alpine pasture	3–6 months	3 months
Departure downwards	Third week of September	Third week of September
Days spent on journey	2–7 days	20 days
Arrival at lowland base	First week of October	First week of October
Stay in lowlands	8 months	7 months

crop and hay harvest. Nomads start their upward journey from early May to the last week of June, when the wheat is harvested in areas near their winter grazing (Table 11.10).

Sedentary graziers travel on the main road, stopping at seven sites for one night, where they give the livestock hay. Nomads use three routes: many move along ridges and mountain tops on the left and right sides of the Kunhar River; a few use the main valley road. They make 23 stops on right or left sides and 13 stops on main roads. At each stop, they stay for one or two nights and graze the livestock. They cover 15–24 km daily before camping.

At their final camp sites, both groups herd their stock daily for 9–11 hours. Water is provided daily and salt once in 9–10 days. Sedentary graziers use Suj to Besal pastures in summer, and Kaghan, Balakot and Shohal in autumn and winter. A few move some stock, particularly buffaloes, to Haripur for winter feeding on sown crops; in such cases only a few men move. Nomads graze about eight of the pastures in summer, and Haripur, Khanpur, Taxila and Attock pastures in autumn through spring.

HOME AND HOUSEHOLD

Nomads drive all their stock to high altitudes with the whole family; they have no permanent hutments in the winter grazing areas, so everybody has to move. Sedentary graziers have houses in lower parts of the Kaghan valley; one or two milch animals remain at home to meet the needs of household members who stay behind. Sick and elderly people do not move with livestock. Male members move between the summer huts and permanent homes in the lower valley to take care of the remaining members and stock. Households decide independently on livestock movements, sale and purchase of stock and products. Decision-making processes vary between groups. Decisions are said to be made by male household heads among sedentary graziers. Nomads consult their wives and make collective decisions.

GRAZING RIGHTS AND FEES

Local communities have rights and concessions for grazing and grass cutting in all the State forests of Kaghan valley; these are exercised by local people, unless prohibited on silvicultural grounds, in part of the forest land. Similarly, full rights and concession are exercised in the community forests, known as *guzara* in NWFP. Grazing on common lands, and individually owned land after harvesting hay, is allowed. The catchment of Lake Saif-ul-Maluk belongs to the famous Sayed community of Kaghan but is used by a mixed usufruct group from Phagal village and other nomadic and semi-nomadic people. The semi-nomadic group hail from Balakot, Kohistan and a few more localities of Mansehra district, while nomads bring livestock from as far as Taxila and Hassanabdal (Punjab province) and Khanpur and Haripur.

Graziers from Phagal and its vicinity have tenancy rights, so do not pay grazing fees to landowners. Other graziers pay a pre-fixed fee, so they have demarcated the area arbitrarily and recognize *ghair mahsuli* (rent free) and *mahsuli* (rented) areas, and have built *Dharas* (huts) or tents there. There were seven units (sites for Dharas) with different names. Of these, graziers of Dheri and Kach Dara pay fees to the owners; other units are grazed free. Graziers of free grazing units do not allow outside graziers access, unless there is consensus; if so, nomads are allowed to graze stock for a nominal fee. Usually outsiders are not allowed. Nomads shift their camp sites during the grazing seasons within the allowed limits.

Tenants of Sayeds residing in the revenue jurisdiction of Kaghan town – from village Loharbanda to Naran town – graze free of cost as a tenancy right. Other sedentary graziers from Kaghan valley pay nominal grazing fees: PRs 2.00 per cow or buffalo; PRs 0.25 per goat or sheep; and PRs 0.50 per horse or mule. These rates were fixed during the first settlement of the District, in 1872, and, though not officially increased, are no longer applicable, and a fee not less than PRs 5 per head per season, or a lump sum, is charged for a particular site. A group buy it and pay according to the number of their stock. For example, there are two main owner families of Kaghan grazing: one charges PRs 100 000 per season for his chunk of grazing. These rates and fee arrangements apply to Burawai, Besal and Jalkhad sites. The graziers of Gittidas pay no fees as they claim it is their community land.

WINTER GRAZING AREAS

These are dry subtropical, broad-leaf forest grazing lands. Most of Haripur district (NWFP) is in this zone. Haripur and Khanpur are two cities with large areas in the ecozone, where there are scrub forests (*Olea-Acacia*) and large tracts of grassland. Nomads graze their stock in and around these forests in winter and spring. Attock, Rawalpindi and Fateh Jang are adjoining districts of Punjab, with similar forests and grasslands. The area of winter grazing totals 75 456 ha: 21 616 ha in Haripuir-Khanpur, 8 135 ha in Taxila, 1 011 ha in Hassanabdal, 29 328 ha in Attock and 15 366 ha in Fateh Jang.

Most of these are guzara forests, particularly in Haripur; the rest is state owned. Large areas of community and individually owned grasslands are available for free grazing in winter in the foothills and lower slopes of the Himalayas, the Salt Range and Kalachitta, between subtropical thorn forests and subtropical pine forests, between 450 m and 1 525 m. A long dry season is tempered by winter, spring and monsoon rain. Precipitation is from 250 mm to 760 mm annually. Temperatures are high in June–July, with mean maxima from 29.4° to 33.3°C. December–January is the coldest period, with mean minima of about 10°C. Frost may occur in winter.

BOTANICAL COMPOSITION

Characteristic trees are *Olea cuspitada* and *Acacia modesta*. Shrub genera include *Dodonaea*, *Withania*, *Rhazya*, *Gymnosporia*, *Monotheca* and *Carissa*. Fifteen grasses were recorded, but only seven forbs. Shrubs (8 species) and trees (6 species) are much more important. Only two grasses are important: *Chrysopogon montanus* (13–15 percent) and *Heteropogon contortus* (9–14 percent). Forb cover was insignificant. Shrub cover was about 11 percent, of which *Acacia modesta* (4–6 percent) and *Adhatoda vesica* (1–3 percent) had some importance. For shares of the protective cover types, see Table 11.11.

The winter grazing lands of the nomads are also the summer grazing land of local communities, who harvest hay in September-October. Thereafter the areas may be grazed till spring. Nomads' stock graze such areas both in spring and in late autumn and winter; there is very little forage available for winter grazing-browsing, and that is leftover stubble or re-growth. These ranges are overgrazed. They were evaluated once, in October-November, when available forage was 467 kg/ha air-dry material. This is too low for winter and spring use by large numbers of nomadic livestock (Table 11.12).

GRAZING RIGHTS AND FEES

Most forests in these areas are closed and nomads have no grazing rights. Illicit grazing in the forest occasionally leads to violent confrontation with the Forest Department. Graziers usually rent winter grazing or have arrangements with private landowners, to whom they give manure or other livestock products. It is difficult to procure grazing, and some buy fodder for grazing or stall feeding.

LIVESTOCK

Both semi-nomads [those who drive their livestock for summer grazing only, while

TABLE 11.11
Protective cover (percent) of Dara (Khanpur) and Thatha Khalil (Taxila) areas.

Material	Dara	Thatha Khalil
Plant Base	10.8	12.8
Litter	4.4	13.0
Cryptogams	–	–
Rock pavement	14.4	19.6
Bare soil	70.4	54.6

TABLE 11.12
Forage production of winter range(kg/ha air-dry material).

Site	Grasses	Forbs	Shrubs	Total
Dara (Khanpur)	186	9	257	452
Thatha Khalil (Taxila)	304	15	163	482
Average	245	12	210	467

residing in the valley, or who similarly move livestock to the plains in winter] and nomads keep all types of stock: cattle (milch, draught and dual-purpose); buffalo (mostly milch); sheep (wool and meat); and goat (milk, hair and meat). They also have ponies, mules and horses. Cattle and buffaloes are usually nondescript crossbreds of the important breeds of the plains.

The Kaghani breed of sheep is small to medium sized, and are mostly white; males have horns. The liveweights of male and female are 22 and 28 kg, respectively. Annual wool yield is about 1.5 kg per head. Some Kaghani sheep have some Rambouillet blood, resulting in better quality wool and weight; males weigh 60–65 kg and wool yield per head is 2.5–3 kg/year. Gaddi and Kaghani goats are kept in Kaghan Valley. Gaddi goats are generally black, fairly large and hairy; adult males and females weigh about 42 and 50 kg, respectively; they are raised for milk and hair. Milk is about 125 litres in 150 days; hair yield is 2 kg/head/year. Kaghani goats are usually black, with a well developed, compact body covered with long dense hair. Adult male and female weights are 35 and 42 kg, respectively. Hair yield is 2 kg/head and twins are common. The local cattle in the valley are Achi-gabrali, mostly crossbred with Jersey or Friesian or both. The weight of adult cattle varies from 300-350 kg. These are kept for meat, milk and draught; their milk yield is comparatively low.

Buffaloes are bought from the plains and brought to the valley for milking. The average age at maturity is 30 months for males and 36 months for females. Adult males weigh 500–600 kg and females 300–400 kg. Milk yield per lactation is 1 700–2 200 litres, with over 6 percent butter fat. In the Kaghan Valley, their weight and milk yield are lower. This could be due to the different environment, as well as mixed breed.

The high altitude alpine pastures are grazed continuously in summer by both nomads and semi nomadic graziers. Besides ecological adaptation, there are social, political and economic factors that force the graziers to continue this centuries-old practice.

- Most nomads are landless and their household economy depends on livestock, so they move from place to place in search of grazing.
- Some semi-nomadic graziers have grazing rights on alpine pastures, which they use seasonally.
- Foothill and middle hills pastures are closed in summer for haymaking, but are open to grazing in winter, free or at nominal charge, to landless graziers.
- Nomads consider that their livestock cannot tolerate the summer heat of the foothills of NWFP and Punjab.

The average number of livestock per household was calculated from data collected through questionnaires. The herd size of nomads was 149 head, of which 108 (72 percent) were goats, 40 (27 percent) sheep and 1 (0.8 percent) equine; they did not keep buffaloes or cattle. Sedentary graziers, on average, kept 12 head, of which 5 (42 percent) were goats, 5 (42 percent) cattle, 1 (8 percent) buffalo and 1 (8 percent) equine. Interestingly, they had no sheep. Yaks are not reared in this part of the country.

Nomads have clearly specified periods for breeding and lambing. Two-year-old sheep or goats are mated in September–October and lamb in February. For every 100 females, they keep 2 males, which are herded separately in non-breeding periods. Sedentary graziers have no specified time period for breeding or calving and lambing. The breeding age for cows or buffaloes is 4–5 years, with about 16 months calving interval.

LIVESTOCK PRODUCTS

Milk, ghee (butter oil) and wool are the main livestock products of transhumant graziers. Buffalo lactations are about 8 months and cows 7 months; milk production per animal is very low, with monthly ghee yields of 5.7 and 3.5 kg/month, respectively; small ruminants have lactations of 4–5 months and give 2 kg/month ghee. Sheep are sheared twice yearly and yield about 800 g wool each. The market structures for sale of livestock and these products are known to the graziers, but the graziers consume almost all products (milk and ghee), except wool. Dung is used by the sedentary graziers in their fields; nomads according to terms and conditions, give it to their house owner or to landowners.

LIVESTOCK HEALTH

The graziers reported that fever, cold and tuberculosis are common diseases of transhumant livestock. They treat the sick and weak livestock with the antibiotic and anthelmintic medicines available in the markets. Most treatments are given in winter, when stock are near towns or cities. Medicinal plants are used when livestock are in alpine pastures. According to veterinary staff, the following diseases are common: anthrax, eczema, enterotoxaemia, haemorrhagic septicaemia, piroplasmosis (Red water) and pneumonia.

WILD HERBIVORES

Major wild herbivores, such as ibex (*Capra ibex*) and musk deer (*Moschus moshiferous*), were once found in these pastures; their present numbers are not known; probably they are very rare. A few goral (*Naemorhaedus goral*) may be present. There are herbivorous rodents in the alpine zones.

FODDER AND FEED SUPPLY

Hay, maize stover and wheat straw are the major winter fodders available to the sedentary grazier, both from their own or rented lands and bought. Green grass is available to them for grazing and stall feeding from April to October. Sedentary graziers face serious feed scarcity in January and February. Nomads purchase some fodder (*Trifolium* spp.) and feed it together with tree leaves and twigs to livestock from January to April. Gazing is available from June to September. However, livestock in nomad flocks mostly depend on grazing throughout the year, and also face feed scarcity in January and February. Rarely, supplementary feed in the form of oilcake, molasses or grain is fed to weak or sick animals.

Hay is taken from the winter grazing areas (the temperate and subtropical humid zones in Kaghan Valley and the subtropical subhumid zone in the foothills of NWFP and Punjab province) of the nomads and semi-nomadic graziers. These areas are protected from grazing from mid-July to mid-September, and from mid-September to mid-October are cut by sickle for hay. Small bundles of cut herbage are air dried at site; after three or four days of drying the bundles are tied together to make bigger ones. These bundles (8-10) are stooked for further drying in the field. Finally, the made hay is collected and brought, as head loads, close to the stock huts or farmer's house, and stored in the open – on the ground or occasionally in trees – where leaching of nutrients by sun and rain is common. These grasslands have medium-tall to tall grasses; a few are desirable, while most are intermediate to undesirable; all are harvested for hay at maturity. Hay quality, though not evaluated, is poor due to overmaturity at cutting, and poor storage conditions.

CONSTRAINTS OF THE SYSTEM

Analysis of the production and utilization subsystem indicates a number of constraints related to the resource, its management and plant growth. These are considered below.

- **Faulty land tenure** One community owns the pasture land, but it is grazed by others. This encourages overuse as owners are interested in revenue while the users and buyers want to maximize its seasonal use. Hence no group makes any input to its proper management.

- **Inadequate knowledge of the users** Almost all graziers lack knowledge or skill in proper pasture use. Grazing is uncontrolled, which leads to either overuse or underuse. They do not follow the concept of range readiness, but bring their stock as early as June, when soil is soft due to snow melt or snow is still present, and plants are in the earliest stages of growth.

- **Difficult topographic factors** High altitude, steep slopes, very dissected terrain, deep gorges, barren peaks and varying micro-aspects are not conducive to good forage production, proper animal distribution and proper use.

- **Climate** Poor distribution of seasonal rain during the growing season causes moisture stress and poor plant growth. Very low temperatures cause stress and retard vegetation growth, and the growing period is very short.

- **Soil erosion** Glacial processes cause a range of erosion types, which include deep gully formation, soil slips, debris flows, rock falls and rock disintegration, so that the vegetation on valley floors is covered and damaged.

- **Shallow soils** Most of the area has shallow residual soils, which have poor water infiltration and moisture retention characteristics. Soil fertility may not be a problem as the nutrient levels suffice for good growth.

- **Patchy distribution of vegetation** The pastures consist of different vegetation patterns at different scales. Generally, individual plants of less palatable species have big patches and have rendered most of the area less productive for forage production or grazing. Their elimination, to give space to desirable species, may not be economically and environmentally feasible.

Both grazier groups keep livestock mainly to meet their domestic needs, and sell stock when they need cash for social needs. The inefficiency of the system is obvious from its low productivity, resource constraints, livestock management factors and marketing problems. Important factors include:

- **Seasonal weight loss** Livestock lose a lot of weight during travel and also in searching for feed on the scanty pasture, so milk production is very low. Reproduction rates are low, so the graziers have hardly any livestock or surplus produce to sell.

- **Lack of land for growing fodder** Most graziers are landless. A few may rent land, but for cereal production only. They generally do not grow fodder for winter feeding or supplementary feed.
- **Inadequate veterinary services** Sick animals are either treated with traditional medicinal plants or whatever medicines are available. Nomads have no access to an organized veterinary service.
- **Low prices** Herders usually only have access to intermediary buyers, who take most of the profit, so prices to the herder are unfairly low.

CONCLUSIONS
Pastoralists' perceptions of problems and needs

The prevailing land tenure and tenancy systems and the traditional land use patterns in the Kaghan valley are driving forces for transhumance to the high alpine pastures. Unequal land distribution forces less privileged people to move with their stock since they rely on privately owned common lands and public land for subsistence. [The term "privately owned common lands" means that a particular piece of land is collectively owned by the village or community and belongs to only the bona fide residents and land owners. The area is open to use by tenants and others (landless persons). Such tenants and landless persons are termed "rights holders" while the others are "land holders" or "land owners."]

Nomads try to cope with the fodder and forage requirements of their livestock through transhumance, moving to pastures in different ecozones and purchasing crop residues and fodder crops for winter feed. Sedentary grazi-

ers neither grow fodder crops nor make silage. The absence of any technical input by the State to improved pasture management, and lack of appropriate technology, leaves them dependent on the traditional system. Production is not market oriented, although a marketing structure does exist. Livestock are kept for domestic use, with only surplus produce sold. Animals are sold according to the household's cash needs.

Decisions regarding livestock are made by household heads; they are made individually according to household priorities. Sustained food and fodder supply and self sufficiency are the motivation and objectives. There is great potential for a participatory approach to improve systems if the State wishes to improve pasture management and productivity.

Detailed perception analysis and discussion in this regard was not carried out, but participants were asked about their problems related to livestock production. Both types of grazier, though in small numbers, raised five issues. Their problems were related to absence of permission to graze in forests; fodder shortages; losses of animals in transit; lack of facilities for transport of livestock; and restrictions by local people on access to grazing.

Nomads seem unaware of or unconcerned by their landless state, their lack of permanent settlements, lack of access to education and other basic necessities of life. Probably they have become inured to their hard, nomadic life over many years. Their life is very difficult and they are surrounded by poverty, yet they are determined to struggle hard. They face these problems with courage and hope for the best.

Potential of the systems

- **Forage** The clipping study showed that resting for a year increases forage production. This indicates the high grazing pressure on the pasture and the inappropriate management. It also shows a reasonable potential for improving pasture productivity under rational management.

- **Livestock** Improved breeding stock, appropriate veterinary care, appropriate transport for animals and proper and nutritious feed could enhance livestock production. Proper marketing structures and pricing systems would improve household incomes.

- **Environment** Environmental values would improve with improvement in the physical factors. With careful husbandry, the grazing lands have the potential to ensure that there is good quality water in quantity for downstream consumption.

- **Biodiversity values** Many species are surviving under poor conditions. The area has the potential to recover species that have disappeared due to overgrazing.

- **Aesthetic values** Good management would rehabilitate the plant cover and add more colour to already diverse vegetation, improve wildlife habitat and attract more tourists.

Prospects for improving management

The pastoralists of high altitude alpine pastures of the Kaghan valley follow age-old transhumant subsistence livestock production. Apparently they are not looking for change in the near future. Pasture production is constrained by physical environmental factors and is declining. Major causes of low productivity include poor shallow soils, steep slopes, dissected topography, loose rocks and stones covering large areas, scanty precipitation, low temperatures leading to short growing periods, cold winds and frosty nights. Superimposed on this, heavy grazing, lack of technical inputs, unsuitable tenure arrangements and poverty also take their toll.

Despite these constraints, application of sound management principles could improve the system. There is no, or negligible, scope for artificial seeding as most of the level to moderately sloped land is being cropped, and is still being converted to sloping fields. Natural improvement could be achieved through deferment and rest. Intensive grazing plans for remote and less used portions of the ranges could be another option. Patches of weeds could be cleared manually and resown with promising forages. Abandoned, sloping fields could also be sown with forages. Soil moisture shortage could be improved through water spreading and soil and moisture conservation measures. The owners and users of these pastures could be bound by rational land use policies. Trained and dedicated staff should be posted for such works. The range management service would have to be made a career-oriented agency.

Foothill ranges have great improvement potential. Rational and pragmatic policies, rules and regulation for their improvement and utilization would have to be drawn up. Unproductive forest areas could be converted into productive open woodland grazing and developed into productive forage reserves for the nomads if assigned on long leases to graziers.

Winter forage shortage in the Kaghan valley must be addressed. Fallow lands could be sown with winter forages and fodder supply could be improved from other areas.

This study attempted to analyse the high altitude alpine pasture pastoral production and utilization systems and assembled baseline data. However, this study highlights the need for comprehensive and precise interdisciplinary research. For holistic understanding of the systems, specialized contributions by both natural and social scientists are needed. This should lead to the identification of the most important elements and variables that influence the system. To achieve this, research will be needed in disciplinary application-oriented areas, including institutional improvements; grazing land rehabilitation and management improvement; livestock improvement; and fodder and cereal crop yield improvement.

Chapter XII
Pakistan case study 2: High altitude pastoral systems in Malakand Division, Pakistan

Khan Sanaullah and Ahmed Mukhtar

SUMMARY

Swat has been a traditional winter grazing area for transhumant herders, who graze the alpine pastures of north-eastern Pakistan in summer. Changes in political structures and land use patterns over the past thirty years has led to a great reduction in the grazing area available to nomads (who are of a different ethnic group from the landowners, and raise sheep and goats) in winter, as well as blocking many of their transhumance routes. The incorporation of Swat into Pakistan in 1969 weakened traditional relationships between landowners and landless graziers. The revision of land ownership in 1972 led to the privatization of much land that previously had been regarded as communal grazing – the ensuing legal disputes are still not yet settled. Landowners formerly rented grazing on a seasonal basis to nomads, but this is also much reduced because of fears that it might compromise litigation.

Large afforestation programmes from the mid-1980s have created large areas of private plantation that are closed to grazing, and many block traditional transhumance routes, although such forestation has had a very positive environmental effect and, until the canopy closes, provides large quantities of forage for cutting. Herd travel on roads is difficult because of high traffic density, and night travel on roads carries risks of armed robbery. Increased cultivation and plantations have increased the labour needs of herding; previously, a herder could handle one to two hundred head of small stock; now the average is 33, so nomads' herd sizes are falling. Among the settled population, who mainly keep large ruminants, stock are now mainly stall fed. Cattle numbers have fallen sharply and there are more buffaloes, which are easily stall fed and give richer milk. Some nomads have managed to settle, but many have left herding for labouring jobs elsewhere. The drift from herding has been mainly in the past twenty years, during which the number of herders has fallen by 60 percent.

INTRODUCTION

This chapter is based on the results of a rapid appraisal study, undertaken to gain information on the livelihood of nomadic graziers and trends in hillside development that affect them. Malakand Division is in the North West Frontier Province of Pakistan (NWFP). The area concerned begins about 150 km NNE of Peshawar (Site I in Figure 9.1).

Since the merger of the State of Swat with Pakistan in 1969, many social and political changes have affected the use and management of natural vegetation on the hillsides, land ownership and the distribution of ownership and user rights. The impact of these changes on communities differs according to the population group. Nomadic and semi-nomadic graziers seem to have been affected by three major developments:

- New settlements and purchased ownership by tenants and Gujars has resulted in the transformation of grazing lands into fields or areas with severe restrictions on access.
- Privatization of hillsides.
- Afforestation on lands formerly used as winter grazing. Plantations not only decrease winter grazing but form barriers across traditional trekking routes between summer and winter pastures. At the same time, such forestation since 1985 has improved vegetative cover and composition, increased the availability of grass and shrubs, and improved aesthetic value. This benefits the whole population, but more directly the landowners.

There is a worldwide trend for nomadic lifestyles to disappear as rapidly expanding populations reduces the amount of grazing land available; the nomadic life is hard and those with a reasonable alternative will definitely change their way of living, but in NWFP many families still live by transhumant herding and they cannot be ignored. The main objective of the study was to discover the trends, options and constraints of hillside development and the seasonal patterns of grazing.

OBJECTIVES OF THE STUDY

The main objectives of the study were to:
- assess and map the increase of new-owner areas (purchase of ownership) in the grazing lands;
- assess the decrease in free grazing land due to closure of afforested lands during the past fifteen years through the Environmental Rehabilitation Project (ERP) and the Watershed Project;
- assess and map the present grazing areas under qalang [a traditional system

of rent for grazing]; free grazing areas; ERP afforestation areas closed for grazing; upper water catchment plantations closed to grazing; and upper water catchment plantations opened to grazing;
- assess changes in livestock numbers, and the causes, for all population groups during the past thirty years;
- assess the use of increased grass production, harvesting methods and shifts in user groups;
- prioritize problems related to hillside development and seek possible solutions for improvement, involving all stakeholders; and
- study the impact of afforestation on pressure on summer and winter grazing land.

Nine villages linked with ERP were chosen for study. Selection criteria were: presence of different user and owner groups in the village area; different rates of afforestation; and no major disputes between owners and users. Six of the villages – Kuza Bandi, Kanju, Gado, Dadahara, Parrai and Kucha – were in Swat, in an area where much plantation has taken place and graziers have many problems related to hillside development. In Buner, three villages were chosen – Pantjar, Kingeralai and Kuhai – and, in addition, four non-ERP villages – Balera, Techma and Bampoocha – were included to compare villages with extensive plantations and those with none. The survey team comprised ERP and Forest Department staff. Questionnaires were used to collect data from Village Development Committee (VDC) representatives and nomadic graziers; they were interviewed separately. In non-ERP villages, only nomads were interviewed. For mapping, one or two VDC members and Ajars were asked to join the team and inspect the village area. Topographical sheets and existing ERP range base maps were used to plot past and present land ownership, grass cutting and qalang areas, and block plantations. Field data collection was done in February.

Some local terms have to be used, defined here as follows: Ajars are nomadic or semi-nomadic commercial livestock raisers, mostly keeping goats and sheep and producing meat and wool. They are of Hinko origin and speak Gujroo. Gujars are mainly settled or semi-nomadic commercial livestock raisers, mostly keeping cattle and buffaloes and producing milk. They are descendants of original Ajars and also speak Gujroo. The main difference between Ajars and Gujars is the type of livestock they keep. The confusion, however, comes when the settlement pattern is examined, with several types each of Ajars and Gujars distinguished.

Ajars
- Have neither permanent shelter nor land: this is the "real" Ajar.
- Have permanent shelter, but no land: this is a semi-nomadic Ajar. Some families stay permanently in the winter grazing area where they have a house. A few family members move to the summer grazing with the livestock. Some also have a house in the summer grazing area.
- Have both shelter and land. This is also a semi-nomadic Ajar, often keeping cattle, which remain with the family throughout the year, as well as small ruminants. Only small ruminants go on transhumance. Such Ajars might

gradually call themselves Gujar, as small ruminants are replaced by cattle.

Gujars
- Have shelter but no land. These usually work for landowners in return for the use of grazing and crop by-products. They depend on grazing and grass-cutting, and sell livestock products; they are semi-nomadic.
- Have both shelter and hillside land. These have purchased or claimed a piece of hillside where they graze their stock and cut grass. They often start rainfed cropping near their homestead.
- Live in the main village; their animals are stall fed with purchased crop residues. These are mainly found near large settlements.
- The "real" nomadic Gujar – not identified in the project area.

The terms Ajar and Gujar are confusing, even to local people. There is a gradual move from nomadic to settled Ajar. With increased settlement there is a shift from small ruminants to cattle; this is a gradual change and results in confusion between the terms Ajar and Gujar. Many Gujars call themselves Ajars as that was their original background; similarly many Ajars call themselves Gujars.

GENERAL TRENDS IN HILLSIDE DEVELOPMENT
Land ownership and settlement
Land ownership and settlement can be categorized into four periods:
- Establishment of government and land consolidation; Father of Wali of Swat period, 1917–1949.
- Strengthening of government and area development. Wali of Swat period, 1949–1969.

- Tragedy of the commons – 1969–1995; merger with Pakistan, 1969; Bhutto Period, 1971–1977; ongoing conflicts develop between landowners, Gujars, etc.
- Revival of village government and social institutions (ERP: 1995–present).

Most land was owned by inheritance groups (khels) or was communal during the Wali period; there were hardly any private hillsides. During the Bhutto period, many communal hillsides were divided between khels. Purchased (new) ownership increased, especially among tenants, then Ajars. Over the past ten years, individual purchase of hillsides has decreased due to high prices. Redistribution continues of hillsides purchased earlier by Ajars and tenants.

About 21 percent of the once communal land is now privately owned. Communal hillsides, as well as khel-owned ones, are also often divided between shareholders, without marked boundaries on the ground. These areas are not yet, however, registered as being individually owned and are considered to be communal. They are often given on lease (qalang) as a whole. Qalang is usually paid to the head of the khel. Due to increased individual ownership, areas given on qalang have been significantly reduced.

In the Wali period, people lived in clustered villages; owners lived in the main village, surrounded by the landless and artisans. Tenants lived in the village or near their crop land. Gujars either lived on the fringes of major towns or in small hamlets on the hillsides. With population explosion and increased land ownership, a more scattered settlement pattern has developed. Gujars and Ajars began to live further up the hillsides, often cultivating

small areas once they bought housing and land. In this way, 42 percent of Ajars purchased land recently in Swat (Dadahara and Kulai), 26 percent had in the past 30 years purchased hillside, compared to 1 percent in the four non-ERP villages. The main villages show explosive growth, especially those on the main road in the Swat valley. In Swat, the encroachment upon high hillsides and conversion into terraced crop land is much greater than in Buner.

Plantation

The six Swat villages have afforested 15 percent of their hillsides with the help of the Watershed Project and 48 percent with assistance from ERP. In Buner, 28 percent of hillsides have been planted. Plantations cover just over half of the hillside area. With protection, the quantity and quality of the vegetation has increased and the catchment area has been improved. Almost everybody interviewed was positive about the results of afforestation and enjoy the increased availability of grass. Afforestation gave many poor and landless people temporary employment. Now livestock raisers are more dependent on grass cutting for stall feeding because of the temporary closure of young plantations. Nomadic and semi-nomadic graziers have more difficulty in finding winter grazing than before. In Swat, qalang areas for winter are down by 91 percent, of which 38 percent is due to afforestation. Some plantations block traditional seasonal trekking routes.

The overall trend is that the number of livestock per family is decreasing among all classes, with a shift from small ruminants to cattle and buffaloes. Data collected on stock numbers are few and probably not very reliable, but the rough trends can be discerned from this survey.

The number of sheep and goats owned by Ajars is decreasing rapidly; figures for Swat show a decrease from 340 to 140 goats and sheep per flock. In Buner, flock size fell from 200 to 140. According to IUCN (1998), the average flock size in NWFP was 110 small ruminants. The main reason given for the reduction is the scarcity of winter grazing due to afforestation, increased crop area, privatization of hillsides and closure of trekking routes. The number of stock per family has decreased (by 48 percent for small ruminants), as well as the number of families. Comparing field data with that from the Livestock Survey (1976–1986), similar trends are found. In Buner, livestock is mostly goats as the vegetation is mainly scrub; in Swat sheep predominate. According to Ajars, 20 small ruminants is the minimum flock size needed to marginally sustain a family (equal to a daily wage of PRs 70.00 [US$ 1 = PRs 51 at time of writing]); this minimum number ignores the risks of theft, accident or disease. About a quarter of Ajar families have sold all their livestock and found jobs in agriculture or as urban labourers.

Livestock, especially cows, of landowners, tenants and Gujars has decreased on a per family basis,. The number of cattle per land-owning family in the past was three to twelve, and one or two buffaloes. Now a family has one to five cows and one or two buffaloes. Tenants show the same pattern. Gujars used to have 15 to 30 cows and two to five buffaloes; now they have reduced cows to between four and six and increased buffaloes to between two and ten. Buffaloes give richer milk and are easily stall fed.

A survey in the adjacent Social Forestry Project, Malakand and Dir, shows the same pattern: 59 percent of the 200 respondents had switched to stall feeding due to the ban on grazing in afforested areas; and 39 percent had reduced livestock numbers, especially tenants and landowners (Nizami, 1998). The Livestock Census of 1976–1986 showed an annual increase in buffaloes and cows of 5.25 and 0.91 percent, respectively.

Impact of hillside development on nomadic graziers

The main source of income for nomadic herders has always been small ruminants, and they have depended entirely on a transhumant system. In summer they graze alpine and subalpine pastures (Upper Swat, Kohistan), moving in winter to the lower altitude hillsides or the plains. In the past, hillside grazing was communal and Ajars paid rent (qalang) in cash or kind (wool, manure, ghee, etc.) to the owners. There was harmony between owners and graziers on the use of respective hillsides. Gujars had the same pattern of movements, although their animals had different requirements in terms of fodder and terrain. Gujars tend to stay near agricultural land or mountains that are not too steep, rough or rugged.

In 1973, with the passing of the land reform act, disputes over land ownership arose between tenants, Gujars and landowners. Tenants and Gujars began to claim hillsides without the owners' consent. Landowners began to divide communal land between themselves to strengthen their claims to ownership, to be able to manage it more strictly and give it more protection. This has affected the area available on qalang to nomadic graziers, especially in Swat.

In the mid-1980s, forestry-related

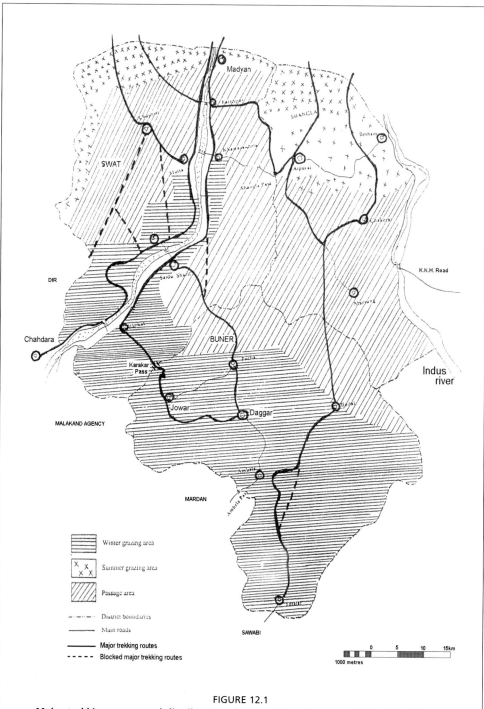

FIGURE 12.1
Major trekking routes and distribution of seasonal grazing areas in Swat and Buner.

projects accelerated the restriction of the grazing areas and increased pressure on graziers seeking winter grazing. Since 1994, with the launching of ERP in Swat and Buner, more hillside grazing has come under protection due to afforestation. In the nine villages surveyed, 51 percent of the total hillside has been afforested since the mid-1980s. This is perceived by the owners as insurance (or confirmation) of their ownership, and has resulted in an expansion of protected areas. New-purchase owners (both tenant or grazier communities) protect their land from grazing by outsiders and thus increase pressure on landless Ajars to reduce their herd size or seek grazing elsewhere. Owners are reluctant to open old watershed plantations to grazing due to the many land ownership conflicts and court cases that are still pending over land claimed by Gujars and tenants.

Trekking routes are centuries old (see map – Figure 12.1). Nomads used to move their stock from the lowland winter grazing to subalpine and alpine summer grazing, and mostly passed along hillsides on their way to and from the summer pastures. Most spent five or six months at summer pasture, of which three were on subalpine pasture (Chail, Lalko, Bishigram, Behrain Kalam, Maydan, etc.) and two to three on alpine pasture (Mahodand, Mankial, Saigadi Lol Panghalai, Daral, etc.). The remaining six months were spent on winter grazing.

A number of problems concerning migratory movements were identified in the individual questionnaires. Traditional routes have been blocked by plantations, which cannot be traversed. The herders have to take alternative routes, such as main roads. There are problems of travel and stopovers while travelling, including lack of fodder and access to grazing along the route. The old routes are blocked and there are plantations along the main roads so it is difficult to feed the stock during migrations and to camp overnight. Those who can afford it use trucks to move animals quickly. Trucks are expensive and not all Ajars can afford their hire.

Traditional and current trekking routes in Swat and Buner are basically the same, but now many nomads use trucks and follow main roads. Major changes in trekking patterns have been forced on herders:

- Mingora – Mangalwar to Kalam. This route was formerly walked; now many travel by truck due to lack of accessible grazing because of new settlements and protected plantations.
- Nawagai – Daggar – Barikot – Mingora. As for the above. Major barriers due to plantation are Barikot–Amlook Darra – Ghaligay.
- Daggar – Pir Baba – Djambil – Mingora. This is still travelled on foot, but follows the main road. There are no major barriers except in the Kokarai, Samangul and Fizagat area.
- (Dir) – Dhamozai – Suigalai – Kanju – Shakadara – Maidan – Mankial. Some plantations now block the way, such as at Suigalai and Biakand. Graziers from Dir in particular have changed their route because of the plantations near Biakand. The number of days taken to cover the route has been reduced because of scarcity of grazing. Many go by truck from Kabbal. Others travel, quickly, on foot along the main road.
- Totalai – Budal – Alpurai – Fatehpur –

Maydan and onward.

This shows that the major changes are in the Kabbal area (Suigalai, etc.) and Matta (Biakand, etc.). Minor short-cuts have disappeared in the Saidu Range (Barikot/Amlook Darra – Ghaligay). It is of great importance for the future to keep the Alpuri – Fatehpur (Swat) track and others in Buner open.

Nomads formerly travelled in a piece-meal fashion, going to and from seasonal pastures and grazing their stock on the way. It was accepted that a nomadic grazier would not stay in an area en route for more than two nights, and only one flock per season would be allowed. Now, with protection of individually owned land, it is difficult to find forage for one- or two-day stops. Another reason for trucking is the high traffic density on the roads, which makes droving very dangerous. Theft of livestock and armed robbery is frequently reported during night travel on the road.

The number of Ajars leaving herding in the past thirty years is indicated in Table 12.1. Field findings gave a huge range of answers, so it is difficult to interpret average data, but the main trends can be discerned. In the nine villages in the three periods – the Wali period, the Bhutto period, and the recent period – 3 (1 percent), 30 (8 percent) and 95 (37 percent) left herding. Nomads are increasingly seeking other employment, mostly on farms or as day labour. The shift in jobs by Ajars has mainly occurred in the past fifteen years. Those still in herding have reduced their flock numbers considerably and some have moved their winter grazing to the plains around Mardan and Peshawar. The amount of labour required to herd a flock has increased due to the restriction of areas by cropping and plantation. Whereas a herder could manage 100–200 small ruminants; now they can only tend, on average, 33.

Nomadic graziers' perception of problems

Ajars and Gujars were invited to one-day workshops, one in Kabbal and another in Matta, before the case study was designed, to list problems related to herding and livestock production; prioritize problems and suggestions on how to solve them. The main problems raised were:

- Lack of grazing land, especially in winter. The total area is decreasing because of plantations, and flock size has had to be reduced, leading to decreased income.
- Plantations are a barrier across trekking routes and obstruct grazing.
- Lack of watering points limit the use of hillsides for grazing.
- Lack of coordination between VDC and Ajar community; Gujars and Ajars are not adequately represented on VDCs.
- Animal health is a problem since free medicine is no longer available.
- Uncertified, unskilled "veterinarians" who roam in the herding areas cause problems in disease treatment.
- Protection of stock from armed robbers is hindered since the government will not grant firearms licences.
- It is difficult for the children of nomads to receive education.
- Frequent need to attend court cases (subsequent to damage reports by the Forest Department) is a severe constraint on nomadic life.
- Lack of good breeding stock and need for improved sires.
- Scarcity of equipment, especially for

TABLE 12.1
Numbers of Ajars at different periods and those leaving herding.

	Wali period	Bhutto period	Recent period
Swat – total	195	198	95
Swat – left herding	2	26	50
Buner – total	61	77	74
Buner – left herding	–	3	9
Non-ERP – total	80	85	78
Non-ERP – left herding	1	1	32
Total left herding	3	30	91
Total families	336	360	247

shearing.

- Market prices of livestock are low and not based on weight.
- Tax and octroi are charged above the official rates.
- Market places lack watering points for both livestock and people.

The Ajars' suggested solutions include opening up plantations to grazing after 5–7 years; provision of mobile education; and provision of watering points and tents during migration.

Ajars and Gujars in Swat stressed the problem of winter grazing, and put the whole blame on plantations. Study results show about an equal impact from privatization of hillsides.

CONCLUSIONS

i. The six villages in Swat have afforested 63 percent of their hillsides so far. In Buner, 28 percent of the area has been planted. The average plantation over the whole area is 51 percent.

ii. *Qalang* grazing areas have been reduced during the past 30 years due to plantation (31.5 percent), privatization of hillsides (21 percent) and other reasons (20.3 percent), including low qalang rates. Qalang was still available on 24.1 percent. The winter grazing area – important

for survival – has been reduced. Due to protection, areas have become greener and produce more and better forage, but grass cutting is too labour demanding to maintain large flocks, and small ruminants are not adapted to indoor life.

iii. Grass cutting without charge is permitted by VDCs on half of the plantation area and seasonal controlled grazing is allowed on half. Taking the entire hillside area, 24 percent is now under controlled cutting instead of free cutting. In a few cases, users have to pay for grass.

iv. Villagers, as well as nomadic graziers, are positive about the results of afforestation and enjoy the improved availability of vegetation, especially grass and trees. Many people have had temporary employment in afforestation and some are permanently employed by VDCs as chowkidars [guards].

v. A reduced grazing area means fewer animals, especially small ruminants. This also means a reduced use of the higher pastures; these are underutilized because of lack of winter grazing, so the overall resource is underused while demand for livestock products is rising. This is a negative development.

vi. Average numbers of stock per family is falling in all classes of society and there is a shift from cows to buffaloes by landowners, tenants and Gujars. There has been a sharp decrease in the size of Ajar flocks. Landless people have less access to grazing because of afforestation and privatization.

vii. The development of hillsides has affected the livelihood of nomadic graziers.
- First,
  - their migration routes have been disturbed: blocked routes due to plantation has led to the use of alternative routes, such as roads;
  - there are problems of finding forage and campsites while travelling, so trucks are being used by those who can afford them; and
  - trekking is increasingly expensive.
- Second, their traditional livelihood is under pressure as a result of:
  - closure of winter grazing areas and trekking routes; and
  - increases in qalang prices (only mentioned in Buner).

Alternative jobs are mostly found in agriculture or as day labour; the drift from herding has been highest among Ajars in the past fifteen years.

RECOMMENDATIONS

- Include more users, especially graziers, in the design and implementation of village land use planning. Even at advanced stages of such planning they can be made part of the VDC. If their needs are incorporated in the plans it will improve the choice, implementation and maintenance of many activities.

- At the planning phase of village land use planning, the following aspects should be added to those considered:
  - trekking routes through village areas;
  - carrying capacity of grazing lands and selection of best grazing lands; and

  total area required for grazing of stock, including planting where appropriate.

  In this way villages could attain larger and more sustainable plantations without creating serious problems for livestock owners.

- Develop a uniform policy for the use of established plantations (>5–10 years), whatever their original funding. In order to maximize return from these plantations, a silvipastoral system is proposed; since herbage production decreases as the tree cover thickens, grass cutting will no longer be profitable. Grazing will improve the recycling of water, nutrients and energy and is less labour demanding. These areas could be made available on qalang, with prescribed rules and regulations for use drawn up by the VDC. Controlled grazing, implemented in conjunction with nagha (a traditional system of punishment for defaulting graziers). This would go some way to solving the problem of winter grazing, with benefit to all parties.

- The Forest Department can, with ERP project support where appropriate, play a leading role in the management and use of established plantations. Project plans should pay attention to the future management of established plantations. Institutions such as the Pakistan Forest

Institute could explore the constraints to grazing in plantations, compared to grass cutting.

- The study of major trekking routes could be extended to the whole of Malakand Division to get a complete picture of the seasonal movement of nomads. That map would become an essential tool in all planning work related to hillside development.

- Enhance the dialogue between nomadic graziers and local government and, in collaboration with the Livestock Department, facilitate problem resolution.

Chapter XIII
The eastern Himalaya

SUMMARY

In the eastern Himalaya, transhumant herding is important in Nepal, Bhutan and Sikkim. This zone is generally wetter than the western Himalaya and large ruminants much more important than small; yak and mithun are kept in addition to cattle and buffaloes. Systems are more stratified altitudinally, since yak prefer low temperatures and can survive in colder places than other stock. The same pasture may be used by different species and different herding groups at different seasons of the year – the summer pastures of cattle × yak hybrids may be the winter grazing of yaks, and in turn the winter grazing of the hybrids may be the summer grazing of buffaloes and cattle from lower regions. In one Bhutanese system, cattle are entrusted to another group for part of the year and migrate, while their owners remain stationary. Three case studies are presented: two from Bhutan and one from Nepal; summaries are provided for each study. The first study (Chapter XIV) describes a mixed herd system in which some families entrust their stock seasonally to others; the second (Chapter XV) describes a yak-based system, and the third (Chapter XVI) describes two chauri-based grazing systems in Nepal.

INTRODUCTION

The Himalayas, which form a barrier between the Tibetan Plateau and the alluvial plains of India, run obliquely from northwest to southeast for about 2 500 km. Their height is such that they protect the subcontinent from cold winter air from the north and thus have a profound effect on climate. The grazing zones go further north than the true Himalaya, to the Karakoram foothills and the Hindu Kush. The latitude range of the studies is some twelve degrees, from about 38°N in Pakistan and Afghanistan to 27°N in Bhutan. This vast distance obviously involves considerable changes in climate and vegetation.

The western Himalaya, discussed in Chapter IX is mostly arid to semi-arid, and its flora shows considerable influence from western and central Asia. Rainfall increases from northwest to southeast and the vegetation changes. The wild olive gets as far east as western Nepal, which for our purposes is the western limit of the eastern Himalayan grazing systems. In all cases, the Himalayas abut on to great alluvial plains, but there the terrain and vegetation also change: in Punjab the foothills are in acacia forest, while the Nepal Terai is under dipterocarp (sal – *Shorea robusta*) forest, reflecting the much higher rainfall and warmer conditions.

The main areas of transhumant herding are in Nepal and Bhutan, and to some extent the part of India (Sikkim) that separates them. One of the earliest records by a professional botanist of wild white clover in the high eastern Himalaya (Hooker, 1855, Vol. II, p. 189) is from Sikkim, below the Donkia Pass where its seeds were brought over from Tibet by yaks. "White clover, shepherd's purse and chickweed are imported here by yak."

Large ruminants prevail in the eastern Himalaya and species unknown or little known in the west are locally important – yak and their hybrids at higher altitude and, in Bhutan and parts of India, mithun (*Bos frontalis*) and its hybrids are also kept.

The whole region is very steep and mountainous and transhumant systems are widespread. In some cases more than one group may use a pasture at different seasons of the year; as shown in the case studies, the summer pastures of crosses may be the winter pastures of yaks, and the winter pastures of these crosses are the summer pastures of cattle and buffaloes from lower latitudes. One Bhutan case study describes an unusual system in which the livestock migrate but two groups of owners look after them at different seasons.

BHUTAN

The Kingdom of Bhutan is the smallest (46 500 km²) and the most southerly and easterly of the Himalayan countries, lying between 26° 40′ and 28° 20′ N and between 88° 45′ and 92° 7′ E. It is landlocked, surrounded by China to the north and India elsewhere. A Pasture Resource Profile with more details is on the FAO Web site (Kinzang Wangdi, 2002).

Bhutan is divided into three physical regions from north to south: the Great Himalayas, the Lesser Himalayas, and the Duars Plain. It is dissected by numerous rivers. The main rivers from west to east are the Amo (Torsa), Raidak (Wong), Sankosh (Mo) and Manas. All the rivers flow southward from the Great Himalayas and join the Brahmaputra River in India.

The country is mountainous, with elevations ranging from 150 up to 8 000 m traversing south to north with a great diversity of environments. However, its mountainous nature leaves only about 8 percent of the total land suitable for crops; over 70 percent has forest cover and 4 percent is registered pasture (*tsadrog*). The great altitude range gives rise to many climatic zones, from wet subtropical in the lower areas (starting at 150 m), through humid-subtropical, dry subtropical, warm temperate, cool temperate and finally alpine above 3 500 m.

More than 80 percent of Bhutan's population in engaged in agriculture and related activities; livestock account for 10 percent of the gross domestic product (GDP). Although the contribution of livestock to GDP is estimated to be relatively low, the value of that livestock extends beyond milk, meat and fibre production – the main reason for keeping them is to provide draught and manure for crop production. Mountainous, rugged terrain limits mechanization and accessibility, so alternatives to manure and draught animals are difficult to find. The number of cattle and yaks was estimated by the Ministry of Agriculture in 1995 at 304 000 (Siri cattle – 224 555; Jersey and crosses – 25 570; Mithun crosses – 54 268; and yak 30 162), with buffalo – 1 022; equines – 25 762; sheep – 31 300; and goats – 16 030. Cattle, yak and buffalo are dual purpose, used for both draught and milk, and provide manure. Large ruminants, therefore, account for about 90 percent of domestic herbivores.

There are three distinct types of large ruminant production systems. The transhumant yak system is limited to the alpine–cool-temperate areas; with migratory cattle in the temperate–subtropical area. These two systems take advantage of the variations in climate and vegetation as herders migrate with their animals according to the seasons. The third system is sedentary livestock rearing in semi-urban and other rural settlement areas.

NEPAL

The overall pasture situation in the country is described by Pariyar (1999). Nepal, like Bhutan, is landlocked and lies along the southern slopes of the Himalayas between India and Tibet. It has a population of 20 million, and an area of 147 180 km². It is 800 km from east to west, varies from 144 to 240 km north to south, and lies between 80–88° E and 26–31° N.

The south of the country is the Terai, a northern extension of the Ganges Plains of India. The topography is flat and ranges from 25–32 km in width. Rising above the Terai, and aligned east-west, are ranges of hills generally referred to as the "mid-hills" (1 300–2 500 m), and the "high hills" (2 500–5 000 m). To the north of these high hills are the Himalayas proper, which include the highest mountains in the world (5 000–8 848 m). Their rugged topography constitutes almost 78 percent of the land mass of Nepal.

The Terai and mid-hills are zones of sedentary agriculture, although livestock are important (Plate 59). The transhumant systems are mainly in the high hills and alpine zones. Large ruminants dominate the livestock sector: buffalo are important in the lower zones; and cattle in all but the highest areas, where yak and cattle × yak hybrids take over. In 1997, there

Plate 59.
Terraced farming in the mid hills of Nepal. Stock from here go to the high hills in summer.

were 7 million cattle (yaks and hybrids included), 3.4 million buffaloes, 5.9 million sheep and less than a million goats, which are mostly kept in the hills and the Terai. Sheep are mainly in the hills and mountains. Transhumance is practised in the temperate, subalpine and alpine regions where cattle, buffaloes, sheep and goats migrate from one place to another throughout the year. In earlier times there was trans-border transhumance of yaks into Tibet, but this was halted by the Chinese authorities to protect their grazing lands, with consequent fodder problems in the Nepalese districts affected.

The lower, agricultural areas are very densely populated and cultivated; there is practically no grazing land and livestock rely heavily on crop residues. Grazing land is concentrated in the mountains, and some of it is seasonal because of snow, with 17 percent of grassland in the middle mountains, 30 percent in the high mountains and 49 percent in the high Himal.

Temperate pasture lands are associated with oak or mixed broad-leaved species such as *Quercus* or blue pine. These pastures are very important, but due to heavy grazing for many years, less palatable species have become prominent. Thus, *Andropogon tristis* has been replaced with less palatable species such as *Arundinella hookeri*. The common forage species are *Arundinella hookeri, Andropogon tristis, Poa* spp., *Chrysopogon gryllus, Dactylis*

glomerata, Stipa concinna, Festuca spp., *Cymbopogon* spp., *Bothriochloa* spp., *Desmodium* spp. and *Agrostis micrantha.*

Subalpine pasture lands are associated with a variety of shrubs; common genera are *Berberis, Caragana, Hippophae, Juniperus, Lonicera, Potentilla, Rosa, Spiraea* and *Rhododendron*; in many areas, *Pipthantus nepalensis* has invaded productive pasture lands once dominated by *Danthonia* spp. The common grasses are *Elymus* spp., *Festuca* spp., *Stipa* spp., *Bromus himalaincus, Chrysopogon gryllus, Cymbopogon schoenanthus* and *Koeleria cristata. Elymus nutans* is of great importance in pastoral systems at high elevations.

Alpine pasture lands are associated with *Rhododendron* shrubs. The main types of vegetation, based on the specification of areas, are *Kobresia* spp., *Cortia depressa*, and *Carex–Agrostis–Poa* associations. Common plant species are *Kobresia* spp. and *Agrostis* spp.

A considerable amount of study has been done on pasture improvement and many temperate forages can be grown in the higher areas; these have, however, little practical application for many reasons, including the steepness and inaccessibility of the terrain, the need for fertilizer to establish and maintain higher-yielding forages, the dubiousness of economic returns and the poor access, requiring that inputs be taken over long distances by porterage.

Chapter XIV
Bhutan case study 1: Transhumant cattle raising in western Bhutan
Tsering Gyaltsen and B.N. Bhattarai

SUMMARY

Naja *geog* has thirteen villages and is between 2 600 and 3 000 m altitude; livestock are very important in the economy but summer crops are grown on restricted areas. Cattle and cattle × mithun (*Bos frontalis*) hybrids are by far the most significant; small ruminants are few. Summer grazing is on high altitude pastures up to at least 4 200 m (which are also winter pastures for yak belonging to another group), and winter grazing is in low altitude forests, down to 300 m. Grazing rights to specific areas are registered and hereditary. Many herders have more than one pasture, often in different zones. Migration routes are traditional and herders have no right to linger. A system of entrusting the care of stock to other groups for part of the year is described – in this case for the winter. Grazing and forest loppings, according to season, are the main feed but supplements of meal and oilcake are fed to milch cattle and calves. Herders plant fodder trees near winter camps and there is some sowing of pasture in higher areas. A transect of the transhumance routes is described.

Problems include heavy grazing of summer pastures, landslides and floods on the summer journey, and severe overstocking around winter camps. Toxic plants are a problem at high altitudes when unaccustomed stock arrive for the first time. Butter and local cheese are the main products marketed from summer pastures; when winter camps are close to towns, then fresh milk is sold; there is a growing urban demand for milk and herders are increasingly settling in lower areas and keeping Jersey stock.

STUDY AREA

There have been many studies on various aspects of livestock production in Bhutan, but this is the first integrated study covering the overall transhumant system, including forage resources, grazing management and herders' socio-economic status (for study site, see Site V on the map in Figure 9.1). This study took a broad view of transhumant livestock production systems and focused on herders' movements between seasonal quarters. Most movements are over many kilometres, in some cases hundreds. The study attempts to identify the strengths and weaknesses of the system so as to guide appropriate research strategies and demonstrate how the system could be improved rather than how it could be done away with, as is sometimes suggested. Transhumance is embedded in local tradition and is an efficient way of making use of seasonally available forage.

Naja is a *geog*, between 2 600 and 3 000 m elevation, in Paro *Dzongkhag* [administrative region], with most records of transhumance in the western *Dzongkhags*. It has 276 households, with a population of 2 162 (1998–1999) and

TABLE 14.1
Crop areas and yields – Naja geog, Bhutan.

Crop	Area (ha)	Production (kg)	Yield (kg/ha)
Potato	127.1	755 328	5 941
Wheat	78.0	6 9512	891
Barley	41.5	4 183	101
Cabbage	19.6	261 414	13 369
Paddy	13.7	(18 257 deys)[1]	2, 531
Chilli (dried)	3.7	19 300	5 243
Pea (green)	17.9	78 300	4 380
Apple (fruit bearing)	1 917 trees	178 040	

Note: (1) 1 dey of paddy = 1 5 kg.

TABLE 14.2
Najap stock numbers.

	Cattle	Jersey cattle	Mithun crosses	Mithun	Sheep	Horses
Male	1 071	98	362	7	30	224
Female	1 728	268	452		38	

Source: Livestock Extension Centre, Naja.

comprises 13 villages. The major source of livelihood is sale of agriculture produce: butter, cheese, potatoes and vegetables. Crop land comprises: wetland – 12.1 ha; dryland – 302.1 ha; orchards – 194 ha; and gardens – 19.7 ha. The study area covered five districts of Western Bhutan, with both summer and winter grazing sites of the migratory cattle.

Potatoes, wheat and barley are the main crops, but vegetables are also very important (see Table 14.1). Crops are looked after by women, in summer, while their partners tend the herds.

There were 1 137 farmers in 13 villages in Naja; village populations varied between 290 and 52. Those not directly involved in farming were civil servants and shopkeepers. According to the 1997–1998 census, Najaps [people from Naja] attach great importance to stock rearing and are those who migrate with the herds. The figures shown in Table 14.2 is their share only; partners (*nothoue*) who belong to another area record their share separately in the livestock census.

The *nothoue* arrangement

Since *nothoue* figures throughout this section, some explanation is in order. It is an age-old, traditional relationship between herders for transhumance, organized such that both partners function symbiotically. *Nothoue* is intricate and requires the trust of both parties. It is common in Chukka, Haa and Paro Dzongkhags. Only limited information was collected.

Nothoue arrangements are commonest within the district of Paro; a few farmers of Naja, being closer, have *nothoue* with Haa *Dzongkhag*. A few Naja keep cattle for summer grazing (May to August) in Jodokha, Nabina, Chambithang, Nalikha, Montongmo, Tseplengha and Tsentong, where they have their registered pastures about half a day away.

From September to April, the counterparts from Haa take over the cattle and move to Samse *Dzongkhag*, where they have *tsadrog* [registered grazing land or pasture rights] at Dorokha and Setina (three days journey from Haa). For the rest of the time, the Naja farmers take over the cattle and migrate to Chukka *Dzongkhag* (September to April), where they have their registered pasture land. General parts of the arrangement include:

- There should be an equal share of cattle of the same type in the herds. If the breeds differ then the balance is calculated and cash compensated accordingly.
- On the fourth Bhutanese month, the *nothoue* from Shaba, Iduna, Shari, Dawakha take over from the different *nothoue* of Naja, Geling, Dunga and Metab for summer grazing sites for four months (Plate 60).
- In the ninth Bhutanese month, the *nothoue* from Naja, Metab, Geling and Dunga take over for winter grazing sites for eight months.
- In the event of mortality, meat is shared between the *nothoue*; if sharing is not possible, for example when the animal has been eaten by wild beasts, proof of death of the animal, skins, heads etc., should be produced to the other partner. Occasionally the meat is sold for money, but this is uncommon.
- During their respective tenures as *nothoue*, milk and dairy products are not shared but used by the *nothoue* in question.

Feed and fodder resources

In summer, migratory herds graze meadows in the alpine *tsadrogs*; in winter, they are in forest, grazing trees and shrubs and given loppings of fodder trees in the *tsadrog*.

Plate 60.
Transhumant cattle (mithun crosses and siri) on summer pastures at 3 200 m in August in Naja geog, Paro, Bhutan, just before the downward trek, when cattle will be handed over to partners for the winter 8-month period under the nothoue *system.*

Supplements, such as salt, maize flour and mustard cake, are fed to milking cows and calves in both summer and winter. During migration, salt is fed weekly or fortnightly at 250 g per adult; milking cattle are given about 1 kg daily of a mustard cake and maize meal mix, as a porridge; whey is fed to calves.

Sedentary cattle are kept for draught, manure and milk; their feed comprises forest grazing, cut-and-carry from improved pastures, stubble grazing, fodder trees (*Quercus* spp.), straws and stovers, common grazing, crop by-products, cabbage, weeds, hay, brewing residues, salt, maize flour, mustard cake, and winter fodder (maize and soybean).

Fodder seed is distributed free by the government. At Naja, most households grow improved pasture for the improved cattle (these are outside the *nothoue* system), mainly on rainfed land or intercropped in orchards; farmers mow the pasture four to five times yearly. Maize and soybean are grown for working bulls, which migrate later than the herds, following preparation of the wheat land. In Naja *geog*, there was an average of 770 m² of improved pastures in 1996–1998. For the fodder cultivars used and the recommended seed rates, see Table 14.3.

Seed requirements are estimated by the *Dzongkhag* [District] Animal Husbandry units; seed is produced by the National Fodder Seed Production Centre, through contract growers. Rhizobial inoculant is distributed with the seed as required.

Samples of native fodder shrubs and trees were taken at all sites visited and their vernacular names, production potential and suitable growing sites were discussed. At the Omna winter site, 22 out of the 41 species reported during interviews were found. Herders plant fodder trees in their *tsadrog* in April–May. Saplings are collected in the forest, and the choice of species takes into account their palatability. Preferred trees are: Dagpo (*Ficus roxburghii*), Omshing (*Ficus nemoralis*), Tashim (*Ficus cunia*), Dumsi (*Saurauia nepaulensis*), Jogsa/Jathshang (*Ficus* sp.), Sisi (botanical name uncertain), Besum (botanical name uncertain), Dapchu (*Ficus lacor*) and Chemla (*Bauhinia purpurea*); lopping begins after three years. Herders indicated that these trees were all palatable and digestible, increased milk production, were fast growing and good yielders of green forage, with figs considered the best.

During migration, improved stock get paddy straw and concentrates as well as tree loppings and salt. Maize flour and oilcake, usually bought in Phuentsholing or Jaigoan (India), are fed as porridge at the rate of 1 kg/head daily. Five bundles of straw (2 kg each) and salt at 200–300 g/month are also given.

Most herders own one or more pastures, individually or as part of a herding community. They pay a nominal fee to the government, irrespective of size or area of registered *tsadrog*. In the winter grazing areas of yaks, yak herders own winter grazing rights, while cattle herders (rarely of the same community) own summer grazing rights for the same pasture.

Some grazing land is owned by a community, or a section of a community, especially around settlements. Most herders treat pasture as a family inheritance; however, the Land Act (1980) clearly states that grazing land belongs to

TABLE 14.3
Pasture cultivars, seed rates and costs.

Forage	Cultivar	Seed for mixture (kg/ha)	Cost (Nu) [1]	
			Nu/kg	Nu/ha
Trifolium repens	Ladino	3.3	217	716.1
Festuca arundinacea	Barcel	6.6	50	330.0
Lolium multiflorum	Lipo and Defo	4.4	36	158.4
Dactylis glomerata	Amba	11.0	66	726.0
Total	–	25.3	–	1930.5

NOTE: (1) Bhutanese ngultrum (Nu), on par with Indian Rupee.   Exchange rate: Nu 45 = US$ 1 at time of reporting.

the state and herders only have grazing rights. Rights to *tsadrogs* are important household possessions and are passed down from generation to generation.

Summer grazing sites include registered *tsadrog* in blue pine (*Pinus wallichiana*) forest clearings and extend up to or above the tree line (4 200 m). The meadows are extensively grazed by migratory stock (mithun, mithun crosses and siri cattle).

Some *tsadrog* between 3 000 and 4 000 m belong to the group or to others and are grazed by cattle in summer and yak in winter. Cattle from Chentok *geog* share yak pastures at Soe Thombu in summer at an altitude of 4 300 m. Some pastures (Plate 61) that serve as winter grazing for yak and summer grazing for cattle are dominated by dwarf bamboo (*Yushania microphylla*).

Plate 61.
*Winter grazing for yak (and also summer grazing for cattle) at 3 500 m near Pelela Pass in Bhutan. Ground cover is dominated by dwarf bamboo (*Yushania microphylla).*

Pastures at Thombu

Preliminary vegetation surveys of alpine meadows were carried out in western Bhutan by Harris (1987) and in eastern Bhutan by Miller (1989). The dominant grass genera in summer pastures above 3 900 m are *Agrostis, Festuca, Bromus* and *Poa. Carex* and *Juncus* are widespread in alpine pastures. Among the many genera of broad-leaf forbs, *Potentilla, Bistorta, Bryophyta, Gentiana, Primula* and *Iris* are the most prolific. *Rumex nepalensis* is the commonest weed and is especially obvious around camp sites, from the subtropical zone up to over 4 000 m. *Eupatorium adenophorum* is a serious weed in the subtropical zone; it soon dominates other plants.

Thombu is an open valley at 4 100–4 400 m; it has good grazing land, about 5 km long. The environment offers a considerable challenge for pasture development; the growing season is short and the quality of the vegetation generally low. Growth starts between April and June, and finishes in September or October (4–6 months). Winter sites are subject to very high, probably worsening, grazing pressure. Yaks graze almost all the Thombu (Soe Yasksa) complex, from April to June and September to October; in July and August it is grazed by cattle from Paro. It is owned by seven herder families, of whom two are from Soe Yaksha and others from Chentog Paro, a yak *tsadrog*. Cattle from Bida,

Changlam and Chib Phub Tshering graze the same pasture.

Sites for measuring production were selected in keeping with stress caused by yaks and cattle. Two locations, representative of the whole area of Thombu, were chosen. Botanical composition and vegetation cover were measured by 1.5-m transects with 30 point readings. Each site had a circular area of 12 m radius, with an iron pin at its centre. Eight metal cages, with a base of 70 cm × 70 cm, and 60 cm. high, were installed on 11 April 1999 at both locations for recording herbage production. Cages were rotated, avoiding previously harvested areas. The first location represented about 40 percent of Thombu tsadrog, at an altitude of 4 300 m with a slope of 30 percent and aspects south and southwest. The second site represented the plain areas of Thombu, about 60 percent, at an altitude of 4 200 m and with a south and southwest aspect.

Forage was to be harvested twice yearly, but in 1999, due to the weather, it was only possibly to clip once, on 6 October. The results are summarized in Table 14.4. Analytical data from grazed and ungrazed samples are shown in Table 14.5. From the first year's results, it is clear that grazing pressure was very high.

Winter pastures in Chukka *Dzongkhag* were visited and herders interviewed at Omna in Lochina *geog*, Dungna *geog*, Sadhumandhu in Phuentsholing *geog*,

TABLE 14.4
Herbage yields at Thombu.

Location of cage	Dry matter (kg/ha)		Average height (cm)	
	Inside cage	Outside cage	Inside cage	Outside cage
Thombu 1	721.6	127.6	12.0	3
Thombu 2	1303.8	212.0	16.25	2

TABLE 14.5
Nutrient contents of grazed and ungrazed herbage (percent).

Sample	Ash	CP[(1)]	Ca	Na	K	P
Thombu 1 – inside cage	5.9	9.3	0.83	0.0	1.31	0.12
Thombu 1 – outside cage	7.7	13.4	0.82	0.01	1.41	0.17
Thombu 2 – inside cage	6.3	10.6	0.90	0.01	1.21	0.23
Thombu 2 – outside cage	7.9	13.2	1.11	0.06	1.19	0.35

NOTES: (1) CP = crude protein.

Kamzhi in Geling *geog* and Metab geog. Winter *tsadrogs* are in subtropical broad-leaved forest with open areas and clearings in and around camp-sites. Cattle are fed lopped fodder – branches are usually lopped recklessly and sometimes the tree is felled. About a quarter of the trees belong to the following group (from a study by Dr Lungten Norbu (Norbu, 2000) in Gedu and Geling *geog*): *Aïsandra butyracea*, *Brassaiopsis hispida*, *Cordia obliqua*, *Eriobotrya petioklata*, *Erythrina stricta*, *Euodia fraxinifolius*, *Ficus neriifolia*, *Glochidion thomsonii*, *Ilex* sp., *Macropanax undulata*, *Pentapanax recemosus*, *Saurauia nepaulensis* and *Turpinia pomifera*. Cattle also browse, and so the undergrowth is practically devoid of seedlings of palatable fodder plants. Fodder trees are more common near camp sites than in far-off forest areas, confirming that herders plant them.

According to Dr Lungten Norbu's study, the decline in forage can be attributed to overgrazing, since census data suggest that cattle numbers have been increasing. Herders from Naywkha used to migrate to Suntolakha, near Geling, but have settled in Suntolakha, probably due to the remoteness of their previous area and the damage caused by wild animals to their crops and livestock.

Migrating herds follow traditional routes; herders know that they can stop for a night at others' *tsadrogs* without payment. If they cannot move the next day, due to rain or other unforeseen events, they must approach the *tsadrog* owner, inform him, and give him some foodstuffs. At stopping places in transit, herders pitch tents; they only have permanent shelters in their summer and winter *tsadrogs*. On the migration to winter pastures from Naja, cattle grazed meadows until their first halt at Chaye, 2 700 m, and thereafter browsed bamboo (*Yushania microphylla*), nettles and trees, with little or no grazing. They usually set out early, at or before 06.00 hours, and reach the halting place around 11.00; a day's journey is usually less than 15 km.

On the return journey in summer, even small streams as well as rivers are in flood, and landslides common. A herder recounted that he lost 26 cattle swept away in a stream in 1993. The Kazonochhu stream on the main migration route has to be forded twelve times; herders have to cross many other streams before reaching Dunga, all difficult to cross after or during rain. Herders often wait for hours until cattle can ford the stream. A further problem is the narrowness of the tracks that pass along steep cliffs and contribute to stock losses. Leeches, sand-flies and other bloodsucking pests damage livestock health.

The major migration route, which was also the main trading route before a vehicular road was made to Phuentsholing, still serves as the main transhumance route for Naja, Dopsari and other *geogs* of Paro *Dzongkhag*, and Wanakha *geog* of Chukka *Dzongkhag*; 80 percent of herds in the western *dzongkhags* use it.

The longest route takes about 10 days each way, with altitudes ranging from 300 m to 3 420 m.

Herders must carry movement permits issued by the Livestock Extension Centre or Veterinary Hospital of their *Dzongkhag* when travelling to other *dzongkhags*. The permit gives records of vaccinations, etc. A new permit must be obtained for the return journey.

Although milk and milk products are mainly used domestically, some are sold at Phuentsholing. The herders buy Jersey cattle at Ron Jaigoan and Hashimara if business turnover is good; Friesians were found to be unsuited to high altitudes. Jerseys are much more profitable; prices vary from Nu 6 000 to Nu 12 000. The Government has supplied a Jersey bull to Naja to improve and promote the breed. Herders collect non-timber forest products (NTFPs) in winter and sell them in Phuntsoling. Seasonal sales included cane shoots (Nu 600); Od Dumru (*Elatostema lineolatum*) (Nu 200); fern (Nu 300); Pan (betel leaf; *Piper betle*) (Nu 600); and brooms (Nu 200). In summer, Naja farmers get cash through sale of livestock products and horticultural crops. Butter and cheese are sold through intermediaries, who in turn sell in Thimpu. Butter prices were Nu 130–150/kg, and cheese was Nu 6–10 per ball; income from dairy products (excluding domestic consumption) averaged Nu 5 818 per household.

THE REASONS FOR TRANSHUMANCE

Herders state that transhumance is a well established, deeply-rooted tradition and an inseparable part of their life and that of the community. They, with their family, move to lower altitudes in winter to manage land holdings, do business (plantation crops) and have better grazing for their stock in their inherited *tsadrog*. Herders gave the following reasons for migration:

- Climatic factors and lack of grazing at high altitudes and ownership of low altitude *tsadrogs*; *nothouc* arrangements.
- Ownership of orange orchards in lower *tsadrogs*; many also own cardamom plantations.
- Opportunities for trading: some subcontract orange crops; sale of NTFPs; and employment opportunities (pack pony rental and porterage).
- Ease of sale of livestock and products and ease of access to goods.
- Some had no registered high-altitude *tsadrog*.

Yaks do not graze below 3 000 m in winter nor above 5 000 m in summer. Cattle do not venture above 4 200 m in Thombu and in summer graze between 2 600 and 3 700 m; their lowest winter grazing is at 300 m. Herd composition on the high pastures of Soe Yaksa (Harris, 1987) was yak – 88 percent; cattle – 1 percent; horses and mules – 10 percent; and goats – 1 percent. Jersey cattle do not travel with the herds; they are taken by truck to Phuentsholing and are kept around the Torsey river bank and Norgey Cinema. These herders are occupied in orange business from October until the beginning of February. Transport from Naja to Phuentsholing is Nu 3 000–4 000 per truck.

Almost every herd had its own bulls; *noblang* (siri) bulls are individually owned. The government supplies Jersey bulls to remote communities; both mithun and

TABLE 14.6
Average milk production parameters of bovine species in Bhutan.

Breed	Lactation (days)	Lactation yield (kg)	Fat percentage
Siri cows	240	180	4.6
Mithun cow cross	253	316	7.9
Jersey cross	246	492	4.5
Yak	280	196	6.7

Jersey crossbreeding facilities are readily available through artificial insemination where there are motorable roads. Mithun bulls are supplied by the government but are managed at communal level and migrate with other cattle. The government has mithun breeding farms at Chukka in eastern Bhutan. The price of a bull is currently Nu 10 000. Wild mithun are undergoing gradual degeneration, perhaps due to inbreeding and the degradation of their habitat, even in Aranachal Pradesh (Tshering, 1994).

The mithun or gayal, locally known as *bamey*, is the domesticated form of the gaur, *Bos frontalis* or *Bos gaurus*. It is indigenous to neighbouring parts of India (Aranachal Pradesh and Assam), Bangladesh and Myanmar. Mithun cross freely with cattle; the male of the cross, the *jathsa* is a huge and very strong draught animal compared to indigenous cattle; it is usually sterile. The female – *jathsam* – is a good milker with high butterfat. They are liked for ease of maintenance in Bhutan's difficult terrain, and are good at grazing on steep hills and slopes and feeding on native pasture and browse. Traditional practice is to mate female hybrids back to Siri bulls for four successive generations. If a *jathsam* is mated with a mithun bull she frequently fails to conceive or aborts and calves born of such a cross (*menchi*) are weak and die early, so they are of little use.

Daily milk yield of the various breeds and crosses was estimated by herders to be 2–3 bottles for *jatsham*, 2 bottles for *thabum* and *yangkum* and 2–3 for quarter-cross Jersey. In a study on Bhutan's high altitude ranges by Pema Gyamthso (1996), the milk production of the various species was as shown in Table 14.6.

There are no fixed rates for produce: prices vary according to the scale of production, season and place. Herder produce is sold in the open market or on demand; price ranges are Nu 120–140/kg for butter and Nu 7–8 per ball of cheese. Herders usually sell milk in winter in the most convenient markets: Phuntsholing, Phuntsholing–Chukka roadside sites of Kamzi and Suntolakha, Gedu and Chimakothi.

Foot-and-mouth disease and black quarter are the most serious problems in cattle. Haematuria is also sometimes seen. Predators, parasites and toxic plants are subjects of concern. Cattle graze to the Indian border and there is a worry about contact with infected stock. Poisonous plants are common at higher altitudes; mainly newborn and newly-introduced stock from lower areas are likely to be poisoned. Poisonous plants, including *Senecio* sp. and *Ligularia* sp., are found at the highest pass on the migration route, Lumilakha and in most summer pastures (between 3 000 and 4 000 m). Ticks and leeches are the most serious external

TABLE 14.7
Transhumance system constraints and herder suggestions for improvement.

Constraint	Suggestion for mitigation
Fodder scarcity in March–April	Improve *tsadrog* management by controlling grazing; plant good quality fodder trees; improve pasture in clearings; cull unproductive stock.
Natural calamities in May (heavy rain, landslides, rivers in flood)	Modify timing of transhumance to summer pastures; research intervention to improve fodder supply at that season.
Bad tracks and narrow cliff-side routes for migration	Improvement of main track by community and the *Dzongkhag* authorities.
Diseases, parasites, predators and toxic plants	Improve contacts with local Livestock Extension Centres (LEC); timely vaccination and deworming; promotion of vigilance groups at village level to provide feedback; documentation of toxic plants and awareness campaigns.
Lack of information on cattle movements during migration	Pass information from LEC to LEC through herders (movement permit/health certificate); inform herders of information need.
Bush encroachment by *Juniperus, Rhododendron*, etc., in high altitude meadows	Research is needed on the dominance of non-fodder over fodder species.

parasites; because of distance it is often difficult to obtain medicines from the *Dzongkhag* extension service, so traditional treatments are used:

- for ticks: salt, *Xanthoxylon* and garlic, well crushed and made into a solution with a little water is applied locally to affected animals;
- for leeches: salt, tobacco and lime – either alone or in combination – are used on both livestock and herders; and
- sand-flies and flies are repelled by burning incense vegetation like *Artemisia*, blue-pine leaves and other shrubs and herbs.

TRANSECT WALK

To study grazing sites from Sadhumadhu Phuntsoling *geog* to Omna in Lokchina *geog*, a transect walk was undertaken.

During the transect walk, big, well established orange orchards were seen in the *tsadrog*; one was at least 50 years old as a herder, now 73, was 20 when it was established. Almost all the herders were met and samples were taken of the fodder trees they use. In discussions with herders, some constraints of the system were indicated; these, together with suggestions for their mitigation, are listed in Table 14.7.

GENERAL RECOMMENDATIONS

After considering the information gathered during the study, a number of conclusions and recommendations emerged.

Traditional transhumance benefits farmers and has advantages

These include registered *tsadrogs* in warm areas; ownership of rainfed land, wetland, orchards and cardamom; fodder available seasonally at high altitudes; access to markets for sales and purchases; better prospects for income generation (oranges and NTFPs); manuring of fields and orchards; nothoue develops very strong bonds of friendship and mutual partnership; herders are exposed to development activities in other centres and areas whereas high areas have few field activities in winter.

Disadvantages of the system

Loss of grazing through conversion of *tsadrog* pasture into orange groves; bare patches are appearing in forests due to constant, uncontrolled lopping and overharvesting of NTFPs; damage due to trampling in forest, especially when wet; spread of diseases due to animal movements; difficulties of access to animal production and health services, including vaccination and training; in some areas farmers have settled in warmer areas, abandoning registered land at higher altitudes.

Strategies suitable for immediate implementation

- Improve forage production in *tsadrogs*. Encourage further planting of fodder trees and develop pasture in clearings and within orange groves. Improve management of natural pasture and fodder trees.
- Support regular training programmes for herders regarding the rational use of fodder resources.
- Develop adapted extension programmes applicable to transhumant herders, including livestock production and health, grazing and forest management.

Chapter XV

Bhutan case study 2: Yak herders in Soe Yaksa, Chentok Geog, Bhutan, in 1999–2000

Tsering Gyaltsen and B.N. Bhattarai

SUMMARY

The Soe Yaksa community is wholly dependent on yak herding for their livelihood. They have permanent homes in the lower part of their territory (around 4 000 m), and the herds, with enough people to look after them, move to high pastures in summer, above the tree line, up to 5 000 m. Most children now attend school in the provincial capital, two days journey away. No crops are grown, only a few vegetables. Hay is made close to the houses and a little wheat is grown for hay, mostly on winter yak pens. Stock numbers have risen very steeply from the levels reported in 1987, and pastures are generally very hard grazed. The pastures visited and studied were in good condition. Bush encroachment is troublesome and is exacerbated by a ban on pasture burning to improve wildlife habitat. Blue sheep (*Pseudois nayaur*) are competitors for grazing on the high pastures.

The transhumance is vertical and relatively short, one to two days travel from the villages. Yak and a few ponies are the livestock; sheep are not kept. Some of the stock are tended on behalf of monasteries. Dairy products, especially dried cheese, as well as live animals and yak-hair products, are marketed or bartered for grain and necessities. Herders mainly live off dairy products and cereals; animals are usually slaughtered only for ceremonies. Gathering incense and medicinal plants is a secondary source of income.

The demand for fuelwood, needed for cheese making as well as domestic cooking and heating, is such that families have to go farther and farther to get supplies. Winter mortality of young and weak animals due to malnutrition is a major problem; hay-meadows do not produce enough to see stock through the winter. Improved pasture forages can be grown on the better soils but, unless protected, are destroyed by overgrazing. Fencing is a problem. Oats have shown considerable promise and are more productive than the traditional green wheat, but seed supply has still to be organized.

BACKGROUND

Soe Yaksa is mostly in Chentok *geog* of Paro *dzonkhag*, and comprises 9 villages with 18 households; villages are about half an hour apart on foot. Two of the villages are under Lango *geog* and one under Shari *geog*, the rest are under Chentok *geog*. The altitude range is 3 900–4 200 m. The inhabitants are pastoralists, totally dependent on livestock; yaks are mainly raised for meat and milk; dairy products may be sold on the markets of Paro and Thimpu. Horses also earn a good income in the tourist season. Transhumance is usual throughout the yak-rearing zone but, unlike many other areas, Soe people have permanent dwellings and usually one or two family members remain at home when others move to temporary summer yak pastures, although sometimes the whole family moves. At the onset of winter they move back to their lower base and feed yak on hay made in summer, but the amount of hay is inadequate and the stock are put to graze on barren pastures.

The only crops grown are in small kitchen gardens (radish, potatoes and turnips). Wheat fodder is grown in sheltered areas – yak winter pens – and made into hay. Some herders have small areas of improved pasture near their dwellings. There was no government infrastructure at the time of the visit, but in 1999 most of the villages got piped water and no longer have to fetch it from a stream. Most herder children go to school in Paro, two days journey away. Two village leaders are elected annually to assist the headman of the block in passing messages, organizing public meetings, etc.

GRAZING LANDS

There are two kinds of registered land rights: *tsesa* (household plots) and *tsadrog* (pasture). The average registered *tsesa* is under 1 000 m²; a *tsadrog* would cover hectares in area, and stretch from the village for two days' journey. Land near the village is winter pasture; summer pastures are at one or two days' travel, at altitudes up to 5 000 m. Grazing land belongs to the state and herders have only grazing rights. Grazing rights at Soe Yaksa mostly belong

to the Monastries-Dhatshangs of Thimpu and Paro; nominal fees are paid annually to the government to renew them. Livestock does not migrate to other *geogs* but remains within their locality.

In summer, the herds graze, moving five to six times from one grazing ground to another. In winter, morning and evening, they are fed hay and some concentrates such as millet, oilcake, maize flour, mustard oil, and maize and millet dough mixed with ground hay; during the day they are let loose to graze what they can find. Yaks do not take salt voluntarily and it has to be administered by hand – placed in the mouth and washed down with water; it is given monthly at 300–350 g for adults and 100–150 g for young.

The growing season is short and pasture quality is generally low; growth begins between April and June and ends in October or November. A grassland monitoring trial was set up on natural pasture at three sites at altitudes between 4 000 and 4 300 m, corresponding to winter, spring-autumn, and summer grazing areas. Sample areas were circular and covered 452 m². Eight metal cages, 70 × 70 cm tapering to 40 × 40 cm, and 60 cm high, were placed in each trial to record yield. Preliminary results, the average of two years, are given in Table 15.1.

TABLE 15.1
Production from natural pasture (average of two years; kg/ha).

Site	Altitude (m)	In Cage	In Open
Lamilakha 1	4 200	1 976	1 699
Lamilakha 2	4 060	1 677	1 791
Kamgung 1	4 130	1 058	237
Kamgung 2	4 100	1 716	408
Thombu slope	4 300	722	128
Thombu plain	4 200	1 304	212

TABLE 15.2
Botanical and vegetation cover at six sites (percentage).

Site	Altitude (m)	Grass	Sedge	Broadleaved	Fern	Moss	Bare
Lamilakha 1	4 200	6.7	65.3	26.7	–	–	1.3
Lamilakha 2	4 060	8.6	26.7	63.3	0.6	0.8	–
Kamgung 1	4 130	9.4	51.9	25.0	0.3	11.7	1.7
Kamgung 2	4 100	9.7	43.9	33.0	–	13.1	0.3
Thombu slope	4 300	5.8	63.8	8.8	–	18.0	3.3
Thombu plain	4 200	8.9	63.6	18.1	–	8.0	1.4

The fodder of sites at Lamilakha, Kamgung and Thombu slope was harvested before the yaks arrived for winter grazing. The difference between in-cage and outside was due to grazing by blue sheep (*Pseudois nayaur*) and horses. Fodder yield outside cages at Thombu are from intensively grazed summer pasture; grazing livestock included yaks, cattle, horses (including tourist horses) and blue sheep. Botanical composition and vegetation cover were recorded using a transect of 1.5 m and reading 30 points at 5-cm intervals, with 12 transects recorded at each site (Table 15.2).

The vegetation of Soe Yaksa contains a large number of species – further study is needed to see changes with time. Specimens collected from grazing areas during the study were identified by the Renewable Natural Resources Research Centre, Jakar, and the Royal Society for the Protection of Nature, Thimpu.

Grasses and sedges: *Agrostis pilulosa, Brachypodium sylvaticum, Bromus* sp., *Calamagrostis lahulensis, C. scabrescens, Carex hamata, Danthonia cumminsii, Elymus dahuricus, E. nutans, Festuca* sp., *Kobresia prainii, Poa* sp., *Stipa* sp., *Trisetum* sp., and six grasses and sedges not yet identified.

Broadleaved plants: *Allium wallichii, Anemone* sp., *Aster falconeri, Cyananthus lobatus, Epilobium?* sp., *Gentiana prolata,* *Geranium nakaoanum, G. polyanthes, Inula rhizocephala, Leontopodium jacotiatum* (*Anaphalis* sp.), *Ligularia?* sp., *Onosma hookeri, Pedicularis* sp., *Polygonatum hookeri, Potentilla* sp., *Pterocephalus hookeri, Ranunculus* sp., *Rhodiola* sp., *Rubus fragaroides, Saussurea* sp., *Saxifraga paranassifolia, Taraxacum* sp., *Thermopsis barbata,* and twenty broadleaved species still to be identified.

According to Harris (1987), the common shrubs of the area are: *Berberis angulosa, Cassiope* sp., *Cotoneaster* sp., *Juniperus indica, J. recurba, Potentilla fruticosa, Rhododendron anthopogon, R. setosum,* five other *Rhododendron* spp., *Salix* sp. and six unidentified shrubs.

Soil samples were taken from six sites at the three locations; pH ranged from 4.8 to 6.5; phosphate and potassium were low. This would have implications on species choice if hay meadows were to be improved.

Pastures accessible to grazing animals are claimed to be overgrazed. Pressure is very high in one of the most important pastures at Thombu, where yaks graze in spring and autumn and cattle graze in summer. The closure of the Chinese border and the denial of traditional grazing areas is another cause of overgrazing in Soe and Lighsi. The increase in yak numbers may be partly due to the good

TABLE 15.3
Percentage cover by plant group in seasonal pasture at Soe Yaksa, 1987.

Plant group or pasture type	Winter pasture	Spring–autumn pasture	Summer grassland	Shrub land
Grasses	24.4	29.3	14.1	16.5
Cyperaceae	3.8	10.8	13.5	12.0
Juncaceae	8.2	7.2	15.2	12.7
Broad-leaved herbs	50.3	39.4	38.6	29.1
Bryophyta	3.4	2.0	10.9	9.4
Pteridophyta	1.2	2.8	0	0
Thallophyta	0	0	0.2	0
Shrubs	8.8	8.3	7.3	20.4

SOURCE: Based on Harris, 1987.

TABLE 15.4
Percentage ground cover at Soe Yaksa in 1987 by pasture type.

	Winter pasture	Spring–autumn pasture	Summer pasture	Shrub land
Vegetation	65	85	70	66
Litter	27	7	19	19
Bare soil	--	4	2	2
Rock	8	4	9	13

SOURCE: From Harris, 1987.

veterinary services provided by the Royal Government.

However, most of the *tsadrogs* visited were in good condition, with good vegetation cover, but the destructive effect of marmots through burrowing and grazing was evident in some places. The entrances of marmot burrows cover a radius of 30 m in stony meadows between 4 000 and 4 500 m in the Laya pastures (Gyamthso, 1996). These entrances are used by yaks to sharpen their horns and, with further expansion, serve as resting pits for yaks; eventually they become very large and foci for erosion. Scars were seen on almost all pastures in the study area. Herders claim that, in all pastures, unpalatable plants like *Rhododendron*, *Juniperus*, etc., are spreading due to restrictions on the burning of pasture. Herders used to burn unwanted vegetation as part of traditional management and

would like, once more, to burn for shrub control and grazing improvement. Apart from shrub encroachment, other weeds include docks (*Rumex nepalensis*) which rapidly colonize camp-sites due to fertility accumulation.

Senecio and *Ligularia*, which are poisonous and can cause problems for livestock, are common in many areas of forest grazing at high altitudes; stock generally avoid such plants but may eat them in times of feed scarcity; during the study no herder reported mortality due to toxic plants.

The community pasture of Soe-Thongbu is a day's journey over the Thongbu pass at 4 600 m; a nice open valley at 4 100–4 500 m with rich open grazing land and about 5 km long. The valley runs southeast to northwest; southwest facing slopes are mostly open grazing while northeast facing slopes are almost completely covered by shrubs. At the end of the valley, on the ridge, are 3 ha of fir forest. There is marshy land on both sides of the stream, with black soil rich in organic matter; the marshy area is about 15 percent of the total area. On the lower part of the northeast slope, 4–5 ha of rhododendron had been burnt to allow better grass regrowth. Herders bring their yak twice yearly, March–May and August–October. In June and July, cattle (siri and mithun cross) of herders from Chentok *geog* graze. The area is on a major trekking route of tourists and traders, so tourist horses also graze in the camping season.

Yak are by far the most important live-stock, with horses, a few goats and some dogs; there are no sheep. Stock numbers at the time of the study were: yak – 1 655, of which 60 percent were female; 89 horses and 25 goats. Harris (1987) reported a yak population of 897 in Soe Yaksa, so there had been an increase of 85 percent in 13 years! The goat population had also increased, from 9 to 25; goats have no eco-nomic role but the initial stock was given to a herder as *tsethar* [saving them from being slaughtered] – belonging to a reli-gious foundation – and the numbers have increased to 25 from the original pair.

Yaks have played, and continue to play, a very important role in the economy and social activity of the people of Bhutan. They are an integral part of the Kingdom's pastoral systems and are mainly reared in the north of the country. They are kept by pastoral groups known as *Jop* in the west and *Brokpa* in the east – in both cases meaning yak herders.

The yak of Bhutan are multipurpose animals for draught and meat and milk production. Demand for yak dairy products and meat, high internally and in neighbouring states, ensures that yaks will remain important in the Bhutanese economy for the foreseeable future. The value of the yak should be viewed not only on the basis of its meat and dairy production, but also as it is the only domestic animal that can survive and produce under extremely cold temperatures and convert alpine herbage into products for human use. It is also valuable for pack-work, draught in crop production and as a source of hair and down. The main yak products are milk, butter, cheese, hair products, *philu* (clotted cream), meat, tails and hide. The total dairy commercialization at Soe Yaksa is 520 litres per week of milk, 356 kg per week of butter and 623 kg per week of cheese.

Herders milk only once daily during the first year after calving, in the morning, leaving the rest for the calves. From the second year, herders milk twice daily: in the morning between 5.30 and 7.30 and in the evening between 17.00 and 18.30. Both men and women milk. Yak milk is valued for its fat content as well as medici-nal qualities, attributed to herbs in alpine meadows eaten by the yaks. The qualities of these plants is thought to be transmit-ted to milk, butter and cheese. It is proba-bly for this reason that yak dairy products fetch a premium in the market compared to cattle products. The composition of yak milk averages 17–21 percent dry mat-ter, 5–6 percent protein, 6–9 percent fat, and 1 percent ash (Sasaki, reported by Gyamthso, 1996).

The average daily yield of a yak is reported to be two bottles (1.5 litres, inclusive of suckled milk). Milking begins from the second month after calving, from May to October; because of feed scarcity, herders do not usually milk in winter, except a few animals for domestic consumption. Milk yield over a lactation (excluding that suckled) is 220 litres in 223 days.

Milk must be churned very fresh since the buttermilk is used to make *chugo*, a high-value product that cannot be made from sour milk. Churning is done daily in summer, after the morning milking, and takes one to two hours. The butter is removed and the liquid poured into a pot for chugo making. The skimmed liquid is heated, stirring all the time; after about an hour the chugo is ready and is put in a cotton cloth and pressed between stones overnight; next morning it is solid and is cut into pieces 10 × 5 cm and these are strung into rings of 24 pieces, which thereafter are smoke dried. Chugo making uses a lot of fuelwood. *Tachu* is made in the same way, but is cut into smaller pieces – 2.5 by 1 cm – and boiled in milk to make it white and sweet; after boiling, the pieces are strung into rings of 24 pieces and sun-dried. Tachu requires more labour, fuel and milk than chugo, and its manufacture is less popular with herders; it is sold locally, whereas chugo is marketed in bulk in towns bordering India.

Livestock products are marketed in Paro and Thimpu, although chugo is marketed in Phuntsholing and the border towns of Kalimpong and Darjeeling. Prices quoted in 2000 were butter – Nu 180/kg; chugo – Nu 100–120/kg in Paro and Thimpu, but Nu 117.5/kg in Phuntsholing and Nu 125–137.5/kg in Kalimpong and Darjeeling, India; tachu – Nu 20–24 per string of 24 pieces; plilu (cream) from milk – Nu 180/kg; beef with bone – Nu 100–120/kg; boneless beef – Nu 130–140/kg; hides – Nu 150 per unit;

yak-hair rope – Nu 200–300 per piece; and saddle bags – Nu 1 000 per pair.

Herders barter livestock products for local red rice and milled flour. At the time of writing, rates were 1 kg butter for 8 deys [15.2 kg] of rice, and 1 kg of wet cheese for 2 deys [3.8 kg] of rice. Most herders are moving from barter to selling for cash. Sale of live animals, mainly yak bulls, is now common in Soe Yaksa; they are purchased either by herders or people from Paro in the lower valley. Prices are from Nu 19 000 to 23 000 per adult bull. Live animals are taken down to Dophu village and sold to butchers at a profit margin of Nu 3 000–4 000 per head. Thereafter they are slaughtered for sale in Paro and Thimpu. The season for selling yak meat is from September to January. Old female yaks are also sold to butchers at Nu 8 000–10 000; bulls are preferred as they cut out better. Tshering (1994) reports the weight of adult males to be 480 kg, with castrates at 400 kg and adult females at 340 kg. Herders slaughter two yaks annually for religious purposes and bartering or selling for rice. A butcher, hired to do the slaughtering, charges 20–25 kg of meat and fat.

Herders used to sell yak-hair products to tourists but due to the way in which contractors now organize tours, there is little opportunity for such selling.

The commonest disease is gid (caused by a tapeworm, *Taenia multiceps*, the intermediate stage of which is known as *Coenurus cerebralis*), for which dogs are intermediate hosts, and there are occasional cases of liver fluke. Routine deworming is done quarterly and vaccination six-monthly; diseases like foot-and-mouth and black quarter are controlled. Livestock mortality is mainly due to malnutrition in winter, especially calves and weak animals; April and May are the worst months for such losses. Snow leopards also attack yak and horses; herders report losses of 4–5 horses and 6–7 calves annually due to leopards; the victims are usually weak animals.

The government supplies breeding bulls. Those from Haa Dzonghag are regarded as superior, and are exchanged between areas to avoid inbreeding. Only pure yaks are reared – no hybridization is done. The mating season is July–August; both government and private bulls are used. Frozen yak semen from China has given promising results but widespread artificial insemination is unlikely to be feasible since there are no roads and the herds are at 5 000 m in the breeding season. Yak cows are first served at three to four years of age; calving is from April to July; a yak should give birth to a minimum of five calves; the calving interval is 23 to 24 months. Herders expect a minimum lactation of 10 months and a maximum of 24.

Blue sheep compete for grazing in high areas. Gibson (1991) reported that since blue sheep and marmots occupy the high places for all or most of the year, and yak for only three to four months, it is reasonable to assume that where the numbers of blue sheep and marmots are high they cause more environmental damage by overgrazing than do domestic stock. Herders claim that there are about a thousand blue sheep in Soe Yaksa and do not think that they compete seriously for grazing; the blue sheep graze on areas that are too steep and rocky even for yaks. Snow leopards prey on blue sheep. During the study, several flocks were sighted of between 20 and 80; competition by wild-

life may be more serious than is realized. Wangchuk (1994) concluded that there is considerable dietary overlap between blue sheep and yak; observations indicate that both preferred leafy foliage and avoided woody parts. He concluded that, whether or not there was competition for feed, overgrazing and bare, eroded pastures were becoming increasingly common in the Lingshi area.

Large animals reported to be in the area are blue sheep (*Psuedois nayaur*), bear (*Melurus ursinus*), takin (*Burdorcas taxicolor* – observed for the last five years in the Thombu area), snow leopard (*Panthera uncia*) and wild dog (*Cuon alpinus*), of which at least two were seen recently.

IMPROVED PASTURE AND SOWN FODDER

Some improved grasses and legumes can be grown at high altitudes if soil conditions are suitable, but temperatures above 3 500 m are considered too low for introduction of improved forages and fertilizer application to improve productivity. Earlier trials above 3 500 m in Bumthang in Lingshi and Merak Sakteng were unsuccessful for various reasons. The only successes seem to have been the development of hay fields in intensively managed individually owned plots that are protected from grazing. During the ADB-supported Highland Livestock Development Project, some success was reported with *Trifolium hybridum* at Merak and Saktens, with protection and mineral fertilizer.

A few herders at Soe Yaksa have hay plots, usually established on old winter yak pens; most such plots are now old and past their prime. Forages include *Trifolium repens*, *Dactylis glomerata*,

Festuca arundinacaea and *Lolium multi-florum*. Manure is applied annually after irrigation; two cuts are taken from unirrigated plots and three from irrigated. Average plot size is small, from 100 to 150 m², and they are fenced with wooden slats. In 1999, oats (*Avena sativa*) and rye (*Secale cereale*) were given to two farmers to compare their performance against traditional fodder wheat. Both grew successfully at over 4 000 m and herders were very pleased with them. Seed supply may be a major constraint, as at present herders would have to go to Paro to buy oat seed.

Herders spend over a month every year making hay from natural herbage, which includes broad-leaved plants and is done before yaks return to the village for winter. Each herder has their designated hay area close to the house; grass from knolls and steep cliffs is also cut. Hay is usually twisted into ropes and hung to dry in the roof or from trees; hay from broad-leaved species is half-wilted and stacked in the field.

COLLECTION OF WILD PLANTS

Fuelwood is collected in the vicinity of the village, mainly in spring. Fuelwood for the summer pastures, which are above the tree line, is taken from the village by pack animals. *Juniperus, Betula, Salix* and *Rhododendron* trees are used. The distance to go to find fuelwood is now much greater than in the past.

Incense collection is a significant source of income for the poorer of the population; major plants are *balu* (*Rhododendron anthopogon*), *sulu* (*Rhododendron setosum*) and *shrub* (*Juniperus*); *pang gey, jagey, gey pey* and *tong key* are collected in minor quantities. Some plants are uprooted and the whole used, while only parts of others are harvested. Medicinal plants are gathered, often illegally, on the summer pastures; those most extensively taken are *Cordiceps sinensis* (a mushroom) and *Fritillaria delavayi*; others collected intensively include *Picorrhiza kurroa, Corydalis* sp. and *Gentiana* spp. Some herders dig *Onosma hookeri* to sell in the valley for religious purposes as a red dye.

TRADITIONAL CULTURE

Herders of Soe Yaksa have their traditional festivals. *Ten zou* is the offering of an animal to the local deities without slaughtering it; this helps bring good luck and avoids evil events to the herd and family. One of the most important female deities in which the herders believe is *Tsheringma*, a goddess of longevity, wealth and prosperity. A male yak is offered to male deities and a female to female deities. The animal offered is identified by coloured yak hair on its ear, tail and rump. *Ten zou* animal are celebrated, with incense and tying coloured yak hair, in the sixth and seventh Bhutanese months. *Ten zou* animal are exchanged when old or replaced on death; old *ten zou* animals are sold or slaughtered.

There are three local festivals annually. *Da-tsa* is celebrated in the village, on the third day of the second Bhutanese month (March) for three to four days, which has a special community hall for it. Men have archery competitions; women look after the catering and dancing – dancing is a speciality of young women. This is the only festival where a large group gathers and every household joins in. Food is contributed and a herder, selected by the group, provides enough yak meat for all. The selection is done, in rotation, by offering a scarf (*Khadar*). This festival is a farewell before the herders move to the summer pastures.

Loe-cho is an annual religious ceremony observed by every household in the first Bhutanese month, February. It is performed by a priest from Paro in the lower valley. A family member from every household will bring some rice, *ara* (local liquor) and join the *Loe-cho*, they are treated as guests and served a good meal and drinks. Priests are given butter as their fee. Herders also celebrate *Lomba* at the beginning of the eleventh Bhutanese month.

CONDITIONS GOVERNING THE KEEPING OF MONASTERY YAKS

There is a traditional relationship between monastic bodies and herders. Most Soe Yaksa herders tend monastery stock. The number of animals remains the same; any increase belongs to the herder, but he has to replace mortalities. There is a formal account of livestock at the time of handing over by the monastery. A milch yak with calf = three head; a female yak = two head; a two-year-old male yak = one head; a four-year-old male yak = two head. Payment is in butter at four *sang* (1.3 kg) per head per year. The monks usually collect in person. At least 86 yaks are herded by Soe families for monasteries from Thimpu and Paro.

CONSTRAINTS PERCEIVED BY HERDERS

Constraints identified in discussions included:

- mortality of young and weak stock in winter;
- encroachment of *Rhododendron* and *Juniperus* on grazing land due to restrictions on burning pasture;
- gid in young yak, and calf mortality due to liver fluke;

- winter feed scarcity; and
- pasture degradation is common, but overstocking was not emphasized by herders, despite the massive increase in stock numbers.

SUGGESTIONS FOR INTERVENTION

Overcoming the winter feed scarcity is a priority. Assessment of current practice and the economics of feed supplementation in winter is needed for better understanding of seasonality of feed supply and the responses of yaks in terms of body weight, growth, fertility, milk production and mortality so that interventions can be targeted more strategically. Increase in hay supply and an improvement in quality is needed; summer oats may be part of the solution and more study is needed, including the seed supply.

Depending on tsadrog conditions, controlled burning of shrubs should be permitted on pasture land on a trial basis; the effect of fire on wildlife habitat will, however, have to be monitored. More detailed inventory of pasture land and pasture quality trend studies are needed as part of a programme to bring stock numbers into equilibrium with pasture production.

Probably the major technical difficulty in improving pastures, hayfields and fodder plots is the lack of fencing. Some technology is available for increasing winter fodder and for pasture improvement. The fencing problem can only be alleviated with the involvement of the communities themselves, before the initiation of any fodder improvement programme. With some effort from the community, the fencing problem could be resolved.

Chapter XVI

Nepal case study: High altitude pastoral systems of Sailung and Thodung regions, Ramechap District, Nepal

S.M. Pradhan, D. Pariyar, K.K. Shrestha and **J.R. Adhikary**

SUMMARY

Two grazing systems were studied, both based on raising bought-in *chauris* for milk. The first system, in Thodung, is highly commercialized and based around a milk-purchasing organization; the second, in Sailung, has no outlet for fresh milk so only ghee and local dried cheese is sold. This difference in market opportunities gives rise to marked differences in incomes. Grazing areas are between 2 500 and 3 100 m in Sailung; up to 2 800 m they are in the vicinity of forest, while higher pastures are open and treeless. The rangelands of Thodung are between 2 600 and 4 000 m, with grazing up to 2 800 m in the vicinity of forest, while higher areas are treeless. There are problems of overgrazing, compounded by the summer grazings being also the winter grazing of yaks belonging to other communities, and the winter areas are used in summer by buffaloes from the lower areas. In both places, *chauris* (yak-cow hybrids) are the main stock, purchased elsewhere; calves are slaughtered at a few days. Old and unproductive chauris are sold to traders, often over the Tibetan border. Herds stay in the lower areas for about four months and spend four months in the highest areas. During their passage between seasonal grazing lands they use the transitional pastures for about four months (in March–April and September–October). The distance between camping points is about 1–2 hours walk. In summer, and at transition points, chauris graze around the camps.

In Sailung, herd size is about 20; milk is made into *chhurpi* and butter. Two contractors collect *chhurpi* and butter. The dominant sward species are *Danthonia cachemiriana, Agrostis* sp. *Potentilla fulgens, Duchesnea indica* and *Onychium* sp. An annual income of US$ 81.18 per chauri is obtained from dairy products over a 7–8 month period (April to October). Average income is US$ 984 to US$ 2 460 annually, depending on herd size.

In Thodung, chauris are the main stock and no sheep are kept, in contrast to the herd composition in Sailung; herd size is 22. Sale of fresh milk is the major source of income. There are three public milk collection centres and three from private dairies. Little difference in vegetation was found from 2 800 to 3 300 m; the predominant species at 3 300 m were *Danthonia* sp., *Pogonatherum paniceum* and *Anaphalis contortus*. In open grassland at 3 170 m, the dominant species were *Danthonia* sp., *Pogonatherum paniceum* and *Trifolium repens*. In the fenced area, the dominant species were *Pogonatherum paniceum, Danthonia* sp., *Trifolium repens, Caltha palustris, Anaphalis contortus* and *Galium aparine*. The average number of chauri in a herd is 22 and the annual income from milk sale is US$ 3 057, with almost half of it spent on management, feed and medicine, giving a net profit of US$ 1 529 from a herd with 22 *chauri*.

BACKGROUND

Two grazing systems were studied, both based on raising bought-in *chauris* for milk. The one system is highly commercialized and based around a milk-purchasing organization; the other system has no outlet for fresh milk, so sells only ghee and local dried cheese. Livestock provide milk, meat, fibre, manure and draught for the population of the hilly and mountainous tracts, but production per animal is very low due to undernutrition, mainly because of overstocking. Household production systems involve crops, livestock, forestry and some trade.

Explosive population growth in the last decades has upset the balance previously secured by local ingenuity and left herders with no technical solution to their problems. They have been forced to cultivate steep slopes, unfit for sustained farming, even with astonishingly elaborate terracing (Rajbhandary and Pradhan, 1981). Mountain agriculture can no longer support population growth. According to the Land Resource Mapping Project (LRMP, 1986), the grazing area of Nepal covers about 17 000 km², or 12 percent of the total land area. However, only 37 percent of the pasture is available or accessible to livestock (Pariyar, 1998). The grazing areas, which are unique ecosystems with a high level of endemism, are slowly being turned into barren land (Yonzon, 1998). Common property has been misused due to lack of stewardship and ownership. In some areas, rotational grazing is organized by communities and herders pay a fee to graze their animals on specific areas.

Households in the high mountain and Trans-Himalayan region keep 15 to 30 *chauris* (the female hybrid of yak and cattle) and at least 60 to 70 sheep and goats. They are in transhumance most of the time, returning twice yearly to their settlement, to sow and harvest barley. The whole terrain appears to be semi-arid desert. Their main source of income is from livestock (Rajbhandary and Pradhan, 1981).

Ramechap district in the hill and mountain region, at 27°28′–27°50′ N and 85°50′–86°35′ E, has several grazing lands in the high mountain area, including Sailung and Thodung (Site IV in Figure 9.1). Much of northern Ramechap is at high altitude (1 000–4 848 m), while the south is in the mid-hill region (700 m). The climate sequence from south to north is cool, temperate and alpine. The average annual minimum temperature for the whole district is about 11.9°C and the maximum is 21.3°C; temperatures in the high pastures are, of course, very much lower. The average annual precipitation is 2 025 mm.

Out of a land area of 150 194 ha, cultivated land is 26.6 percent (40 050 ha), uncultivated land is 12.7 percent (19 130 ha), grazing land is 8 percent (11 429 ha), forest is 44 percent (66 152 ha), with 8.7 percent (13 433 ha) classed as "other". The cereals grown are rice, maize, finger millet, wheat and barley; potato, oilseed rape and sugar cane are cash crops. The food deficit of the whole district is estimated at 2.5 percent (NRA, 1997), but is severe at high altitudes.

Reaching Sailung involves a 4-hour drive from Kathmandu, reaching about 1 500 m, and followed by a trek of 5–6 hours, with a climb of 1 500–2 000 m to the grazing area. Thodung is farther than Sailung from Kathmandu – an 8-hour drive and a trek of 7–8 hours, with a climb of 1 800–3 100 m to the grazing.

The unique character of the *chauri*-rearing system (Plate 62) of Sailung is the involvement of different ethnic groups from Ramechap and Dolakha districts. In Thodung, all the herders are from the Sherpa community.

High altitude transhumance is common from east to west in Nepal along the foothills of the Himalayan range and Trans-Himalaya. Since the closing of Tibetan grazing to Nepalese stock, the number of *yak* [male] and *nak* [female] has fallen and that of *chauris* increased. *Yaks* are crossed with local low-mountain cattle to produce crosses called *Urang chauris* (yak × aule cow), which can graze down to 2 000 m. With the introduction of cheese making, coupled with traditional *chhurpi* cheese production, *chauri* keepers have no problem in marketing milk and milk products. *Yak* cheese is tasty and famous among tourists; Kathmandu and the trekking route to Mount Everest base camp are the markets for *yak* cheese and hard dried *chhurpi*.

The study aimed to obtain information on the traditional high altitude pastoral system; major constraints and problems of *chauri* rearing; productivity and condition of different pasture lands; and indigenous knowledge on maintaining and sustaining a high altitude pastoral system. It was hoped that, after identification of the major constraints and problems through a participatory approach, strong linkage could be established among herders, researchers and extension workers to conserve and improve production from existing herds.

In many parts of the country, each village, in addition to the lands nearby, uses pasture in distant places, usually at

Plate 62.
Chauris grazing at just below 3000 m near Sailung, Ramechap District, Nepal.

higher elevations than the settlements. Generally, the inhabitants have the right to use the pasture close to their village, whereas several villages may share a grazing area away from the settlements (Rai and Thapa, 1993). In Kalingchowk (central Nepal), collective right to grazing rests among groups of herders who have banded together for communal moving of the herd; this is ruled by tradition, and each household in the village in principle has the right (provided it has paid the summer pasture tax) to use the village-owned pasture area. Gibbon *et al.* (1988) reported that in Cheeskam (Solokhumbu), the neighbouring district, only local clan groups have rights to grazing and fodder collection. Members of the same clan group who live elsewhere do not have access to these lands, which are so controlled that specified areas are closed at specified seasons and others reserved for the winter, when large amounts of fodder are needed to feed livestock on the terraces.

Since 1989, there are no specific grazing rights in Sailung. *Chauri* herders pay annual taxes decided by the Village Development Committee (VDC) and the money is used for schools, roads and social welfare. In general, each herd has to pay US$ 16–20 annually. Sherpa herders from a neighbouring district use the rangelands in Sailung because only a few of the Sailung Tamang community keep *chauris*. Similarly in Thodung, an annual contribution of US$ 7–15 per herd is made to the VDC. The herds of Thodung graze in the administrations of Chuchure VDC, Bamti VDC and Gumdel VDC. Traditional demarcation in the use of grazing areas is still maintained.

The study was by interview, field survey and sample collection. Questionnaires were used to record information on stopover and camping points, duration of stay at different points, livestock and their production systems, breeding and calving patterns, health care and mortality, livestock products, productivity and marketing. Similarly, information was recorded on grazing systems, pasture conditions, toxic plants, grazing rights and socio-economic status. With the assistance of herders, grasses, legumes and forbs were identified in the field. Samples were pressed and carried to Kathmandu for identification. A 1 m² quadrat was used to assess green biomass production. Herbage production was assessed by clipping at 2.5 cm above the ground, and major species were recorded. Soil samples of about 1 kg, to 20 cm depth, were taken from 7 grazing areas. Standard sampling procedures were followed. For data on herd composition, 15 herdsmen in Sailung and 58 herdsmen in Thodung were contacted. For household size, literacy, cropping systems and their production, 15 herders in Sailung and 19 herders in Thodung were interviewed.

THE SAILUNG SYSTEM

Herding families have almost equal proportions of males and females: 57 percent are adult and 43 percent are young. Literacy is very low in males, 20 percent, and poor to negligible in females, 2.2 percent. Ten herdsmen own a total of 8.75 ha of cultivated land. Potatoes are a major crop. Among cereals, wheat, maize and finger millet are grown and annual yields are wheat – 3 tonne; maize – 5.4 tonne; and finger millet – 2.2 tonne. As families can grow only about

TABLE16.1
Sailung grazing lands.

Grazing area	Area (ha)	Elevation (m)	Aspect	Average slope (%)	Biomass (tonne/ha)
Baske	12	2 690	SW	10–12	2.7
Thulachulighati	8	2 750	NE	20–25	2.0
Kaberkaji	8	2 850	–	25–30	2.5
Panichour lower	10	2 600–2 650	EW	30–35	1.8
Jhakrithal	10	2 820	SW	20–25	1.0
Todkepani	9	2 820	W	35–40	3.5
Balbisani pani	11	2 970	N – W	35	1.8
Mulkharka	22	2 950	SE	10–20	1.4
Kholakharka	10	2 920	SE	40	1.2
Panichour upper	16	2 900–2 920	W	40	1.4
Thulochuli	9	2 820	EW	45	1.2
Dhanbir	8	2 600-2 900	E – S	40–45	n.a.
Dhodale	12	2 700-2 780	S – E	40–45	n.a.
Bagdhunga	25	3 100	S – E	40–45	n.a.

NOTE: n.a. = not available.

20 percent of their grain requirement, they are very dependent on *chauri* rearing.

Grazing areas are between 2 500 and 3 100 m in Sailung. They vary in size, elevation, aspect, slope and area. Grazing up to 2 800 m is in the vicinity of forest, while higher pastures are open and tree-less (Plate 63). Some characteristics of the grazing lands are described in Table 16.1. Soil samples from different grazing lands were analysed. Of the macro-elements, K_2O and N were high, but phosphorous was low; OM was high; and the soil was acid. The average pH value of the samples was 5.2 (range: 4.7–5.9), available K_2O was 538.95 kg/ha (range: 216–1 306 kg/ha), OM was 9.6 percent (range: 6.4–18.2 percent), total N was 0.43 percent (range: 0.29–0.92 percent) and available P_2O_5 was 18.22 kg/ha (range: 10.3–41.2 kg/ha).

The herding system

The route of each herd is fixed throughout the year. Three camping points are used by 16 herds in two major seasons: winter and summer. The camping points, based on their use, are winter (November to February), transitional while going up in March and April and returning in September and October, and summer camping in May to August. There are four distinct routes and, in general, three or four herds follow each route (Figure 16.1). Herds stay in the lower areas for about four months and spend four months in the highest areas. During their passage between seasonal grazing lands they use the transitional pastures (in March–April and September–October). The distance between camping points is about a walk of 1 to 2 hours. In summer and at transitional points, chauris graze lands of either camping point.

Chauris are the main stock and each herd contains about 20. Goats and sheep are kept for additional income, with an average herd having 4 goats and 4 sheep. Generally, three herds share a breeding bull; about half of the herders keep poultry. The main mating season for *chauris* is June–July; calving is in February–March. Although green feed is very scarce, farmers prefer calving then due to good returns from off-season production. For sheep and goats, three young in two years is common in highland pastoral areas. Lambing is generally in September–October and in March–April, particularly in the lower lands, where kidding twice a year is common. Occasional cases of mastitis and foot-and-mouth disease are seen in *chauris*. Lambs and kids are sometimes seriously affected by pneumonia.

Milk and dairy products are the major source of income. Milk is made into *chhurpi* and butter. During a lactation, lasting 8–9 months on average, a *chauri* gives 1.5 litre of milk daily in the peak period, and half a litre daily in the dry season. *Chhurpi* is made from skimmed milk. A *chauri* produces 15 kg of *chhurpi* and 19 kg butter per year; these are sold to intermediaries at US$ 2.13/kg and US$ 2.59/kg, respectively. *Chauris* are

rarely sold; calves are killed within three to seven days of birth to assure continued milk production. Sheep and goats are used domestically for meat. To establish a new herd, 10-20 *chauris* are bought from Solukhumbu District through traders; the cost per *chauri* is on the basis of age. A three- to five-year-old *chauri* costs US$ 200–250, and is kept up to 12 years of age.

Sheep are shorn twice yearly, using shears made locally, in February–March and September–October. An adult produces 500–700 g annually; the wool is used to make *radi* (blanket) and *pakhi* (carpet) for domestic use. Collection of manure from camping points of high altitude and transitional areas is not common. At winter camping points, villagers collect manure for their fields. Calf skins are used as bedding.

Plate 63.
Pastures grazed by chauris near Sailung at 3100 m in Ramechap District, Nepal. Note the high mountains in the distance.

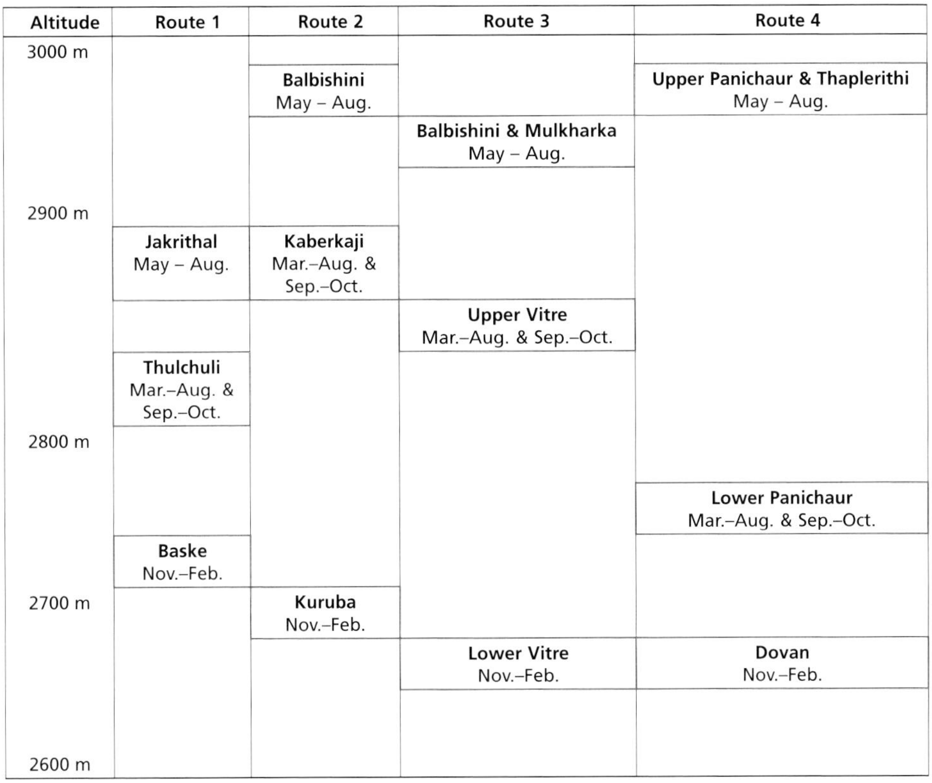

Altitude	Route 1	Route 2	Route 3	Route 4
3000 m				
		Balbishini May – Aug.		**Upper Panichaur & Thaplerithi** May – Aug.
			Balbishini & Mulkharka May – Aug.	
2900 m				
	Jakrithal May – Aug.	**Kaberkaji** Mar.–Aug. & Sep.–Oct.		
			Upper Vitre Mar.–Aug. & Sep.–Oct.	
	Thulchuli Mar.–Aug. & Sep.–Oct.			
2800 m				
				Lower Panichaur Mar.–Aug. & Sep.–Oct.
	Baske Nov.–Feb.			
2700 m		**Kuruba** Nov.–Feb.		
			Lower Vitre Nov.–Feb.	**Dovan** Nov.–Feb.
2600 m				

FIGURE 16.1
Routes and camping points of the Sailung herds.

There is no cheese factory, so milk is made into *chhurpi* and butter, which two contractors sell in Kathmandu; the herders have no marketing problems. The prices of *chhurpi* and butter are US$ 2.13/kg and US$ 2.59/kg respectively. An annual income of US$ 81.18 per *chauri* is obtained from dairy products over 7–8 months from April to October. Herd owner income is US$ 984 to US$ 2 460 annually, depending on herd size.

Ruminants are reared on forage from the grazing lands in a transhumant system. Rotational grazing is prevalent. In winter, grazing is short, 5–6 hours, while 8–9 hours is usual in summer. Herders bring *chauris* to camp for milking and they stay around the shed at night.

The *chauri* industry is based on grazing, but there is feed scarcity for three months (January–March) so at that time maize flour is boiled, cooled, mixed with salt and fed to animals. Lactating *chauris* are fed salt and flour daily. Each *chauri* receives about 40–50 kg of maize flour in a year.

Feeding tree fodder is very rare; it is given to *chauris* for 2 to 10 days after calving. There are few trees on grazing areas; fodder is lopped by villagers in winter; *chauri* herders have little chance to do so. The fodder trees are *Quercus* sp. (Plate 64), *sirlinge* (unidentified) and *sisi* (*Lindera pulcherrima*). Annual production is less than one *bhari* [30–40 kg] per tree from *Quercus* and one bhari from three to four sisi and sirlinge.

A total of 45 plant species were collected from the different grazing lands of Sailung. The dominant species were *Danthonia cachemiriana, Agrostis* sp., *Potentilla fulgens, Duchesnea indica,* and *Onychium* sp. Herbage estimation was done in four summer grazing areas, six transitional grazing areas and one winter grazing area, using 0.25 m² quadrats. On average, 1.9 tonne/ha of green herbage was available to the animals. Yield in cages was 9.4 tonne/ha in September. No weed or toxic plant problems were reported, although bloat sometimes occurs when

young leaves of *angeri* (*Lyonia ovalifolia*) and *chyatu* (*Chlorophytum* spp.) are eaten. Grazing lands are in poor condition as a result of overgrazing, with an increase of unpalatable shrubs and inedible plants lowering their productivity. There are no water point problems, except at Bagdhunga, a summer grazing area, where monsoon rain is the only source of water, while water scarcity is common in upper Panichur during April and May.

THE THODUNG SYSTEM

Herder families had 52 percent females and 48 percent males. The proportions of adults and young people were similar; average family size was 5.3. Literacy was poor: male literacy was 26 percent and female was 18 percent. Nineteen herdsmen owned 25.45 ha of cultivated upland (*bari* land – cultivated upland where most of

Plate 64.
Oak trees heavily lopped for fodder, Nepal.

TABLE 16.2
Thodung grazing lands.

Grazing area	Area (ha)	Elevation (m)	Aspect	Average Slope (%)	Soil pH
Chamru	18	2 950	SE	10–12	4.2
Camaru (Serding-2)	19	3 000	NW	10–15	4.4
Dhupi Kharka	25	3 600	N	40–45	4.5
Surke	12	2 890	NW	40–45	4.2
Thodung	15	3 170	NW	10–20	4.2
Dovan	15	3 450	SW	35–40	4.6
Serding-1	10	3 400	SW	5–10	4.2
Pancha Pokhari	12	4 000	NW	40–45	4.0
Bhirkarka (Sebuk)	15	3 170	NW	35–40	4.2
Pumnasa	11	3 450	NW	30–40	4.0
Gamigaps/Dumsetu	10	3 600	NW	35–45	4.2

the crops are grown, generally under rainfed conditions, but with supplementary irrigation in hard times) – an average of 1.27 ha for each family.

Maize, wheat, finger millet and potato were grown in the lower bari land (2 600–3 000 m) of the high altitude pastoral system under a well-thought-out management system: the cultivated area is demarcated according to the need and potential for growth. Maize is sown in February and harvested in August; wheat is then sown in the same plot in September and harvested in May. In another plot, finger millet is transplanted in June and harvested in November. In the third plot, potatoes are planted in January and harvested in August. This system is said to produce two crops in 18 months. Rotation of the area for maize and wheat and the area for potato is common. Cropping systems are different in the higher bari land (3 000–3 800 m), with one crop in a year; generally land is demarcated into cereal and potato areas. Wheat, naked barley or barley are sown in September and harvested in June. Potatoes are planted in January and harvested in September. In the household survey, maize, wheat,

finger millet and potato produced 3 271.2 kg, 4 384.8 kg, 1 060.8 kg, and 21 715.2 kg respectively, giving a cumulative total yield of 30 432 kg from 25.45 ha, equivalent to an annual production of 1 518.5 kg from each 1.27 ha family plot. An adult is considered to require 626 kg of cereal grain for a year (excluding milling waste and reserved seed), so family requirements (average family size = 5.3) are not met by crops (actual yield of 1 518.5 kg versus requirement of 5.3 × 626 = 3 318 kg, so only 46 percent of total food requirements is covered). This is the prime reason for the people moving towards enterprises generating more income, such as *chauri* rearing.

The grazing lands of Thodung are between 2 600 and 4 000 m (see Table 16.2). Altogether, 1 200–1 300 *chauris* from 60 herds use the vast grazing area. Grazing up to 2 800 m is in the vicinity of the forest, while higher areas are treeless grassland. Soil samples from seven grazing areas were analysed. The average pH was highly acid at 4.27 (range: 4.2–4.6). Available phosphorus (P_2O_5) was low, in the range of 14.2 to 30.05 kg/ha (average: 20.04 kg/ha). A full recommended dose

Altitude (m)	Route 1 Thodung	Route 2 Thodung	Route 3 Deurali	Route 4 Sebuk	Route 5 Chamru
4 200					
4 100					
4 000			Panch Pokhari		Panch Pokhari
3 900					
3 800					
3 700	Sawune		Pakhuri		Bhale Pokhari; Dovan
	Dhupi Kharka	Dhupi Kharka	Dhupi Kharka	Siran Katera	Dhupi Kharka
3 600	Gwasa	Danfebhir	Gairi; Dovan		Pakhuri; Gairi
		Pangjung			
3 500		Dovan			
		Gairi		Majh Katera	
3 400			Dumsetc		
			Serding		Serding
3 200			Sermiyo Gyang; Jambuk		
	Phaarmu; Balam	Trishuli; Kadbu			
3 100	Thodung	Thodung			
	Trishule; Sebuk	Chitre		Kosing Kharka	
3 000			Thodung		
			Phokate		
2 900			Chitre		
2 800		Nunthala: Tukding			
		Bhanjyang		Thotne Kharka	
2 700	Hille	Barse; Surke			Chamru
	Phokte				Jambuk
2 600				Devsthan	
				Nayaban	
2 500			Deurali		

FIGURE 16.2

The major stopover points and rangeland for the different grazing herds in high altitude areas of Thodung, Ramechap District, 1999.

of phosphorus would have to be applied to get optimum forage production from these lands. As is general in high altitude areas, average available potash and OM were high – 493.03 kg/ha and 11.02 percent, respectively. Texture varied from sandy loam to loamy sand.

The 60 herds use different grazing lands, moving by five distinct routes through the year. The stopover points of each herd are fixed. Herds following Route 1 have three stopovers, Routes 2 & 4 have four stopovers, while Routes 3 & 5 have five stopovers. Almost all herds spend 4–6 months in winter at low altitude, i.e. 2 600–2 800 m, and 2–4 months on transitional camping points at 2 900–3.200 m while going up in March–June and descending in September–October. The summer grazing season at 3 300–4 000 m is short, only 1–3 months in June–August (Figure 16.2). The 56 herders had a total of 1 279 chauris, 57 local breeding bulls and 78 goats. All the *chauris* were in milk and not a single sheep was kept, in contrast to the herd composition in Sailung, where sheep and fowls were kept, along with the *chauris*. Non-productive *chauris* were traded over the Tibetan border. On average, there were 22 *chauris*, 1 bull and 1.3 goats per herd.

To form a herd, herders go to Namche Bazaar and Khumjung in Solukhumbu and buy 12–18-month-old females, which are kept for another 18 months before mating. They calve at four years old. A *chauri* may be kept for 9–10 lactations, until it is 13–14 years old. Yield reduction is apparent from the ninth lactation. In general, herders sell *chauris* to Tibetan traders after the eighth lactation. Some herders purchase 18-month-old *chauris* for US$ 40–45, keep them to 6 years old, or for two lactations, then sell them for US$ 220–300 each.

The main mating season for *chauris* is in June–July, with calving in February–March. Again, farmers prefer calving during this period because of good returns from off-season production. With goats, three kids in two years is common in higher areas, with kidding twice a year common in the lower belt region.

Red water, mastitis and foot-and-mouth diseases are seen occasionally. Kids are seriously affected by pneumonia. Local herbs are used to treat the animals. Some death of *chauris* occurs due to falls from steep mountains, and in such cases it is traditional to spread the cost by sharing the meat among the herders.

Sale of fresh milk is the major source of income; there are three milk collection centres of the Dairy Development Corporation and three for private dairies. Collection centres have permanent infrastructure at different altitudes, with small, permanent sheds built from local materials, made by herders at stopovers. Milk collection centres are so sited that herders have to walk a maximum of two hours to deliver milk. The lactation of a *chauri* is about 240–270 days. Milk yield is around 3 litre/day in April–May, rising to 4–5 litre/day in June–August. Milk yields start to fall in September and about 1–1.5 litre/day per animal is obtained in December. Milk production of a *chauri* during a lactation of 270 days is estimated to be 630 litre. Sale price of milk is US$ 0.22/litre and the total income averages US$ 138.97 per animal per year. The average number of *chauri* in a herd is 22 and so annual income from milk sale is US$ 3 060. Almost half of this is spent on management, feed and medicine, so the net profit from a herd of 22 *chauri* is US$1 530.

The raw milk is sold daily, and the dairy subcentres make cheese, which is mostly sold in Kathmandu; some is sold to hotels, which resell to tourist agencies in Solukhumbu or to large expeditions. There is no market problem.

Chauri hair is not commonly collected, but *chamar* (*chauri* tails) are sold for religious ceremonies. They are classified according to colour: mixed (black and white – *til chamar*), brown (*khairo*), or whitish (*seto*). The price is around US$ 2.94–$11.76 per unit. Whitish *chamar* commands the highest price, followed by mixed, with brown the cheapest. *Chauri* hides are used as bedding.

Up to 3 200 m, dung is collected and stored, but above that it is difficult to collect, store and transport. It is stacked on the sward to dry then powdered and carried to the bari land in sacks or *thunse* (bamboo baskets). Even large amounts of manure can easily be transported thus; it is put in a pit to decompose for about a month before use.

Each *chauri* is given 50–100 g of salt weekly. Maize flour is fed at and after calving for two weeks; it is also fed to weak animals. A *chauri* is given 11 kg of maize flour annually; those of Thodung are sustained by forage, maize flour and salt. Medicines are rarely used. Opinions and grazing systems differ from those of Sailung graziers. Thodung herdsmen keep no sheep because they believe that, like *chauris*, sheep graze deep below the surface and compete for nutritious and palatable herbage. They prefer to keep goats, which browse and do not compete with *chauris* for forage. They believe that sheep urine and dung have a bad smell and *chauri* avoid soiled areas. Goats are grazed up to 3 200 m, and above that level the herd consists of chauris only.

Feeding tree fodder is very rare for the high altitude ruminants, although leaves and twigs of *Arundinaria* sp. (a shrub) and *Quercus semicarpifolia* (a tree) are fed for about 10 days after calving. These grow up to 3 100 m; annual fodder production from a *Quercus* tree is 30 kg, with about 810 kg from an *Arundinaria* plant.

A total of 47 native and naturalized plant species were collected from Thodung. Among them were a large number of forbs (25), followed by grasses (9), shrubs (8), trees (4), only one legume, and five species that could not be identified due to poor sample quality. There

were no native legumes in the pasture. *Trifolium repens* cv. Huia was introduced in 1974–75. It is still productive within the protected areas of milk collection centres. At some stopover places and due to rotational grazing, white clover is still growing well.

Herbage recording was done in nine randomly selected grazing areas situated at altitudes of 2 800, 3 100 and 3 300 m. Three samples of 1 m² were taken from each area. In addition to open grassland, data were also recorded from the fenced area of Thodung Milk Collection Centre. From 2 800 to 3 300 m, little difference in vegetation was found; the predominant species at 3 300 m were *Danthonia* sp., *Pogonatherum paniceum* and *Anaphalis contortus*. Green matter yield was 500 kg/ha at the first cut in May–June 1999. Three cuts can be taken in the growing season of May–August, giving an average annual yield of 1.5 tonne/ha of available green forage; the yield under cages was much higher. In open grassland at 3 170 m, the dominant species were *Danthonia* sp., *Pogonatherum paniceum*, *Trifolium repens* and a mixture of other species; they produced almost 2.8 tonne/ha (based on an average of three cuts in a growing season). However, in the fenced area, the dominant species were *Pogonatherum paniceum*, *Danthonia* sp., *Trifolium repens*, *Caltha palustris*, *Anaphalis contortus* and *Galium aparine*, and these species yielded 7.0 tonne/ha of green matter (based on an average of three cuts in a growing season).

In the lower altitude rangelands of Derail–Yaknagi, *Anaphalis contortus*, *Pogonatherum paniceum* and *Anaphalis margaritacea* were dominant and yielded 2.4 tonne/ha (based on an average of three cuts in a growing season).The vegetation cover in grazing lands around 2 800 m was 40–70 percent; at 3 170 m (open grassland) it was 60–70 percent; and at 3 300 m it was 70–90 percent.

There was an acute problem of toxic plants, principally *jukabikh* (*Anemone elongata*), *choto* (*Chlorophytum* sp.) and *bulu* (*Pieris formosa*). Herders rate *Chlorophytum* sp. as very dangerous to all ruminants. *Chauris* and goats die within two hours of eating it and there is no effective local treatment; it is fatal to newly arrived *chauris* because they lack selectivity and graze *Chlorophytum*; acclimatized stock avoid it. Seemingly, young *Chlorophytum* sp. – which resembles *halhale* (*Rumex nepalensis*) at a younger stage – is much more dangerous than old, semi-dried plants. As *Chlorophytum* is increasing rapidly and invading some grazing lands, herders have requested assistance to eradicate it. *Anemone elongata* and *Pieris formosa* are much less toxic and rarely has an animal died after eating them, but they cause bloat and indigestion which lasts for at least three days, resulting in decreased milk production.

The condition of grazing is poor to medium. At low altitudes (2 600–2 800 m), where animals stay almost six months, overgrazing is common. There is much more pressure on grazing lands up to 2 700 m because these areas are also grazed regularly by the livestock of a lower belt. Grazing lands at this altitude in Sailung are close to the villages and therefore are extensively used by water buffaloes and cattle in summer, up to 2 830 m. In winter, *chauris* are brought to lower altitudes because of snow cover at the higher elevations. Vegetation cover of lower grazing lands (2 600–3 400 m) is 60–70 percent. The degree of utilization is over 90 percent to Thodung (Routes 1 & 2), Phokate (Route 3), Koshi Kharka (Route 4) and Serding (Route 5). Due to favourable climatic condition, easy access for materials and easy stay, herds stay for long periods (8–10 months).

Grazing lands above 3 400 to 4 000 m are not overgrazed and contain a palatable native plant called *tapakir* (*Caltha palustris*). The degree of utilization is less than 50 percent. Due to the harsh climate, difficult access for materials and difficult living conditions, herds remain in this belt for a shorter period (2–3 months). There is no problem of watering points in the major grazing lands. The VDC has helped the herders by constructing trails and drinking water facilities, and charges herders an annual contribution of US$7.35–14.7 per herd.

CONSTRAINTS AND SUGGESTIONS
Major constraints identified
- *Toxic plants* Invasion of the grazing lands by *Jukabih* (*Anemone elongata*), *Chlorophytum* sp. and *Pieris formosa* is a major concern of the herders in Thodung. Occasional death due to *Chlorophytum* has occurred in new stock, and its instant fatal effect has led to economic loss in *chauri* herds.
- *Overgrazing* There is an overgrazing problem below 2 900 m, where buffaloes from lowland villages also graze to 2 830 m.
- *Low productivity of pasture* Although there are large areas of grazing, its productivity is poor. Absence of legumes and low productivity of native species could be due to lack of proper protection coupled with overexploitation (1 200 *chauris*), resulting in loss of soil

fertility. Regrowth of the grasses is poor due to overstocking.

- *Animal diseases* Red water, mastitis, foot-and-mouth disease, and pneumonia are the main diseases.

Suggestions by herders

- An effective initiative should be taken by government to eradicate toxic plants, and Village Development Committees should bring this the notice of District Offices.
- An orientation programme should be launched or training organized to create awareness among the herders towards finding ways to improve and sustain rangeland productivity.
- A study should be carried out on the introduction of high yielding native species, as well as improved low-fertility-demanding forages, applying an Integrated Research and Development Approach, in which system extension workers, scientists and users share equally all responsibilities.
- The herders should receive training in animal health care, in parallel with introducing an effective animal health treatment programme through District Level Offices of the Department of Livestock Services (DLS).
- There should be clear demarcation between forest and grazing land. The grazing should be managed by users' groups, actively supported by the Department of Livestock Services and the Nepal Agricultural Research Council, for better use and higher productivity.

Chapter XVII
Future directions

SUMMARY

Two kinds of transhumant systems have developed under different geographical conditions. Those in the Himalaya overwinter in lower, warm areas; in cold semi-arid Asia they have no access to warm pastures. Grassland is by far the most important vegetation type; browse is important in the subtropical end of Himalayan systems. Cyperaceae form a major part of the forage in the highest areas, especially in yak grazing. Lack of clarity in grazing rights was identified as a serious problem; this has been exacerbated in those countries that earlier had collectivized extensive stock rearing, since livestock were distributed at decollectivization without definition of grazing rights. Methods of decollectivization varied, as has their impact on the herding industry. Conflict of interests between settled farmers and herders is increasing with rising population pressure and intensification of agriculture throughout the Himalayan zone.

Poor pasture condition figures highly among technical constraints. Since there is no base data, the evolution of degradation can only be guessed; there is a serious need for more monitoring of pasture condition and trends as a management tool, and to measure environmental impact. Winter and spring feed are major problems and winter shelter is highly desirable in cold semi-arid areas. Water supply is a local problem. Fire is little used as a pasture management tool and does not seem to be a serious problem.

Technical problems are not the main ones facing transhumant herding; the major ones are socio-economic. The importance of clarifying problems of grazing rights is overweening. The "technical" approach that has been advocated for improving extensive pastures and livestock production in the past has not been successful, and in most cases an integrated methodology would be needed. Educational levels among herding communities in the study areas vary greatly but it is not obvious that the level of literacy affects the main traditional herding skills. In the Himalaya, herders were generally perceived as being poor, but in cold semi arid Asia they are in the mainstream population and are not a poor group. The studies have shown that most of the usual technical "grassland" suggestions for improving pasture management and herding productivity (better grazing management, reseeding with high-yielding species and herder training) are impracticable, although localized fodder production is an option in some areas.

INTRODUCTION

The main methods of improving pasture condition involve manipulation of grazing pressure and grazing management. It is necessary, therefore, that the grazing rights to the land involved be clear, that the necessary laws and regulations be in force and that the mechanisms exist to see that they are respected. Application of regulations for improvement – such as only grazing land at the correct season and regulating the overall stocking rate – require the agreement and compliance of all who have rights to graze a particular piece of land. Participatory methods are indicated, but the whole issue may be very complicated. Where the human population is dense, and the pasture – even correctly managed – cannot provide a reasonable livelihood, it is very difficult to get agreement on destocking. Throughout most of the area there is lack of information on pasture condition and trends, although China has just completed a national grassland survey; even areas are often only approximately known. If management of grazing land is to be improved, more information is required for both planning of work and monitoring vegetation trends. Transhumant systems are potentially less damaging than sedentary ones because they exploit the herbage at fixed seasons, and leave it to recover for the remainder of the growing season. While many herders would prefer a more settled life, and many governments would like to settle nomads, alternative employment would have to be found; in the Himalayan context this would mean finding livelihoods in a labour market that is already oversupplied; in the cold semi-arid zone, extensive herding seems to be the only practical way of earning a living from the land. It is likely that transhumant herding will continue for many years yet. In the Himalaya zone, the settled stockowners who use the same pastures as transhumants have considerable opportunity for improving feed supply through growing hay crops.

Two very different kinds of transhumant herding systems have been identified, which have developed under different geographical conditions. Those in the Himalayan region can overwinter in lower, warm areas, but in cold semi-arid Asia they have no access to warm winter pastures. The Himalayan group have followed their ancient routes more or less undisturbed (except for increas-

ing encroachment by sedentary farmers), whereas all the herding industry of cold Asia was collectivized for a large part of the twentieth century and decollectivization has only taken place in the past two decades: there the reconstruction of herding systems is still ongoing.

Transhumant systems are an efficient way of using extensive grazing land that cannot be exploited in a sustainable manner by sedentary agriculture, as well as for making use of highly seasonal pastures, notably alpine grasslands. Provided that the basic rules of grassland management concerning stocking and movement are observed, transhumance is a far more ecologically friendly way of grazing than the uncontrolled grazing practised by sedentary groups where these overlap with transhumants – as in the Himalayas.

Herders mostly keep mainly local breeds of livestock. Attempts at "improvement" have had little impact, except sometimes with cattle, since exotic stock are less hardy and do not travel as well as local landraces. In cold semi-arid Asia, multispecies herds are the norm (although the species may be herded separately) and horses are important both for riding and as a source of food. In the Himalaya, herding groups tend to specialize in either large or small ruminants, and equines are unimportant. Yaks are kept where conditions are too cold for other cattle and feed is adequate.

THE PASTURES

There is a wide range of pasture types over the great area involved; they are described in the individual studies. Grassland is by far the most important vegetation type; browse is locally important in the subtropical end of Himalayan systems, both as forest grazing and from trees retained in arable land. Herbaceous pasture legumes are generally scarce, although they are important in some high-altitude sites in Pakistan; elsewhere they probably suffer from a dry pedoclimate or low soil fertility, or both; Trifolium spp., as well as Lotus, Medicago and Trigonella, are present throughout the region on favoured sites. Technicians in the Himalayan zone seem particularly interested in the scarcity of legumes. Non-gramineous plants are, however, very important as forage. Cyperaceae form a major part of the grazing in the highest areas, especially in yak grazing. Artemisia spp. are very important throughout the drier areas, according to species, both as browse and invasive pasture weeds. While trees are unimportant as fodder in the cold semi-arid zone, they are – where present – very useful for shelter, as well as their other uses: fuelwood and timber.

MAJOR PROBLEMS AND CONSTRAINTS
Legal and land tenure problems
Land tenure, or lack of clarity in grazing rights, were identified as a serious problem in most of the Himalayan zone, although less so in Bhutan. There are traditional rights in most areas. In some of the temperate tracts of India and Pakistan, these rights were documented over a century ago at the time of land settlement, but much has changed since then, including vast increases in the settled population and in the proportion of land under crops. For land under the jurisdiction of Forest Departments, laws and regulations on access, stock numbers, timing of grazing and grazing fees were enacted long ago, but regulations have little effect unless there is both political and popular will to enforce

them. Fees have remained minimal and no attempt has been made to keep them in line with present values. The problems of land tenure in countries that collectivized extensive stock rearing are discussed below; in most cases livestock were distributed at decollectivization long before any attempt was made to define grazing rights.

Impact of political and social change
There have been many political and social changes throughout the region during the past century, which have had an impact on herding and transhumance. The collectivization, and subsequent decollectivization, of livestock in the communist era had a marked effect, as described in Chapter II – the end result varied from country to country but, in general, those systems that maintained mobility and used hardy landraces have proved the most sustainable. Border closure to transhumant herds, as has occurred between Nepal and China, has increased grazing pressure on many Nepali pastures – but has probably protected Chinese ones. The disputed territories of Jammu and Kashmir are great areas of transhumant stock rearing; the troubles since partition must have had an effect on migration routes, although it has not kept herders from using the alpine pastures. Prolonged civil war in Afghanistan initially led to most of the livestock leaving the country, but herd numbers in both the settled and transhumant sector rapidly returned to normal once conditions in the countryside became quieter, so peace is not a prerequisite for herding – especially when borders are open to herds moving to market.

In central and northern Asia, livestock ownership has been privatized but grazing resources have not, and the problems of grazing and hay-cutting rights (and maintenance of grazing resources) have still to be resolved.

Conflict of interests between settled farmers and herders is increasing with rising population pressure and intensification of agriculture throughout the Himalayan zone. This is clearly described in one of the Pakistan studies, where agricultural and silvicultural development, with a double role of income generation and catchment protection, has been very successful in achieving its own aims, but has simultaneously created many barriers to traditional transhumance.

Changes due to decollectivization

Most of the countries of the cold semi-arid zone underwent a period of collective agriculture. Political and economic changes towards the end of the twentieth century resulted in decollectivization everywhere. The methods of decollectivization varied, as did the impact on the herding industry.

In Mongolia and Kyrgyzstan, stock were distributed to members of the collectives without much thought for the impact on management or to distribution of grazing rights or to assuring technical and marketing support for the livestock industry. The results have been generally unsatisfactory. Mongolian herders are currently suffering great economic difficulties, with problems in obtaining veterinary and other services, and grazing disputes are common. Fear of losing winter grazing land is disturbing transhumance routes since some herders are afraid to go too far lest squatters take over traditional winter camps.

The Kyrgyz livestock industry, which had become dependent on imported feed

and "improved" but less hardy breeds, has almost collapsed. China took a more positive approach and codified the use and allocation of extensive grazing land. The Xinjiang case study describes a different approach, where areas of land throughout the transhumance system are leased to households, who are obliged to manage them correctly to retain the lease, on a "family responsibility" system. Services have been maintained. The Tibet and all-China studies indicate that the national preference is for sedentarization, even on lands of very low carrying capacity.

TECHNICAL CONSTRAINTS
Poor pasture condition

This is widespread and is due to overstocking and poor management techniques. Much of the overstocking is due to increases in human population and a lack of alternative means of earning a livelihood. Mismanagement is exacerbated by lack of defined rights to grazing, by lack of grazing rules to assure proper land use or by lack of will to apply either. Degradation varies from changes in the specific composition, through drop in yield, to invasion by undesirable plants and erosion.

Winter and early spring are problem seasons throughout the area. Systems vary in their ways of dealing with the problem. Some make hay, but usually in quantities wholly inadequate to do more than provide some roughage to assist survival of a few weak stock. Those that are in contact with agricultural areas may have access, usually for payment, to crop residues, stubble grazing and grain. The Himalayan systems overwinter in areas of mild climate where there is usually browse and some grazing, as well as agricultural land. The systems of the steppe, however, have no natural winter forage resource and traditionally have had to rely on getting their stock fat enough to survive the winter.

In the cold zone there are two situations: systems that rely on grazing, with very little feed other than grazing – fattening their stock in autumn to survive winter and spring, of which Mongolia is the classic example; and those other systems that use, or have used, large quantities of supplementary feed. Supplementary feeding, whatever its economics, is obviously beneficial to the livestock; it keeps them in good condition through winter and early spring; it should reduce losses and allow the overwintering of larger numbers of stock. It reduces the amount of forage grazed and is not additive to grazing.

The environmental impact of winter feeding of transhumant herds, however, is often very negative. In systems totally dependent on grazing, overall numbers tend to be kept in check by how many can be overwintered. When concentrates are fed, however, large numbers can be maintained through the lean season. This greatly increases the pressure on the grazing land, especially if the livestock are allowed to graze before the herbage has fully recovered in spring, which is, unfortunately, often the case. Winter feeding seems to have been largely responsible for the serious degradation of Kyrgyzstan's pastures during the collective period, and may be a contributing factor to pasture problems in Inner Mongolia.

Extreme examples of the effect of the negative impact of concentrate feeding can be found in some semi-desert grazing lands of western Asia. Jordan is one example (Al Jaloudy, 2001). Subsidized cereals were made available to herders and this greatly increased their capacity for overwintering. In addition cheap fuel and open country allowed transport of water, feed and sometimes the stock, and allowed grazing wherever rain had brought on a flush of green. Previously, the duration of grazing had been limited by the availability of drinking water and the speed at which flocks could walk. Vast areas of grazing have been destroyed in this manner. The constant use of motor transport on fragile vegetation is also very damaging. Winter feeding has a definite role in transhumant systems, but it must be used in a rational manner.

Winter shelter is important in the cold-semi-arid zone, where herders cannot migrate to milder areas in winter. Natural shelter, through correct selection of winter campsites, is of primary importance, considering aspect, seeking foothill valleys with some protection from wind, and using forests. The value of artificial shelters has been well demonstrated in many areas during collective times, and there is a strong need for such shelters to be repaired and maintained.

Other technical constraints

Poisonous plants are mentioned in many of the studies, but nowhere seem to be a serious problem, although transhumant stock unfamiliar with such vegetation may be more susceptible than those that graze the same land all the time. Predators are a problem in some areas – with conflicts of interest between conservationists and herders.

Poor access to services – especially veterinary – and to good breeding stock is mentioned in several studies, with the problem varying greatly in intensity between countries. Veterinary care can probably not be expected to extend to the highest alpine pastures, but herders have a right to access to routine vaccination and facilities when on more accessible parts of their routes. No serious incidences of disease were reported, but the transition from free, state-supplied care to private causes double problems in some countries: herders are unwilling to pay for what they had become used to receiving free, and veterinarians find it difficult to make a living in areas of extensive stock rearing.

Transport of tentage and equipment is very labour demanding in those areas where motorized transport was once supplied by the state, and herders now have to use pack animals or pay for lorry hire.

SOCIO-ECONOMIC CONSTRAINTS

Technical problems are not usually the main ones facing transhumant herding. The major ones are socio-economic. The overweening importance of clarifying problems of grazing rights has been discussed above. The "technical" approach that has been advocated for improving extensive pastures and livestock production in the past has not been successful, and in most cases an integrated methodology would be needed. This would involve not only technicians, but also the administration to provide a suitable legal framework, and sociologists to deal with the organization of the herders and other groups involved. This is not a traditional approach and would require, amongst other hard tasks, the training of sociologists in the basics of pasture, land and livestock management.

Educational levels among herding communities in the study areas vary greatly. Mongolian herders have all completed at least junior secondary school and are among the most literate in Asia. Chinese herders also generally have a good standard of literacy. In the Himalayas, herders are minority groups and generally have less access to schooling than do settled farmers in the same area, and their level of literacy is very low. It seems to improve from west to east. It is not obvious that the level of literacy affects the main traditional herding skills, although it could hinder any training programmes that might develop. Low educational levels, of course, limit access to outside employment and, perhaps, to markets.

In the Himalayan studies, herders were generally perceived as being poor. No direct comparisons are made, however, with settled, subsistence cultivators in the hill tracts. Herders certainly have a hard lifestyle and can carry few possessions, but they do have considerable capital in their herds. With a series of good years, they can accumulate wealth to invest in, amongst others, land. The groups studied generally owned medium-sized flocks; larger flockmasters may be quite rich and even employ shepherds for the transhumance while carrying on some other business, including stock trading. In cold semi-arid Asia, herders are in the mainstream population and are not a poor group.

MARKETING

Technical improvements in livestock production must be accompanied by adequate marketing facilities if they are to lead to better livelihoods for the producers. Therefore marketing will have to be kept in mind in any programme of grazing management improvement. Marketing of stock and produce was a problem in many of the areas studied. The Nepal study was different in that the specialist milk producers were linked to cheese making or marketing organizations. Groups far from main markets complain of lack of infrastructure and unscrupulous dealers – a complaint heard in many other stock-rearing zones. Absence or breakdown of trekking routes is also a problem locally. Loss of or diminution in processing capacity is also having adverse effects. In the cold semi-arid zone, large volumes of stock are slaughtered in autumn, so abattoirs with freezing capacity are necessary to handle this; the system was well organized, allied to trekking stock over large distances, but financial difficulties have reduced capacity and this affects offtake.

World markets for meat and wool are, at present, depressed; this is clearly felt even in remote herding areas. Wool in particular is affected, and most of that produced by herding systems is short, rather coarse and dirty; it cannot compete with imports from Oceania. In Afghanistan, mechanized wool-washing facilities have ceased to function; now traditional hand-knotted carpets are being made from Oceanian wool imported via Pakistan – although local wool may be used for the carpet web.

CONCLUSIONS BY ZONE
Conclusions from the Himalayan studies

The main conclusions of the series of Himalayan studies were brought together at the Meeting of the Working Group, held in Peshawar in June 2001. They are summarized by Morrison (2000b):

- Overuse is a common feature and range condition is generally poor.
- Forage production is low, partly as a consequence of a short growing season.
- Alpine pasture contributes only a small

part of annual feed (ca 30 percent) in goat/sheep and cattle migratory systems, but in the chauri (yak hybrid) systems subalpine pastures are used for year-long grazing.

- Seasonal feed shortages, mainly in late winter and the early part of the grazing season, are common and critical.
- Changes are occurring – e.g. reduction in herd size – and pastoralists are becoming sedentary – e.g. Pakistan and India.
- Migration – more detailed knowledge of livestock and household movement has been collected.
- Grazing rights – information has been recorded on traditional grazing rights, but the studies have also exposed uncertainties about these traditional grazing rights.

Several gaps were identified in the information available.

- There is need for more information on growth in exclosure cages to measure response to specific periods of defoliation and rest for the determination of stocking rates and formulation of site-specific improved range management practices.
- Better identification is needed of opportunities for fodder intervention – oversowing for fodder banks or pasture improvement and integration of sown fodder on arable land.
- There is a lack of cost-effective methods for controlling unwanted plants.
- Clarity is needed in grazing rights and land ownership so that communities and households have the appropriate rights to manage and benefit from their range resources.

The views of herders were recorded in some studies. They would welcome "improved" seeds for oversowing, provided that the government provides them. None are willing to pay higher grazing fees. All would like to see reduction in weeds and more veterinary attention.

The Himalayan studies overall have shown that most of the usual technical "grassland" suggestions for improving pasture management and herding productivity are impracticable. Common suggestions are: better grazing management, reseeding with high-yielding species; and providing herder training. However, any management improvement would require major changes in the present vague allocation of grazing rights (especially in some of the cases where two or three very different groups use the same land at different seasons). Reseeding could only be done if all the management faults that caused the degradation had been resolved and suitable ecotypes of desirable forages identified, tested and seed supplies assured – before deciding on the economic sustainability of the activity and the operational problems of reseeding in very inaccessible regions on steep slopes. As to training, what can a technician tell a herder who has no real secure right to land nor protection from trespass? Herders probably know full well the grosser faults of their practices: grazing too early in spring, overstocking, and so on, but usually they have no choice but to feed their stock as they can today since they have not the finance to plan for the longer term.

Pasture condition in the Hindu-Kush-Himalaya

Most of the case studies from the Hindu-Kush-Himalaya state that pastures are generally in poor condition; this may not apply to all the pastures of the zone but most are said to be seriously overstocked.

The causes of pasture degradation are the usual ones associated with poor pasture management: overstocking, putting stock to graze too early in spring before there is adequate herbage growth and keeping them on pasture too late in the season (where there is no snow cover); grazing every available piece of pasture all the time without spelling may also cause damage; the stock of sedentary owners may be more culpable than those of transhumants, since the latter move seasonally. Further degradation of the vegetation is caused by excessive felling of trees, and uprooting of shrubs for fuelwood and harvesting of medicinal herbs.

Many of the middle-altitude hay lands in the Himalayas are closed to grazing throughout their growing season and only mown at the end of the monsoon. This probably explains why they generally maintain a good cover, generally of a few grasses (Chrysopogon is often prominent), with very few herbaceous legumes since these are shaded out by the management regime.

Some of the studies, notably that from Nepal, record very high stocking rates indeed. Many countries and localities have grazing rules and regulations, often old but quite logically formulated and designed to maintain the natural vegetation while allowing livestock production to continue along traditional lines, especially in forest areas. It is clear, however, that these have little effect in controlling stock numbers or in improving grazing management. Rules are not a solution in themselves, they require the means for their application and a political will, at all levels, to see that they are respected.

Fortunately, it appears that most of the pastures are quite resilient and respond to resting, so management changes could be used as a means of improving their vegetative cover. The effect of short-term protection has been shown in many of the enclosed versus open cutting trials. Another demonstration of rapid regrowth of rested pasture was that of Afghanistan during the troubles, when most of the livestock had left the country.

Manipulation of grazing pressure and management is only likely to affect the pasture vegetation – improvement of the tree layer may be more difficult.

Conclusions from the Cold Semi-Arid studies

The systems are almost purely pastoral with little or no interaction with crop-growing groups. The thermal growing season over most of the zone is too short to allow easy crop production or the use of sown forage. Extensive, mobile herding of mixed herds, using hardy landraces, is the traditional, and most sustainable strategy. Survival through winter and early spring is mainly assured by having the stock as fat as possible, through skilful grazing, in autumn.

The Mongolian studies describe how migration routes develop to suit the terrain, climate, available grazing and livestock types. They also show how political change, and lack of attribution of grazing rights, can have a disruptive effect on migration patterns, leading to overuse and unseasonable grazing of some areas while others are underused. The second study demonstrates the feasibility of making hay from natural vegetation, by herders, using simple equipment. It also showed, however, that yields are generally low and only some hay for emergency use could be produced. This technology, however, is only suited to some zones, notably the

mountain steppe, and to situations where hay land is close to where the hay will be required, the spring and winter camps. In the mountain steppe, transhumance distances are usually short and meadows relatively abundant.

Conserved winter feed is usually limited, therefore, to a small amount of mediocre hay. The Altai study describes the effect of introducing quite large amounts of high quality legume hay into the winter feeding of transhumant stock. Not surprisingly, the effects are very positive. However, the situation of the project is special: abundant water for irrigation is available and the hay growing area in the Junggar Depression is at much lower altitudes than most of the zone and with a growing season of about six months. The abysmally low average hay yield attained by herders, compared to the crop's proven performance in the area, confirms that it is not easy to convert herders to competent farmers in a short time.

POSSIBILITIES FOR PASTURE IMPROVEMENT – FEASIBILITY

The management of natural pasture, especially in areas with unclear title to land and grazing rights, is complicated both legally and technically. Sometimes, as in many of the Himalayan studies, grazing land is interspersed with forest and both land uses have to be taken into consideration. Protection of catchments and minimizing damage to and siltation of downstream works may also be an issue, although these are probably of little direct interest to the users of mountain grazing. Attempts at "improvement" of grazing are futile without rectifying the management faults that are to blame for the initial damage.

The main practical methods of improving pasture condition involve manipulation of grazing pressure and grazing management. It is necessary, therefore, that the grazing rights to the land involved be clear, that the necessary laws and regulations be in force and that the mechanisms exist to see that they are respected. Application of regulations for improvement, such as only grazing land at the correct season and regulating the overall stocking rate, require the agreement and compliance of all who have right to graze a particular piece of land – participatory methods are indicated, but the whole issue may be very complicated. Where the human population is dense, and the pasture even correctly managed cannot provide a reasonable livelihood, it is very difficult to get agreement on destocking.

If pasture improvement (or arrest and reversal of degradation) is to be brought about on a large scale, and catchment protection considerations would often indicate the desirability of this, then a very broad and integrated approach would be needed. The legal framework would have to be in place, the interests of all users – local graziers, transhumant herders, foresters, wildlife and those downstream who benefit from better flood control – would have to be taken into account. Where the land is no longer sufficient to support an increased human population, then the authorities will have to tackle the problem of providing alternative livelihoods – this may include, as is being done in parts of the Northern Areas of Pakistan, education and training of the youth so that they can seek employ elsewhere. Particular care would also have to be taken to see that localized development and improvement does not bar transhumance routes.

Control of stock numbers in a particular area notoriously just moves most of the stock elsewhere to cause more damage – this could only be dealt with by planning on very large areas indeed.

Accurate and detailed information on many technical matters is essential in planning improvement work. In addition to the pasture-animal complex, many social factors have to be taken into account, as well as forest and livestock matters. From the pasture point of view, present management systems, vegetation composition, condition and trends over time, stock numbers and condition, other land uses and many other details must be known, and usually information from those isolated areas is fragmentary at best. Point-of-time surveys of vegetation may assist in project formulation, but they do not represent a solid enough foundation for making serious interventions in the management of large areas of vegetation. As Pratt (1997) points out:

> *Participatory Rural Appraisal (PRA) may suffice to get a process project started, letting monitoring data guide subsequent inputs, but embarking on development in a state of relative ignorance is always a high-risk strategy.*

INTERVENTIONS ON GRAZING LANDS IN THE LIGHT OF CONSTRAINTS INVOLVED

Can pasture condition and productivity be improved under the conditions of the production systems described in the studies?

In the Himalaya

Several authors propose herder training. During early discussions of the FAO Temperate Asia Pasture and Fodder

Working Group, many participants were keen on re-seeding with "high-yielding forages". Interventions like overseeding and fertilization, even if they had a chance of being profitable, could only have a positive effect once the defects in the management which brought about the deterioration had been rectified! While fertilizer application would have a positive effect on yield (no information is available on what long-term effect it might have on species composition over time) it is impossible that it could be profitable on the grazing land as a whole; transporting fertilizer to and spreading it on steep, broken terrain far from motorable roads makes such an operation almost impossible. No cultivars suitable for reseeding of high altitude grazing land have been identified, and any disturbance of the natural vegetation is liable to do more harm than good. Collection of native pasture ecotypes is possible, but collection in itself does not mean that these ecotypes are suitable for reseeding, nor that their seed could be produced cheaply and in quantity.

Targeted sowing of forage on bottom land for hayfields, or close to dwellings, may be locally feasible on protected, privately- or group-owned land. Some experience of reseeding is mentioned in the studies on the eastern Himalaya (where rainfall is higher): failure was common but causes are not given, other than unprotected plots being grazed continually and excessively from the time of their emergence.

Herder training in pasture management also seems to have little promise at present in the Himalayan zone. Technicians have little of practical use to tell them. Grazing management will be difficult to improve until such time as problems of grazing

rights and control of stock numbers are dealt with by the authorities. Most of the problems associated with overpopulated land are not technical. Some improvement of social organization may be possible, through a fully participatory approach to discussing grazing management and rights, but with severe overpopulation, several communities involved – both settled and transhumant, and sometimes land rights belonging to third parties, this will not be easy.

For cold semi-arid areas

In this zone, pastoral lands are usually large and discrete; there is little or no interaction with agricultural and agropastoral groups. Because of the climate, transhumance routes cannot avoid the severe winters, and opportunities for production and conservation of fodder are also limited. Therefore, herding systems must rely on optimum use of the natural pasture to ensure survival of herds through winter and spring.

The zone has seen considerable political change over the past century and this has had a marked effect in breaking down traditional herding systems and social organization. India and Pakistan also saw vast political changes with independence, but this does not seem to have had a very marked effect on their herding communities as they are marginal to the mainstream. The effects of decollectivization have varied according to the country, as described in Chapter II. All attempts at improvement involve organization of grazing management – in the widest sense – and some social organization.

The Chinese option, described in Chapter V, is allocation of land on contract; reseeding and investment in infrastructure, including fencing, is encouraged. This is supported by a considerable technical and research establishment, at both national and local levels.

Mongolia is typical of areas where extensive, mobile systems have been maintained. Stock numbers have risen since decollectivization, but there are technical and social problems; grazing rights have yet to be allocated, herders are not yet socially organized, and only collaborate at the level of small groups. A large class of urbanized rural poor has arisen, including "new herders" who lost administrative and technical jobs on the disbanding of the cooperatives, but that is not a problem with a technical solution.

Where grazing must be very extensive and mobile, it is essential that herders be so organized socially that they can agree on the overall management of vast areas of land within a "four season" system, avoiding trespass and conflict while still maintaining the flexibility necessary for risk avoidance in bad seasons. In parts of Mongolia there is collaboration on herding tasks by small groups, but there is still a vast task to organize the entire herding population.

Reseeding and artificial pastures are not an option in the harsher parts of the zone. Sown fodder would only be possible under oasis conditions, such as the project described for Xinjiang Altai, and some areas of western Mongolia, where some irrigated lucerne has been grown. In the rare situations where such production is possible, its improvement merits study. Haymaking is being greatly encouraged by the Mongolian authorities, but the areas are limited where this can be done profitably by herders. It can be encouraged where suitable vegetation is available

and where hay can be made close to where it is needed – winter and spring camps.

Need for more information on vegetation and trends

A common feature throughout most of the area is the lack of real information on pasture condition and trends, although China has just completed a national grassland survey. Even areas are often only approximately known. Pasture surveys are often only local, conducted for a specific project, and lack follow-up to determine pasture trends. In some cases where surveys have been carried out they are now out of date. Pasture deterioration is reported in many of the studies; this is almost certainly true, but there are no baseline data to confirm it. If management of natural grazing land is to be improved, then more information is required for both planning of work and monitoring vegetation trends. On the scale and topography of the lands involved, this would be a vast task, which would have to be organized at national level.

The need for more information is particularly acute in those areas, like the Himalaya, which are important watersheds and where the impact of grazing in not only local but can affect land and infrastructure far down the catchment. The deleterious effects of flooding and siltation may cross national boundaries, such as much of Nepal's flood water. In such cases, the cost of survey, and much of the rectification of deteriorated vegetation cover, could not be met by the herders alone and funding would have to take into account beneficial environmental effects.

Environmental impact

Do transhumant systems differ from sedentary ones in their impact on the pastoral environment? They are potentially less damaging than sedentary systems because they exploit the herbage at fixed seasons, often at the peak of its production, and leave the vegetation to recover for the remainder of the growing season. Like all grazing systems, however, their impact on the herbage depends on the stocking rate, the timing of grazing and the length of time for which the livestock remain on the pasture. Since there has generally been little monitoring of pasture condition and composition, especially in the more remote grazing areas, except for local and usually short studies, the evidence for pasture degradation is anecdotal, but in many places damage is so severe that it cannot be denied.

Pasture degradation is usually even worse along transhumance routes than on the summer pastures. Where herders traverse settled areas, as in the Himalayan zone, they are often blamed for destruction of the pastoral vegetation but, in almost all cases, the settled population has risen greatly during the past century and their flocks and herds have increased in proportion. Transhumant stock pass fairly rapidly through transit areas: sedentary stock are there all the time and graze wherever there is a green leaf available.

Felling of trees and uprooting of shrubs for fuelwood causes considerable damage in populous areas, especially in the vicinity of agglomerations, where it may be more damaging than grazing. Collection of medicinal plants is locally important; its effect on the vegetation cover is not known, but, if uncontrolled, such collection can harm biodiversity.

In the cold semi-arid, more truly pastoral systems, pasture degradation may be linked, at least in part, to the degree of modification of traditional systems, limitation of mobility and artificial winter feeding regimes. Mongolia, for example, which retained a high degree of mobility and maintained native breeds as the basis of the system, has suffered far less environmental damage than other countries in the subregion, which opted for degrees of sedentarization and "intensification". That Mongolia has suffered as a result of unusually severe weather in two recent years is not a fault of the system.

High levels of winter feeding from external sources appears to be an almost certain way to pasture degradation unless stock numbers and timing of grazing are in tune with the natural vegetation. This was discussed earlier in more detail.

The vegetation in the more northerly lands of Mongolia and the Xinjiang Altai is in somewhat better condition, while still giving cause for concern. They are less important as sources of rivers, and irrigated agriculture is much less important than in the south. Mongolia has few rivers and these mainly drain internally, apart from the Selenge system that flows into Lake Baikal. The Chinese side of the Altai is partly on the Arctic Ocean catchment: the Irtych joins the Ob; the other major river, the Ulungur, is internal, flowing into Fuhai lake. The overall situation in the pastoral areas of China is serious and while the "Long-term contract grassland use system" has been applied throughout most of the pastoral lands, pasture degradation has increased over the past decade (Table 5.9); changing pasture trends takes time and the contract system has not had enough time to show whether or not it will improve the pastoral vegetation as well as livestock output.

The status of wildlife on the pastures varies greatly from country to country; both destruction of habitat and indiscriminate hunting are taking their toll. In Pakistan and Afghanistan, the situation seems to be particularly serious. Wildlife is effectively protected in Bhutan. Mongolia, with its relatively low population density and herding lifestyle, still has a relatively abundant fauna; in some areas where mechanized water points have broken down, domestic herds can no longer enter or can only use the pastures for very short periods. This has led to an increase in gazelle numbers; rodent numbers have risen with the reduction of control and their predators are also more numerous. Herders usually co-exist with wildlife and do not usually hunt a lot; other sectors of the community, in some countries, do hunt and destruction of habitat is serious where land is being cleared and forests felled.

THE FUTURE OF HERDING AS A LIFESTYLE

In much of the area under discussion, herding is under stress from incursions by agriculture and the stock of settled groups, loss of grazing land, and interference with traditional migration routes. There are also serious problems associated with increasing human and livestock populations. Modern transport and means of communication have raised the awareness of many of the herding community to other ways of life and to the attractions of urban or settled life. In some areas, such as the Northern Areas of Pakistan, improved education has encouraged the young to seek employment in "more skilled" jobs; but then other ethnic groups have taken over the herding tasks, so the pastures are still used.

Some authors (e.g. Blench, 2001) consider that nomadic herding is anachronistic and that it will have disappeared by the middle of this century; in the area under consideration, however, it is difficult to imagine herding's demise. While many would prefer a more settled life, and many governments would like to settle nomads, alternative employment would have to be found for them; in the Himalayan context this would mean finding livelihoods in a labour market that is already oversupplied. If one group settles, then it is likely that others will arrive to scrape a living from the pastures.

In the cold semi-arid zone, extensive herding seems to be the only practical way of earning a living from the land; wildlife and tourism may have a niche but it is so cold and isolated an area that such prospects are probably limited. It is likely that Mongolia's pastures will be exploited by livestock, under extensive grazing systems, for a long time to come. Recent information from Kyrgyzstan indicates that part of the population are returning to traditional herding. Transhumance need not exclude herders from access to services and education, and this was demonstrated clearly during Mongolia's collective period.

In semi-arid and arid areas where the climate is harsh and herding risks high, mobility is very necessary to allow skilled herders room for risk-avoidance strategies; this is even more important in situations where they have no access to agricultural products for use as emergency feed.

Herding is a low external input, labour intensive system that provides employment in lands where other work is scarce; it provides both subsistence and income.

Ranching is the "modern" capitalist system of using extensive grazing land for livestock production; it is far less labour intensive than traditional systems. Subsistence herders are the only secondary users of vegetation who depend on milk much more than meat. All others, from carnivores to ranchers and capitalist herders, depend on meat. No commercial dairy producer would choose arid and semi-arid grazing as the basis for their production. The logic for relying on milk is that it is available daily, but meat only sporadically, and the system can provide subsistence for far more people per unit area than any other arid zone production method. No data are available for temperate Asia, but, for African conditions, Jahnke (1982) estimated that if arid countries like Mauritania and Somalia organized their land use as modern ranching, they would have to reduce their human population by a factor of fifty.

For many authors, the need for continuing herd mobility and the need for planners and policy-makers to consider the special conditions of the extensive grassland environments remains. Merkle (2002) notes that Scholz (1995) proposed a modern form of mobile livestock keeping, but suggests that policy-makers and planners need to give priority to subsistence rather than market-oriented husbandry, to job security rather than to increased productivity, and to resource conservation rather than increased yields. Richard (2002), when reviewing the potential for rangeland development in yak-rearing areas of the Tibetan Plateau, notes that planners must recognize that animal husbandry and livelihoods on the Plateau are still subsistence based, and that the environment upon which these livelihoods depend is marginal, with limited potential for intensification. She recommends a number of policy guidelines, which include:

- promoting livestock mobility to prevent environmental degradation,
- developing legal mechanisms to protect both individual and communal rights to resource access,
- building on the strengths of local communities, and
- increasing social cohesion through collaborative management of rangeland resources.

A recent article in the The Economist (Anonymous, 2002) suggests for Mongolia that "there is a desperate need ... to restore mobility".

Possible interventions for settled or agropastoral stock owners

While the main object of the studies was transhumant systems, quite a lot of insight was gained, at least in the Himalaya–Hindu Kush zone, on problems of the settled stock owners who use the same pastures. Feed scarcity is a major constraint and winter feed scarcity may be more serious for some settled groups than for transhumants, who can move to more clement areas.

Possibilities for improving feed supply

Improved pasture management is often mentioned, but, with grazing rights constraints, often multiple users of pastures, and high levels of stocking, this is only likely to be possible in a few areas. Cultivation of fodder is one option available to farmers.

Fodder from arable land is a possibility for those with adequate land (and sometimes irrigation) resources where it is economically interesting. Extra fodder does not, despite the hopes of many projects "take some of the strain off the grazing land", but it does improve animal performance. Sown fodder, however, is a crop like any other and must compete with them on economic terms for land and inputs. Supplementation for milch cattle and fodder, conserved or fresh, to help survival in the lean season would seem to be the main applications. Better conservation and use of crop residues is an important part of improving fodder output from arable land. There has been considerable progress in parts of the Himalayan zone on winter fodder production in recent years. Berseem (Trifolium alexandrinum) is already well known in the lower areas. Introduction of improved, multi-cut oat cultivars in Pakistan in the 1980s resulted in that crop becoming a major fodder on the plains, for use for both farms and urban dairies; as described by Bhatti and Khan (1996). Oats have proved to be very successful in mountain areas as well, notably in the Northern Areas, where they have been widely adopted (Dost, 2001). Berseem is

now also used there, up to above 1 300 m; this was introduced in the context of the overall cropping system, with parallel work on the main cereals (Dost, 1996). Oats have now been successfully introduced as a fodder in Afghanistan and are promising in Bhutan, as mentioned in Chapter XV.

Haymaking is useful where forage resources and climatic conditions favour it. In much of the Himalaya, overripe hay of low quality is made after the monsoon, but, for climatic reasons, it seems difficult to improve it. Better hay can be made under steppe conditions, if growth is adequate (see Chapter IV). Irrigated fodder for hay is traditional in some areas, notably Afghanistan and parts of China; lucerne is the major crop, with shaftal (Trifolium resupinatum) in Afghanistan. Haymaking from irrigated lucerne is described in Chapter VII. Oat hay has become commercially important in Pakistan (Dost, 2002). Haymaking for pastoral conditions and conservation of crop residues is discussed in detail by Suttie (2000a).

References cited and other sources used

ADB [Asian Development Bank]. 1998. Mongolia Agricultural Sector Development Program Interim Report. Prepared by Sloane, Cooke and King.

Al Jaloudy, M. 2001. *Country Pasture/Forage Resource Profile for Jordan.* see: http: //www.fao.org/WAICENT/FAOINFO/ AGRICULT/AGP/AGPC/doc/Counprof/ Jordan.htm

Animal Husbandry and Veterinary Medicine Division of Agriculture Ministry of China, Grassland Institute of Chinese Academy of Agricultural Sciences, Integrated Survey Committee of Chinese Academy of Sciences. 1994. [*Data on the Grassland Resources of China.*] (in Chinese). Beijing: China Agricultural Science and Technology Press.

Animal Husbandry and Veterinary Medicine Division of Ministry of Agriculture, National Animal Husbandry and Veterinary Medicine Station. 1996. [*Rangeland Resources of China.*] (in Chinese). Beijing: China Science and Technology Press.

Anonymous. 1908. *Imperial Gazetteer of India.* Gyaraspur to Jias. Vol. XIII (Hazara District). Oxford Press. pp. 75–84.

Anonymous. 1981. *Population. Census of Pakistan.* District Census Report, Hazara. pp. 1.3-1.20.

Anonymous. 1993, 1998-1999. *Livestock Census Book, Turgen sum.* Uvs aimag.

Anonymous. 1993, 1998-1999. *Livestock Census Book, Rinchinlkumbe sum.* Khuvsgul aimag

Anonymous. 1995. *Statistical Digest.* Department of Statistics, Himachal Pradesh Government, Shimla, India

Anonymous. 2002. Nomadism in Mongolia: the last best place. *The Economist*, 365 (8304): 48–50.

Arsvoll, K. 1995. *Agriculture in Norway.* pp. 3–5, *in: Mountain Grassland Biodiversity and Agriculture Value.* FAO, Rome, Italy.

Baas, S., Erdenbaatar, B. & Swift, J.J. 2001. Pastoral risk management for disaster prevention and preparedness in Central Asia – with special reference to Mongolia. *In: Report of the Asia-Pacific conference on early warning, prevention, preparedness and management of disasters in food and agriculture.* Chiang Mai, Thailand, 12–15 June 2001. FAO RAP Publication No. 2001:4. Ref. APDC/01/REP.

Badarch. N. 1971. [*Climate of Mongolia.*] (in Mongolian). Ulan Bator: Academic Press of the Academy of Sciences of Mongolia.

Bai Tao. 1994. *Rural and agricultural reform in Tibet.* Tibetology Publication House.

Bhatti, B. & Khan, S. 1996. *Fodder production in Pakistan.* Islamabad: Pakistan Agricultural Research Council, and Rome: FAO. ISBN 969-8288-03-01.

Blench, R. 2001. "You can't go home again." Pastoralism in the new millennium. London: ODI.

Buyanorshikh, D. 1994. [*Uvs aimag: vegetation and natural hay and pasture.*] (in Mongolian). Ulan Bator-Ulaangom.

Cai Li & Weiner, G. 1995. *The yak.* Bangkok: FAO Regional Office for Asia and the Pacific. ISBN 974 89351-0-8.

Champion, Sir Harry G., Seth, S.K. & Khattak, G.M. 1965. *Forest types of Pakistan.* Peshawar, Pakistan: Pakistan Forest Institute.

Chen Baoshu. 2001. [*Cultivation of forage grasses and forage crops.*] (in Chinese). Beijing: China Agricultural Science and Technology Press.

Chen Shan. 1994. [*Grassland forage plants resources of China.*] (in Chinese). Shenyang: Liaoning Nationality Press.

Chen Youchun. 1990. *Characteristics of Chinese Yellow Cattle ecospecies and their course of utilization.* FAO/Chinese Academy of Agricultural Sciences, Agricultural Publishing House, China.

Christensen, D. 1999. Meeting the basic human needs in Tibet. *Report of CIDA Mission in Tibet.*

Dost, M. 1996. Improved fodder in smallholder livestock production in northern Pakistan. *World Animal Review*, 87: 74–77.

—— 1999. *Pastoral resource profile for Pakistan* http://www.fao.org/WAICENT/FAOINFO/AGRICULT/AGP/AGPC/doc/Counprof/Pakistan.htm

—— 2001. Fodder success story: improved fodder crop production in the Northern Areas of Pakistan. *Integrated Crop Management,* 4: 1–23. FAO, Rome, Italy.

—— 2002. The introduction and use of oat (*Avena sativa*) cultivars in Pakistan. http://www.fao.org/WAICENT/FAOINFO/AGRICULT/AGP/AGPC/doc/pasture/spectopics/oatspakistan.html

Drew, F. 1875. *The Jummoo and Kashmir.* Reprinted 1980 by Indus Publications, Karachi.

Editorial Board of Cattle Breeds of China. 1988. [*Cattle breeds of China.*] (in Chinese). Shanghai: Shanghai Science and Technology Press.

Editorial Board of Sheep Breeds of China. 1989. [*Sheep breeds of China.*] (in Chinese). Shanghai: Shanghai Science and Technology Press.

Ehlers, E. & Kreutzman, H. (eds). 2000. *High mountain pastoralism in northern Pakistan.* Stuttgart, Germany: Franz Steiner Verlag. ISBN 3-515-07662-X

Erdenbaatar, B. 1995. Livestock and grazing management in various ecological zones of Arkhangai province: review of current knowledge. Study report for FAO Project FAO/MON/TCP/4553.

—— 1996. Socio-economic aspects of the pastoral movement patterns of Mongolian herders. *In: Culture and Environment in Inner Asia,* vol. 1.

FAO. 1959. *Grasses in agriculture.* Prepared by R.O. Whyte, T.R.G. Moir and J.P. Cooper. *FAO Agricultural Studies,* No. 42.

—— 1992a. Report on the round table on pastoralism. FAO Technical Cooperation Programme, Project TCP/IRA/2255. Rome.

—— 1992b. Employment, income and expenditure of Mongolian herders. Prepared by S. Luvsandorj, D. Shombodon and G. Narangarel. Rome.

—— 1996. *Trends in pastoral development in central Asia.* Rome.

—— 2002. *Nenne and Babuh discovering the natural resources of the Hindu Kush – Himalayan region.* Illustrated booklet for young people, prepared by FAO and ICIMOD. 79 pp. + 31 pp. Teacher's Guide. FAO, Rome.

Fitzherbert, A.R. 2000. *Pastoral resource profile for Kyrgyzstan.* http://www.fao.org/WAICENT/FAOINFO/AGRICULT/AGP/AGPC/doc/Counprof/kyrgi.htm

Gibbon, D., Schultz, M., Thapa, M.B., Upadhya, M.P. & Joshi, Y.R. 1998. Report on a study of agricultural potential of Cheeskam Panchyat. Pakhribas Agricultural Centre, Dhankuta. Technical Paper, No. 95.

Gibson, T. 1991. Forest management and conservation: Bhutan. Forest grazing study. Working Document, No. 26, of FAO/

UNDP Project FO:DP/BHU/85/016. Department of Forestry, Thimpu.

Gyamthso, P. [1996]. Assessment of the condition and potential of high altitude rangelands of Bhutan. PhD Thesis submitted to Swiss Federal Institute of Technology, Zurich.

Harris, P.S. 1987. Grassland survey and integrated pasture development in the high mountain region of Bhutan. Consultancy report prepared for FAO TCP Project TCP/BHU/4504.

—— 2001. Grassland resource assessment for pastoral systems. *FAO Plant Production and Protection Paper*, 162. ISBN 95-2-104537-2.

Ho, P. 1996. Ownership and control in Chinese rangeland management: the case of free riding in Ningxia. *ODI Pastoral Network Paper,* 38d.

Hooker, J.D. 1855. *Himalayan journey.* John Murray, London. Reprinted 1980 by Today & Tomorrow's Printers and Publishers, New Delhi.

Hong Fuzeng. 1989. [*Regional division of cultivated perennial forage grasses of China.*] (in Chinese). China Agricultural Science and Technology Press.

Hou, G.L., Li, J.Y. & Zhang, Y.G. 1991. [*Climatic resources of Chinese agriculture.*] (in Chinese). Beijing: Chinese Peoples University Press. pp. 57–168.

Hu, Songjie. 1995. *Conspectus of Tibetan agriculture.* Sichuan Science and Technology Publishing House.

Hu, Zizhi & Zhang, Degang. 2001. *Pastoral resource profile for China.* see http://www.fao.org/WAICENT/ FAOINFO/AGRICULT/AGP/AGPC/ doc/Counprof/

Hu, S.T.P., Hannaway, D.B. & Youngberg, H.W. 1992. *Forage Resources of China.* Wageningen, The Netherlands: Pudoc.

Hussain, Ijaz. 1968. Role of alpine grazing lands in the management of watersheds in (West) Pakistan. pp. 205-212, *in: Proceedings of the First West Pakistan Watershed Management Conference.* Pakistan Forest Institute, Peshawar.

ICIMOD [International Centre for Integrated Mountain Development]. 1995. Analysis of the feed situation and livestock carrying capacity in Ghorka District. pp. 11–23, *in: Applications of GIS for planning agricultural development in Gorkha District. MENRIS Case Study Series,* No. 3.

IUCN [International Union for the Conservation of Nature]. 1998. Background paper and draft strategy for the sustainable management of grazing lands in the North West Frontier Province, Pakistan.

Jahnke, H.E. 1982. *Livestock production systems and livestock development in tropical Africa.* Kiel, Germany: Kieler Wissenschaftsverlag.

Jiang, W.L., Mu, X.D. & Cheng, Q.G. 1996. [Optimum model for grassland husbandry in Yunnan-Guizhou Plateau. 1. Optimization of grazing system with Shantong fine-tail sheep on pasture.] (in Chinese). *Acta Pratacultura Sinica*, 1: 67–74.

Karagoz, A. 2001. *Pastoral resource profile for Turkey.* http://www.fao.org/WAICENT/ FAOINFO/AGRICULT/AGP/AGPC/ doc/Counprof/Turkey.htm

Khan, C.H. & Anwar, M. 1971. Range management in Hazara District (NWFP). Board of Economic Enquiry, University of Peshawar.

Kharin, N., Takahashi, R. & Harahshesh, H. 1999. *Degradation of the drylands of central Asia.* Centre for Remote Sensing (CEReS), Chiba University, Japan.

Kinzang Wangdi. 2002. *Pastoral resource profile for Bhutan.* http://www.fao.org/

WAICENT/FAOINFO/AGRICULT/ AGP/AGPC/doc/Counprof/Bhutan.html

Kosayev, E. 2002. *Country pasture profile for Azerbaijan.* http://www.fao.org/ WAICENT/FAOINFO/AGRICULT/ A G P / A G P C / d o c / C o u n p r o f / Azerbaijan.html

Land Management Bureau of Tibet Autonomous Region. 1992. *Land use in Tibet Autonomous Region.* Sciences Press.

—— 1994. Rangelands resources in Tibet Autonomous Region. Sciences Press.

Larin, I.V. 1953. [Liman irrigation for fodder crops and problems for its further study.] *Bot. Z. SSSR,* 38: 315–329.

Li, D.Q., Sun, C.Y. & Zhang, X.S. 1998. [Modelling the net primary productivity of the natural potential vegetation in China.] (in Chinese). *Acta Botanica Sinica,* (No vol. no.) 560–566.

Li-Menglin, Yuang Bo-Hua & Suttie, J.M. 1996. Winter feed for transhumant livestock in China: the Altai Experience. *World Animal Review,* 87: 38–44.

Ling Hui. 1998. Rangeland degradation in Tibet: Status, rehabilitation, management and strategies. Paper presented at *An International Workshop on Tibet Biodiversity Management and Conservation.*

Liu, G.D., Zeng, X.B. & Cai Rong. 1999. [Vegetative agriculture and sustainable development of prataculture in the south of China.] (in Chinese). *Acta Prataculture Sinica,* 2: 1–7.

Liu Shuzhen. 1999. *Studies on the grassland degradation and desertification of Naqu Prefecture in Tibet Autonomous Region.* Tibet People's Press.

Liu Yanghua. 1992. *Land production potential: assessment of land resources in Tibet Autonomous Region.* Science Publication House.

Liu, Z.X. 2001. [The great role of grassland industry endowed by history.] (in Chinese). *China Green Times,* 11 Sept. 2001.

Lkhagvajaw, N. 1998. [Use and improvement of natural pastures in Khangai region.] (in Mongolian). Ulan Bator. (PhD thesis).

LRMP [Land Resources Mapping Project]. 1986. *Economic Report.* Survey Department, HMG, Kathmandu, Nepal/Government of Canada/Kenting Earth Sciences Ltd.

Lunnan, T. 1995. A survey of the agriculture in the high altitude inland district of southern Norway. pp. 6–10, *in: Mountain grassland biodiversity and agriculture value.* FAO, Rome.

Luobsang Linzhiduojee (ed). 1992. *Development environment of Qinghai-Tibet Plateau.* Tibetology Publishing House.

Ma Rong & Li Qu. 1993. The impact of system reform on pasture use and environment in Inner Mongolia. A case study. Paper presented at *Conference on the grassland ecosystem of the Mongolian Steppe.* Racine WI, USA.

Ma Yushou & Li Qinyun. 1999. [Study on control of weeds and poisonous plants on "Black Soil Type" deteriorated alpine meadows.] (in Chinese). *Pratacultural Science,* 3: 46–60.

Leber, D., Holawe, F. & Hausler, H. 1995. Climate classification of the Tibet Autonomous Region using multivariate statistical methods. *GeoJournal,* 37(4): 451–473.

Makhmudovic, M. 2002. *Pastoral resource profile for Uzbekistan.* See http: //www.fao.org/ WAICENT/FAOINFO/ AGRICULT/AGP/AGPC/doc/Counprof/ Uzbekistan.html

Merkle, R. 2002. Nomadism: a socio-ecological mode of culture. pp. 128–133, *in:* H. Jianlin, C. Richard, O. Hanotte, C. McVeigh and

J.E.O. Rege (eds). *Yak production in central Asian highlands.* Proceedings of the Third International Congress on Yak, Lhasa, PRC, 4–9 Sept. 2000. Nairobi: ILRI.

Miller, D.J. 1989. Rangeland resources of Bhutan. Booklet published under the ADB Highland Livestock Development Project.

—— 1995. Herds on the move: Winds of change among pastoralists in the Himalayas and on the Tibetan Plateau. *ICIMOD Discussion Paper Series,* No. MNR 95/2.

Miller, D.J. & Craig, S.R. 1997. *Rangelands and pastoral development in the Hindu Kush-Himalayas.* Kathmandu, Nepal: International Centre for Integrated Mountain Development (ICIMOD).

Misri, B. 1995. Range and forest grazing in the Himalaya. pp. 28–33, *in:* P. Singh (ed). *Proceedings of the First Meeting of the Temperate Asia Pasture and Fodder Sub-Regional Working Group.* Kathmandu, Nepal.

—— 1996. Nomadic graziers of the Himalaya: the Gujars of Jammu and Kashmir pp. 53–60, *in: Proceedings of the Second Meeting of the Temperate Asia Pasture and Fodder Working Group.* Dehra Dun, India.

Misri, B. & Dev, I. 1997. Traditional use of fodder trees in the Himalaya. *IGFRI Newsletter,* 4(1). Jhansi, Uttar Pradesh, India.

Misri, B. & Sareen, S. 1997. Regeneration dynamics of mid-hill grasslands of the Kangra Valley. *Envis-Bulletin – Himalayan Ecology and Development,* 6(2): 3–5..

Misri, B.M. 1999. *Pastoral resource profile for India.* http://www.fao.org/WAICENT/FAOINFO/AGRICULT/AGP/AGPC/doc/Counprof/India.htm

Morrison, J. 2000a. Constraints and interventions for Himalayan alpine pastoral systems. *In:* Rafique, 2000, q.v.

—— 2000b. Country range system studies: Final conclusions. In: Rafique, 2000, q.v.

Nan, Z.B. 2000. [Establishing sustainable management systems for disease of pasture crops in China.] (in Chinese). *Acta Pratacultura Sinica,* 2: 1–9.

National Bureau of Statistics, People's Republic of China. 2000. *China Statistics Yearbook 2000.* Beijing: China Statistics Press. (in English).

National Examining and Approval Committee for Forage Cultivars. 1992. [*Registered grass cultivars of China.*] (in Chinese). Beijing: Beijing Agricultural University Press.

Niamir-Fuller, M. (ed). 1999. *Managing mobility in African rangelands.* Published for FAO and Beijer International Institute of Ecological Economics by Intermediate Technology Publications, London.

Nizami, A. 1998. Users survey in Social Forestry Project, Malakand and Dir. SFPMD, Saidu Sharif (NWFP), Pakistan.

Noble. C. 1987. *Over the High Passes.* Collins, Glasgow, UK.

Norbu, L. [2000]. Cattle grazing – an integral part of broadleaf forest management planning in Bhutan. Unpublished PhD Thesis. Swiss Federal Institute of Technology, Zurich.

NRA [National Research Associates]. 1997. Nepal district profile. National Research Associates, Nepal.

Pariyar, D. 1998. *National Biodiversity Action Plan (1998): Institutional development, capacity building and conservation of rangeland biodiversity.* Kathmandu: Department of National Parks and Wildlife Conservation, Ministry of Forestry and Soil Conservation, HM Government of Nepal.

—— 1999. *Pastoral resource profile for Nepal.* http://www.fao.org/WAICENT/FAOINFO/AGRICULT/AGP/AGPC/doc/Counprof/Nepal.htm

Pratt, D.J. 1997. Food security in arid rangelands. An assessment of issues and approaches. Paper for the UN Conference of the Parties to the Convention on Desertification, Rome, 29 September – 10 October 1997. AGPC, FAO, Rome.

Przevalsky, N.M. 1883. *The third expedition in Central Asia.* Saint Petersburg. Quoted by Kharin, Takahashi and Harahshesh, 1999. p. 56.

Rafique, S.M. (ed). 2000. *Proceedings of the Fourth Meeting of the Temperate Asia Pasture and Fodder Network.* Held at the Pakistan Forest Institute, Peshawar, Pakistan, 6–11 June 2000.

Rai, N.K. & Thapa, M.B. 1993. Indigenous pasture management system in high altitude Nepal: A review. *in:* Policy Analysis in Agriculture and Related Resource Management. HMG Nepal Ministry of Agriculture & Winrock International, Kathmandu.

Rajbhandary, H.B. & Pradhan, S.M.S. 1981. Appropriate technology for livestock development in hill farming systems. Paper presented at a seminar on Appropriate Technology for Hill Farming Systems, 22–25 June 1981. Published by the Department of Livestock Development and Animal Health, Extension and Training Section, Nepal.

Ren, Jizhou. 1985. [*Grassland survey and planning.*] (in Chinese). Beijing: Agricultural Press.

Ren, J.Z., Hu, Z.Z. & Zhang, Z.H. 1999. [A preliminary discussion on grassland ecological region in China.] (in Chinese). *Acta Pratacultura Sinica,* 8(Suppl.): 12–22

Ren, J.Z. & Wan, G.C. 1994. [System coupling and desert-oasis agro-ecosystem.] (in Chinese). *Acta Pratacultura Sinica,* 3(3): 1–8.

Ren, M.E. & Bao, H.S. 1992. [*Natural vegeta-*

tion and its renovation and exploitation in China.*] (in Chinese). Beijing: Science Press.

Research Group on Sustainable Agricultural Development in Karst Regions of China, Chinese Academy of Engineering. 1999. [Strategy and tactics for solution of sustainable agricultural development problem in karst regions of China.] (in Chinese). *Acta Prataculturae Sinica,* 8(Suppl.): 32–42.

Richard, C. 2002. The potential for rangeland development in yak-rearing areas of the Tibetan Plateau. pp. 11–18, *in:* H. Jianlin, C. Richard, O. Hanotte, C. McVeigh and J.E.O Rege (eds). *Yak production in central Asian highlands.* Proceedings of the Third International Congress on Yak, Lhasa, PRC, 4–9 Sept. 2000. Nairobi: ILRI.

Sardar, M. Rafique. 1997. Indigenous production and utilization systems in the high altitude alpine pasture, Saif-ul-Maluk, NWFP, Pakistan. Pakistan Forest Institute, Peshawar. 47 pp.

Scholz, F. 1995. *Nomadismus. Theorie und Wandel einer sozio-okologischen Kulturweise.* [Nomadism. Theory and change of a socio-ecological mode of culture]. Stuttgart, Germany: Franz Steiner Verlag. 300 pp.

Singh, P. 1996. *Proceedings of the Second Meeting of the Temperate Asia Pasture and Fodder Network.* Dehra Dun, India.

Statistic Bureau of Tibet. 1996–2001. *Statistic Year Book of Tibet (1995-2000).* China Statistic Publishing House.

Sun, Shangzhi (ed.). 1994. *Economic Geography of Tibet.* Xinghua Publishing House.

Suttie, J.M. 2000a. *Hay and straw conservation for small-scale farming and pastoral conditions.* FAO Plant Production and Protection Series No. 29. 303 pp. Rome.

—— 2000b. *Pastoral resource profile for Mongolia.* http://www.fao.org/WAICENT/

FAOINFO/AGRICULT/AGP/AGPC/doc/Counprof/mongol1.htm

Swift, J. 1999. Pastoral institutions and approaches to risk management and poverty alleviation in Central Asian countries in transition. Report prepared in collaboration with S. Baas, FAO Rural Development Division. Available online at: http://www.fao.org/sd/rodirect/roan0018.htm

t'Mannetje, L. (ed). 2000. Silage making in the tropics, with particular emphasis on smallholders. *FAO Plant Production and Protection Paper,* 161. ISBN 92-5-104500-3.

Thieme, O. 2000. *Pastoral resource profile for Afghanistan.* http://www.fao.org/WAICENT/FAOINFO/AGRICULT/AGP/AGPC/doc/Counprof/AFGAN.htm

Tibetan Bureau of Land Planning. 1992a. *Assessment of range land in Tibet.* Science Publishing House.

—— 1992b. *Land use in Tibet.* Science Publishing House.

—— 1992c. *Rangelands resources of Tibet.* Science Publishing House.

—— 1992d. *Soil resources in Tibet.* Science Publishing House.

Tserendash, S. 1999. [Importance of natural resources in the livestock economy of Mongolia: theoretical and practical tendencies.] (in Mongolian). MDRC, Ulan Bator.

Tshering, L. [1994]. Yak husbandry in Bhutan. Unpublished report of the Animal Husbandry Department, Thimpu, Bhutan.

Tulachan, P.M. & Neupane, A. 1999. *Livestock in mixed farming systems of the Hindu-Kush-Himalaya.* Joint FAO-ICIMOD Publication. Kathmandu, Nepal: International Centre for Integrated Mountain Development. ISBN 92-9115-071-1

Tulachan, P.M., Mohamed-Saleem, M.A., Makki-Hokkonen, J. & Partap, T. (eds). 2000. *Contribution of livestock to mountain livelihoods.* Proceedings of a symposium. Kathmandu, Nepal: ICIMOD. ISBN 92-9115264-1

Tumanian, R. 2001. *Country pasture profile for Armenia.* http://www.fao.org/WAICENT/FAOINFO/AGRICULT/AGP/AGPC/doc/Counprof/Armenia.htm

Van Hove, C. 1989. *Azolla and its multiple uses, with emphasis on Africa.* FAO, Rome. 53 pp. (available in English and French).

Van Veen, T.W.S. 1995. Kyrgyz sheep herders at crossroads. *ODI Pastoral Network Paper,* 38d.

Verma, V. 1996. *Gaddis of Dhauladhar.* New Delhi: Indus Publishing Company.

Wangchuk, T. 1994. *Competition between blue sheep (*Pseudois nayaur*) and domestic yak (*Bos grunniens*) in the Jigme Dorji Wildlife Sanctuary.* University of Maryland, USA.

WAPDA. 1997. *Pakistan Snow and Ice Hydrology Project, Lahore.* (Official Records).

Wu Zhengyi. 1980. [*Vegetation of China.*] (in Chinese). Beijing: Science Press.

Xiao, Huaiyuan. 1994. *Marketing livestock production in Tibet: issues and strategies.* Tibet People's Publication House.

Xinjiang Animal Husbandry Bureau. 2001. Annual Report (2000) on [the FAO-supported] Studies on traditional nomadic Kazak transhumant system and a Kazak transhumant system where herders return to settled winter farms in Burjin County, Altai Prefecture, Xinjiang. Foreign Funds Project Executive Office, Xinjiang Animal Husbandry Bureau.

Yang, Gaihe. 1995. *Land resource productivity and its carrying capacity of population in Tibet.* People's Publishing House.

Yang, Z.Y., Xin, G.R., Chen, S.Y., Liang, Z.Z., Lu, Z.H. & Zhang, Y.Y. 1977a. A case study on benefits of Italian ryegrass–rice rotation system. *Pratacultural Science,* 14(6): 35–39.

Yang, Z.Y., Yue, C.Y., Xin, G.R., Jian, S.G. & Yang, Z.R. 1997b. [Effect of winter cropping of *Lolium multiflorum* in a rice field on growth of succeeding rice and a preliminary approach to its mechanism.] (in Chinese). *Pratacultural Science,* 14(4): 20–24.

Yonzon, P. 1998. Biodiversity conservation of Nepal. *In: Procceding of the Third Meeting of the Temperate Asia Pasture and Fodder Network,* Pokhara, Nepal, 9–13 March 1998.

Zhang, R.C. 1989. [*Yak of China.*] (in Chinese). Lanzhou: Gansu Scientific Press.

Zhang, Xiaopin. 1997. *Tibet: Marching towards 21 Century.* China Tibetology Publishing House.

Zhou, G.S. & Zhang, X.S. 1996. [Study on NPP of natural vegetation in China under global climate change.] (in Chinese). *Acta Phytoecologica Sinica,* 1996: 11–19.

Glossary

Word, acronym or phrase	Explanation	
aimag	Main administrative division, equivalent to province; there are eighteen aimags in Mongolia.	MON
Ajar	Type of Gujar q.v.	PAK
AJK	Azad Jamu and Kashmir.	PAK
alsyn nuudel	Migration between autumn pasture and winter camping.	MON
bag	Subdivision of a sum; it is an administrative unit of population and is not necessarily delimited geographically.	MON
bakarwals	Transhumant herders.	PAK
barani	Rainfed crop land.	PAK
bari (land)	Rainfed cultivated land.	NEP
bhari	Weight measure of produce (= 30–40 kg).	NEP
bhoosa	Chopped straw, often wheat.	PAK
bod	Traditional large animal livestock unit: a camel is 1.5; cattle, yaks and horses are 1; and 6 sheep or 7 goats = 1 bod (there is also a small animal unit, the bog).	MON
chang	Beer.	BHU
chauri	Hybrid of *Bos taurus* and *B. grunniens*.	NEP
chhurpi	Cheese from chauri milk.	NEP
chowkidar	Watchman.	PAK
chugo	Smoke-dried, hard, yak cheese.	BHU
dey	Container for measuring grain – about 1.9 kg rice.	BHU
Dzonghka	National language of Bhutan.	BHU
dzongkhag	District.	BHU
ERP	Environmental Rehabilitation Project.	PAK
geog	Administrative block of a district.	BHU
ghasni	Grassy area.	IND
ghee	Clarified butter.	PAK
gol	River.	MON
Gujar	Ethnic group of herders.	PAK

gur	Unrefined sugar, artisanally produced.	PAK
guzara	Communal (forests).	PAK
kacha	Built in rammed earth; unripe; unsurfaced.	PAK
kanal	Land measure (one twentieth of a hectare).	PAK
khair	*Acacia catechu*	BHU
kharif	Cropping season based on the monsoon.	PAK
khavarjaa	Spring camping areas.	MON
khel	Inheritance group.	PAK
kholyn nuudel	Transhumant systems.	MON
khormoi	A traditional measurement unit equal to 3-5 kg of dry or frozen materials.	MON
khot-ail	A group of a few families that work and camp together – with or without family links.	MON
khot	Area where herders are camped.	MON
kolkhoz	A cooperative agricultural enterprise operated on state-owned land.	KYR
maldar	One who gains a living from livestock.	PAK
mahlundi	Owner of grazing rights.	IND
mithun	Domesticated *Bos gaurus*.	BHU
nak	Female of *Bos grunniens*.	NEP
namarjaa	Autumn pastures.	MON
negdel	The cooperative unit in collective times; boundaries were those of the present sums.	MON
Northern Areas	A territory administered by Pakistan, comprising the disputed territories other than Azad Jamu and Kashmir – the former Gilgit Agency.	PAK
nothoue	Partnership in rearing cattle.	BHU
nuudel	Generalized term for any kind of moving of things, including livestock.	MON
NWFP	North West Frontier Province.	PAK
otgonne	Herding movement to find better feed – similar to Mongolian otor.	KYR
otor	Herding movement, often to distant pasture, to find better feed.	MON
pan	Betel leaf.	BHU
panchyat	Lowest level of local administration.	IND
PFI	Pakistan Forest Institute.	PAK

philu	Cream skimmed from milk before churning.	BHU
pukka	Of a house: in stone or baked brick.	PAK
pulhals	Hired herders.	IND
qalang	A traditional system of rent for grazing.	PAK
rabi season	Autumn-sown, spring-harvested cropping season.	PAK
radhari	Check points for levy of forest grazing fees.	IND
RNRRC	Renewable Natural Resources Research Centre.	BHU
ropani	Land measure.	NEP
sovkhoz	State-operated agricultural estate, organized on industrial lines.	KYR
sum	Subdivision of aimag (= district).	MON
tachu	Sun- or air-dried yak cheese.	BHU
tahsil	Administrative unit – below district.	PAK
tamang	Ethnic group.	NEP
tenzou	Offering an animal to local deities without slaughter.	BHU
thunse	Bamboo basket.	NEP
tsadrog	Registered grazing land.	BHU
tsesa	Household plot.	BHU
tsethar	Animal saved from slaughter.	BHU
uvuljuu	Winter camping and grazing sites.	MON
WAPDA	Water and Power Development Authority	PAK
warisi	Hereditary grazing rights of Gaddis.	IND
yak	Male of *Bos grunniens*.	NEP
zamindar	Land owner.	PAK
zo	Yak × cow hybrid.	CPR
zud	Term covering various types of weather-related disaster – associated with winter precipitation, usually too much or too little snow.	MON
zuslan	Summer camping areas.	MON

Key to UNDP Country Codes:

BHU	=	Bhutan
CPR	=	People's Republic of China
IND	=	India
KYR	=	Kyrgyzstan
MON	=	Mongolia
NEP	=	Nepal
PAK	=	Pakistan

INDEX

A